Stable and Sustainable Growth of a Large Open Economy

Zhang Xiaojing

Stable and Sustainable Growth of a Large Open Economy

An Empirical Study of China

Translated by Liu Shiying

PETER LANG

New York · Berlin · Bruxelles · Chennai · Lausanne · Oxford

Bibliographic information published by the Deutsche Nationalbibliothek.
The German National Library lists this publication in the German National Bibliography; detailed bibliographic data is available on the Internet at http://dnb.d-nb.de.

Library of Congress Cataloging-in-Publication Data

Names: Xiaojing, Zhang, 1969- author
http://id.loc.gov/authorities/names/n2025016505
http://id.loc.gov/rwo/agents/n2025016505
Title: Stable and Sustainable Growth of a Large Open Economy : an empirical study of China / Zhang Xiaojing.
Description: First edition. | New York : Peter Lang, [2025] | Includes bibliographical references.
Identifiers: LCCN 2025002335 (print) | LCCN 2025002336 (ebook) | ISBN 9783034356077 hardback | ISBN 9783034357692 ebook | ISBN 9783034357708 epub
Subjects: LCSH: Economic development--China http://id.loc.gov/authorities/subjects/sh2009124570 | China--Economic conditions--1949- http://id.loc.gov/authorities/subjects/sh85024016 | China--Economic policy--1949- http://id.loc.gov/authorities/subjects/sh85024023
Classification: LCC HC427.9 .X53 2025 (print) | LCC HC427.9 (ebook) | DDC 330.951--dc23/eng/20250411
LC record available at https://lccn.loc.gov/2025002335
LC ebook record available at https://lccn.loc.gov/2025002336

Cover image: Sujono sujono, Shutterstock.

ISBN 978-3-0343-5607-7 (print)
ISBN 978-3-0343-5769-2 (E-PDF)
ISBN 978-3-0343-5770-8 (E-Pub)
DOI 10.3726/b22765

Published by Peter Lang Publishing Inc., New York, (USA)

info@peterlang.com

This edition is an authorized translation from the Chinese language edition.
Published by arrangement with Chinese Social Sciences Press.

This publication has been peer reviewed.

www.peterlang.com

Table of Contents

List of Figures

List of Tables

Preface

1. Two Facets of an Open Economic Catch-up

China's opening-up could be a double-edged sword: On the one hand, an open China is integrated into and gains benefits from the system of globalization. It is driven to carry out or deepen its domestic reform as a positive impact and an encouraging experience in its miracle of growth. On the other hand, stable growth can be affected or even threatened by negative shocks from the outside world. For example, the Latin American debt crisis and the Asian financial crisis are believed to have been at least partially triggered by their opening-up, although internal factors should primarily be held responsible. The so-called middle-income trap is now interpreted by more scholars from the perspective of opening-up. The seemingly stable domestic systems with insufficient resilience may be poorly responsive to, malfunction, or even collapse under marginalization of international division of labor or volatile impact of international capital flows and financial turbulence or crisis, leading to economic stagnation or even regression. Moreover, an open economy will rely more on the outside world, inviting a wolf into the house and bringing new threats to the industrial and supply chains under some extreme circumstances. Therefore, the impact on domestic sustainable and stable growth in the era of globalization is a real issue the macroeconomic administrators, or governors must face.

When open to the outside world, developing countries can access more advanced knowledge, technology, systems, management, or "best practices," etc., getting on a faster track of growth and finally catching up, achieving convergence, that is, close per capital income with the developed economics. On the other hand, however, this process will inevitably result in distorted factor prices, prioritized key industries, financial repression, forced saving, preference of consumption to investment, tariff protection, capital control, and other distortions.

These distortions, represented by forced government intervention, as well as implicit government guarantee and the potential moral hazards of market entities including state-owned economic sectors, corporate local governments, and some local government-backed private sectors can give rise to more risks, thus affecting economic stability and hindering sustainable growth. How to properly response to these two faces of a catching-up economy, namely, how to minimize distortions and achieve sustainable growth while striving to catch up with a developed economy, is a major test for state governors.

The coming chapters will show us how an open China is building up risks in development due to various distortions while benefiting from the globalization. This process sees subtle tensions between rapid growth and sustainable growth. A country generally pursues "a faster speed" in the early stage of catching up with the developed economies, as demonstrated by a host of our policy slogans. Nevertheless, this "faster speed" may make the country more unstable, warning us to pay more attention to the sustainability of growth. Although China benefited from the so-called "great moderation" and did not become "more unstable" from 2001 to 2007 since its accession to the WTO, it had to "repay the price" when more risks built up under the new normal of "dealing with the slowdown in economic growth, making difficult structural adjustments, and absorbing the effects of previous economic stimulus policies." The United States finally ascended to the world's top economy after an average annual growth of 3% for over one hundred years. For China's future growth, the concern for sustainability will be more significant than that for growth rate. This is likely one of the key points in understanding and adapting to the new normal of the economy. Of course, growth needs to be continuous; a sudden fall or a sharp fluctuation in growth would also find the society and economy to their costs. Therefore, both speed and sustainability must be taken into consideration in an economy to be healthily developed.

2. An Influential Big Open Country That Grew from a Humble Position

A big country in economics refers to an influential economy that is not passively affected by others, that can cause two-way (instead of the old one-way) spillover effect with every move. For instance, China used to be affected by the United States and other major developed economies but, it is now influencing the world. With its economic size and international influence, China has risen from a humble position to an influential power. The whole international community is discussing how to adapt to the new normal of

China's economy—while China is adapting itself to the world, the world can hardly develop without China.

China is now a truly big country, for according to the data of the International Monetary Fund (IMF), it ranked first in 2014 in GDP at purchasing power parity (PPP). Besides, since its accession to the WTO in the beginning of the new century, China has made great headway in economic and trade strength, further open-up and right of speech in global system.

China's open economy is developing rapidly and occupies a notably higher position in international economic and trade pattern. 1) China's RMB is included in the SDR currency basket. 2) China is recognized as the No.1 manufacturer in the world. In 2012, with a manufacturing output value accounting for about 1/5 of the world's total, China surpassed the United States and rose to be the No.1 manufacturer in the world. In 2014, China continued to rank the first in the manufacturing industry, with more than 220 industrial products staying on the top of the global lists. Its industry has stepped into the middle and late stages. 3) China has joined the rank of major economic and trade powerhouses and became a major investor. In 2009, China's exports rose to buck the trend, surpassing Germany and ranking the first in the world, and its imports were the runner-up only after the United States. In 2013, China outperformed the United States in total imports and exports and became the world's largest trader. While trade continued to expand, its international investment cooperation also grew steadily. In 2014, the actual use of foreign direct investment was USD 119.6 billion, ranking the first in the world. In 2014, China's foreign direct investment reached USD 116 billion, second only to the United States and Japan and ranking third in the world since 2013. 4) China has become an important engine of world economic growth. Since 2008, China has surpassed the United States to be the largest contributor to global economic growth. From 2009 to 2011, China's contribution to world economic growth reached more than 50%. In recent years, its average contribution rate has also exceeded one third.

China is gaining more right of speech in global governance institutions. China takes advantage of existing platforms such as the United Nations and APEC, as well as newer platforms such as the G20, the BRICS Summit, the Council of Heads of SCO Member States, and the China-Africa Forum to actively participate in and continue to promote innovation in global economic governance. In the above-mentioned summits, China's initiative to establish the Asian Infrastructure Investment Bank, the BRICS Development Bank and the Silk Road Fund has attracted extensive attention from the international community. For China, the governance platforms in regional or global level have become increasingly significant.

On January 27, 2016, IMF announced that its share and governance reform plan for 2010 came into effect, which means that China has officially become the third largest shareholder of IMF, followed by Germany, France, and the United Kingdom, and only after the United States and Japan. This is not only the most important governance reform plan of IMF since it was established 65 years ago, but the largest share transfer plan for emerging markets and developing countries. At the meeting held in Washington in November 2009, the organization decided to increase the share of the "BRIC countries" (China, India, Russia, and Brazil) in the "New Loan Arrangement," that is, from the original USD 80 billion to USD 100 billion. In this way, the voting rights of the four countries in the organization exceeded 15%, and they actually had a collective veto on major issues.

On October 1, 2016, IMF announced that the RMB was officially included in the SDR (Special Drawing Right), five years since the last round of assessment. IMF President Lagarde said at the press conference: "The entry of RMB into the SDR will be an important milestone for China's economy to integrate into the global financial system, and a recognition of the Chinese government's progress in the reform of the monetary and financial system in the past few years."

In addition, since the 18th National Congress of the Communist Party of China (CPC), China has successively introduced a series of reform measures, making solid strides in building a new system of opening-up. The Foreign Investment Law of the People's Republic of China (draft) was published, abolishing the case-by-case approval system established by the three laws on foreign investment, and exploring the management model of pre-entry national treatment plus negative list. The newly revised Catalogue for the Guidance of Foreign Investment Industries substantially reduces restrictive measures. Four pilot free trade zones, that is, Shanghai, Tianjin, Guangdong, and Fujian, have basically established a foreign investment management system with negative list management as the core. The comprehensive reform of the negative list has a clear "timetable." From 2018, China will officially implement a nationwide unified negative list system for market access.

3. Improvement of Openness and Governance and Sustained and Stable Growth

Achieving sustainable and stable economic growth under the conditions of opening-up is to rely on improved open governance. First, open competition is an important guarantee for sustainable growth. In the most general sense (i.e., from a non-economic perspective), open systems are safer than closed systems. According to the "entropy law," open systems will bring order and bring forth new vitality, while closed systems will lead to disorder and death. Closure will generally form a temporary or occasionally a long stability and a static security like in some dynasties in ancient China. However, from a dynamic point of view, closure leads to institutional rigidity and social inertia and will even collapse under turbulence. Opening-up is to remove all kinds of prejudices and discrimination, thresholds and barriers, allow exchanges of ideas, and let all resource elements flow freely. In comparison, we can identify the gap, promote the flow of elements based on the gap, learn from others, seek common ground while reserving differences, narrow the gap and gather positive forces. From the perspective of institutional economics, the evolution of internal and external institutions is driven not only by reactive responses to international trade and factor mobility, but also by proactive adjustments to institutions to better compete for market shares and mobilize factors of production. Globalization has led to "institutional competition." In particular, since the 2008 global financial crisis, rebalancing, structural adjustment, and reform have become the main theme of global development. The Third, Fourth, and Fifth Plenary Sessions of the 18th CPC Central Committee made a comprehensive deployment of China's reform and development. The United States, Europe, and Japan have also launched structural reform plans and long-term growth strategies, opening the prelude to reform and competition. Open competition is not only an important driving force for an economy to get rid of institutional inertia, but an important prerequisite for sustained growth.

Secondly, the new challenges of opening-up put forward new requirements for governance. The outbreak of the international financial crisis in 2008, the sharp contraction of global trade, the reshaping of international trade and investment rules dominated by developed economies, and the rebalancing and structural adjustment of China's economy under the new normal all indicate that China's economic opening-up is facing new challenges in the new stage. (1) New challenges under the constraints of new international rules. On the one hand, higher standards of international economic and trade rules are in the making, such as the Trans-Pacific Partnership Agreement (TPP), the Trans-Atlantic Trade and Investment Agreement (TTIP), the Trade in Services Agreement (TiSA), and the Japan Europe Economic Partnership Agreement. On the other hand, there are new changes in the international monetary system. On October 31, 2013, the Federal Reserve, the European Central Bank, the Swiss Central Bank, the Bank of England, the Bank of Canada, and the Bank of Japan announced that they had reached a long-term multilateral currency swap agreement, forming an exclusive super international reserve currency supply and demand network centered on the Federal Reserve that involves the central banks of major developed economies.

How to gain the dividends of globalization under the constraints of new rules has become a new challenge for open governance. (2) International policy coordination under the influence of global value chain and financial cycle. The big country spillover effect is mainly realized through trade channels and financial channels. The rise of global value chain has created a new form of international policy spillover effect, because government policies that affect the domestic components of the international production chain will also affect the overall value of the production chain. Supply chain trade provides a new perspective for domestic policy spillovers. In terms of financial channels, the newly emerging financial cycle theory points out that the main factor affecting the global financial cycle is the monetary policy of the central country. Therefore, the spillover effect of the monetary policy of this central country is very significant. As far as peripheral countries are concerned, to prevent the adverse external spillover effects of the global financial cycle, the central country needs to exercise self-discipline in its policies or supervise and constrain its monetary policies. The big country spillover effect requires strengthening international policy coordination and urging countries to implement responsible economic policies. (3) The impact of further economic and financial openness. The construction of a new system of open economy means further all-round opening. As a result, it will also bring greater external impact. Responding to the impact of the new opening-up calls for sound market development and regulatory governance. The management of a gradually internationalized currency, including the outflow and return of RMB and its impact on macro stability, is an important aspect; as well as the impact of changes in the exchange rate formation mechanism, such as the exchange rate reform on August 11, 2015.; the risk of capital going out and the obstacles to the global allocation of capacity; operation and governance of the AIIB; the geopolitical impact and countermeasures of the Belt and Road strategy. These are all new challenges brought about by all-round opening-up, calling for more effective and efficient open governance.

Third, we need to further improve the capacity of open governance. In the final analysis, to improve the capacity of open governance, the market should play a decisive role, and the government render better services. For the market to play the decisive role, the key is to promote the relative free flow of domestic and foreign elements, to form more reasonable element prices. In this way, both "domestic and foreign markets and resources" can play their respective due roles to promote the optimal allocation of resources at home and abroad; More space will be tapped for domestic development and overseas expansion, to gain more benefits from globalization. For the government to render better services, we should focus on the order and extent of openness, especially the market maturity and macro prudential supervision required for deeper openness. This requires us to not only learn from the experience of mature economies and improve the relevant regulatory framework in broader ways but also enhance our right of speech in the game of international rule making and the formulation of global governance systems. In addition, we should properly grasp the long cycle and new normal of the world, better understand the cyclical pattern of the global economy and finance and strengthen international policy coordination. All these are of great importance in improving the capacity of governance in opening up and symbolic of a government with great competence.

4. Origin and Arrangement of the Book

This book is the fruit of the author and the research team's exploration of China's macro-economy from an open perspective. The study of China's macro stability has gone through an evolution process in China. The first part of the book concerns the impact of the dual track system on macro stability. For example, Fan Gang's *Outline of Macroeconomic Theory of Public Ownership* discusses this topic in depth, a main theme from the late 1970s to the early 1990s. The second part is about marketization and macro stability, highlighting the impact of economic marketization on macro-operation. Zhang Shuguang's *Marketization and Macro Stability* illustrates the main theme of the socialist market economy from the mid-1990s to the beginning of the new century. Then came openness and macro stability. Liu Shucheng's *Financial Opening-up and Macro Stability* illustrates the main theme of China's economic opening-up in the new century, especially after China's accession to the WTO. Of course, such arrangements may be somewhat subjective (e.g., some themes overlap in the period), but it can reflect well the progressive understanding of domestic researchers on the importance of factors affecting macroeconomic stability.

This book is mainly based on the partial results of the major bidding project of the National Social Science Foundation "Implementing the Scientific Outlook on Development and Improving the Macroeconomic Control System" (approval No. 07&ZD004) and the major project of the Chinese Academy of Social Sciences "Macroeconomic Stability Research under the Open Economy" led by the author. The book covers the relevant research since 2004, all of which has been put to the press. These studies reflect our understanding over a period of time. These understandings, whether farsighted or defective, are all presented here for future investigation. The basic logic of the open economy discussed above is reflected in each chapter, but these chapters do not cover all the new challenges and countermeasures of the open country. Therefore, the preface may serve as a necessary supplement.

This book is the pearl of teamwork. The chapters are arranged as follows: Chapter 1 (written by Zhang Xiaojing, Zhang Ping), Chapter 2 (by Zhang Xiaojing), Chapter 3 (by Yuan Fuhua, Wang Hongju, Zhang Xiaojing), Chapter 4 (by Wang Hongju, Zhang Xiaojing), Chapter 5 (by Zhang Xiaojing, Sun Tao), Chapter 6 (by Sun Tao, Zhang Xiaojing), Chapter 7 (by Sun Tao, Zhang Xiaojing), Chapter 8 (by Tang Duo, Zhang Xiaojing), Chapter 9 (by Sun Tao, Zhang Xiaojing), Chapter 10 (by Zhang Xiaojing, Wang Hongju, Chang Xin), Chapter 11 (by Zhao Zhijun).

I would like to thank all colleagues of the Institute of Economics of the Chinese Academy of Social Sciences, namely Zhang Ping, Zhao Zhijun, Wang Hongju, Chang Xin, Yuan Fuhua, and Tang Duoduo, for their help and support in my academic research. I also want to thank Dr. Sun Tao, a former senior economist of the IMF, for his close cooperation with me. My thanks also go to Ms. Wang Yin, the Editor in Charge of this book, without her dedication to work the expedited delivery of this book will be impossible.

In the process of collating the manuscript, my son watched me working in front of the computer and said: "I really hope you can finish this earlier so that you can play with me for a while." This should be the supervision and encouragement of my academic research!

Economic Growth and Policy Choice in China's "Opening-Up" Period

1.1 Introduction

In 2003, China's economy entered "an accelerating track," hitting a shocking growth of 9.1%. Its growth was mainly benefited from the cumulative effect of structural adjustment and changes in capital flow (Frontier Research Group on Growth, 2003), while the new "opening" factors apparently got more relevant with its economy. Trade frictions, and expectations of RMB exchange rate fluctuations, especially foreign capital inflows, have greatly affected the money supply and other issues, putting "economic growth and policy choices in opening up" under hot theoretical and practical discussions.

Opening-up is a key factor for a country's growth. Madison (1997) summarized the development history of the world economy over the past two hundred years and concluded that, in the long run, the sustained high growth of per capita output was determined by four factors: technological progress, material capital accumulation (including technological progress), human capital accumulation and opening-up For the leading countries, opening-up and accumulation of more materials and human capital are the keys to their catching up with others. The World Bank also pointed out in The East Asian Miracle (1995) and Reflections on the East Asian Miracle (2003) that opening up and accumulation paid the way for the Asian miracle. However, opening-up may also be costly, as the external shocks (especially the financial shocks) triggered the Asian financial crisis, causing low growth and post-crisis macro and micro-structural adjustments.

The opening-up and growth has been long discussed. Opening-up was first understood more as trade opening-up. With the development of financial globalization since the 1980s, financial opening-up has received more and more attention. According to mainstream theory, trade opening-up can bring relatively fixed benefits, but the benefits of financial opening-up are controversial. In the wake of the Asian financial crisis, in particular, the whole academia reflected upon the financial opening-up. The IMF, which had been advocating financial liberalization and financial opening-up, reported recently that the financial opening-up's rule in stable promotion of economic growth cannot be justified by empirical data. Therefore, the IMF is not as eager to push capital account liberalization in developing countries as before (Prasad, Rogoff, Wei, and Kose, 2003). In addition, the latest literature also showed that in countries with medium financial development such as China, financial opening-up would bring economic instability (Aghion, Bachetta, and Banerjee, 2004).

A number of empirical studies are conducted in China on the issue of opening-up, mainly from the perspective of the contribution of FDI and trade to China's growth, from China's excessive trade dependence, high foreign exchange reserves, and from exchange rate regime. In general, these empirical studies focus on trade opening-up, while the exploration on the impact of financial opening-up, such as capital account liberalization, is limited to reference from international experience and normative research.

The existing international experience and research show that opening-up and high capital accumulation are the driving forces of growth, but there may be some negative effects. The high accumulation model itself shows clear marks of resources mobilized by the government. High accumulation can cause an imbalance between domestic and external demand, and the distortion of the economic structure. Before and after the Asian crisis, plenty of scholars criticized the high resource accumulation model mobilized by Asian governments from the perspective of total factor productivity. In the couple of years after the crisis, Asian countries have been making structural adjustment to improve the resource allocation model. After its accession to the WTO, China is speeding up its opening-up process, and now vulnerable to external impact. In a closed system, the "structural distortion" of state intervention may promote development at a certain stage, but with active flow of foreign capital with the opening-up in the financial sector, the distorted structure will be "forcibly corrected" by the market. Therefore, how to make full use of external resources to accelerate China's non-agricultural process, eliminate institutional distortions, optimize resource allocation, reduce external impact risks, and promote economic growth will be discussed in this chapter.

1.2 Trade-Oriented Strategy and Economic Growth

1. China's Trade-Oriented Strategy

With the rapid development and integration of the global economy over the past two hundred years, trade has been recognized as the engine of growth.

At present, the global total import and export has accounted for 40% of the global GDP. Global resource flow directs economic development.

Countries adopt trade strategies that vary with what national conditions they have and which development stages they are in. Import substitution and export orientation were once the most popular proposed trade strategies. When the free trade theory is exclusively adopted, the developing countries can only specialize in some low-end industries and will be stuck in the backward conditions. Under this circumstance, they should implement the import substitution strategy to cultivate the domestic market, achieve economic take-off and catch up with developed economies by importing only necessary high-tech capital goods or intermediate goods and focusing on independent production to replace imported goods. The export-oriented strategy is adopted given that export is conducive to expanding external demand, increasing employment opportunities and upgrading the industrial structure in international competition. In practice, Japan is considered a successful model of the import substitution strategy, while the Asian Four Dragons is deemed to have risen from the export-oriented strategy. While this distinction may help highlight the merits of trade, it may lead to a one-sided understanding and "opposition" between export and import. In fact, the synergy between export and import is the key to promoting growth. The World Bank seriously appraised East Asia's economy, which was famous for its export, and concluded that the miracle of East Asia's economy was "trade-oriented rather than export-oriented growth" (World Bank, 2003). Although not a clearly defined strategic idea as an import substitution and export orientation, trade orientation is more common in practice, and is of more practical significance, especially for big countries.

As a large developing country, China has a very strong trade orientation. Its economic growth is highly correlated with trade growth, but poorly correlated with net exports. Only in some years, like 1990 and 1994, when its trade surplus increased significantly, its net export growth made large contribution to GDP growth. In fact, when the export strategy is only measured by the contribution of net export to GDP, South Korea and Singapore, both of whom are renowned for their opening-up, cannot live up to their reputation, for they registered trade deficits during their "take-off" period, that is to say, their net export made negative contribution to GDP. China's net export has not contributed much to GDP, but many scholars have indeed perceived the opening-up's great contribution. This is certainly not a simple issue simply relating to import or export, but the result of China's rapid trade-oriented development.

Before the 1990s, China had generally seen trade deficit and an industrial structure inadaptable to the rapidly changing consumption structure, the country thus had to import large volume of consumer goods and related capital goods. Following the sharp depreciation of the RMB in 1994, the J effect was obvious, the export sector showed apparent competitiveness, and the subsequent export tax rebate policy further encouraged exports. On the other hand, China has always encouraged the import of capital goods with tax policy - most notably, production-type VAT is adopted in China, and is not deductible for investment goods, but deductible for imported equipment. In the development zones, with the implementation of a series of preferential policies on foreign investment like "two exemptions and three reductions" [1], much foreign capital was attracted and the import of capital goods sector stimulated. This shows that China has always maintained a "two-way incentive" rather than a simple export orientation in trade import and export policies.

The contribution of exports to economic growth has been hotly argued (Lin and Li, 2002). In particular, by taking advantage of the comparative advantage of low labor costs, the export sector can readily complete its accumulation, transferring more rural labor to the modern industrial sector. However, there are few studies on the improvement of factor input quality from the perspective of import. Recent studies have noticed this and have also proved the contribution of import to the improvement of total factor productivity theoretically and empirically—the same with the empirical analysis on the import and export effects of Japan and South Korea (Shen et al., 2003; World Bank, 2003). As a large country, China has never upheld the same model in essence, implementing both the import substitution and export-oriented models. For example, Guangdong is mainly labor-intensive export oriented, while the Yangtze River Delta prefers capital-intensive import substitution (Lu, 2003). The economic growth and allocation efficiency have been greatly promoted via two-way trade deployment, effectively increasing the non-agricultural employment and the improvement of total factor productivity— trade orientation constitutes the growth path of China's structural optimization.

---

1 The policy of "two exemptions and three reductions" refers to that productive foreign-invested enterprises with an operating period of more than 10 years can enjoy the exemption from enterprise income tax for 2 years and reduction of enterprise income tax by half for 3 years from the profit-making year.

2. The Sustainability of Trade-Oriented Strategy

China's trade-oriented strategy has proved successful. China's rural labor transfer and productivity improvement need to be expanded through trade orientation. However, can the trade-oriented strategy continue today when trade frictions are frequent and increasingly fierce? First understand the position of China's trade growth in global trade if you would know.

First of all, Table 1 shows that in the position in world trade, China was inferior to Japan in the 1960s and 1970s, and the so-called "China threat" is absurd. Besides, China achieved an export growth of 11.9% from 1978 to 2002, lower than those of South Korea, Japan, and newly industrialized countries and regions (see Table 3).

Table 1. Share of China and Japan in world exports (1953–2002) (%)

Year / State	1953	1963	1973	1983	1993	2000	2002
Japan	1.5	3.5	6.4	8	10	7.7	6.6
China	1.2	1.3	1	1.2	2.5	4	5.1

Data source: WTO, Direction of Trade Statistics and CEIC.
The figures in 2002 are calculated by the author.

Secondly, according to Table 2, China, Japan and South Korea account for 10.7%, 10.4% and 3% of the U.S.' import, showing China is not "going too far." Even today, Japan and China still hold approximate share of the U.S. import market. In the history, Japan's share of U. S. imports rose steadily from the 1960s to 1970s and reached a peak of 22% in 1986 (the serious Japan-U.S. trade frictions in the mid-1980s was not groundless). Regardless its fastest trade growth in the past 35

Table 2. Shares in the U.S.' import (2002) (%)

Countries and regions	Share of imports
North America	29.6
Western Europe	21.1
China	10.7
Japan	10.4
Korea	3.0
Others	25.2

Data source: U.S. Census Bureau website.

years, South Korea did not occupy a large share due to its small size (compared to China and Japan). Even so, in the late 1980s, South Korean's export still accounted for 4.5% of the U.S. import market (Prasad and Rumbaugh, 2003).

Thirdly, the international community tends to worry about the "externality" of China's trade growth, which is intentionally perceived as a negative Chinese factor seeking an increasing share of the international market for itself while squeezing out that for others, but evidently the contribution of China's trade growth to global trade should never be ignored. Data shows that China's import increased from USD 53.4 billion in 1990 to USD 412.8 billion in 2003. China has surpassed Japan as the world's third largest importer, after the United States and Germany. China's import ratio (the proportion of import to GDP) has risen from 15% in 1990 to 29% in 2003, and will soon reach 30%, far higher than Japan's 8% and the U.S.' 14%. When this positive externality of China's trade growth is taken into account, China's trade growth is not so "problematic."

Finally, compared with the 27, 35, 28, and 31 years of export growth of Japan, South Korea, Malaysia, and newly industrialized countries, although China has achieved 1/4 century of fast export growth (see Table 1–3), China has not reached its limit, and there's still room for this process.

Table 3. Comparison of export growth among countries

Countries and regions	Period*	Years	Growth rate (%)
Japan	1954–1981	27	14.2
Korea	1960–1995	35	21.5
Malaysia	1968–1996	28	10.2
China	1978–2002	24	11.9
NIEs (newly industrialized economies)**	1966–1997	31	13.1

Data Source: IMF, Direction of Trade Statistics.

*The period starting from the continuous export growth until the three-year mobile average export growth rate falls below 10%

**NIEs refer to Hong Kong of China, South Korea, Singapore, and Taiwan (China)

The above analysis shows that: (1) As China is inferior to Japan back then in trade, including share of global trade, share of the U.S.' import or and export growth (China faces the claims for more advanced stages on trade deficit and appreciation of the home currency against Japan back then), China's trade growth should not be fussed about taking into account its contribution to global trade. (2) The comparison of export growth among countries also indicates that China's trade growth still has potential. (3) China's rich resources of cheap labor can offer concrete support to the long-term growth of its trade.

Nevertheless, in 2003, China's trade dependence was as high as 60%, making it more and more difficult to continue the high growth of trade. It is time to lift the distorted structural policies of state intervention such as the "two-way incentive policy" in China's trade orientation. The focus of trade growth should shift from trade surplus to trade balance, and from trade volume to the trade-oriented strategy of improving productivity and promoting sustainable international competitiveness.

1.3 Capital Formation Under the Condition of Labor Transfer

Trade-oriented economic growth has greatly promoted a country's savings and capital formation in the following manner: (1) the traditional sector increases its savings while its surplus labor serves the export sector; (2) more foreign capital is used; (3) import brings higher productivity to the capital goods sector, increasing its savings. Savings are transformed into the investment to stimulate growth, thus breaking through the "poverty cycle," ushering in a virtuous circle of capital accumulation - growth - saving improvement and removing the traditional "two gaps." The gap in capital formation, however, can still be very big, as long as there are still a large number of surplus rural labor in China that need to be transferred and combined with capital.

1. The Traditional Two-Gap Model and the "Disappearance" of China's Savings Gap

A classic theory in development economics, known as the two-gap model, was proposed by Chenery and Straw (1966) to interpret how to use foreign capital to develop the domestic economy, and can be expressed by the following simple relations:

$$Y = C + I + (X - M)$$
$$I = Y - C - (X - M)$$
$$I = S + (M - X) \quad (1)$$

The above relations are the transformation of national income identity. Among them Y = Gross Domestic Product; C = Final Consumption, I = Investment, X = Export, M = Import; S = Savings.

Relation (1) indicates that domestic investment is restricted by S and (M-X). The former is savings (S) restriction, and the latter the trade restriction or foreign exchange restriction caused by import exceeding export. In order to further explore the impact of foreign investment, we can introduce the current account surplus CA:

$$CA = \left(X - M\right) + NFI + NTRA \tag{2}$$

NFI = income account surplus (including outward remittance of foreign direct investment income), $NT - RA$ = current transfer account surplus. For a more convenient presentation, we hereby omit the last two terms of the above formula, namely, the income account surplus and the current transfer account surplus (the conclusion will not be affected), then:

$$CA = X - M \tag{3}$$

We introduce the capital account (referred to capital and financial account in China) KA, then obviously:

$$CA + KA = \Delta FR \tag{4}$$

Where:
$\Delta FR =$ Changes in foreign exchange reserves.

According to formulas (2), (3) and (4), we can get the following variant:

$$I - S = KA - \Delta FR \tag{5}$$

Formula (5) indicates that the savings gap ($I - S$) can be made up by capital inflow ($KA - \Delta FR$).

Next, we will study China's introduction of foreign investment to see whether it conforms to the above-mentioned two-gap model.

The simplest way to measure whether there is a savings gap is to compare China's savings rate with its investment rate, where:

Investment rate = gross fixed cost formation/ GDP by expenditure method

Savings Ratio = (GDP by expenditure method-final consumption)/GDP by expenditure method

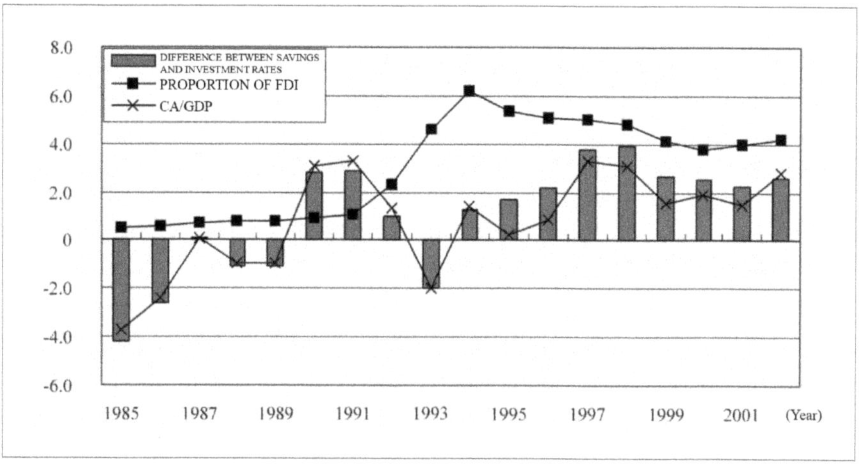

Figure 1. Investment-savings gap, current account surplus, and FDI

Data source: China Statistical Yearbook 2003, State Administration of Foreign Exchange.

Figure 1 shows that from 1985 to 2002, the investment rate was higher than the savings rate in only five years, including four years before the 1990s. That is to say, before the 1990s, China had a savings gap, but after the 1990s (except 1993), the savings gap disappeared.

Further analysis shows that before the 1990s, the savings gap and the foreign exchange gap co-existed, which conforms to the two-gap model. That is, an investment well above savings can bring high imports, making imports exceed exports, resulting in a current account deficit. That the current account surplus is almost identical to the investment savings gap in Figure 1 is not surprising, which can be indicated by transforming formula (1) to $I - S = M - X = -CA$. The slight difference in Figure 1 is caused by our assumptions about CA (the earnings of income items and current transfer items are omitted) and the error in statistics.

The above two gaps can be made up by the introduction of foreign capital. However, the existence or size of China's two gaps is measured with the inflow of foreign capital, we are going the opposite way. There was a two gap before the 1990s, regardless of the low inflow of foreign capital, and FDI accounting for less than 1%. Since 1992, FDI has been pouring in in a large amount, staying above 4%, while the savings gap was gone in China. It is obviously not feasible to explain the inflow of foreign capital with the savings gap given China's development in recent years. With the filling of the savings gap, China no more needs to introduce foreign capital because there's no more savings gap to be closed by foreign investment based on the two-gap model. Some scholars have also expressed the same view (Song Guoqing, 2003; Yasheng Huang, 2001). Of course, even if there is no savings gap, China still has good reasons to introduce foreign capital. However, we should be clear: Has China's savings gap really disappeared? Or did we look at things from a wrong angle?

2. The Two-Gap Model of Additional Employment Target and the "Emergence" of China's Savings Gap

The traditional two-gap model takes GDP (or GNP) growth rate as the target (6%–7% annual growth rate) (Chenery & Strout, 1966), and deduces the savings gap, without considering the matter of employment, and the employment target was far less important than the GDP target, at least in the eyes of experts from international organizations. The employment is a matter of great concern for China - besides the large number of workers laid off in reform and structural adjustment, a large new labor force comes out and a large number of rural surplus labor forces must be transferred from the rural land every year.

Therefore, we decide to add the employment target in the two-gap model or impose the employment restriction on the basis of the saving restriction and foreign exchange restriction. The said employment target restriction can be interpreted as a certain investment level to achieve the specified employment target. The potential investment demand determined by the employment target may exceed the savings, forming a savings gap.

To explore the relationship between investment and employment, assume the production technology is Leontief production technology[2], that is, a certain output requires a fixed proportion between capital and labor, while there is no substitution relationship between capital and labor (see Figure 2).

---

2 In a completely competitive and sound factor market, the demand for capital and labor can be met, and there is no technical problem in the substitution between the two. In this case, it is assumed that Cobb Douglas' production technology is reasonable. However, due to the imperfect factor market in China and the existence of a large number of surplus labor, the demand for capital cannot be met. It is unrealistic to expect to absorb all surplus labor through labor replacing capital. In this case, it is assumed that Leontief production technology is in line with China's national conditions.

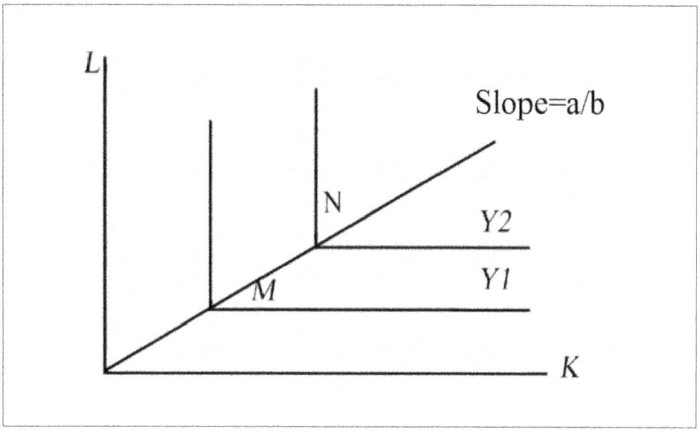

Figure 2. Leontief production technology

Figure 2 shows an L-shaped production curve under Leontief production technology conditions. Obviously, for producers, the best factor-combining point should be the inflection point of the L-shaped production line (M, N points in the figure). Therefore, its desirable output is expanded based on a fixed proportion of the slope a/b.

With the large number of surplus labor, capital restriction is dominant in China. In fact, when the SOE reform was launched, to ensure a job for everyone, the capital combined with labor exceeding a fixed rate, resulting in hidden unemployment which would not increase but even reduce output based on the features of Leontief production technology. With the promotion of market-oriented reform, hidden unemployment has turned into laid-off workers and overt unemployment. We assume that hidden unemployment is no longer a typical situation in the current Chinese economy, and producers prefer to combine factors according to the optimal ratio. Therefore, we get a simple relationship between labor and capital $aK = bL$, which reflects a functional relationship between investment and employment creation:

$$L = \frac{a}{b}K = \alpha K$$

Thus:

$$\dot{L} = \frac{a}{b}\dot{K}$$

L means new jobs, which can also be expressed by actual labor demand L^d. K refers to new investment or I, therefore:

$$L^d = \frac{a}{b} I$$

$$I = \frac{b}{a} L^d = I\left(L^d\right) \tag{6}$$

It should be noted that although Leontief production technology is assumed, the ratio between labor and capital is not constant. Note that the fixed ratio assumption is relaxed here, but it is still assumed that there is no strong substitution relationship between labor and capital. A rising α means labor intensive, and a falling α indicates capital intensive, provided that $\alpha > 0$. Under capital intensity, unit capital can create less jobs (see Figure 4).

Substitute formula (6) into formula (5) to get:

$$I\left(L^d\right) - S = KA - \Delta FR \tag{7}$$

Next, we will take into account the two-gap model with employment target restrictions, under the scenario of urban employment. In China, the annual supply of urban labor L^s is generally composed of laid-off workers, new working-age labor force, and the transfer of rural surplus labor. Thus:

$$L^s = L_x + L_n + L_r$$

Where L_x= the number of laid-off workers

L_n= the number of new working-age labor force
L_r= the number of the transferred rural surplus labor

Suppose the employment target L^*= (1-β)L^S, where β is an acceptable level of unemployment rate. Obviously, $L^d \leq L^*$, and it can be deduced according to Leontief production technology that:

$$I\left(L^d\right) \leq I\left(L^*\right) \tag{8}$$

This actually means that the investment needed to achieve the employment target will not be less than the actual investment, but according to China's situation, it should be far greater than the actual investment. Substitute formula (8) into formula (7), we get the two-gap model with employment target:

$$I\left(L^{d}\right)=S+\left(KA-\Delta FR\right)\leq I\left(L^{*}\right) \tag{9}$$

If the employment target restriction in formula (9) works, the following formula holds:

$$S+\left(KA-\Delta FR\right)=I\left(L^{*}\right)$$

Thus, the new savings gap becomes

$$I\left(L^{*}\right)-S=KA-\Delta FR \tag{10}$$

Next, we will discuss whether there is a savings gap in China with additional employment restrictions, that is, to examine the size and trend of $I\ (L^{*})$ and S.

2.1. China's National Savings

China's savings rate always stays at a high level. Since 1993, the average savings rate has exceeded 41 %. However, considering the off-set effect on savings by other factors below, the real savings rate is not so high.

1. Bad debt of banks: Since bad debts are usually calculated afterwards and cannot be eliminated from the GDP of that year, the real national savings should be less because of the bad debt factor (this cannot be ignored in China).
2. The impact of future aging: China's current high savings rate is related to specific factors. On the one hand, the uncertainty brought about by the reform has more or less restrained consumption and promoted savings; on the other hand, from the perspective of demographic changes, China is in a period when the working-age population accounts for a very high proportion of the total population. Young people will save more, so the savings rate is high. Once they reach the aging stage, savings will decline. Research shows that the proportion of the working-age population will tend to decline after reaching its peak around 2010, and the proportion of the elderly population increase rapidly from around 2010 (Cai et al., 2001). This demographic change will obviously lead to a decline in the savings rate.

2.2. Employment and Investment in China

Investment growth is required to achieve the employment target. How many jobs can a certain investment create? Figure 3 shows the change in capital stock per worker in China since 1978. The increase of capital stock per worker not only shows capital deepening, but also (e.g., from the perspective of employment) demonstrates less jobs created by each unit of capital stock.

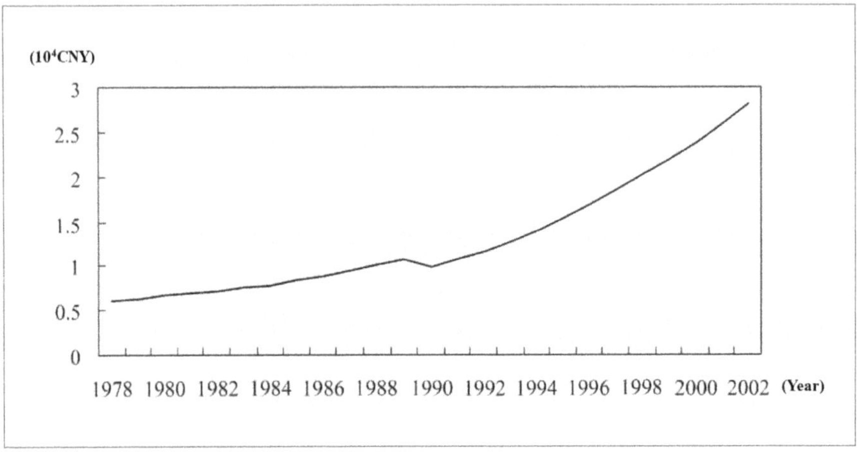

Figure 3. Capital stock per worker in China (1978–2002)

Data source: China Statistical Yearbook.

Note: The capital stock data from 1978 to 1998 is from Zhang Jun (2002). Data from 1999 to 2002 is calculated by the author.[3]

However, note that the number of labor force in Figure 3 is the sum of urban and rural labor forces. Obviously, the capital stock of the rural labor force is much less than that of the urban labor force. Given the fact that farmers migrate to cities, more capital is needed for each additional unit of urban labor force. Figure 4 offers a brief picture of this situation: From the late 1970s to the early 1990s, the newly fixed asset investment required for new employment every year was significantly lower than that from the late 1990s to the early twenty-first century. In other words, the ability to create jobs per unit of newly fixed asset investment is declining.

The declining capacity of the investment to create jobs since the 1990s can be attributed, to a certain extent, to the state-owned enterprises' poor employment

[3] The calculation method of capital stock is as follows: capital stock of the current year = capital stock of the previous year (constant price in 1990) + (fixed capital formation in the current year -depreciation)/fixed asset investment price index. The depreciation here is uniformly calculated at 5% depreciation rate.

capacity caused by the deepened reform of state-owned enterprises that laid off their former employees who were in a potential state of unemployment. In addition, since 1998, the government has increased investment in infrastructure, which had a weak employment-driving effect, thus affecting job creation. The declining capacity of the investment to create employment conforms to the falling capacity of GDP to drive employment. As estimated by the National Bureau of Statistics, in the 1980s, every 1 percentage point of economic growth could increase 2.4 million jobs, but since the 1990s, only 700,000 jobs could be created, showcasing the marked inability of economic growth in stimulating employment. According to the research of the International Monetary Fund, after controlling the wage effect, the employment elasticity of China's GDP stood at 0.52 from 1978 to 1993 and 0.20 from 1993 to 2000. This means before 1993, every 1 percentage point of GDP growth brought a 0.52 percentage point of employment increase, while after 1993, every 1 percentage point of GDP growth only drove a 0.2 percentage point of employment increase (Brooks & Ran, 2003).

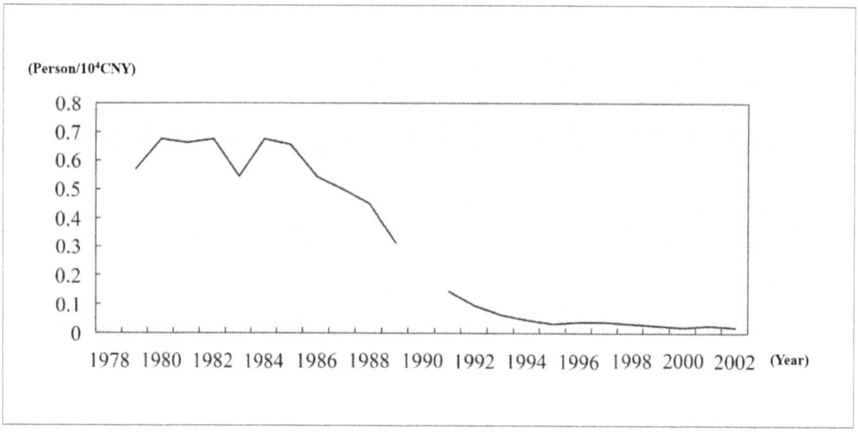

Figure 4. The proportion of new employment and newly fixed assets investment every year (1978–2002)

Data source: *China Statistical Yearbook* of 1978–2002.

Note: Fixed asset investment is calculated at the constant price in 1990.

According to China Statistical Yearbook in 2003, an output of 26.51 million yuan was created by the new urban workers in 1990, which obvious included those missed in the 1990 census. In addition, the newly fixed asset investment in 1990 was negative. For the convenience of analysis, the "abnormal point" in 1990 is set as missing.

The declining capacity of an investment to create employment means that more unit investment is required to create one job. So, how big is our current employment gap? According to the statistics, 109 million people were transferred from rural to urban areas in the last 20 years from 1982 to 2000. At present, the number of urban laid-off workers is 14 million. Every year, about 10 million people reach the working age. About 150 million surplus rural labors need to be transferred. To complete this process in the next 20 years, 7.5 million people will need to be transferred every year. In recent years, only about 8 million jobs are created annually. What a big employment gap!

Moreover, comparison among countries more intuitively shows the employment pressure of China in the future. According to Table 4, China has the highest proportion of working-age population in the world, which together with the future working-age manpower (people under 15 years old) will account for 93% of the total population, the highest in countries and regions other than underdeveloped countries. Given the short life expectancy of many underdeveloped countries and some incomparable factors, China is deemed to have the most abundant labor supply. It is not hard to imagine the immense employment pressure considering further the total size of China's labor force.

Table 4. Comparison of population status among countries (%)

Countries and regions	Under 15 years old	15–65 years old	Over 65 years old
China	23	70	7
Less developed countries (except China)	36	60	4
Developed countries	18	67	15
East Asia	22	70	8
United States	21	66	13
Japan	17	67	16
Western Europe	14	66	18

Data Source: 2002 World Population Data of the Population Reference Bureau.

Considering China's grave employment issue, we intend to add employment target restrictions in the two-gap model. In theory, in the face of such a huge employment gap, further investment growth is undoubtedly necessary. However, it is unrealistic to expand employment simply by increasing investment. After all, our investment rate has exceeded 40%, a pretty high level. By contrast, in investment rate, namely the ratio of investment to GDP calculated at constant prices, among the Four Asian Tigers, Hong Kong achieved over 40% in the early

1980s, which then reached a plateau around 30%; Singapore reached 10% in the 1960s, 39% in 1980, and 47% in 1984.; South Korea achieved 5% in the 1950s, 20% in the 1960s, 40% in 1991, and about 30% in the late 1990s, while Taiwan registered 10% in the 1950s, 27% in 1975, which then reached a plateau around 22% (Young, 1995).

According to the experience of the Four Asian Tigers with investment-driven economy), an investment rate of 40% is the upper limit. Therefore, we cannot count on more growth room for China's investment rate even if there is such room. However, given the employment targets, we must maintain a high investment rate even above 40%.[4] And further considering that China's declining savings rate in the long run, there will be a potential savings gap in China. Inevitably, an open China still has to fill its savings gap by attracting more foreign capital.

3. China's Savings Gap and the Net Outflow of Resources

The above analysis shows that although the real savings gap has disappeared since 1993, the potential savings gap exists. In order to truly utilize external resources and fill the savings gap, what changes should be made to the balance of payments?

In terms of China's external balance, these years see net outflow of resources, rather than net inflow of resources. According to formula (10), $\Delta FR - KA$ can measure the outflow of net resources. Because $\Delta FR - KA = CA$ and the current account surplus CA or the net export these years always stays above 0, the net outflow of resources is obviously greater than 0. The total net outflow of resources refers to the difference between the total accumulated foreign exchange reserves and the total accumulated capital account surplus.

Obviously, to realize the net inflow of resources, the current account, when the potential savings gap is taken into account, should be less than 0, that is $\Delta FR - KA < 0$. Two conditions are required to satisfy this formula: a declining ΔFR, that is, to reduce the increment of foreign exchange reserves decreases; a rising KA, that is, to attract more foreign capital. Note that in China, the surplus in the capital account is dominated by introduced foreign capital.

According to relevant research, there are few countries keeping sustained double surpluses like China (Song Guoqing, 2003). In fact, current account deficits and capital account surpluses are common in the development of many countries

[4] In fact, only a high investment rate is not enough. Structural adjustment and other measures conducive to employment are also needed. For example, we need to vigorously develop labor-intensive industries, remove micro regulations that are not conducive to labor mobility and employment, etc.

including South Korea and Singapore. Only in this way can the savings gap be made up with foreign capital.

From this point of view, maintaining a large current account surplus and a large amount of foreign exchange reserves runs counter to the use of external resources. Rather, the foreign trade surplus should be reduced, the current account balance or a slight deficit maintained, and the increment in foreign exchange reserves meanwhile reduced. Even the overall foreign exchange reserves can be cut, which implies a negative increment in reserves. In this way, we can not only make use of external resources but also reduce the cost of holding a large amount of foreign exchange reserves.

We have explained the necessity of continuing to introduce foreign capital from the capital formation gap under the condition of labor force transfer. This does not rule out the positive spillover effect of foreign capital in technology, management, and system, among others, but China should pay more attention to the contribution of foreign capital in filling the savings gap, especially when a large number of surplus labor needs to be combined with capital.

1.4 Distortion and Risk Accumulation of Trade and Capital Formation Mechanism

The trade orientation and high accumulation have promoted the rapid growth of China's economy, but due to the serious distortion of government intervention in the mechanism of trade and capital formation, the risk of "structural distortion" plagues the process of growth. Under the circumstance of further opening-up, a distorted economic structure is most vulnerable to external impact—a vital lesson from the East Asian crisis. From international experience, China's current trade dependence and investment rate are at a high level (see Table 5). It is actually very difficult to promote trade growth through the two-way stimulus of government policies and for the government to mobilize resources to significantly increase the investment rate.

1. Distortion of "Two-Way Incentive" in Trade and Foreign Investment Policies

China's opening-up has been advancing along the two-way incentive of trade and foreign investment policies: (1) The two-way incentive of import and export has greatly stimulated the volume of trade, established a trade-oriented economy, while the dependence on trade has increased rapidly from 30% in 1990 to 60.3% in 2003, a pretty high level given only Germany reaches a trade dependence of 54% and Japan just gets 13% among major countries. (2) The policy of

Table 5. Comparison among countries of macro indicators such as per capita income, capital formation, and trade dependence

Country and type	Gross national income per capita (USD)	Gross national income per capita in PPP (USD)	Agriculture (%)	Industry (%)	Services (%)	Household consumption (%)	Capital formation (%)	ratio of trade dependence. (%)
China	890	4260	15	52	33	48	39	60
Middle-income countries	1850	5710	10	38	52	59	25	51
lower-middle-income countries	1240	5020	12	41	46	57	27	50
Upper-middle-income countries	4460	8730	7	35	59	62	22	52
East Asian and Pacific countries	900	4040	14	48	37	53	31	60
High-income countries	26710	27680	NA	NA	NA	61	17	38

Data Source: World Development Report 2003.

Note: Gross national income: 2001 data; the proportion of the added value of agriculture, industry, and service industry in GDP: 2000 data; others: 2000 data (China's trade dependence: 2003 data).

introducing foreign capital is distorted. To attract more foreign capital, various preferential policies have been introduced, which puts multinational companies in a favorable competitive position in China. These foreign-funded enterprises still enjoy a comparative advantage in international competition as they can access cheap labor (who are paid with hard-earned wages), exchange depreciation, and export tax rebates. As a result, on the one hand, we adopt a large number of preferential policies to attract foreign capital and encourage exports to earn foreign exchange (a certain policy distortion); on the other hand, we buy the low-yield U.S. Treasuries with the hard-earned foreign exchange reserves, and the gains and losses hereof have aroused great concern in recent years. Most of the existing arguments involve the imbalance between China's import and export and between domestic and foreign development caused by policy distortion, and the cost of policy distortion.

2. Mechanism Distortion in Capital Formation

China's persistently high investment rate and return on capital have been declining for a decade since the mid-19902, accompanied by the rising wave of urbanization. The urbanization in 1993 and 1994 was mainly triggered by the speculation on "the valuable land previously considered priceless," while the substantial urbanization arising from the infrastructure construction promoted by the national active fiscal policy and the bank consumer loans under low-interest rates in 1998 was significant. Based on our calculation, the whole society was investing in infrastructure and real estate development related to urbanization, while the ratio of added value created by social investment continued to fall. The continuous high investment rate and low rate of return could be more or less explained by the rapid development of urbanization and the corresponding changes in the capital process (Frontier Research Group on Growth, 2003). However, this model, especially the capital formation mechanism in which the government mobilizes high investment, is unsustainable.

China's capital formation mechanism is obviously dualistic in that its resource is allocated under the direction of the market and government. Traditionally, all resources were allocated by the government. With the launch of reform and opening-up, the market could allocate resources more efficiently, but the government can still effectively mobilize and allocate resources by industry access, taxation, land, finance, and other means. The proportions of non-state-owned assets in financial assets, short-term loans of non-state-owned enterprises in all short-term loans of financial institutions, interest rate regulation and other financial resources are still poorly marketized (Institute of Economics and Resource Management, Beijing Normal University, 2003). The government mobilization mechanism is applicable when: (1) More than 80% of the medium and long-term bank loans are invested in infrastructure and real estate related to urbanization (Frontier Research Group on Growth, 2003), attracting funds to high capital-intensive heavy industries such as steel, electrolytic aluminum and cement. These investment behaviors cannot truly reflect the scarcity of funds in China. (2) Foreign capital more quickly flows into China under the preferential policies of the government, such as tax exemption, land subsidies, and local financial returns. China then purchases U.S. Treasuries with the foreign exchange reserves earned, which causes serious efficiency losses. (3) The government has been relying on the stock market for financing, which, regardless of its low market returns, has helped a lot of state-owned enterprises out of difficulties. (4) In terms of finance, a rising debt ratio, together with overdraft by export tax rebate countries from banks (if any), gives rise to a high deficit level, making the government more unable to directly mobilize resources.

Government-led capital, land and fiscal taxation distort factor prices and deviate from the medium - and long-term sustainable development goals, as: (1) the cost of capital is reduced, giving rise to the tendency of excessive funds and affecting employment; (2) the excessive competition of local governments in attracting foreign capital leads to the loss of the efficiency in introduction of foreign capital; (3) distortion in the price of land elements, excessive occupation of agricultural land in the process of urbanization and low compensation for agricultural land turn farmers into citizens. However, the supporting social security and employment system is established, while the financial department has paid the price to support the land price inversion in the industrial development zone, and the land elements are used at cheap prices.

3. Risk Accumulation and Opening-up Impact

A poverty-stricken country has low savings on the one hand, which discourages investment, and on the other hand, receives low income, and thus develops no purchasing power—a condition Nax defined as the "vicious poverty cycle" trap. To break the poverty trap, we must increase savings and create demand, in which the government can play a significant role. The East Asian model is a government-led one: (1) the government reduces the savings-investment risk through "guarantee," greatly increasing savings, and directing the allocation of resources; (2) through intervention policies, the government promotes exports, creates demand, and effectively eliminates poverty. However, government intervention has also built up a number of risks. Problems such as bad debts of banks and excessive burden of fiscal productive expenditure are all risks arising under the "guarantee" of the government. As the state intervenes in the prices, the investment intension is strong, but efficiency is improved slowly. These risk-bearing mechanisms of government intervention cause structural distortion and build up macro risks while promoting economic growth. In a closed economy, the government may still have room and ability to "consciously and actively" resolve the risks brought by distortion one by one, but under the conditions of financial opening-up[5], the situation is completely different. After

5 With China's accession to the WTO, the opening-up of the financial industry, the introduction of QFII, ODII, and many other measures, capital flows will be more frequent than before, and the gradual opening-up of the capital account is also imperative. At present,

the financial opening-up, the government has poorer ability to intervene, and international investors will "forcibly rectify" the distorted structure through generalized arbitrage.

International arbitrage mainly arises: first, under the opportunities provided by distorted factor prices and distorted structures, and second, because of asymmetric arbitrage income and risk–the government has taken much risk of distorted structure, while foreign investors can access the arbitrage income in the short term without taking risks or taking few risks. However, this does not mean that foreign investors do not know that the distorted structure will build up a country's macro risk, but they believe that the country's macro risk accumulation has not reached a critical point in the short term, and the government can afford it, so these foreign investors carry on with their arbitrage. These arbitrage behaviors further aggravate the exposure of national macro risks. Foreign investors pay close attention to the accumulation of the said macro risk. Once noticing the government will be "unable to afford" these macro risks, they will shift the flow of their capital, giving rise to a crisis. This is exactly the case of the Asian crisis. Therefore, in the new stage of financial opening-up, efforts should be made to eliminate structural distortions and reduce national macro risks, to crack down on hot money arbitrage and prevent crises.

1.5 A Policy "Mix" with a New "Opening-Up"

China's economy is entering the new stage of financial opening-up from that of the trade opening-up. Considering that the distorted structure formed by policy intervention is vulnerable to impact under financial opening-up, the policy package for the new opening-up aims to eliminate the "structural distortion" caused by government intervention, optimize resource allocation, reduce macro risks and external impact, and maintain stable economy and sustainable development.

1. Reduction of Structural Distortion

Elimination of the above-mentioned policy distortion under two-way incentives for trade and foreign investment policies: properly reduce various incentives

in terms of the capital account, China has implemented partial convertibility. Of the 43 capital account transactions determined by the IMF, four have been fully convertible in China. Eight items are generally convertible, 16 items have strict restrictions, and 15 items are completely prohibited, to prohibit foreign investors from purchasing RMB-denominated securities and assets. In general, China's capital account opening-up has also reached a high level.

for foreign trade and implement national treatment for foreign investment. In terms of resource mobilization, adopt a market-led resource mobilization mode instead of the old government-led resource mobilization mode, and correct the policies that lead to the distortion of factor prices in the government-led resource allocation.

The fixed exchange rate system is not sustainable. The old fixed exchange rate system was designed to serve the opening-up of trade (e.g., to stimulate exports by exchange rate depreciation), but now it is not suitable to serve the opening-up of finance. According to Mondale's Impossibility Theorem, among the independence of fixed exchange rate, capital flow, and monetary policy, we can only choose two. Under the condition of financial opening-up or capital flow, the only option of a fixed exchange rate or independence of monetary policy is available. As a large developing economy, China must maintain the independence of monetary policy, instead of the old fixed exchange rate system. Internationally, the market-oriented reform of the exchange rate is an inevitable trend. The fixed exchange rate system has dropped from 84.8% in 1970 to 46.6% in 2003, while the floating exchange rate system has increased from 15.3% to 53.4%. Therefore, the old fixed exchange rate system should transform into a more market-oriented and managed floating exchange rate system, to more effectively reduce structural distortion.

2. Macro Policy Choices

Given the current "structural distortion," macro policies are implemented in the new stage of opening-up to first reduce the risks in the economic operation. The problems of financial macro debt and bank bad debts reflect the macro risks caused by economic structural distortion. To help eliminate "structural distortion," reduce macro risks, guard against external impact, and maintain economic stability and sustainable development, we should: (1) promote tax reform, unify domestic and foreign income taxes, reduce export tax rebates, and allow the transition from production-type VAT to consumption tax. Only in this way can we effectively shift from national resource allocation relying on national debt to stimulation micro supply through tax reduction, and at the same time eliminate the distortion of tax on two-way incentives for imports and exports; (2) adopt a moderately tight monetary policy to control inflation and reduce macro risks; (3) reduce the vulnerability of finance through shareholding reform of banks and reform of capital markets; (4) use various resources including external resources, improve resource mobilization methods to facilitate capital formation, absorb a large number of surplus labor, and promote non-agricultural employment, for the capital formation gap under the condition of labor force transfer shows that, China will still face the supply problem in the long run, and (5) fully consider the externalities of China's economic growth and macro policies, as well as to the international impact and response of these factor in the new stage of opening-up. Rather than a beggar-thy- neighbor approach, this can create a better external environment for China's growth and is thus a new proposed dimension for China's macro policies in the era of economic globalization.

International Capital Flows, Economic Distortions, and Macro Stability

2.1 Introduction

In 2004, China experienced an unexpected high growth. Unlike previous years, 2004 saw a large amount of international capital inflows, more than USD 200 billion or USD 170 billion of increment in foreign exchange reserves and more capital inflows when trade surplus was deducted. From the macro perspective, as a result of the massive inflow of international capital: (1) The currency is issued not based on the domestic economic situation, but under the pressure of funds outstanding for foreign exchange; (2) The investment grows rapidly, not just relying on the size of loans. In 2004, only around 90% of the loan quota was completed, but the investment growth in the first three quarters reached 43%, 28.6% and 27.7% respectively. In addition to the local impulsion, foreign investment is one of the main driving forces for the high growth of investment: in 2004, the investment by state-owned and state-controlled entities increased by 14.5%, far below the national average, while the investment of foreign-invested enterprises soared by 52.2%. (3) More and more international capital is entering the asset sector. There is a large amount of international capital behind the real estate boom in the central region. Foreign capital has played a very big role in the rise of real estate prices, with marked amplification effect on fluctuations. In 2005, the government promised the "market-oriented reform" of exchange rate and capital flow control, further stepping up the country's opening-up. International capital flows and their impact on macro stability are now hot issues for theoretical research and policy formulation.

Since the Asian financial crisis, the literature on the impact of international capital flows on a country's economy has increased dramatically. These documents focus on the impact of capital flows on the real economy from the perspective of financial liberalization and financial openness. Glick and Hutchison (1999) investigated a large sample of 90 countries in a period of 1975–1990. Their research showed that the opening of emerging markets to international capital flows and liberalization of financial structures made them very vulnerable and prone to double crises, that is, the simultaneous banking crisis and currency crisis.

Demirgüc-Kunt and Detragiache (1998) explored the empirical relationship between the banking crisis and financial liberalization in 53 countries from 1980 to 1995. They found that in an orderly institutional environment (with good legal system, low-level corruption, and faithful contract implementation, the financial liberalization would impose a weak impact on bank vulnerability. These results indicated that the promotion of financial liberalization should be prudent, especially in countries where institutional development such as legal system, contract enforcement, prudent regulation and supervision were not yet mature.

Williamson and Mahar (1998) reviewed the experience of 34 countries in promoting liberalization from 1973 to 1996. They believed that financial liberalization could bring benefits as well as crisis-inducing risks. Financial liberalization has effectuated financial deepening and improved investment allocation efficiency, but it has failed to drive higher savings. Unfortunately, liberalization will give rise to a crisis, and capital account liberalization increases this possibility for most countries. Therefore, the key is to design a proper liberalization plan to avoid the crisis.

Hellman, Murdock and Stiglitz (2000) suggested that we should first formulate a macroeconomic stability policy, then improve the supervision of banks, and finally achieve capital account liberalization—a conclusion close to that of Edwards (2001). He believed that after controlling other variables including total investment, a country with a more open capital account performed better than those with capital flow restrictions. Moreover, the positive impact of capital account liberalization on growth would only take effect after a country has achieved certain economic development, justifying the optimal order of capital account liberalization.

Kaminsky and Schmukler (2002) stressed that financial liberalization would bring pain in the short term but benefits in the long run. Tornell, Westermann and Martinez (2004) also pointed out that financial liberalization would promote growth, but would also bring crisis, that is, financial liberalization had a positive relationship with both growth and crisis. A study organized by IMF titled "The Impact of Financial Globalization on Developing Countries" showed that the benefits of financial opening-up were uncertain (Prasad, Rogoff, Wei, & Kose, 2003). According to Aghion et al., in countries with medium financial development, financial opening-up, especially a large number of incoming portfolio investments, would lead to economic instability (Aghion, Bachetta, & Banerjee, 2004).

Zhao Min (2004) pointed out when analyzing the issue of massive capital inflows that, few successful experiences but many lessons can be learned from the countries dealing with massive capital inflows since the 1990s. One of them was common and the most important, that is, economic distortions were the fundamental cause of large-scale capital inflows and subsequent backflows. Zhang Qi et al. (2003) also mentioned the relationship between financial liberalization and distortion. When various distortions arose from government intervention, financial liberalization would be more likely to cause vulnerability and crisis.

The Frontier Research Group on Economic Growth (2004) also suggested that in a closed economy, the government may still have room and ability to "consciously, actively" and gradually eliminate the risks caused by distortion. However, under financial opening-up, the government's ability to intervene would decline, and international investors would "forcibly correct" the distorted structure through generalized arbitrage, giving rise to fragility and crisis.

In the context of economic globalization, international capital flows are inevitable. On the one hand, capital inflow will bring about economic growth; on the other hand, the incoming international capital would gain more liquidity with the relaxation of controls. In emerging market countries with serious economic distortions, because the benefits and risks are related to the government, foreign capital could "leave in unison," (i.e., large outflows) after high national risks are appraised and reported, which will bring a serious impact to a country. The countries hit by Asian financial crisis are a lesson from the past. Therefore, this chapter will analyze the mechanism of the impact of international capital flows on macro stability and examine how economic distortions magnify this impact.

2.2 Patterns of International Capital Flow and Non-FDI

1. Investment Pattern: FDI and Portfolio Investment

In terms of the strategy of attracting investment, China adopts a favorable policy toward FDI and introduces portfolio investment with caution. Therefore, FDI enjoys various preferences, but there are many obstacles to portfolio investment. Because of this, over the past 30 years of reform and opening-up, China has introduced considerable FDI but has attracted insignificant portfolio investment (see Figure 5). Among 1997, 2000, 2003 and 2004, only 2004 saw portfolio investment exceeding USD 10 billion, and portfolio investment in other years was less than USD 10 billion. However, in recent years, the introduced FDI has reached USD 50 billion and USD 60 billion.

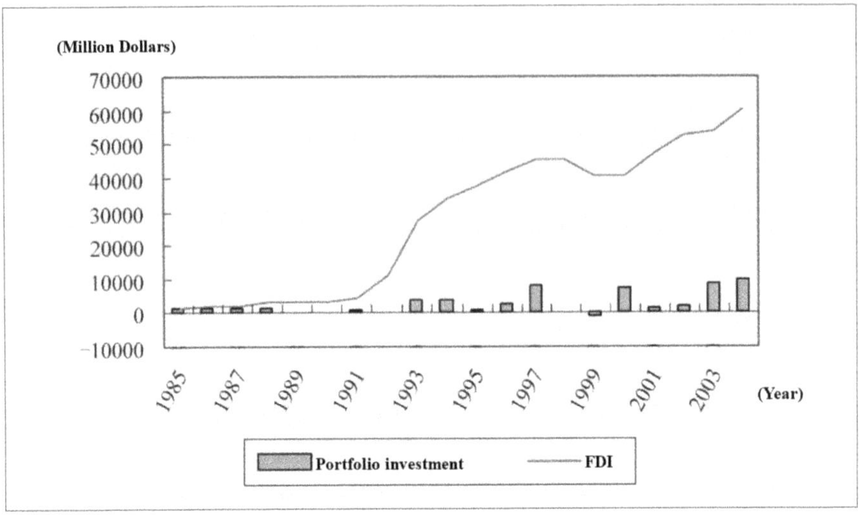

Figure 5. Comparison between FDI and portfolio investment flow

Data source: Statement of Balance of International Payments issued by the State Administration of Foreign Exchange; *China Statistical Yearbook.*

The stock of portfolio investment is also far less than that of FDI. The IMF survey data on China's stock of portfolio investment and the Ministry of Commerce's measurement data on China's stock of direct investment are used here to get Figure 6. According to IMF statistics, China's stock of portfolio investment stood at USD 19.324 billion in 1997, reached USD 20.286 billion in 2001, and remained basically unchanged at USD 20.285 billion in 2002. According to the data of the Ministry of Commerce calculated at an annual depreciation rate of 10%, the stock of FDI absorbed by China reached USD 137.17 billion, USD 158.505 billion and UJSD 168.533 billion in 1997, 2001 and 2002, respectively. These two sets of contrasting data vividly depict China's preference of FDI to portfolio investment.

The above comparison shows that portfolio investment does not seem worthy of attention, which may have caused recent research on foreign capital to focus on FDIs. However, when viewed from broader non-FDI indicators instead of portfolio investment, the international capital flows prove to be an issue far more complex than FDI.

2. Non-FDI Capital Flows in Balance of International Payments

The so-called "non-FDI capital" refers to the balance of changes in reserves minus the balance of current account, and then minus the balance of direct investment in the balance of international payments. Most notably, this index: (1) includes the

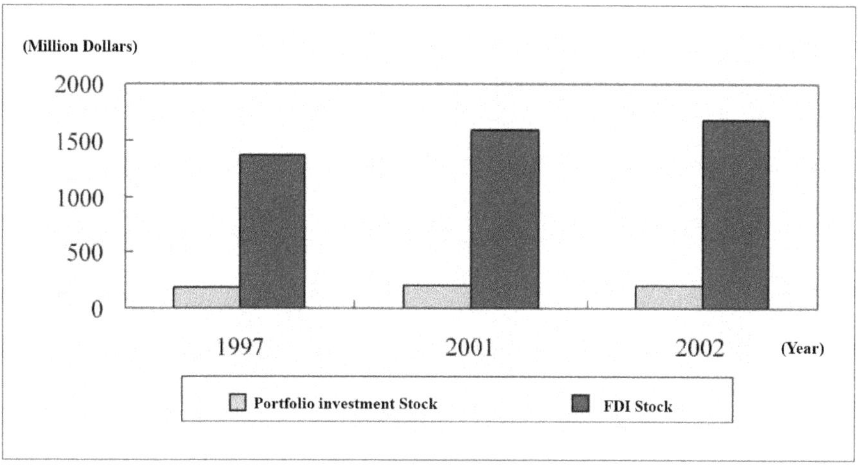

Figure 6. Comparison between FDI and portfolio investment stocks

Data source: IMF, Global Portfolio Investment Survey in 2004, by Ministry of Commerce.

above portfolio investment, and (2) includes errors and omissions, thus reflecting capital flows beyond official control. Through non-FDI, we can more clearly see a country's capital flows (both inflows and outflows).

Figure 7 shows that since the 1990s, China has been experiencing non-FDI outflows (also known as capital flight), which peaked during the Asian financial crisis. After 1998, non-FDI outflows gradually decreased and turned in 2003 to large non-FDI inflows with scale unseen since the reform and opening-up in the 1980s, which reached a peak by 2004.

In fact, when assuming a channel for capital inflows in the current account, we may use such an indicator, namely the balance of change in reserves minus the trade surplus, and then minus the FDI. When the above statistics are adopted, the inflows of non-FDI funds in 2004 will exceed USD 100 billion, which is the ground for the argument that hot money had reached 100 billion US dollars.

When further subdivided according to the balance of international payments, this USD 100 billion is mainly composed of: (1) About USD 32 billion of more foreign exchange settled and less foreign exchange purchased in the actual export, which is reflected in the balance of international payments as an expansion of the net capital inflow of about USD 32 billion. Cause of this settlement and purchase amount: influenced by the expected appreciation of RMB and relatively high interest rate in local currency, enterprises increase their enthusiasm for foreign exchange settlement and weaken their willingness to hold and purchase foreign exchange. They collect foreign exchange in time or in advance and even collect

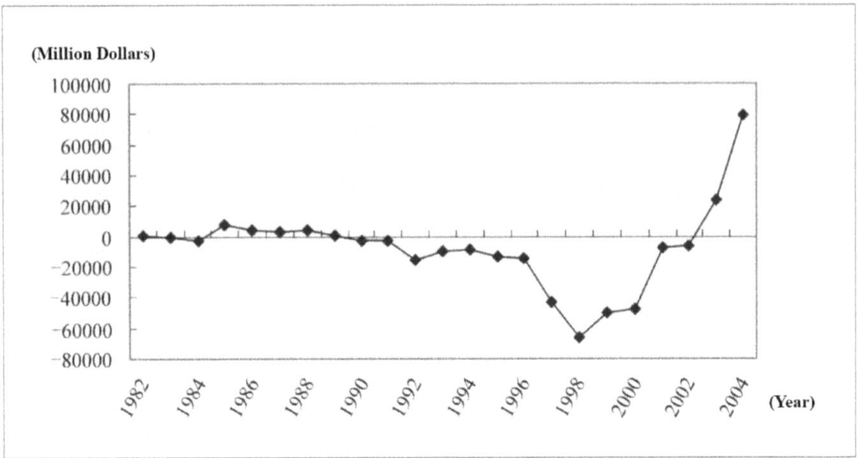

Figure 7. Non-FDI capital flows

Data source: State Administration of Foreign Exchange.

foreign exchange in advance for export and settle it. They use their own foreign exchange for import or borrow foreign exchange for external payment or even delay the payment of foreign exchange. (2) About USD 47 billion of total foreign exchange settlement of overseas loans and foreign direct investment capital, which is reflected in the balance of international payments as an expansion of net capital inflow of about USD 47 billion. (3) About USD 40 billion of the net foreign exchange sold by individuals to banks, which is reflected in the balance of international payments as expanding the net capital inflow of about USD 40 billion. (4) The scale of net capital inflows correspondingly expanded by income from foreign exchange reserve assets. Assuming a 2% yield from reserve investment, there will be a net capital inflow of USD 10 billion.

Compared with FDI, non-FDI capital is featured by strong "liquidity." A capital with strong liquidity is risk-proof for investors, but it is vulnerable to impact for inflow countries. This is why the authorities need to be more cautious with non-FDI capital.

3. Future Capital Flow Pattern

Although there has not been an exact schedule for China's comprehensive opening-up of its capital account, its stepwise relaxation of capital flow channels is universally recognized (Prasad, Rumbaugh, & Wang, 2005).

In 2001, China eased restrictions on foreign exchange purchases for early repayment of home and foreign currency loans, loans converted from foreign debt, and foreign debt. The government gave green light to the purchase of foreign exchange for investment in strategic projects abroad. Self-funded overseas students (undergraduates or above) were allowed to purchase foreign exchange equivalent to USD 20,000 at one time (the previous limit: SUD 2,000) to pay tuition and other fees. Since January 2005, the ceiling of other fees besides tuition fees will be increased to USD 20,000.

In 2002, China introduced the Qualified Foreign Institutional Investor (QFII) system, which allowed non-residents to invest in the domestic stock market (A share) under certain restrictions. So far, 26 QFIIs have obtained a total investment quota of USD 3.65 billion.

In 2003, residents who had got foreign exchange loans from Chinese financial institutions were no longer required to register with the government and obtain government approval when repaying the principal. Domestic enterprises were allowed to retain foreign currency income from overseas contract projects, overseas freight and commissions, and international bidding projects in foreign exchange accounts. In some provinces and regions, not more than USD 3 million (US dollar equivalent, USD 1 million in the past) could be invested abroad. Residents were allowed to carry not more than USD 50,000 of foreign exchange abroad (U.S. dollar equivalent, USD 20,000 in the past) without carrying a Foreign Currency Exit Permit (LCFCA), and could carry not more than USD 10,000 of foreign reserve (US dollar equivalent, USD 4,000 in the past) subject to the approval of the Administration of Foreign Exchange, and could bring not more than USD 5,00 of foreign currently (US dollar equivalent, USD 20,000 in the past) into China.

In 2004, China approved, in principle, the National Social Security Fund (about USD 17 billion under management) and domestic insurance companies to invest a small portion of their investment portfolios overseas. The Chinese government allowed international financial institutions to raise RMB funds in China for overseas purposes. China allowed multinational corporations in China to pool foreign exchange funds and redistribute them in China in the form of trust loans or provide loans to overseas affiliates. At present, Chinese citizens who have emigrated abroad and non-residents who have obtained their heritage are allowed to transfer their personal assets.

In 2005, to effectively meet the demand of enterprises for foreign exchange and reduce the cost of settlement and sales of foreign exchange, the State Administration of Foreign Exchange made the following adjustment to the quota management measures for foreign exchange accounts under the current account: (1) extending the settlement period of foreign exchange beyond the quota from the current 10 working days to 90 working days; (2) expanding the scope of enterprises whose quota of foreign exchange accounts under current accounts should be checked and ratified at 100% of their actual foreign exchange earnings.

The above analysis shows that capital flows (mainly non-FDI flow) are facing less barriers, and national treatment is granted to direct investment (like unifying the income tax on domestic and foreign investment), lifting some preferences for FDI. In this sense, foreign capital now more tends to come to China in non-FDI form instead of in direct investment, giving rise to non-FDI capital flows of greater scale and higher fluidity - a new capital flow pattern China is to face in the future, which conforms to the new trend of international capital flow.

2.3 Capital Flow Impact, Policy Response, and Economic Distortions

1. Impact of Capital Flows on Macro Stability

A large number of capital flows will inevitably impact the domestic economy and financial system, thus posing severe challenges to macro policy and economic stability. Figure 8 depicts the basic mechanism of the impact of capital flows on macro stability with a simple block diagram.

First, capital inflows cause an overheated economy. A large amount of capital inflow will lead to increases in foreign exchange reserves and funds outstanding for foreign exchange. Without taking corresponding hedging measures or insufficient hedging, this increase of funds outstanding for foreign exchange will inevitably lead to the increase of base currency, thus increasing M2, domestic demand, and ultimately cause inflation and economic overheating.

Second, capital inflows cause higher vulnerability. A large amount of capital inflow will, first, ease the credit restrictions. Many enterprises take this opportunity to borrow heavily or even excessively, which will give rise to credit risk, namely the borrower's higher default risk caused by excessive borrowing; second, cause exchange rate appreciation, and the risks caused by exchange rate fluctuations constitute a market risk, and third, be prone to bring liquidity hallucinations, stimulating short-term deposits and long-term loans by banks and resulting in maturity mismatch. Reversed foreign capital flows under a specific impact will lead to insufficient liquidity and risk. The above increases in credit risk, market risk and liquidity risk caused by capital inflow will eventually lead to an increase in vulnerability, imposing a negative impact on macro stability.

Third, with the overheating and increased vulnerability of the economy, the overall risks of the economy are built up. At a certain time, for example, under insufficient external payment capacity of the country caused by rapid deterioration of the current account, foreign capital will prefer sudden stops or even flee. The above situation, together with the flight of domestic capital, will cause massive capital outflows, further worsening the balance of international payments, and resulting in a crisis.

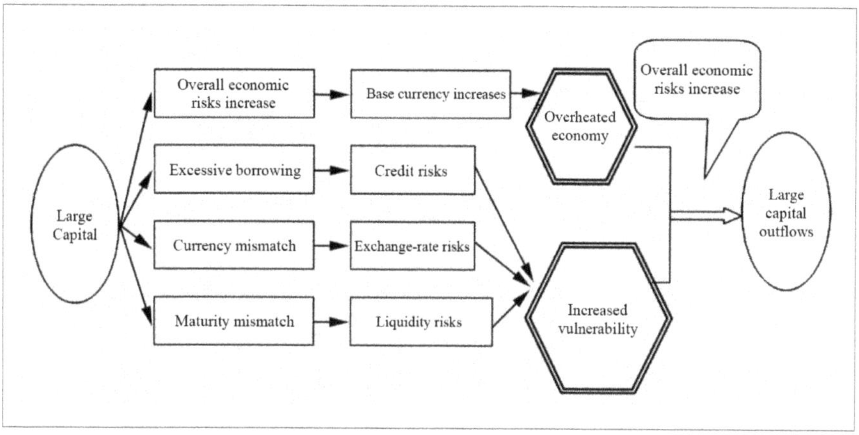

Figure 8. Capital flows and macro stability

The above mechanism presented in a theoretical analysis once happened in practical scenario in Asian crisis countries and Latin American countries. As far as China is concerned, this mechanism is also helpful to analyze the problems brought to us by the impact of capital flows.

First of all, the inflow of foreign capital has caused economy overheating. The latest round of overheating since the second half of 2003 remains fresh in our memory. Although it is hard to say that the inflow of foreign capital has fundamentally changed China's economic fluctuations, the inflow of foreign capital has significantly promoted the economy overheating.

Secondly, capital inflows impose impact on China's economic vulnerability. We should give special attention to the first two types of risks, the credit risk, exchange rate risk and liquidity risk mentioned in Figure 8. Note that liquidity risk cannot be accurately estimated due to the lack of corresponding data. (1) credit risk. At the end of 2004, China's foreign debt balance reached USD 228.6 billion, an unprecedented increase of USD 35 billion U.S. dollars and a growth of 17.6% over the end of 2003. Among them, short-term foreign debt grew faster, accounting for more than 45.6% of China's total foreign debt at the end of 2004, 5.8% higher than that at the end of 2003, and higher than the internationally recognized warning line of 40%. This may have constituted "excessive borrowing" to some extent, which requires close attention. (2) exchange rate risk. China is now implementing an essentially fixed exchange rate system, an equivalent institutional guarantee against exchange rate risk. Although it seems that banks, financial departments and private investors can avoid the risk of exchange rate changes thanks to this institutional guarantee, this risk is actually passed on to the state. For example, while we have a large number of foreign exchange reserves, if the RMB appreciates, foreign assets in the form of dollars will depreciate, bringing the market risk caused by exchange rate changes.

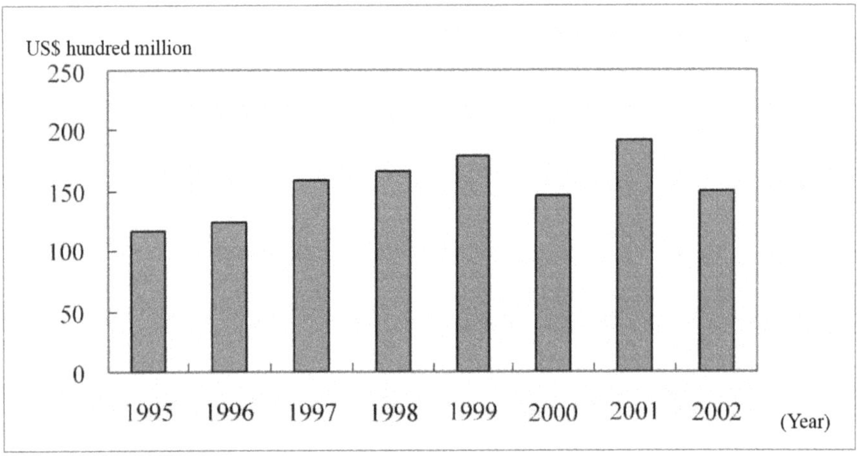

Figure 9. Remittable FDI investment income

Data source: State Administration of Foreign Exchange.

Thirdly, we should be more alert to the large outflow of capital when the overall economic risks are rising. Among the existing capital outflow modes in China, the outward remittance of FDI investment income is of great concern. Figure 9 shows that since the middle and late 1990s, FDI investment income that can be remitted each year has exceeded USD 10 billion. At present, the complete official data on the actual outward remittance of FDI income is still unavailable, but some surveys show a moderate annual outward remittance of investment income, which is conservatively estimated to be no more than 10% of the current year's income.[1] This shows that, on the one hand, the problem of outward remittance

1 A survey conducted by the Jiangsu Branch of the State Administration of Foreign Exchange shows that the total profit retained is much higher than the total amount of remittances. Taking 2000 as an example, the stock of foreign capital profits reached USD 4.54 billion, while the remittance in that year was only USD 440 million, accounting less than 10%.

of FDI investment income is not serious at present; on the other hand, due to the small amount of actual remittances each year, considerable stock of FDI investment income can be remitted. In the case of a large amount of capital outflows caused by disturbances, FDI investment income will be remitted at the same time, imposing a great impact on the balance of international payments. In addition, the relaxation of capital outflow channels, such as encouraging foreign direct investment and QDII, and the deficient capital control system can facilitate synchronized massive outflow of foreign capital, indicating a potential impact on macro stability.

2. Policy Response and Its Limitations

Under adverse impact of capital flows on macro stability, the government often has to take countermeasures, usually hedging and capital control.[2]

2.1. Hedging and Its Sustainability

The massive inflow of international capital will lead to an increase in foreign exchange reserves, a passive increase in the amount of RMB invested in funds outstanding for foreign exchange, and a growing potential inflationary pressure on the market, which will bring hidden dangers to sustained and stable economic growth. The central bank generally adopts hedging operations against this situation. Such hedging operations include open market operations, raising the deposit reserve ratio and restricting rediscount and refinancing. For China, as there is little room for the latter two operations, with the massive entry of foreign capital, the central bank mainly issues central bank bills to reduce the excessive liquidity of commercial banks and ease the excessive growth of base currency. In 2004, the Central Bank carried out 110 RMB open market operations, with a net withdrawal of 669 billion yuan of the base currency. Among them, through repurchase operations including positive repurchase and reverse repurchase, the net withdrawal of base currency reached 184 billion yuan. The remaining 485 billion yuan of base currency was withdrawn mainly through the issuance of central bank bills.[3] This hedging has produced good effects, but in the long run, there are many limitations with the issuance of central bank bills for hedging.

---

2 Other measures include encouraging capital outflow, relaxing foreign exchange outflow channels, and easing the pressure caused by large capital inflows. No detailed analysis will be made here.

3 In 2004, 1507.2 billion yuan of central bank bills was issued, and the balance of central bank bills at the end of the year reached 974.2 billion yuan.

First, hedging is incomplete. Figure 10 shows that the increase in base currency caused by the inflow of foreign capital and the increase in foreign exchange reserves cannot be completely offset by central bank bills.

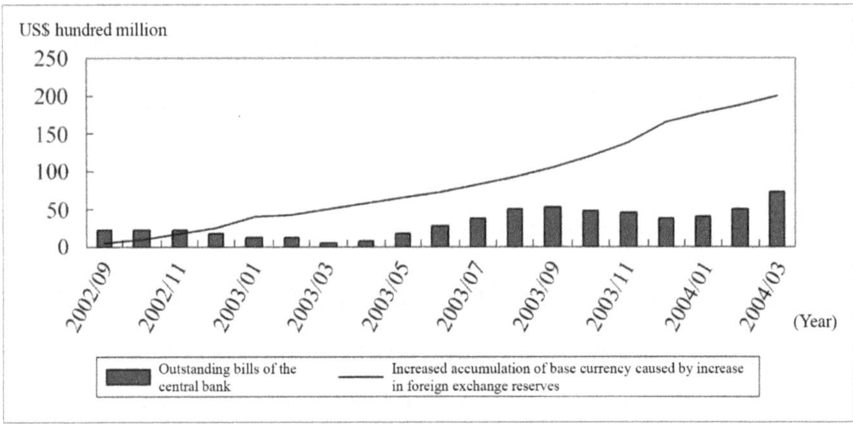

Figure 10. Partial hedging by the central bank in case of large capital inflow

Data source: People's Bank of China.

Second, this kind of hedging is effective in the short term, but there will be problems in the long term. (1) Hedging may lead to quasi-fiscal deficits. If the interest rate paid by the central bank is higher than the yield of its foreign exchange reserves, there will be a deficit. Although the government can force commercial banks to purchase central bank bills at an interest rate lower than the market interest rate, the result is that the financial balance sheet of commercial banks will deteriorate, leading to a banking crisis. Historically, Chile and Colombia have encountered this problem when using open market operations to hedge international capital inflows. As far as China is concerned, the financial costs caused by hedging cannot be ignored. As the U.S. dollar has gradually depreciated since 2001, China's foreign exchange reserve assets are in danger of "shrinking." At the same time, the central bank bills need to pay interest, and the central bank faces rising debt costs. With the continuous increase of issued number of notes, the issuance of notes will not only face the pressure of hedging foreign exchange funds, but also the pressure brought by the maturity of notes and the pressure of interest expenditure. (2) Hedging will cause deflation and interest rate rise, which will lead to further capital inflow. The logic behind it is that hedging means that commercial banks purchase central bank bills with loanable funds, which reduces loanable funds and leads to an increase in interest rates. The rise in interest rates is a new attraction for foreign investment, which is contrary to expectations.

From this perspective, the sustainability of hedging operations is questionable.

2.2. Effect of Capital Controls

In the face of a large number of capital inflows, another way is to impose capital controls to limit capital inflows. However, in practice, capital control is far from watertight and can be avoided in many ways. Therefore, capital control can only work in the short term but has little effect in the long term. After all, the transaction cost of capital transfer is decreasing, while the incentive to avoid regulation is strengthening. There is a wealth of evidence that the effectiveness of capital controls will weaken over time, especially in the case of official intervention against strong exchange rate pressure. The experience of Japan after the collapse of the Bretton Woods system in the 1970s and the experience of Latin American countries during the debt crisis in the 1980s showed that when the exchange rate was under strong upward (downward) pressure, capital controls played little role in limiting capital inflows (outflows). The non-FDI capital flows depicted in Figure 7 have actually shown that China's capital controls are far less effective than expected.

Moreover, capital controls can lead to distortions. Some scholars pointed out that capital control is not sand but mud under the market wheel as Tobin said, meaning capital control hinders the normal operation of the market wheel. Perhaps given the limited effect of capital control and its distortions, the actual strength of capital control in China[4] has declined in recent years (see Figure 11).

[4] Taking 1994 as the base year, considering that there were restrictions on all kinds of capital account transactions back then, but almost no restrictions on FDI, direct investment was scored as 1 point, and securities investment and other investments were scored as 2 points. Thereafter, the increase of openness and the decrease of regulatory intensity will be reduced, the decrease of openness and the increase of regulatory intensity will be increased, and the general adjustment will be 0.5 points, and the major adjustment will be 1 point, so as to obtain the regulatory intensity score (the sum of the scores of direct investment, securities investment and other investments). The higher the score, the higher the control intensity. See Eminent Kim (2004).

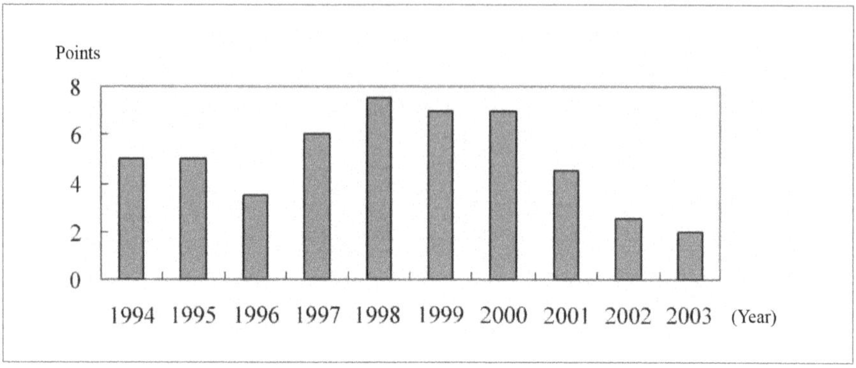

Figure 11. Capital control intensity

Data source: Eminent Kim (2004).

3. Distortion Factors Behind International Capital Flows

There are many factors that affect international capital flows. For emerging market economies, their capital flows are at least affected by growth factors and distortion factors. On the one hand, the rapid economic growth of emerging market economies attracts foreign capital; on the other hand, their existing distortions have also become incentives for foreign investment. There is no dispute about high growth attracting foreign capital, but how to attract foreign capital by distortion factors necessitates analysis.

Economic distortions are a relatively broad concept rather than a rigorous one. Generally speaking, all that may hinder rational allocation of resources can be considered distortions. Distortion is not only related to "congenital deficiency," but also to government intervention. Government intervention is generally carried out to deal with "congenital deficiency." "Congenital deficiency" refers to the deficient legal system, non-transparent policy, or other insufficiently developed systems etc. at the primary stage of development. These distortions are inevitable. The distortion resulting from government intervention encompasses the government's regulation, including capital and interest rate control, its intervention through mechanisms like credit window guidance and market rescue, and its direct participation in activities such as construction investment, all aimed at achieving the established economic development goals. All these distortions, in the long run, will build up a host of risks. Although in general, economic distortions may discourage foreign capital inflows because that economic distortions are considered "bad investment environment," and if the risks caused by distortions are mainly borne by the state[5], there will be an asymmetry between risks and returns: on the one hand, high growth brings high returns, and on the other hand, risks are reduced by implicit government guarantees, which distortions become an incentive for foreign capital inflows.

There are a lot of distortions in China's economy, which form stronger incentive to capital inflow, such as:

1. The externality of the country's risk and partial performance of cross-border contracts will reduce the explicit cost of utilizing foreign capital. Generally, after foreign capital is utilized, "debt must be repaid," and the defaulting party has to pay a price. However, since such cross-border contracts cannot be fully performed, the resulting problems will be addressed by the country. As a result, less costs are actually borne by local governments or enterprises in using foreign capital. This distortion forms stronger incentive to capital inflow.
2. Policies, such as inconsistent income taxes on domestic and foreign investment and other preferential policies given by local governments in the competition for attracting foreign investment, constitute distortions in the economy.
3. Factor price distortions. For example, the prices of capital, land, labor and other factors may be lowered under state intervention, attracting foreign capital for arbitrage.
4. The market is not perfect. Some projects with high returns and high profits, especially small and medium-sized private projects, fail to obtain financing in the domestic market, and have to resort to obtain financing from abroad because of deficient domestic banking system and capital market that are unable to calculate and price the project risks.
5. Some macro policies that seem unsustainable can also lead to distortion. For example, according to the "ternary paradox," the fixed exchange rate system upheld when capital flows are not effectively controlled but the independence of monetary policy is maintained is not sustainable, resulting in distortions.

---

[5] The state assumes the risk for two reasons: firstly, avoiding greater losses. A bailout of a bank, for example, might have prevented a banking crisis or even a financial crisis, as is the case in most countries around the world. Secondly, if these risks are caused by state intervention, the state will be obligatory on bearing the risk. For example, losses caused by having state-owned enterprises take on too much social responsibility would be borne by the state. This is very typical of China.

Two points are key to understanding the meaning of economic distortions on capital flows: First, the hidden costs or risks caused by economic distortions are mainly borne by the state. Second, when the risks are guaranteed by the state, foreign investors can often carry out risk-free (or small) arbitrage (arbitrage in a broad sense), resulting in a large amount of foreign capital inflows. Take the fixed exchange rate system as an example. Either a large amount of foreign capital flowed out during the Asian crisis to bet on the devaluation of the RMB, or a large amount of foreign capital flowed in to bet on the appreciation of the RMB in 2004, was because China promised to keep the value of the RMB stable, so that arbitrage could make steady profits. What are the tricks behind? Take a look at the situation in 1997: a large amount of capital flowed out, which leads to both interest arbitrage and currency arbitrage due to the fact that the U.S. dollar interest rate was higher than the RMB interest rate at that time and the RMB was expected to depreciate. If the Chinese government could not hold on, and the RMB really depreciated, the capital in flight would get double arbitrage. If the RMB remained stable, arbitrage could be realized if capital control was not effective. In 2004, a large amount of capital flowed in, also for both interest arbitrage and currency arbitrage because the interest rate of USD was lower than that of RMB and appreciation of RMB was expected. If the government could not hold on and the RMB really appreciated, double arbitrage would be realized. If the RMB remained stable, arbitrage would be realized. At present, a large number of foreign investors work on real estate, for triple arbitrage—in addition to the aforementioned interest arbitrage and currency arbitrage, they also intend to arbitrage the appreciated benefits of real estate assets away. Generally speaking, arbitrage funds must pay for the huge market risks that may arise due to interest rate changes, exchange rate changes and asset price changes. However, because of the fixed exchange rate system implemented by China and the limit of interest rate adjustment under the fixed exchange rate system according to the ternary paradox, the market risk is mainly borne by the Chinese government, so foreign capital can carry out risk-free or low-risk arbitrage in the market.

2.4 Capital Flows and Macro Stability Model with "Distortion" Factors

A large amount of capital flow will inevitably impose an impact on the economic and financial system (see the analysis above). A "good" system and institution can "resolve" this impact, while economic distortions will magnify this impact, leading to the instability of the entire economy. The previous section gives a theoretical overview of the general mechanism of the impact of capital flows on macro stability. This section focuses on model analysis and discusses how capital flows cause economic instability in the case of economic distortions.

In an economy, producers generally encounter two kinds of restrictions, namely credit restriction and resource restriction.

1. Credit restriction on producers: According to standard economic theory, in an incomplete credit market, due to the agency problem caused by asymmetric information, the amount of loans that producers can obtain is often in direct proportion to their wealth or their cash flow level. This loan ratio or credit multiplier can be expressed by μ or is referred to as the financial acceleration factor (Bernanke, Gertler & Gilchrist, 1998).
2. Resource restrictions on producers: Producers face not only financial limitations, but also limitations of actual resources. The models considering an open economy generally distinguish between tradable goods and non-tradable goods. Thus, the production function includes two types of factors: capital K, and a country-specific factor of production z (considered non-tradable goods). Capital inflow can ease capital (or credit) restrictions, but it fails to immediately ease the restrictions of such domestic unique elements. Due to resource restrictions, credit expansion and production expansion caused by a large amount of capital inflow will inevitably lead to resource tension and bottlenecks, driving up the resource prices.

1. Capital Flow and Macro Instability

According to the previous assumption, a producer with initial wealth W can borrow money μW. The amount of money available for investment is $I=(1+\mu)W$.

The two factors used by the producer for production are K (capital) and z (domestic specific factor or non-tradable goods). To keep things simple, the Leontief production function is adopted, that is $y-\min\left(\frac{K}{a}, z\right)$, namely, if the price of the specific element z is p, the corresponding capital investment is $K=I-pz$.

The producer's optimal decision makes $z=\frac{K}{a}$, and thus $I-pz=az$.

The developing countries have only a small amount of initial wealth (i.e., W is small). When there is no capital inflow, due to credit restrictions, the capital input is insufficient, leading to $\frac{K}{a} < Z$, which means that the supply of specific domestic factors is not used up, thus, $p = 0$. The output is:

$$y_t = \frac{K_t}{a} = \frac{1}{a}(1+\mu)W_t$$

Now consider this closed country opens it up, and there is an inflow of external funds, easing credit restrictions and giving rise to excessive demand for specific domestic factor z, $\frac{K}{a} \geq Z$, then $p > 0$. Thus $y_t = Z$.

The dynamic evolution of W is discussed as follows. The dynamic evolution of W in two consecutive periods is as follows:

$$W_{t+1} = (1-\alpha)\left[e + y_t - r\mu W_t\right] \tag{1}$$

Here e represents the exogenous income, $y_t = \min\left(\frac{I}{a}, Z\right)$ is the output of period t and is equal to the total income of producers in this period. The expression in square brackets is the producer's net income at the end of period t. α represents the fixed consumption ratio and thus the savings ratio is $(1-\alpha)$.

Under the condition that there is no inflow of foreign capital and therefore an excess supply of specific factors, $p_t = 0$, through a simple deduction according to formula (1), we can get:

$$W_{t+1} = (1-\alpha)\left[e + \left(\frac{1+\mu}{a} - r\mu\right)W_t\right] \tag{2}$$

In this way, $dW_{t+1} / dW_t > 0$. This shows that without capital inflow, expanding production through loans will lead to more wealth in the second period than in the first period.

With the inflow of capital, according to the previous analysis, credit restrictions are relaxed, investment is expanding, and the demand for specific domestic factors is rising, which finally gives rise to factor bottlenecks, namely $\frac{K}{a} \geq Z$, $p > 0$. Thus, $y_t = Z$, and

$$W_{t+1} = (1-\alpha)\left[e + Z - r\mu W_t\right] \tag{3}$$

In this way, $dW_{t+1} / dW_t < 0$. This shows that the capital inflow will drive up the price of specific factors, eroding profits and bring less wealth to the second period than the first period.

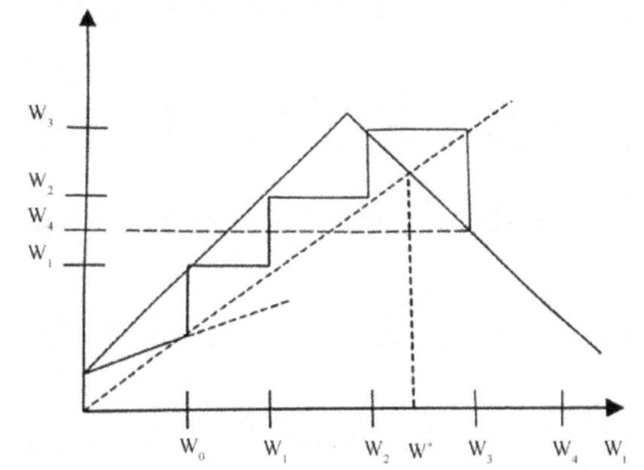

Figure 12. μ shows the fluctuation of wealth (or output) at a moderate level

Then, how are such fluctuations from the increase to the decrease of wealth realized? In other words, what are the conditions for this dynamic evolution? Figure 12 shows that the necessary condition for long-term fluctuation is that the slope of the line inclined to the right and downward represented by formula (3) is less than –1, that is:

$$-(1-\alpha)\mu r < -1, \text{ or, } \mu > \frac{1}{(1-\alpha)r}$$

This shows that the necessary condition for fluctuations is that μ is at a moderate level, neither too small nor too large. If μ is too small, there is not enough investment to drive up the specific factor prices, and the subsequent economic fluctuations will not occur. If μ is too large, there is enough investment demand to ensure that the price of specific factors is always positive. Even if the decline of μ is caused by capital outflow, there will be no price collapse. For example, the U.S. S&L crisis did not impose much impact on its economy. In addition, in the 1970s and 1980s, some developed countries lifted capital controls without causing economic instability. This is all because the developed economies keep a large μ.

Figure 12 shows that, from the initial wealth w_0 to w_3, the entire economy has seen continuous capital inflow, without causing the rise in price of specific domestic factors. Due to the wealth effect, specifically, the wealth of the current period magnifies the investment through the credit multiplier, promoting the growth of wealth in the next period. However, when this growth evolves to w_4, the inflow of capital stimulates excessive demand for specific domestic factors, which leads to an increase in factor prices. This will erode production profits and lead to a decline in wealth (namely $w_4 < w_3$).

Figure 12 depicts the wealth fluctuation mechanism when μ is at a moderate level. Since initial wealth and credit multiplier μ jointly determine the investment level and output level, wealth fluctuation means output fluctuation.

2. Model After Adding "Distortion" Factor

The above analysis is a simplification of Aghion et al.'s model idea (Aghion, Bachetta & Banerjee, 2004), in which the credit multiplier μ is a key, whose size directly determines whether there will be fluctuations.

However, μ is invariant in the above model, but in fact μ is variable. There are many factors leading to μ's change, and economic distortion is an important influencing factor. Therefore, through the functional relationship between distortion and μ, we can incorporate distortion factors into the model analysis.

Under closed conditions, the credit multiplier μ can be regarded as a measurement indicator of the development level of a country's capital market or perfection of its financial system, or a reflection of the imperfection or distortion of its financial system. The change of μ is mainly influenced by the economic cycle. When the economy is in a prosperous stage, the financial leverage of enterprises will expand, and banks are also willing to expand credit, thus raising μ. On the contrary, when the economy turns from prosperity to depression, μ will decrease, as a typical amplification factor formed by the credit channel. Evidently, μ is procyclical. Thus, we obtain the expression of credit multiplier μ_d under closed conditions:

$$\mu_d = \mu_d(\lambda) = \lambda\bar{\mu} \tag{4}$$

λ is a periodic factor, and $\lambda \geq 1$ indicates the rising cycle, while $1 > \lambda \geq 0$ indicates the falling cycle. $\bar{\mu}$ is the average credit multiplier under closed conditions. Cyclical factors will cause the credit multiplier to fluctuate around $\bar{\mu}$.

Under open conditions, the change of μ is mainly affected by both cyclical factors and the ease of credit restrictions by foreign capital inflows. The inflow of foreign capital is affected by economic distortions according to the analysis in the previous section. Therefore, the change of credit multiplier caused by capital inflow can be expressed as:

$$\mu_f = \mu_f\left[f(\tau),\lambda\right] = \lambda\mu_f\left[f(\tau)\right] \tag{5}$$

τ is the degree of economic distortions and $f(\tau)$ the inflow of foreign capital affected by distortion.

The changes in foreign capital inflows caused by economic distortions need further analysis. On the one hand, under a reinforced distortion, the space for foreign capital arbitrage expands, causing an increase in capital inflows; on the other hand, a reinforced distortion indicates that the r the economy is building up more risks. Intending to seek profits and avoid loss, foreign capital will stop entering the recipient when the distortion reaches a critical value $\bar{\tau}$ a typical case for a country in crisis, where the flow of foreign capital will reverse when the risks build up to a point due to distortion. Therefore, the functional relationship between foreign capital inflow and economic distortions is:

$$f = \begin{cases} f(\tau), f'_\tau > 0, & (\tau < \bar{\tau}) \\ 0 & (\tau \geq \bar{\tau}) \end{cases}$$

According to the previous analysis, capital inflows can cause changes in the credit multiplier, so:

$$\mu = \mu_d + \mu_f$$

According to formulas (4) and (5), we will obtain:

$$\mu = \lambda_1\bar{\mu} + \lambda_2\mu_f(\tau)$$
$$\Rightarrow \begin{cases} \mu > \mu_f + \bar{\mu} & (\lambda_1, \lambda_2 > 1, \tau < \bar{\tau}, \tau \uparrow) \\ 0 < \mu < \bar{\mu} & (0 < \lambda_1, \lambda_2 < 1, \tau \geq \bar{\tau}, \tau \downarrow) \end{cases} \tag{6}$$

λ is a parameter. We can draw a functional chart between the credit multiplier μ and the distortion degree τ according to formula (6) (see Figure 13, a simplified linear version).

Figure 13 shows that before the economic distortions reach the critical point, the inflow of foreign capital will increase due to reinforced distortion, resulting in credit expansion. The credit multiplier will become larger, far exceeding the average credit level under closed conditions, and the economy is in a rising cycle. In addition, according to the previous analysis, from credit expansion to production expansion, the demand for specific domestic factors will rise without reaching the bottleneck of specific factors, so this rising cycle can continue.

However, when the economic distortions reach the critical point and the risks build up to a certain point, the flow of foreign capital will reverse, so the credit multiplier becomes smaller, and the economy is in a falling cycle. Further analysis shows that when foreign capital stops flowing in or is even withdrawn, this falling cycle may lead to a crisis, because there will be a sharp decline in demand, a collapse in the price of specific factors, and a contraction in actual production. This crisis is a forced correction of the original economic distortions. Just as Marx emphasized that the frequent economic crisis was a forced correction of the capitalist mode of production, the impact of foreign capital from a large inflow to a large outflow is also a "forced correction" of the economic distortions existing in the recipient. We can see in Figure 13 that when the economy is in a falling cycle, the economic distortions are decreasing from right to left on the horizontal axis.

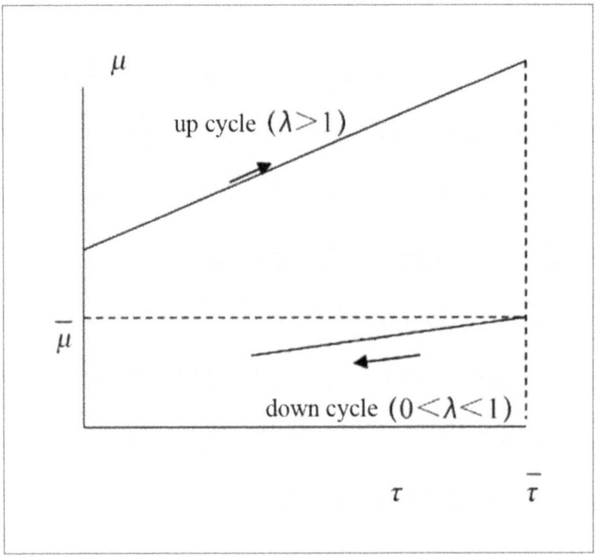

Figure 13. Economic distortions τ, credit multipliers μ and macro instability

Now we conduct analysis combing Figure 12 and Figure 13. Figure 12 shows the mechanism of economic instability caused by capital flow under the assumption that μ is unchanged. Figure 13 focuses on how μ changes caused by distortion aggravate such periodic fluctuations.

2.5 Conclusion and Policy Recommendations

In this chapter we have analyzed the overheating and vulnerability caused by the massive inflow of non-FDI in the new capital flow pattern, and emphasize that under improper policy response (like Asian crisis countries, see García, 2004), risks will continue to build up, and under certain circumstances like the deterioration of the current account, a large number of capital outflows will result in crises. This macroeconomic instability caused by capital flows will be further exacerbated due to economic distortions. Therefore, in the face of the new capital flow pattern, the policy authorities need to:

1. Improve the Non-FDI Flow Monitoring System

Although China has gathered rich experience in dealing with FDI in the past 20 years, it is not ready to deal with non-FDI flows. Due to a lack of experience and a deficient regulatory system, non-FDI flows are not effectively monitored. Compared with direct investment, non-FDI flows enjoy higher liquidity, and thus have greater risks r. Therefore, the policy authorities should step up efforts to improve the non-FDI flow monitoring system and reduce the impact of non-FDI big flows on macro stability.

2. Correct Economic Distortions

Whether in theory or in model analysis, we can see that the economic distortions aggravate the instability caused by capital flows. We do not expect the "forced correction" of various distortions in the original economic structure and economic system by the impact of a large number of foreign capital in the way of the Asian financial crisis, which will result in economic recession or even recession for many years. We need to actively correct distortions in the economy by promoting these reforms: improvement of the micro governance structure, and modification of the macro management framework (Sun Tao, 2004). The improvement of micro governance structure mainly applies to the state-owned economy. State-owned enterprises or banks can promote the improvement of governance structure through equity diversification, so as to enhance their ability to take and resist risks, reduce the legal or moral burden of the country, and more or less defuse the state's risks. To modify the macro management framework is to reduce various kinds of state intervention, including intervention in factor prices and various subsidies or tax distortions.[6]

3. Realize the Transformation of Macro-Control Mode

The quantitative control method against large capital inflows, be it hedging or capital control, can generally be called quantitative control. The limitation of such regulation lies in the poor sustainability of hedging, the unsatisfactory effect of capital control, and the outcome of this practice - reinforced distortions. Therefore, in the face of the new pattern of capital flows, the macro-control model should be changed from a quantitative one to a price-based one. The key to this transformation is to promote the marketization of interest rate while maintaining the flexibility of the exchange rate. The flexibility of the exchange rate is the premise of interest rate regulation. If the exchange rate is fixed and there is capital flow, the independence of monetary policy will be greatly impaired, and interest rate regulation will become empty talk. The marketization of interest rates is the guarantee that the interest rate regulation can be effective. If the interest rate is not marketized, the market's evaluation of capital risk is not accurate, and capital flow can be hardly regulated through interest rate means.

---

6 For the correction of various distortions, please refer to the Frontier Research Group on Growth (2004).

International Correlation of China's Economic Cycle

3.1 Introduction and Relevant Literature

The subprime crisis spread from the epicenter Wall Street to Europe and other emerging market economies, and one country's financial crisis can lead to global recession broke out due to one country's financial crisis—all this makes us feel "the whole world shares warm and cold together"—the cycles among economies in the era of globalization are further linked up. At present, although whether the world economies are under decoupling or convergence is still under debate, the development entirely independent from the outside world is almost impossible, and the global impact of the subprime crisis justifies the old saying that "when a bird's nest is overturned, no egg can remain intact." Under this background, this chapter attempts to discuss the following questions: (1) what is the relationship between the economic cycles of China and the outside world? (2) how badly is China's economic fluctuation affected by external shocks? and (3) to what extent does China's fluctuation affect the outside world? It is well-known that during the Asian financial crisis, China's economy was bound with other economies in the region. Under the influence of the subprime crisis, it is more realistic to explore the relationship between China and the developed economies. Therefore, this chapter focuses on the relationship between China's economic fluctuations and developed economies and analyzes the economic resonance between China and the United States, Japan, and the European Union from an empirical perspective. Our arrangement is based on the following reality: on the one hand, from the perspective of trade correlation, China carries out more than 50% of its import and export trade with OECD countries; on the other hand, under the impact of the crisis, the economic contraction of developed economies has imposed a huge impact on China's economic growth.

Since the 1980s, the acceleration of the globalization process has brought great changes in the cyclical correlation among economies, which are related to both the greater financial and trade times among economies and the rise of emerging economies. According to the purchasing power parity algorithm of the British Economist, at present, the output of emerging economies accounts for about 50% of the world's total output. These changes have important implications for the study of cyclical correlation in the global economy. The theoretical circle has been disputing these years on whether the international economic correlation under the background of globalization is closer or looser or even decoupled: one school argues that globalization has strengthened cross-border economic ties, so the cyclical fluctuations will converge, and the economy grows more sensitive to external impact under more open trade and financial flows. Thus, by expanding the transmission channel of the impact to other countries, the resonance of the global impact will be intensified. The other school points out that the recent strong economic growth of emerging market economies, especially India and China, seems to be immune to the slowdown of some industrialized countries. Some even believe that emerging markets have been decoupled from industrialized countries, which means that the economic cycles of these countries are no longer as closely related to those of industrialized countries as before. So, how do you view this divergence in theory? The theoretical divergence comes from the different assumptions of the correlation premise. For example, the close financial correlation will generate greater cyclical resonance through the wealth effect of external shocks, while the intensified trade correlation will give rise to spillover effects on the demand side and the supply side, leading to a higher output fluctuation correlation. In the standard stochastic dynamic cycle model, an enhanced trade and financial correlation will generally lead to a weakened investment correlation between countries, because "more resources will be transferred" when some capital and current account transaction restrictions between countries are lifted. Capital and other resources can be more quickly transferred from one economy to another more favorable technology-impacted economy (Backus, Kehoe & Kydland, 1995; Heathcote & Perri, 2002). When the production driven by resource transfer is more specialized, and mainly sectoral shocks are encountered, the output resonance among economies will be weakened (Baxter & Kouparitsas, 2005).

As a rising emerging economy, China's development has attracted global attention. In recent years, evaluation of the role of China's economy in the world economic pattern has become a research hotspot, and the international correlation of China's economic cycle fluctuations intrigues more researchers.

1. China and the World

Alan Heap (2005) believed that the world economy was experiencing the third super cycle following the two super cycles from the late nineteenth century to the early twentieth century and from 1945 to 1975. If the first two cycles were driven by the growth of the American economy and the rapid expansion of the post-war European and Japanese economies, the third cycle is driven by the rapid growth of the resource intensive economy induced by China's industrialization and urbanization. China's economic growth plays an important role in the formation of the world economic cycle. Fidrmuc et al. (2008) used the quarterly GDP data (1992–2006) to analyze the nature of the economic dynamic correlation between China and OECD countries, and concluded that in general, regardless of the low economic correlation between China and OECD countries, many countries were closely related to China's economic fluctuations in the short term. Moreover, the national cyclical fluctuations closely related to China's trade and finance showed greater similarity compared with other countries, and the international impact of China's economic fluctuations was significant. In an earlier study, Qin Wanshun et al. (2002) found a weak correlation between the economic cycles of China and the United States through the statistical analysis of the quarterly macro variable series from 1987 to 2000. Ren Zhixiang and Song Yuhua (2004) believed that when deeply participating in the global economy, China would have apparently closer economic ties with the world.

2. China and Asia

From the perspective of bilateral trade, Teng and Wai studied the synergy of economic cycles among India, China and the five founding countries of ASEAN, and noted the intra-industry trade enhanced the synergy of their economic cycles. Genberg (2006) found that after 1990, the economic cycle synergy between Hong Kong and mainland China has steadily increased. The correlation coefficient of real GDP was 0.46 in 2000–2005, and the correlation coefficient of GDP cycle reached 0.92 in 2000–2002. More than 30% of price fluctuations in Hong Kong can be explained by the impact of relevant variables of the mainland.

It is necessary to study the international correlation of China's economic cycle in the light of its economic development stage. The above empirical analysis of the international correlation of China's economic cycle is generally an overall assessment of a long-term series. One point worth discussing is that in the twenty-first century, especially since China's accession to the WTO, China's economy has been growing more vigorously and stably than ever before. In addition, due to domestic and regional factors, China's economic development experienced great ups and downs in the 1990s. Therefore, the international correlation of China's economic cycle should be examined in sections, to more clearly reveal the stage difference of the cycle correlation. Comparing with the existing literature, we are lucky that we can use China's economic development data during the financial crisis to support our analysis and conclusions. Taking full advantage of existing literature, to demonstrate the issues of this chapter we will: conduct a descriptive analysis of the international correlation of China's GDP cycle in Section 2, giving a characteristic description of the correlation; introduce the empirical analysis method and offer data application description of this chapter in Section 3; estimate the international correlation degree of China's GDP cycle around the "worldwide common factors" of economic cycle fluctuations in Section 4. The calculation process reflects our basic understanding of the characteristics of China's economic development stages; conduct a tentative further analysis of "international trade and common factors" based on the particularity of China's international economic correlation in Section 5; describe correlation and decoupling in Section 6. Combining with the performance of China's economy in the subprime crisis, we will provide evidence for the acceptability of the empirical analysis conclusions; and give conclusions in Section 7, delivering our thoughts and suggestions on China's economic cycle correlation.

3.2 International Correlation of China's GDP Cycle: Two Types

From 1993 to 1996, after a soft landing of macro control, China's economy got on a fast lane of steady and rapid growth. After the gloomy deflation and its accession to WTO, China's economy entered a golden era of "high growth and low inflation" in the beginning of the twenty-first century. According to the quarterly GDP growth from 1995 to 2010, as shown in Figure 14, the economy in a dozen years can be roughly divided into four stages: the first quarter of 1996 to the third quarter of 2001, the fourth quarter of 2001 to the third quarter of 2007, the fourth quarter of 2007 to the second quarter of 2009, and the second quarter of 2009 to present. The downward trend of quarterly GDP fluctuation in the first stage was mainly due to the impact of the economic soft-landing policy and the Asian financial crisis. The upward trend of quarterly GDP fluctuation in the second stage was mainly attributed to active domestic investment and a relatively loose international economic environment. The downward trend of the third stage was mainly impacted by the lag effect of the domestic "dual prevention" policy in the previous stage and the global financial crisis since the second half of 2007. The upward fluctuation trend of the fourth stage credited to the containment of the impact momentum of the subprime crisis.

In the context of opening-up and economic globalization, China's economic fluctuations are the result of the double superposition of domestic and international factors. More importantly, with China's deep integration into the world economy, domestic economic fluctuations have been increasingly affected by international economic fluctuations. This is intuitively supported by the international synergy trend of China's macroeconomic variables. Figure 14 is a comparison of quarterly GDP cycle fluctuations which mean values removed between China (CHN) and the European Union (EUU), the United States (USA) and Japan (JPN). The quarterly GDP cycle fluctuations of the three economies were more closely coordinated from the 1st quarter of 1996 to the 3rd quarter of 2010. After 2001, these three economies had a closer synergy on quarterly GDP cyclic fluctuations. Before 2001, the quarterly GDP cycle synergy between China, the EU and the United States was weak, and became significant after 2001. Compared with the EU and the United States, although Japan/China had a strong trend of quarterly GDP cycle synergy before 2001, but a slightly lower synergy after that year. In a word, the trend of correlated quarterly GDP cycles of China and the three major economies showed that, since its accession to the WTO, China has maintained a stronger international correlation of economic fluctuations.

Correlation analysis can provide preliminary evidence for the above intuitive impression. Table 6 reports the correlation coefficient of quarterly GDP, fixed asset investment and household consumption between China and the three major economies. The statistical results are described as follow: (1) In general, from the first quarter of 1996 to the first quarter of 2010, the synergy between China's economic fluctuations and the three major economies was low or even negative. From the quarterly GDP correlation, except for Japan, China was weakly correlated with the EU and the United States, and the t statistic was not significant. The reason for this phenomenon, according to the intuitive impression provided in Figure 14, may be that we did not separate the time factor in the correlation. (2) Taking 2002 as the boundary, the first quarter of 1996 to the first quarter of 2010 is divided into two sub-periods: the first quarter of 1996 to the fourth quarter of 2001 and the first quarter of 2002 to the first quarter of 2010. The economic synergy between China and the three major economies will be easy to explain. From the perspective of quarterly GDP correlation, since 2002, the quarterly GDP cycle fluctuations of China and the three major economies have shown a significantly consistent correlation, with correlation coefficients above 0.50, and the correlation significance has improved significantly.

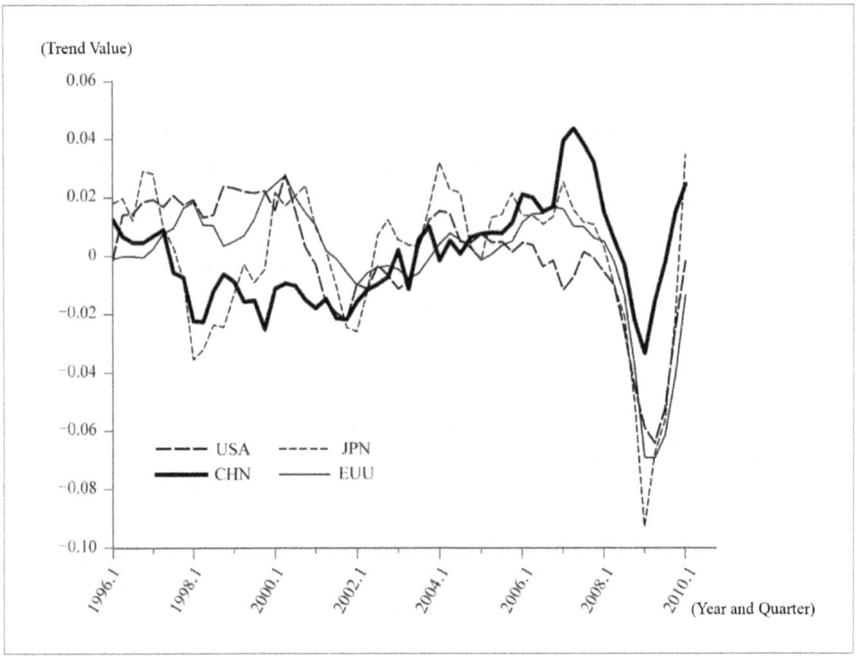

Figure 14. Comparison of GDP cyclical fluctuations (mean values removed) between China and the three major economies from the first quarter of 1996 to the first quarter of 2010

Source of data: The Statistical Database of China Economic Network and the OECD Database. The vertical axis is the GDP fluctuation trend scale (removing mean values), and the horizontal axis is the quarterly indicator.

Table 6. The correlation coefficient of quarterly GDP cycle fluctuation between China and other countries/regions

	China/USA	China/Japan	China/EU
Q1 1996 – Q1 2010	0.11 (0.79)	0.55 (4.88)	0.20 (1.52)
Q1 1996 – Q4 2001	0.24 (1.17)	0.60 (3.55)	-0.37 (-1.88)
Q1 2002 – Q1 2010	0.50 (3.18)	0.65 (4.77)	0.62 (4.38)

Note: figures in parentheses are the t statistics.

The worldwide spread of the international financial crisis in 2008 provides us with a rare opportunity to observe and measure the correlation between China's economy and the world economy. Next, we will focus on the analysis of the relationship between China and the United States, Japan, and the European

Union in the first quarter of 1996–2010 in terms of GDP, consumption, and investment variables, and uses the multivariate random dynamic factor model to analyze common factors of international economic cycle synergy. Based on the discussion on the degree of international correlation of China's economic cycle, we will further measure the impact of trade variables on China's economic cycle and common factors.

3.3 Method and Data

Seeking the commonness of multivariable has always been the focus of statistics and economics, for which many methods have been developed. The traditional factor analysis method has been widely used in the extraction of unobservable common factors thanks to its simplicity. However, as this method is not based on statistical theories, some alternative factor analysis methods have also attracted researchers' attention. For example, Stock and Watson (1989, 1993) employed Kalman filtering to extract unobservable common factors. However, given too many model variables, this method may restrain computational capacity in the application. The evolving Bayesian statistical theory has paved a new path for the study of multivariate commonality. With the development of measurement tools, horizontal factor analysis models, Bayesian dynamic linear model, and other models that widely use Bayesian statistical inference methods have attracted attention in economic literature. Economic literature is recently carrying out a technical exploration to apply the Bayesian dynamic linear model to dynamic factor analysis by the Monte Carlo simulation and Gibbs sampling method and develop from single factor dynamic model to multi factor dynamic model. Otrok et al. (1998) used the Gibbs sampling method to estimate the dynamic single factor model of the manufacturing index in the Midwest of Iowa, USA, including non-agricultural employment, average weekly working hours and the average hourly wage of the manufacturing industry. Kose et al. (2003) estimated the dynamic three-factor model (GDP, consumption and investment) of 60 countries by the Gibbs sampling method, and Kose et al. (2008) used similar methods to analyze common factors of G7 countries in three periods of Bretton Woods system era, the oil shock era and the globalization era. They believed that the common factors were playing a bigger role in the globalization era. Guo Qingwang et al. (2005) used a method similar to Kose (2003) to analyze common, regional and special factors of economic growth in China's provinces and regions.

From the current situation, the three major economies, that is, the United States, the European Union and Japan still play a leading role in the international economy, whether in terms of the overall international impact of economic growth or the local impact of developed economies on developing countries. Since the 1990s, with the deepening of economic internationalization, China and the three major economies have been increasingly relying on each other. In view of this, in the international correlation analysis of China's economic cycle, for the sake of simplification, we naturally focus on the correlation between China and the three major economies. $z_{i,t}$ denotes the macroeconomic variables (GDP, consumption and investment) of different countries i in various periods t. f_t is world common factors. The dynamic single factor model can be expressed as:

$$z_{i,t} = a_i + b_i f_t + \varepsilon_{i,t} \tag{1}$$

Where, $E\varepsilon_{i,t}, \varepsilon_{j,(t-s)} = 0(i \neq j)$, and assume all factors and residual ε_{it} follow an autoregressive process of order p_i:

$$\varepsilon_{i,t} = \phi_{i,1}\varepsilon_{i,t-1} + \phi_{i,2}\varepsilon_{i,t-2} + \cdots\cdots + \phi_{i,pi}\varepsilon_{i,t-pi} + u_{i,t} \tag{2}$$

Where $Eu_{i,t}u_{j,(t-s)} = \begin{cases} \sigma_i^2, & i = j, s - 0 \\ 0, & i \neq j, s \neq 0, u_{it} \sim N\left(0, \sigma_i^2\right) \end{cases}$

The common factor follows the following model:

$$f_t = \varphi_1 f_{t-1} + \varphi_2 f_{t-2} + \cdots\cdots + \varphi_q f_{t-q} + v_t \tag{3}$$

$$Ev_t v_{(t-s)} = \begin{cases} \sigma_f^2, s = 0 \\ 0, s \neq 0, v_t \sim N\left(0, \sigma_f^2\right) \end{cases}$$

In this chapter, we adopt the above single factor model to estimate and compare the correlation of macroeconomic variables between China and foreign countries, to find common factors of economic cycle synergy. The foreign/regional data in the chapter are from the OECD database and China Economic Network statistical database. The selected quarterly macroeconomic data series are all seasonally adjusted constant price series (VIXOBSA. 2000. S1). We obtained China's quarterly macro real economic variable series through: (1) Estimation of quarterly real GDP series. We estimated the actual value of quarterly GDP data based on the annual GDP fixed basis ratio index (1978=100) and the quarterly cumulative GDP growth rate calculated at comparable prices. Firstly, the annual GDP base ratio index was processed by the quadratic function interpolation method to obtain the single quarter GDP index. Then, the first quarter of 1994 was selected as the base period. The cumulative value of each quarter in 1994 was obtained according to the single-quarter GDP of four quarters in 1994. Then, the published quarterly cumulative GDP growth rate was used to restore the actual cumulative GDP index of each quarter. Finally, the actual GDP cumulative index was restored to the actual GDP index of each quarter. The quarterly number of nominal GDP was calculated according to the cumulative value of nominal GDP, and the quarterly GDP reduction index calculated after seasonal adjustment with X11. The annual GDP fixed basis ratio index (1978 = 100), the cumulative nominal GDP and the quarterly cumulative growth rate of real GDP were all from the China Economic Database. (2) Estimation of quarterly actual fixed asset investment and household consumption series. Thanks to the availability of data, we took the real value series of urban quarterly fixed asset investment as the proxy variable of the real value series of social fixed asset investment, and the proxy variable of household consumption was the total retail sales of social consumer goods. Similar to the estimation of the quarterly GDP actual value series, the quarterly completed amount of fixed asset investment over the years was estimated according to the cumulative value of the monthly completed amount of fixed asset investment. After seasonal adjustment with X11, the first quarter of 1994 = 100 was selected, and then the quarterly GDP reduction index obtained above was used to reduce, obtain the quarterly fixed asset investment index. The monthly total retail sales of consumer goods were added to the number of quarters, the quarterly data of total retail sales of consumer goods adjusted with X11, and then CPI was used to reduce the base ratio (the first quarter of 1994 = 100) to obtain the retail index of consumer goods. The cumulative value of monthly fixed asset investment completion and monthly total retail sales of consumer goods were from the China Economic Database. (3) Estimation of quarterly import and export trade data. Similar to the method for obtaining the sequence of quarterly GDP, household consumption and fixed asset investment, we estimated quarterly import and export trade volume and foreign capital used with monthly accumulation and then used the quarterly GDP deflator to discount to obtain the actual numerical sequence.

3.4 The International Correlation of China's GDP Cycle: Empirical Analysis and Comparison

According to the method described above, a convenient method for measuring the international correlation of China's economic cycle is to use factor extraction method to track potential common factors and special factor variables based on China's observation indicators and foreign macroeconomic variables. Finally, the international random impact of China's economic cycle fluctuations can be calculated by the percentage contribution of the observation factor variance to the observation indicator variance.

In this section, we will, according to the Gibbs sampling method, analyze common factors of macroeconomic variables including GDP, household consumption, fixed asset investment in the United States, Japan, China and the European Union based on the above data through numerical calculation with GAUSS9.0 program following formulas (1) - (3). The initial assumption includes common factors and random items lag by 2 periods.

The prior distribution of factor loads is $N(0,1)$ and the prior distribution parameter of the autoregressive polynomial is $N(0,\Sigma)$, in which $\Sigma = \begin{pmatrix} 1 & 0 \\ 0 & 0.5 \end{pmatrix}$. The prior distribution of the variance of residual, σ_i in equation (1), is the inverse gamma function gamma^{-1}(6,0.001). Through 12,000 Gibbs sampling, the simulation results of each parameter are obtained by discarding the data of the first 2,000 samplings, to analyze the average value of simulation data.

1. Division of Sample Time Periods

In the process of reform and opening-up, China participated in the process of economic globalization in an orderly manner, and its accession to the WTO at the end of 2001 is a landmark event. Before and after China's accession to the WTO, there are great differences in the international correlation of China's economy. Since the data of the EU in the OECD database started in the first quarter of 1996, the starting time point of the samples for analysis is also the first quarter of 1996. First, we select the first quarter of 1996 to the first quarter of 2010 as the sample to extract common factors. According to Formula (1), Figure 15 lists the trend changes of common factors (multiplied by factor load) and China's GDP (deducting constant items). The correlation between the world common factor and China's GDP (CHN GDP) showed two stages of difference, namely, the difference between the first quarter of 1996 and the fourth quarter of 2001, and the difference between the first quarter of 2002 and the first quarter of 2010. In the previous period, the changes of the two were not consistent. However, from 2002 to 2010, there was a common trend. When calculating the correlation coefficient between the two (see Table 7), we can find a low and insignificant correlation between China's GDP, investment and common factors from 1996 to 2010, and a negative correlation of consumption and investment with common factors. But this does not mean that China's economy was completely irrelevant to the world economic cycle. When simply regressing China's GDP and common factors and conducting a discontinuity test (see the appendix of this chapter), we can see that the fourth quarter of 2001 was a significant discontinuity. This breakpoint coincided with China's accession to the WTO. Next, we will divide the samples into two periods: the first quarter of 1996 to the fourth quarter of 2001 (1996Q1: 2001Q4), and the first quarter of 2002 to the first quarter of 2010 (2002Q1:2010Q1), to provide a comparison of the international correlation of China's economy.

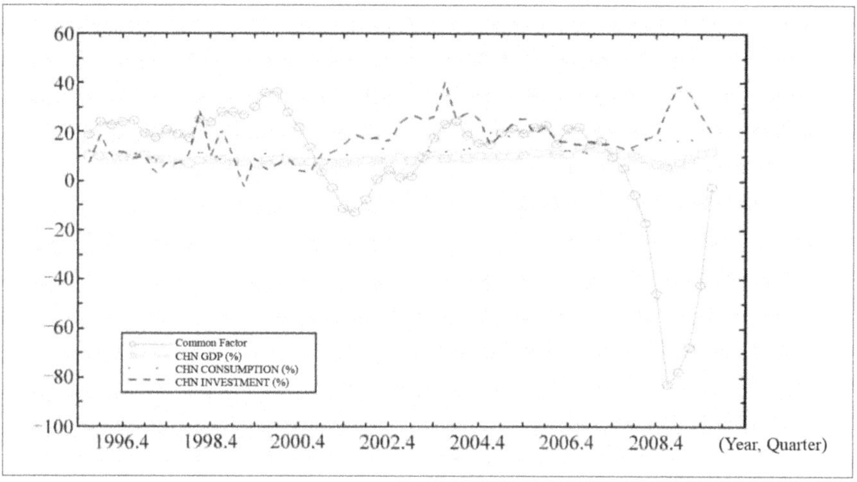

Figure 15. China's GDP, consumption, investment, and the changing trend of world common factors

Table 7. Correlation coefficient between GDP, consumption, investment, and common factors of countries (regions)

	Y	C	I
U.S.	0.93(18.67)	0.85(11.99)	0.91(16.02)
JPN	0.77(8.91)	0.49(4.14)	0.75(8.54)
CHN	0.25(1.88)	-0.47(-3.91)	-0.50(-4.34)
EUU	0.95(22.2)	0.90(15.72)	0.92(17.4)

Note: figures in parentheses are t statistics.

2. Visual Trend of GDP and Random Common Factors from the First Quarter of 2002 to That of 2010

Following the above method, we analyze the data from the first quarter of 2002 to that of 2010. The common factors extracted are shown in Figure 16 (a)–(d).

Figures 16 (a)–(d) provide us with a comparison between common factors of economic fluctuations in the European Union (EUU), the United States (US), Japan (JPN), and China (CHN) and their respective quarterly GDP growth rate trends. Note that fixed constant items are deducted from each series of GDP in the figure, and common factors are added with factor loads of each country. The four figures generally reveal that the common factors of these countries capture the actual trend of GDP growth, that is, the trend consistency between the dotted line (GDP) and the solid line (common factor) in the figure. For each country, the common factor captures the turning point of the quarterly GDP cycle rise/fall. On this point, we can feel this point from the current financial crisis that the world is undergoing. From the perspective of the actual quarterly GDP sequence, after the third quarter of 2007, the GDP growth of all countries showed a continuous downward trend. From the second half of 2009 to the first quarter of 2010, the economies of various countries rebounded. In terms of geographic regions:

1. The trend of EU GDP in this financial crisis was highly consistent with the trend of common factors
2. The GDP growth rate of the United States bottomed out in the second quarter of 2009, and the following recovery was better than common factor
3. Japan's GDP bottomed out in the first quarter of 2009, and its recovery since then was also better than common factor
4. The most prominent is that China's GDP bottomed out in the first quarter of 2010 and recovered vigorously. By the first quarter of 2010, the year-on-year growth rate of GDP exceeded the common factor by about 2.2 percentage points (as shown in Figure 16).

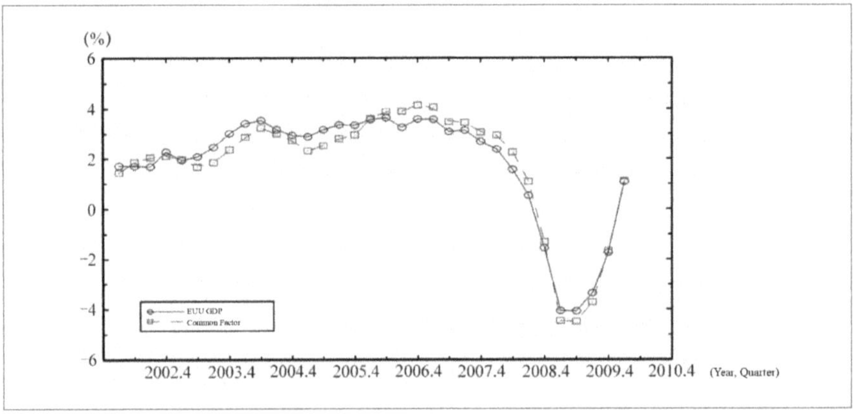

Figure 16. (a) EUU GDP and common factors

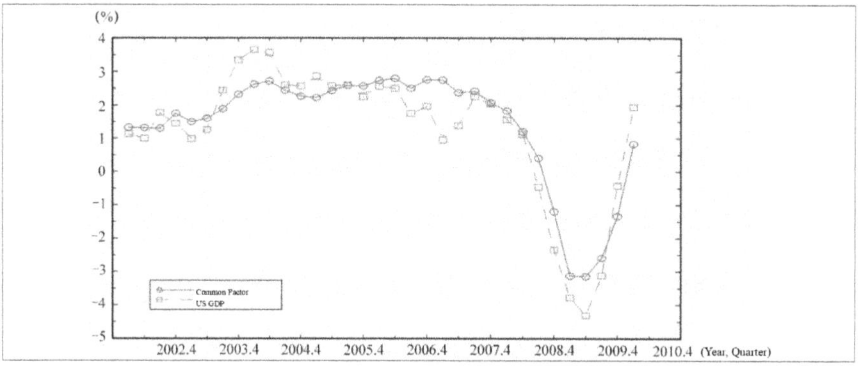

Figure 16. (b) U.S. GDP and common factors

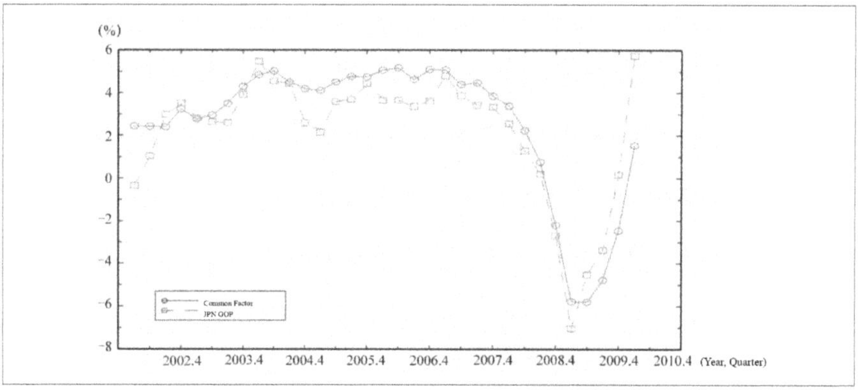

Figure 16. (c) JPN GDP and common factors

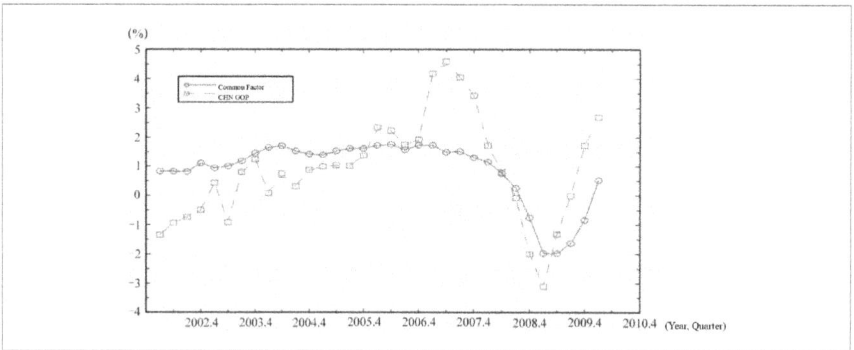

Figure 16. (d) CHN GDP and common factors

Note: Fixed constant items are deducted from each series of GDP in (a)–(d), and factor loads of various countries are added to common factors

3. Factor Variance Contribution

According to the simulation results calculated by the model, the variance contribution of common factors to macro variables of each country—GDP, fixed assets investment, household consumption (S_i) and the variance contribution of domestic special factors ($100 - S_i$) can be calculated by formula (4) and formula (5) respectively.

$$\mathrm{var}\left(z_{i,t}\right) = b_i^2\,\mathrm{var}\left(f_i\right) = \mathrm{var}\left(\varepsilon_{i,t}\right) \tag{4}$$

$$S_i = b_i^2\,\mathrm{var}\left(f_i\right) / \mathrm{var}\left(z_{i,t}\right) \times 100\% \tag{5}$$

Results are shown in Table 8. The variable codes Y, I and C refer to GDP, fixed asset investment and household consumption respectively. In order to get a more intuitive impression, we also list the correlation coefficients between variables and common factors (see Table 9) to study the correlation or importance of the common factors to each macro variable of countries.

Table 8. Analysis on the impact of common factors and special factors of GDP, fixed assets investment, and consumption fluctuation

		World Common Factor Variance Contribution (%)		Variance Contribution of Special Factors (%)	
		1996Q1–2001Q4	2002Q1–2010Q1	1996Q1–2001Q4	2002Q1–2010Q1
U.S.	Y	58.4	86.8	41.6	13.2
	C	46.4	74.2	53.6	25.8
	I	53.0	81.2	47.0	18.8
JPN	Y	5.8	81.2	94.2	18.8
	C	4.5	50.6	95.5	49.4
	I	3.1	81.8	96.9	18.2
CHN	Y	5.0	32.0	95.0	68.0
	C	2.4	15.7	97.6	84.3
	I	1.0	20.5	99.0	79.5
EUU	Y	27.9	95.1	72.1	4.9
	C	24.6	92.8	75.4	7.2
	I	43.8	88.8	56.2	11.2

Table 9. Correlation coefficients between variables and common factors

	Y		C		I	
	1996Q1–2001Q4	**2002Q1–2010Q1**	**1996Q1–2001Q4**	**2002Q1–2010Q1**	**1996Q1–2001Q4**	**2002Q1–2010Q1**
USA	0.907	0.941	0.801	0.870	0.864	0.909
JPN	0.217	0.911	–0.173	0.721	0.065	0.913
CHA	0.186	0.573	0.065	–0.395	–0.048	–0.453
EUU	0.618	0.983	0.576	0.971	0.778	0.950

3.1. The International Correlation of GDP Cycle

From the perspective of the international correlation of the economic cycle, we can seemingly conclude that China has been deeply integrated into the international economy at this stage. According to the divided sample intervals, during the period from the first quarter of 1996 to the fourth quarter of 2001, the variance contribution of common factors to GDP, consumption and investment fluctuations in the United States and the European Union was greater than its contribution to Japan and China. During this period, Japan was experiencing the pain of the "lost decade" after the collapse of the foam economy. In addition, the economic growth was sluggish due to the financial crisis in 1998. The average quarterly GDP growth stood at only 0.8% year on year, while the average quarterly GDP growth of the United States and the European Union reached 3.5% and 2.7% respectively in the same period. Japan seemed to be "decoupled" from the world's leading forces during this period. Although the average quarterly GDP growth rate of China during this period remained at 8.6% year-on-year, the economy was still less affected by the world's common factors, which can only explain 3% of China's GDP cyclical fluctuations. During the period from the first quarter of 2002 to the first quarter of 2010, the international financial crisis strengthened the impact of common factors on the main economic variables in various regions. The common factors made markedly higher variance contribution to GDP, consumption and investment fluctuations in different regions and countries. 32% of China's quarterly GDP cyclical fluctuation can be explained by the impact of random common factors, and the remaining 68% is attributed to domestic special factors. Therefore, the impact of international economic factors on China is significant. The correlation coefficients between common factors and GDP in Table 9 provide similar results. Before China's accession to the WTO, the correlation coefficient between common factors and China's GDP stood 0.186. After its accession to the WTO, the correlation coefficient reached

0.57, showing a correlation substantially matched that of the United States, Japan and the European Union.

3.2. The International Correlation Between Fixed Assets Investment and Household Consumption Fluctuation

The impact of common factors on fixed asset investment and household consumption differs greatly from country to country. From the perspective of investment fluctuation, the variance contribution of common factors to China's fixed asset investment has increased from 1.0% before its accession to the WTO to 20.5% after its accession. Over the same period, Japan has increased from 3.1% to 81.8%, the United States from 53.0% to 81.2%, and the EU from 43.8% to 88.8%. In terms of consumption fluctuation, the variance contribution of common factors to China's consumption increased from 2.4% before its accession to the WTO to 15.7%, while Japan increased from 4.5% to 50.6%, the United States increased from 46.4% to 74.2%, and the European Union from 24.6% to 92.8%. On the whole, the variance contribution of common factors to China's consumption and fixed asset investment is much lower than that of the developed countries and regions in the world. From the correlation coefficient in Table 9, the correlation between the external impact of common factors after China's accession to the WTO and its household consumption and fixed asset investment is negative.

3.3. Problems Revealed by Econometric Analysis and Our Understanding

Compared with the existing literature, an interesting finding of this chapter is that, when the period is divided before and after China's accession to the WTO, we find that since 2002, China's GDP cycle has shown a strong resonance with that of developed economies, but investment and consumption are still determined by domestic special factors. In principle, the GDP calculated by the expenditure method is composed of investment, consumption and net exports. So, in terms of international correlation, why does the international correlation of China's GDP cycle differ significantly from that of investment and consumption? Data caliber can be a possible reason. China has not yet established and improved the quarterly data of expenditure method statistics. We can only use the retail sales of consumer goods and urban fixed asset investment as proxy variables of consumption and investment. The caliber of consumption data and fixed asset investment data we adopt is smaller than that of the GDP expenditure method. A narrowing index caliber may lower the response of consumption and fixed asset investment to external common factors. Xu Xianchun (2009) specified in detail the difference between the retail sales of consumer goods, the total investment in fixed assets of the whole society, and the consumption and investment according to the statistical caliber of the expenditure method. There were both overestimated and underestimated factors, but he did not give a specific quarterly time series of private consumption and investment according to the statistical caliber of the expenditure method. It is a pity that the consumption of the retail series of social consumer goods and investment of urban fixed asset investment series we use are not comparable with the private consumption and investment data of other developed countries or regions. From the proportions of consumption, investment and net exports in GDP which is the ratio of the nominal value after seasonal adjustment (Figure 17), according to our data, the sum of urban fixed asset investment, total retail sales of goods and net exports accounted for less than 70% of GDP in 2001–2002, 65%-97% from the second quarter of 2003 to the second quarter of 2008, and 80%-114% from the third quarter of 2008 to the first quarter of 2010. The narrowing caliber of consumption data and fixed asset investment data before 2002 may be caused by the impact of common factors on investment and consumption. However, considering that the common factors and their impacts in this chapter are estimated on the year-on-year growth rate of macro variables, the impact may not be significant.

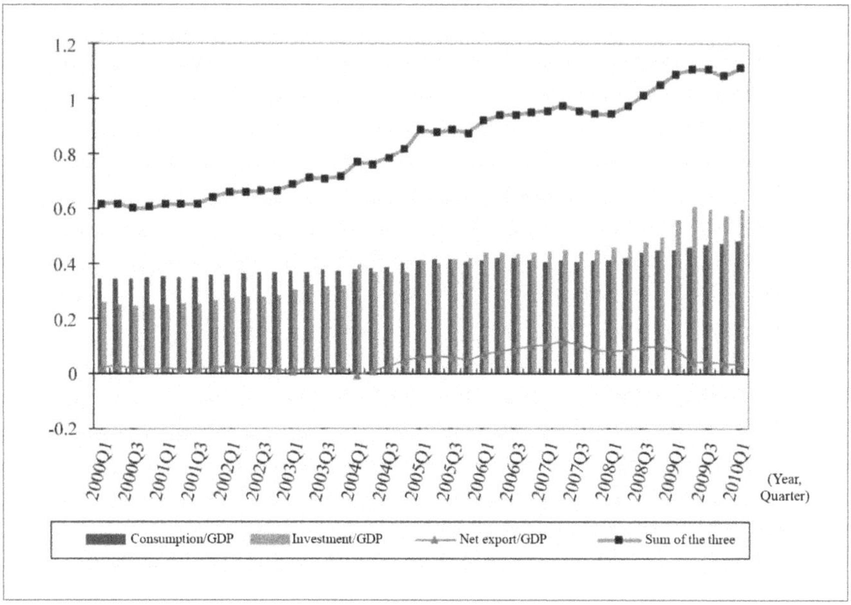

Figure 17. China's consumption, investment, and net export from the first quarter of 2000 to the first quarter of 2010 Proportion of GDP (seasonally adjusted nominal value ratio)
Source: CEIC database.

The second possible reason is China's particular consumption and investment, for example, liquidity constraints and other institutional factors caused by China's backward social security system, degraded consumption levels due to underdeveloped consumer credit, and the impact of external common factors on consumption shielded by the high propensity to save. In addition, China's investment is terribly distorted (research group, 2003 and 2005), which weakens the direct connection between China's investment and external common factors. These factors with Chinese characteristics show that, the weak correlation between external common factors and Chinese household consumption and investment is just an embodiment of the long-term imbalance of China's investment and consumption ratio in the international economic correlation. This reason seems more convincible according to China's current investment system and consumption behavior.

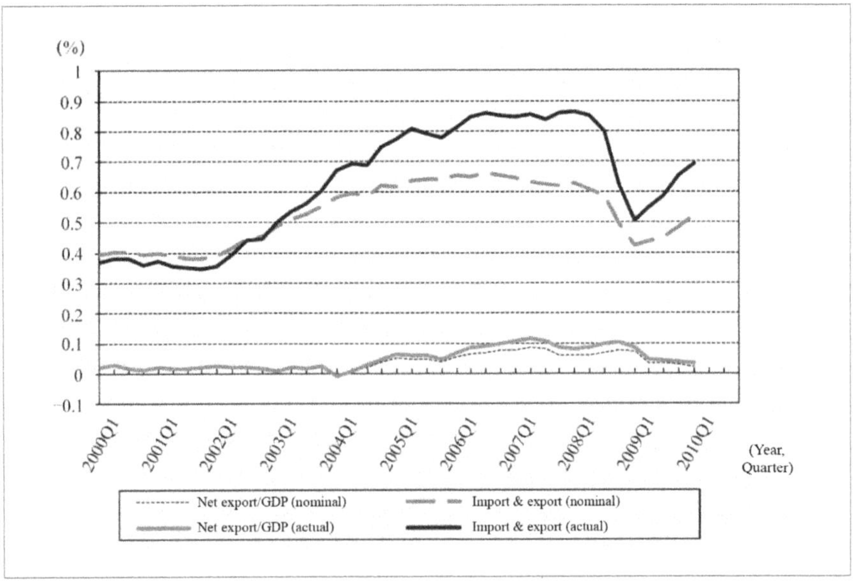

Figure 18. The proportion of China's import and export to GDP from the first quarter of 2001 to the first quarter of 2010

The third possible reason is that the development of China's import and export trade has to some extent made up for the insufficient response of consumption and investment to common factors. Calculation of the proportion of China's net exports of goods and total imports and exports in the real GDP with the RMB real exchange rate index of the Bank for International

Settlements (BIS) (converted to the first quarter of 1994=100) shows that: (1) after China joined the WTO, the proportion of total imports and exports in GDP continued to rise from the first quarter of 2002 to the third quarter of 2006; (2) after the first quarter of 2002, the proportion of the total value of imports and exports calculated according to the actual value was greater than that calculated according to the nominal value (see Figure 18), with a widening gap; (3) after 2005, the proportion of net exports calculated in real terms was also greater than that calculated in nominal terms, which indicated that the actual external dependence of China's economy may be greater than that calculated in nominal terms. In the following section, we will analyze this most direct international correlated transmission factor and try to open the common factor.

3.5 International Trade and Common Factors

Common factors are abstract factors extracted from numerous economic sequences that represent common trends, with rich economic connotation. Crucini, Kose, and Otrok (2008) proposed that oil price, productivity and terms of trade were economic variables that affected common factors of G7 countries' economic cycles. After the subprime crisis in 2007, the financial crisis spread around the world and impacted the economies of countries through financial channels such as international trade, FDI, asset prices, credit as well as the shrinking demand of the real economy, leading to a common trend of the declining growth rate of most economies. A series of chain reactions stemming from the subprime crisis and crisis management policies adopted by countries around the world would become the main variable determining common factors for a long time thereafter.

The estimation of common factors of China's GDP cyclical fluctuations (i.e., the product of the common factor and China's GDP factor load) not only provides data support for the analysis of China's economic cycle synergy but also paves a way for our synergy mechanism discussion below. We further know that such common factors that affect the public cycle may be the results of interaction between international trade and international finance factors. Based on this understanding, in order to make common factor analysis more concrete, we will provide a tentative analysis result below with international trade as the determining factor.

When the common factor of China's GDP cyclical fluctuation is expressed as "chinafactor" as a working concept, and the year-on-year growth rate of the total import and export trade of the European Union, the United

States and Japan and China are expressed as EUU, USA, JPAN and CHN respectively, then the relationship between the four can be intuitively shown in Figure 19. A simple statistical correlation analysis shows that from the first quarter of 2002 to the first quarter of 2010, the correlation coefficients between the common factor of cyclical fluctuation, chinafactor, and the growth rates of import and export trade, EUU, USA, JPAN, and CHN, stood at 0.96, 0.93, 0.90, and 0.74 respectively. In the following section, we will introduce the VAR model to analyze the impact of EUU, USA, JPAN, and CHN.

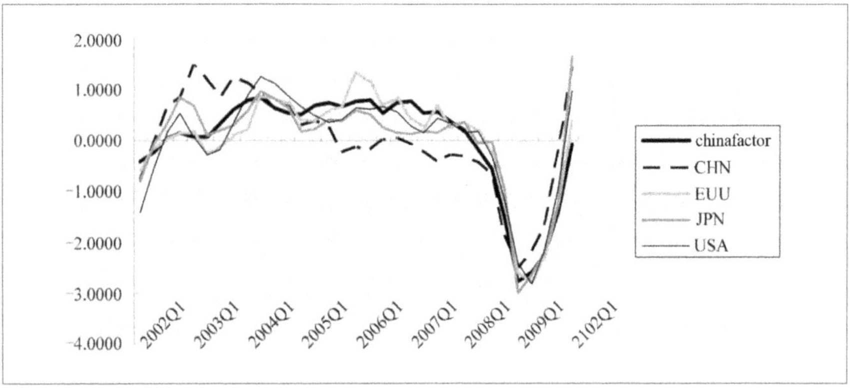

Figure 19. Relationship between the public factors of China's GDP cyclical fluctuation and the growth of import and export trade of EU, U.S., Japan and China (de-averaging)

The stability test of the chinafactor, EUU, USA, JPAN and CHN series (mean values removed) shows that (no intercept term and trend term), the five series are I (0) processes. According to the AIC and SC criteria, 2 is taken as the optimal lag order of the VAR model. In the model setting, chinafactor, EUU, USA, JPAN and CHN are included as endogenous variables. Figure 20 shows the response trend of chinafactor to its own and EUU, USA, JPAN and CHN series change shocks. The figure reveals that common factors show some degree of instability when facing shocks from various variables, and the correlation of trade among the economies has the effect of amplifying such shocks. In Table 10, we list the variance contributions of variables from the first quarter of 2007 (the 21st issue) to the first quarter of 2010 (the 33rd issue). The statistical results show that:

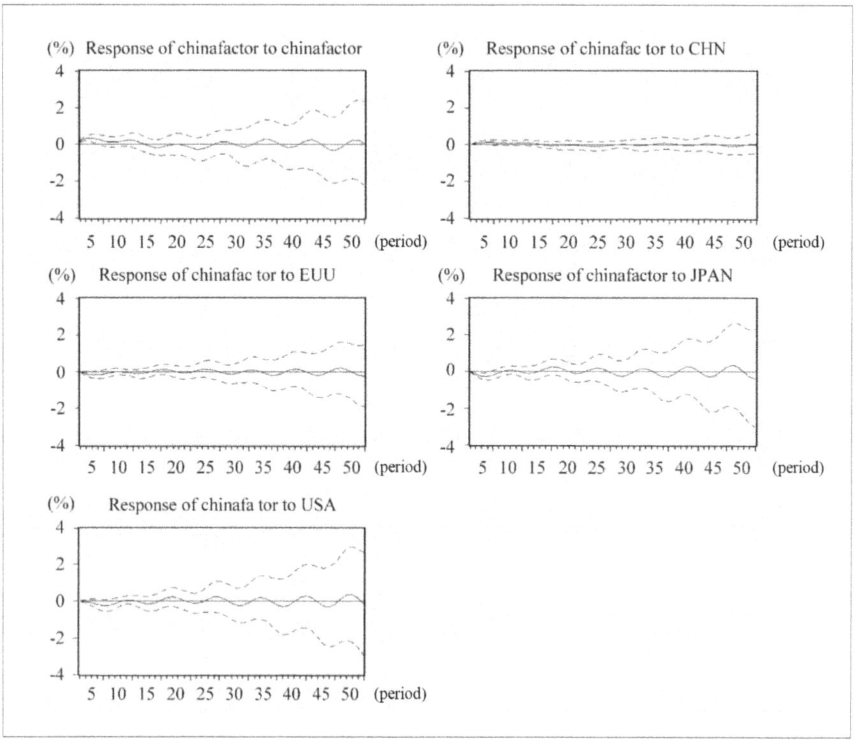

Figure 20. Shock response of public factors of China's GDP cyclical fluctuation to import and export trade fluctuations of EU, U.S., Japan and China (variable de-averaging)

1. From the perspective of common factors of China's GDP cycle, the variance of the import and export growth rate vector of the EU, the United States, Japan and China - namely EUU, USA, JPAN and CHN - explains about 10%, 25%, 24% and 6% (totally 65%) of the variance of the common factor of China's GDP cycle respectively, and the fluctuation from itself explains the remaining 35%.
2. Combining Table 8, the impact of import and export trade on China's GDP fluctuation can be described as follows: the trade growth imposes 3.2%, 8%, 7.7% and 1.9% of impacts respectively (20.8% in total) on domestic GDP fluctuation. Other factors other than trade among common factors explain 11.2% of China's GDP cyclical fluctuation. The total of these four factors reaches 32%, namely the degree of an international synergy of China's GDP cycle, and the remaining 68% goes to the special

factor of domestic GDP cyclical fluctuation- this has been discussed in the previous factor analysis.

3. An interesting cognition revealed by the data simulation is that, judging from China's integration into the world economy in recent years, the fluctuations of trade and other factors are equally important for the random impact of domestic business cycle fluctuations. Therefore, in the process of China's economy integrating into the world economic system, the fluctuations of major economies - through channels such as trade and finance—will, to some extent, lead to fluctuations in the domestic economy.

Table 10. Impact of import and export trade fluctuations in EU, USA, Japan, and China-variance decomposition

Period	chinafactor	CHN	EUU	JPAN	USA
21	40.5	7.0	9.2	22.9	20.4
22	41.4	7.0	9.6	22.8	19.1
23	40.3	7.1	10.2	23.7	18.7
24	38.8	7.0	10.2	23.6	20.3
25	38.4	6.8	9.9	23.0	21.9
26	37.9	6.6	10.1	24.0	21.4
27	36.5	6.4	10.5	25.8	20.9
28	35.3	6.1	10.3	26.0	22.3
29	35.1	6.0	10.0	25.3	23.7
30	34.8	5.9	10.3	25.6	23.4
31	34.1	5.8	10.5	26.3	23.4
32	34.6	5.6	10.1	25.5	24.2
33	35.8	5.4	10.0	24.8	23.9

Order of variables: chinafactor, CHN, EUU, JPAN, USA.

3.6 Correlation and Decoupling: Further Analysis

The empirical results provide a quantitative explanation for the international correlation of China's economic cycle, including periodic common random shocks and their channels to affect China's economy. As for the commonality of China's international economic correlation, this chapter gives an important conclusion different from the existing literature, that is, since 2002, China has shown a significant correlation with the economic cycle fluctuations of developed countries/regions. The main reason for the difference in conclusions lies in that we divide the sample investigation period into two parts with 2002 as the boundary. Without this division, our observation would be substantially consistent with the analysis of existing literature, as revealed by the quarterly GDP wave trend and correlation coefficient between China and foreign countries/regions from 1995 to 2006 in Figure 14 and Table 6. From the historical experience of China's economic cycle fluctuations, since the twenty-first century, the international correlation of China's GDP cycle fluctuations has indeed shown a different trend from the previous period. Therefore, the division of intervals based on this empirical observation is reasonable, and our research on the international correlation of China's economic cycle after 2002 is also valid.

An enlightening result of the statistical analysis is that China and developed economies have very different investment and consumer response patterns under random shocks. As far as fixed asset investment is concerned, developed economies have similar responses against random shocks, but common factors have weak explanatory power for China's fixed asset investment fluctuations and consumption. The domestic macroeconomic environment, a special factor, has strong explanatory power, that is, domestic fixed asset investment and consumption have strong "immunity" to international economic fluctuations and shocks. Considering the differences of micro-investment structure and institutional environment between developed countries and China, the natural extension of this conclusion is that the Chinese government-led investment model and the special domestic consumption environment play a decisive role in investment and consumption fluctuations.

Therefore, there are two forces that control the correlation between China's economy and the world economy: (1) the growing foreign trade and international financial ties. This force has the tendency to "converge" China's economic fluctuations to those of the world economy; (2) the special domestic investment and consumption mode, which tends to "decouple" China's economic fluctuations from those of the world economy. The balance of the two forces has formed the current synergy between the domestic economy and the international economy.

However, as shown by the performance of China's economy after its accession to the WTO, the tendency of "convergence" seems to be more obvious. We have used two typical economic events since 2001 to illustrate this point. One of the events is the U.S. IT foam in 2001. As illustrated by Table 11, the quarterly GDP growth of OECD major countries and the EU in 2001 declined significantly. During this period, China's quarterly GDP did not show a significant upward trend, and did not get on the high-speed track until 2002. The second event is the impact of the rapidly spreading U.S. subprime crisis since 2007. Compared with the growth during the relative boom period from 2002 to 2006, the quarterly GDP growth of OECD major countries declined sharply from 2007 to 2009, and the economic growth of China also declined significantly from 2008 to 2009. Table 12 provides a comparison of China's foreign capital introduction, fixed asset investment and export changes during the financial crisis and the bursting of the IT foam. Compared with the performance of various variables during the period of China's rapid economic growth from 2002 to 2006, the financial crisis has a more obvious inhibitory effect on the foreign capital introduction and export growth.

Table 11. Comparison of quarterly GDP fluctuations between China and foreign countries/regions during the financial crisis and the burst of the IT foam—quarter-on-quarter growth

Countries/Regions Average Growth Rate Year, Quarter	EU	Japan	America	Germany	France	UK	China*
1999Q1–2000Q4	3.5	1.4	4.5	2.7	3.6	3.7	8.0
2001Q1–2001Q4 (During the burst of U.S. IT foam)	2.0	0.2	1.1	1.4	1.8	2.5	8.3
2002Q1–2006Q4	2.1	1.7	2.7	1.0	1.8	2.6	10.6
2007Q1–2007Q4	2.9	2.3	2.1	2.6	2.3	2.6	11.4
2008Q1–2008Q4	0.6	−1.2	0.5	1.0	0.1	0.6	9.6
2009Q1–2009Q4	−4.2	−5.2	−2.4	−4.9	−2.5	−4.9	8.7
2010Q1	0.5	4.2	2.4	1.5	1.2	-0.2	11.9

Data Source: China Economic Network Statistical Database

The performance of China's macroeconomic data under the spreading subprime crisis since September 2008 can serve as some visual evidence of the rationality of the measurement results in this chapter. The GDP growth reached 9.9%, 9.0% and 8.7% in the third and fourth quarters of 2008 and 2009 respectively. Accompanying this downward trend, China's import and export trade continued to decline rapidly from the third quarter of 2008 and turned to negative growth from the first quarter of 2009 (Figure 21).

Table 12. Comparison of changes in China's foreign capital introduction, fixed asset investment and exports during the financial crisis and the burst of the IT foam (%)

Year, Quarter	Proportion of foreign investment in the three major economies in the actual utilization of foreign investment in China	Export		Fixed Asset Investment of the whole society	
		Proportion of foreign capital exports	Export Growth	Proportion of foreign investment	Growth of fixed asset investment in the whole society
1999–2000	29.8	46.7	*	10.7	7.7
2001	27.7	50.1	6.8	10.5	13.0
2002–2006	22.2	56.3	29.6	7.5	24.1
2007	12.0	57.1	25.7	4.6	24.8
2008	10.7	55.4	17.2	3.8	25.9
2009	10.3**	55.9	−16	2.8	30.1
2010Q1–2010Q2	—	54.7	35.2	3.1	25.0

Note: * The export growth in 1997, 1998, 1999 and 2000 stood at 21%, 0.5%, 6.1% and 27.8% respectively. ** The utilization of foreign capital in the EU is estimated by the UK, Germany and France.

Data sources: China Investment Guide, China Gold Coast Yearbook, China Statistical Abstract 2008

In sharp contrast to the continuous declining GDP growth, China's fixed asset investment showed a strong growth trend, with cumulative growth rates of 27.6% and 26.1% in 2008 and 30.1% in 2009, respectively (see Figure 21). In terms of consumption, the year-on-year growth of total retail sales of consumer goods remained at 15.5% in 2009, lower than 22.7% in 2008. However, considering the sharp price rises in 2008 and the deflation trend in 2009, the growth of total retail sales of consumer goods in 2009 was largely the same as that of the previous year. The rise of domestic investment and consumption under the global economic recession is obviously credited to the economic stimulus plan issued by the government at the end of 2008, and the concrete implementation of the ten policies to expand domestic demand, which not only props up the platform for high investment enterprises, but also largely defuses the risk of further shrinking consumer demand under the overall economic downturn, more or less offsetting the negative impact of external demand shocks. Since the first quarter of 2010, China's quarterly GDP growth has rebounded. The cumulative GDP growth reached 11.9% and 11.1% in the first and second quarters respectively, which cannot do without restored import and export trade, the continuous improvement of consumer demand and the sustained growth of fixed asset investment.

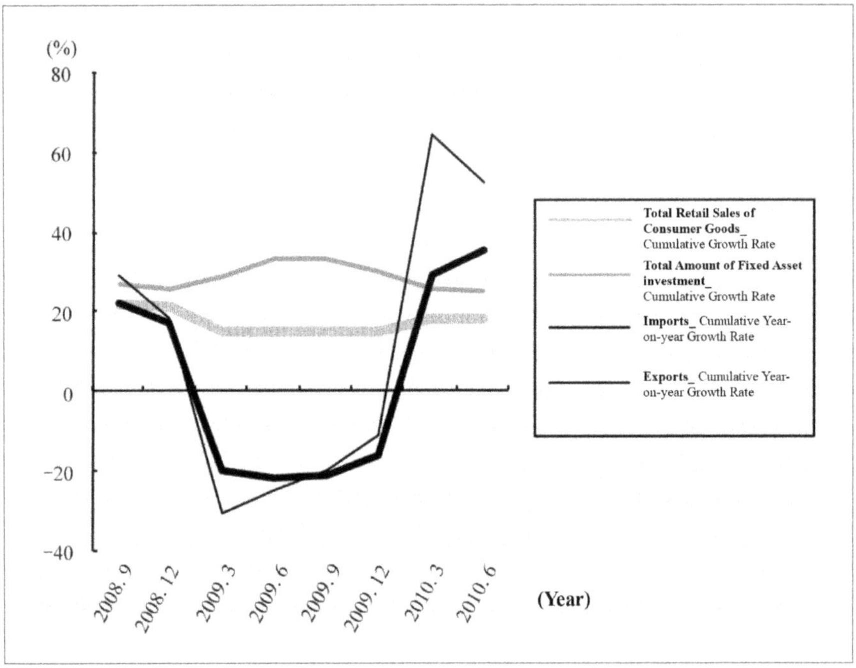

Figure 21. Performance of China's macroeconomic indicators from September 2008 to June 2010

Data source: China Economic Network Statistical Database

3.7 Conclusion

Based on the empirical analysis, our views are summarized as follows: there are two forces that control the correlation between China's and the world's economy. One is the growing foreign trade and international financial links. This tends to "converge" China's economic fluctuations with those of the world economy; the other is the special domestic investment and consumption mode, which tends to "decouple" China's economic fluctuations from the world's. The interaction between the two forces has formed the current synergy between the domestic and the international economy. However, according to the characteristics of the international correlation of China's GDP after its accession to the WTO, the "converging" force is rather stronger. Econometric analysis further shows that about 30% of China's GDP fluctuation gets involved in the world common factors.

Thus, the three policy implications can be derived as follows.

1. China still has great initiative to cope with the crisis. The partial "decoupling tendency" of China's economy reflects the special role of the Chinese government's macro policies under the special stage and mode of development.

In the face of this crisis, the Chinese government has taken strong measures and achieved short-term results. Especially the growth of investment and consumption has largely offset the declining export, which indicates that the world common factors still impose low impact on China's consumption and investment, reflecting the great initiative of the Chinese government to respond to the crisis.

However, the sustainability of this government initiative deserves more attention.

2. The overall recovery of China's economy also depends on an improved external environment. Under economic globalization, China's economic growth, macro fluctuations and the "convergence" tendency of the world economy indicates that China's economy depends heavily on external economies, and its further development cannot be separated from the world economy.

The current subprime crisis is still developing in depth and breadth and will inhibit the recovery of China's economy through the so-called "world common factors." Therefore, we believe that the overall recovery of China's economy cannot do without an improved external environment.

3. China's economic growth model needs to be changed. The impact of globalization on China's economic growth, consumption and investment deserves reflection. If only China's GDP suffers greater external impact from the world common factors under globalization, while consumption and investment are not affected by the same magnitude, China's economic growth has produced extraordinary welfare spillovers, and Chinese consumers cannot share sufficient improved welfare from the world economic growth. For the sake of improving investment, consumption structure and people's livelihood, China's economic growth model needs to be changed urgently.

Appendix: Breakpoint Test of Simple Regression Equation between China's GDP and Common Factors

Chow Breakpoint Test: 2001Q4			
Null Hypothesis: No breaks at specified breakpoints			
Varying regressors: All equation variables			
Equation Sample: 1996Q1 2010Q1			
F-statistic	25.66015	Prob. F(2,48)	0.0000
Log likelihood ratio	37.81175	Prob.Chi-Square(2)	0.0000
Wald Statistic	51.32030	Prob.Chi-Square(2)	0.0000

External Shocks and Internal Inflation in China

4.1 Introduction

The two major uncertainties facing domestic economic growth in 2008 were domestic inflation and the subprime crisis in America. The situation of domestic inflation was grim. In the second half of 2007, the inflation rate exceeded 5% and reached 6.9% in November, a record high in 11 years; in January and February 2008, it even soared to 7.1% and 8.7%. Inflation was getting worse. Meanwhile, large international economies were also facing a rapid rise in price levels. The causes of domestic inflation were multifaceted, but the proposition of "imported inflation" was quite impressive (Fan,2008). In particular, the echo of domestic structural price hikes with global structural rising prices makes it even more convincing. With its deeper integration into globalization, China has become increasingly connected with the outside world. This interconnection has been evidenced by theories of China's "exported deflation" in the previous stage and the recent "exported inflation," as well as by the idea of emerging "imported" soft landing.

Besides domestic inflation, the following impacts of the subprime crisis on China's economy cannot be ignored, specifically:

1. Impact on real economy. The subprime crisis has led to an economic downturn in the United States and a slowdown in the global economy, which will undoubtedly constrain China's economic growth.
2. Impact on capital flow. The crisis affected the way the global capital flows, making a large amount of capital rush around the international market, now to the United States for market rescue, now to the developing countries for profits. Such a huge inflow and outflow will aggravate China's economic fluctuation and financial volatility.

3. Impact on inflation. On the one hand, the subprime crisis has exacerbated the depreciation of the dollar, leading to global inflation. Depreciating the dollar was generally an important measure for the United States to address its massive trade deficit and global imbalances, which was in line with the needs of its economic adjustment.

However, the crisis left people lose confidence in the ever-depreciating dollar, thus exacerbating the depreciation of the dollar. The sharp depreciation has further promoted the rise in global primary commodity prices, leading to global inflation. On the other hand, in response to the subprime crisis, the U.S. government took such measures as fiscal expansion, capital injection and interest rate cuts, which increased the pressure of global inflation in the future. However, considering that the subprime crisis may cause a global recession, this is another downward pressure on inflation. Overall, the net impact of the subprime crisis on inflation is not yet very clear.

Whether it is the impact of "imported" inflation or the impact of the subprime crisis, "decoupling" is just wishful thinking. A recent study by Citigroup (2008) points out that every 1 percentage point drop in the U.S. GDP growth will lead to a 0.34 percentage point drop in the GDP growth of emerging market economies. When the GDP growth rate of the United States is 1 percentage point lower than its potential growth rate, the GDP growth rate of emerging market economies will be 0.54 percentage points lower than its potential growth rate. From this perspective, closely following the growth trends of the United States and the world is of great importance for keeping track of China's economic growth and inflation. It is under such context that this chapter explores the impact of external shocks on domestic inflation.

In recent years, much domestic literature has analyzed the impact of external shocks on China's inflation from different perspectives. Liu Qiang (2005) analyzed the oil price shock in the dual sector model from a theoretical perspective. Other studies adopted the AR model to analyze the impact of international oil prices on domestic CPI, PPI, GDP, investment, and other variables (He, Zhu, 2006). And some studies also verified the effect of exchange rate pass-through (ERPT) (Feng, 2006; Chen, Liu, 2007; Bi, Zhu, 2006) and held that China's ERPT effect was weak. While these studies only examine some aspects of external shocks, this chapter sets out to comprehensively analyze the impact of various external shocks on domestic inflation. It is organized as follows: Section 2 reviews the literature on globalization and inflation. Section 3 introduces the mechanism and stylized facts of external shocks influencing inflation in China. Section 4 offers econometric analysis, using the extended Phillips curve and vector autoregression (VAR) model to comprehensively examine the impact of external shocks on domestic inflation. Section 5 draws a conclusion and makes policy recommendations.

4.2 Globalization and Inflation: Literature Review

Since the 1980s, economic globalization has expedited. In international trade, from 1980 to 2005, after adjusting for inflation, world trade increased fivefold, and its share of world GDP rose from 36% to 55%. After the 1990s, as emerging market countries in Eastern Europe and developing countries of Asia joined the ranks, economic globalization accelerated. In international finance, from 1990 to 2004, the proportion of cross-border financial assets in global GDP increased more than doubled from 58% to 131%; for all emerging market countries, the proportion of FDI in total liabilities rose from 17% to 38%, and the proportion of securities investment in total liabilities increased from 2% to 11% (IMF, 2007a).

Meanwhile, global inflation dropped from 14.5% in 1980–1984 to 3.8% in 2005–2006 (Rogoff, 2006). Extensive literature suggests that globalization has been one of the key factors for the reduction in inflation in developed countries and emerging market countries in the last 25 years (IMF, 2006; Borio&Filardo, 2007).

The channels through which globalization affects inflation mainly include the following.

1. To prevent the negative effects of capital flows on the economy, globalization may prompt central banks of various countries to prefer low inflation targets to promote stable economic growth (Tytell & Wei, 2004).
2. The trade scale expands through intensified competition in product and labor markets, and imports of manufactured goods from low-cost economies will put downward pressure on domestic prices.
3. Globalization competition leads to an increase in labor productivity and total supply, which is conducive to low inflation and stable growth.
4. Labor outsourcing, especially from developed to developing countries, leads to a decrease in labor wage level.
5. As financial system is further open and capital flow expands, the huge trade deficit and the domestic gap can be made up through capital and financial accounts. Economic globalization leads to inflation's lower sensitivity to the domestic output gap. After controlling factors such as the output gap, increased credibility of monetary policy and wage stickiness, the openness index (trade scale/GDP excluding oil) can explain half of the declined price sensitivity to the output gap; meanwhile, the sensitivity of inflation to the

import prices decline is 0.1 and the import price has a short-term impact on inflation. For emerging market countries, wider openness can better explain the lowered inflation rates (IMF, 2006).

6. Cyclical factors, for example, the rising cyclical demand for energy and raw materials in emerging market economies, lead to the rise in the prices of energy and primary commodities. But for developed countries, due to the low proportion of imported energy and primary commodities in all imported products and the low proportion of food consumption, the high prices of energy and primary commodities have no significant impact on the CPI of developed countries.

However, how globalization affects inflation is not a one-sided view (i.e., globalization reduces inflation), but there are a lot of arguments.

Rogoff (2004, 2006) emphasized that in the short run, the Phillips curve has become steeper. Global competition leads to greater sensitivity to changes in prices. In this way, the steep Phillips curve attenuates the short-run output effects of unanticipated inflation, and the monetary authorities have less incentive to deviate from their inflation targets such as monetary expansion. Nevertheless, many empirical analyses argue (Roberts, 2006) that the Phillips curve has become flatter rather than steeper.

According to Mankiw (2007), the discussion of the role of globalization on the price requires an analysis of the effects of globalization on both enterprise pricing and price adjustment. Enterprise pricing depends on marginal cost and markup. In general, the enterprise desired price increases as output grows; and as output expands, its revenue decreases. Moreover, when workers work longer hours, the marginal negative utility of work and real wages rise, thus putting upward pressure on marginal costs and desired prices. It is difficult to say that globalization can change the slope of the labor supply curve or the rate of diminishing returns. In terms of cost markup, obviously, globalization has made the market competition more intense and markups smaller. That is, pricing power has dropped, and the enterprise demand curve has become more resilient. But to understand the current price dynamics, the average markup becomes less important than the sensitivity of the markup to the economic cycle. It is hard to say that the sensitivity of the desired price in a globalized economy to the business cycle is lower than that in a closed economy. Another important aspect is whether globalization has changed the rate of enterprise price adjustment. Why are some enterprises slow to adjust prices? There are menu costs and other frictions. As globalization intensifies competition, reducing the friction that hinders price adjustment, price adjustment will be more sensitive to the economic cycle, rather than the opposite. This, again, shows that the conclusion given by theory is contrary to experience.

Woodford (2007)[1] points out the recent concern that globalization will weaken the ability of monetary policy to control inflation is based on: first, liquidity premium[1] becomes a function of global liquidity rather than of liquidity supply of the central bank for one country (the new LM curve); second, real interest rates depend on the difference between global investment and consumption rather than the difference between a country's investment and consumption (the new IS curve); third, inflationary pressures depend on the global output gap instead of one country's output gap (the new AS curve). Nevertheless, through analyzing the impact of global integration of financial, final goods, and factor markets on the monetary transmission mechanism, Woodford finds that even more complete globalization (i.e., beyond the current extent of global integration) is unlikely to cause a country's central bank to lose control over the dynamics of inflation. However, Woodford mainly focuses on basic model analysis and has not provided enough empirical evidence.

Taylor (2008) argues that although many people believe globalization has led to a decline in inflation, it may be misleading. Because the weakening exchange rate pass-through, the flatter Phillips curve, and the anti-inflation of the past quarter century can all be explained by globalization. As a result, however, the discussion about the monetary policy framework falls into confusion. According to Taylor, without globalization, monetary policy can also work in all these above aspects.

While there is much debate about the impact of globalization on inflation, one point is certain, that is a country's inflation would be one-sided if the impact of globalization, more specifically, the external shocks were not considered. It is under such important theoretical background that this chapter explores the impact of external shocks on China's inflation.

4.3 External Shocks to China's inflation: Mechanisms and "Featured Facts"

The causes of domestic price rises are multifaceted, and external shocks are just one of them. First, excess global liquidity is a major factor causing price rises. It was mainly responsible for the surge of asset prices some time ago, but recently, with the sharp fluctuation of asset prices, excess liquidity's impact on the real economy cannot be ignored. Inflation boils down to a monetary phenomenon.

---

1 Investors should require different levels of extra compensation subject to the specific liquidity of assets they hold.

The accumulation of excess liquidity will inevitably become a hidden risk of future inflation.

Second, the cost-push pressures are caused by factor price revaluation. When industrialization and urbanization reach a certain stage, the costs of various factors will rise - a process that many countries will go through in their development. Under complete marketization, the rise of factor cost is a natural process. However, in China, certain price regulations are still imposed in the field of factors, and will, when reaching some point, cause an outbreak, like the rise of land costs, resource and energy prices, environmental protection costs and labor costs we now face (the implementation of the new Labor Contract Law will have a more far-reaching impact). In addition, the revaluation of the RMB exchange rate has caused a large inflow of foreign capital and the asset price in RMB has risen significantly, promoting the revaluation of factor prices, especially the evaluation of the land and real estate prices, which in turn has promoted the rise of factor costs (Zhang & Wang, 2007).

Third, the impact of the global rise in primary commodity prices on China's inflation. More food is demanded under the demand for bioenergy, markedly driving up the international food prices in recent years. The sharp depreciation and low-interest rates of the U.S. dollar, speculation and other factors have led to the rise of global commodity prices, keeping global commodity prices at an invariably high level. These have undoubtedly contributed to China's inflation.

And some other factors with "Chinese characteristics" also usher in inflation, like PRRS, higher direct costs for farmers to grow food and feed pigs, for example, the rise in agricultural materials and feed prices, and higher opportunity costs for example, rising wages of migrant workers in recent years lure people to leave farming for work), not to mention ice-snow disasters and cyclical factors of agricultural products. We'll say no more of them. This chapter focuses on the analysis of to what extent China's inflation is caused by external shocks. In fact, excess liquidity, factor price revaluation, and primary commodity price rise are all closely correlated with opening factors or external shocks.

Illustrated below are the analysis of the aspects of the transformation of global liquidity, the transmission of international commodity prices, the tightening effect of RMB exchange rate appreciation, the impact of international interest rates and the price distortion effect amplified by external shocks.

1. The Transformation of Global Liquidity

Excess liquidity is a global problem. Although the current subprime crisis has caused a temporary shortage of liquidity in the developed economies of Europe and the United States, the situation of global excess liquidity has not fundamentally changed. Excess liquidity can be caused by a number of factors, including: (1) The loose monetary policies implemented by the major monetary authorities for a long time; (2) Savings surplus, that is, global savings exceed investment. For example, Bernanke (2005) believes that emerging market economies and oil exporting countries have accumulated a large trade surplus, resulting in a global savings surplus; (3) a shortage of high-quality assets (Caballero, 2006; Rajan, 2006). Underdeveloped financial markets in emerging market economies, especially poor corporate governance and unfavorable property rights protection lead to insufficient high-quality collateral assets to support bond issuance. In addition to scarce products such as oil, only developed countries, especially the United States, can issue quality assets acceptable to global investors. In this way, excess liquidity rises when too much global capital chases fewer high-quality assets.

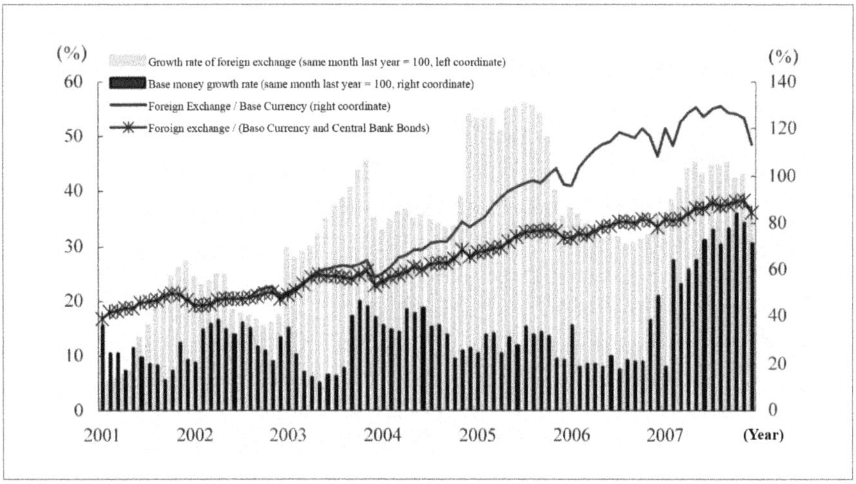

Figure 22. China's external assets and base currency growth

Source: People's Bank of China.

The excess of global liquidity will cause too much international capital to rush around the international market, especially a large amount of capital will flow into China, attracting a large inflow of foreign capital including floating capital. The large inflow, combined with China's massive trade surplus, has built up huge foreign exchange reserves. Due to the lack of exchange rate elasticity, a large amount of funds outstanding for foreign exchange injected into the base money supply, coupled with incomplete hedging by the central bank, have turned this global liquidity into liquidity in the domestic market. From January 2001 to December 2007, the ratio of funds outstanding for foreign exchange to base currency increased by 2.89 times from 39.3 % to 113.4 %. To control the excessive growth of base currency, the central bank hedged by issuing bonds, bills and other means. Over the same period, the proportion of funds outstanding for foreign exchange in the sum of base currency and the bonds issued by the central bank rose from 39.3% to 84.7%. Through hedging, the growth of base currency is much lower than that of funds outstanding for foreign exchange, but the growth of base currency accelerated significantly in 2007 (Figure 22). The increase of base currency can be transmitted to M1 and M2 of the money supply through the money multiplier effect and eventually impose an impact on prices.

2. Transmission of International Commodity Prices

Due to the China's huge economic volume integrated into the world economy and the high growth of the Chinese economy since 2002, much more imported energy, metals and other raw materials have been demanded, and the prices of energy and raw materials in the international market have also risen sharply. From December 2001 to January 2008, the energy price index increased by more than 3.5 times, and the spot price of crude oil by 3.9 times; the prices of non-energy commodities doubled, of which metals rose by more than two-folds, while agricultural primary products and food rose by 31.74 % and 98.19 % respectively.

The prices of most downstream commodities in China have been liberalized. Most upstream products, especially basic products such as energy, are controlled by the state. Domestic oil prices are lower than those of similar international products, but there is a linkage mechanism between domestic and international oil prices. Figure 23 shows that oil and gas prices in China's PPI lag behind international energy prices, but they change in close alignment with each other. Figure 24 shows that the international food price index fluctuates greatly, and China's CPI food price index also lags behind the international food price index.

We have calculated the correlation coefficients between China's PPI and raw material and fuel purchasing price index and international commodity price index (with a 1-month lag) and found that the domestic price index is highly correlated with the international price index.

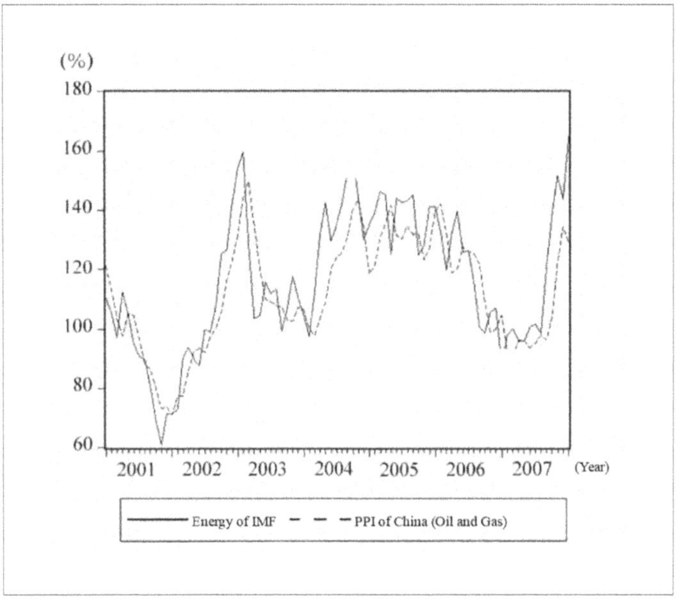

Figure 23. PPI (Oil and gas) in China and international energy prices

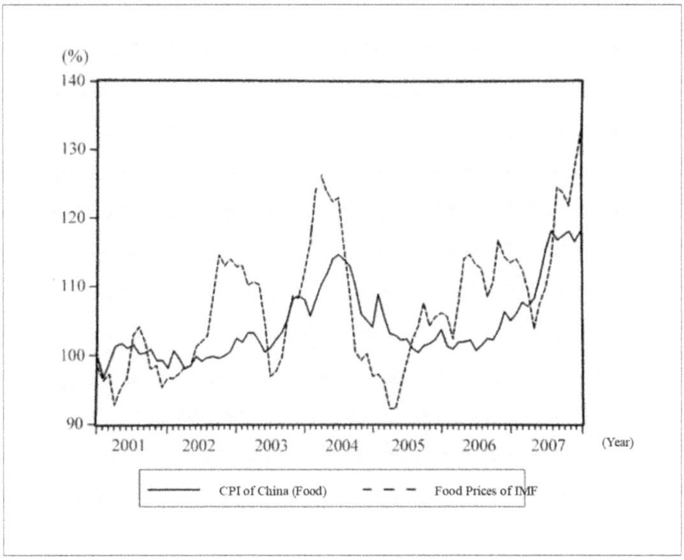

Figure 24. China CPI (Food) and international food prices

Source: CEIC, IFS.

The correlation coefficients between the oil and gas price index and the fuel purchase price index in PPI and the IMF energy price index stood at 0.96 and 0.93, respectively, and the correlation coefficient between the non-ferrous metal purchase price index and the IMF metal price was as high as 0.97. The correlation between China's PPI food price index and the international food price index was 0.65, slightly lower. In summary, the correlation coefficient between China's PPI and all IMF commodity price indexes was also highly correlated (correlation coefficient is 0.86) (Table 13).

Table 13. Correlation between China's PPI Index and IMF Commodity Index (with a 1-month lag) (January 2001–January 2008)

	IMF Energy index	IMF Food index	IMF Metal index	IMF owned Commodity index (all IMF Commodity index)
PPI	0.82	0.44	0.61	0.86
PPI (Oil and Gas)	0.96	0.20	0.36	0.92
PPI (Food)	0.12	0.65	0.22	0.21
PPIRM	0.78	0.40	0.62	0.82
PPI (ferrous metals)	0.42	0.39	0.21	0.42
PPI (fuel power)	0.93	0.15	0.44	0.91
PPI (Non-ferrous metal)	0.41	0.39	0.97	0.59

Source: CEIC, IMF, author's calculation.

Rising global energy and primary product prices have caused two rounds of shocks to China's CPI: (1) Direct transmission channel promoted by cost. The rise in the prices of imported energy and primary products led first to an increase in the purchasing price index of raw materials, fuel and power (PPIRM), then the producer price index of industrial products went up, ultimately affecting the consumer price index (CPI). (2) Income effects. Affected by a price increase, residents may reduce their expenditure or choose other alternative ways of consumption under the income effect, thus partially offsetting the first round of shock. The comprehensive impact of these two aspects needs to be determined through empirical analysis.

3. The Tightening Effect of RMB Exchange Rate Appreciation

Since the exchange rate reform in July 2005, the revaluation of the exchange rate has caused the nominal exchange rate of RMB against the world's major currencies to rise and fall. From July 2005 to January 2008, the RMB appreciated by

12.7 % against the dollar, 8.66 % against the yen, and 1.03 % against the pound. It depreciated against the euro, the Canadian dollar, the Australian dollar, the Singapore dollar, the Swiss franc, and some Nordic currencies. The most prominent depreciation was 7.45 % against the euro and 6.58 % against the Canadian dollar. After trade-weighted and inflation-oriented adjustment, the nominal effective exchange rate has not changed much, and the real effective exchange rate has appreciated (Figure 25).

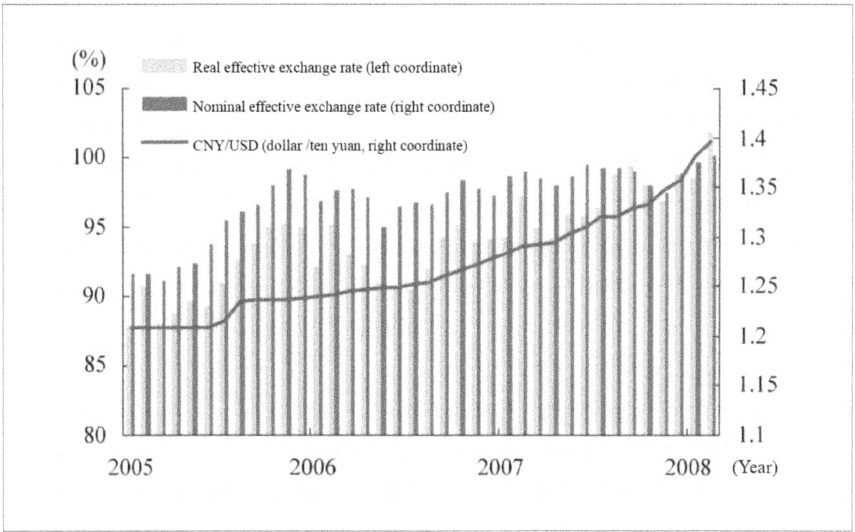

Figure 25. Nominal and effective exchange rates of RMB

Source: Real effective exchange rate from BIS, others from CEIC.

On the one hand, exchange rate appreciation reduces imported inflation. Since most of the imported primary raw materials are denominated in U.S. dollars, the appreciation of RMB against the U.S. dollar can partially offset the direct impact of rising prices of primary products on domestic inflation. Taking imported crude oil as an example, before the exchange rate reform, the RMB exchange rate was largely stable, the oil price converted into RMB was consistent with the fluctuation trend of oil price marked by the dollar, and the importer undertook the fluctuation of international oil price. After the exchange rate reform, especially after the international oil price exceeded $ 90 in November 2007, the RMB appreciation stepped up, the RMB price trend of crude oil deviated from its dollar price, further inhibiting domestic price rise (Figure 26). Specifically, the international oil price in January 2008 was 58.5 % higher than that in July 2005, the RMB appreciated by 12 % against the U.S. dollar, and the RMB-denominated WTI rose roughly by 39.48%. The empirical research on the pass-through effect of the RMB exchange rate shows that the RMB exchange rate imposes weak impact on China's import price and CPI, and the price pass-through effect of the exchange rate is significantly different in various inflation environments. In a period of low inflation, the pass-through effect of the exchange rate on import price is reinforced, but the pass-through effect on consumer price gets weakened (Feng, 2006; Chen, Liu, 2007; Bi, Zhu, 2006).

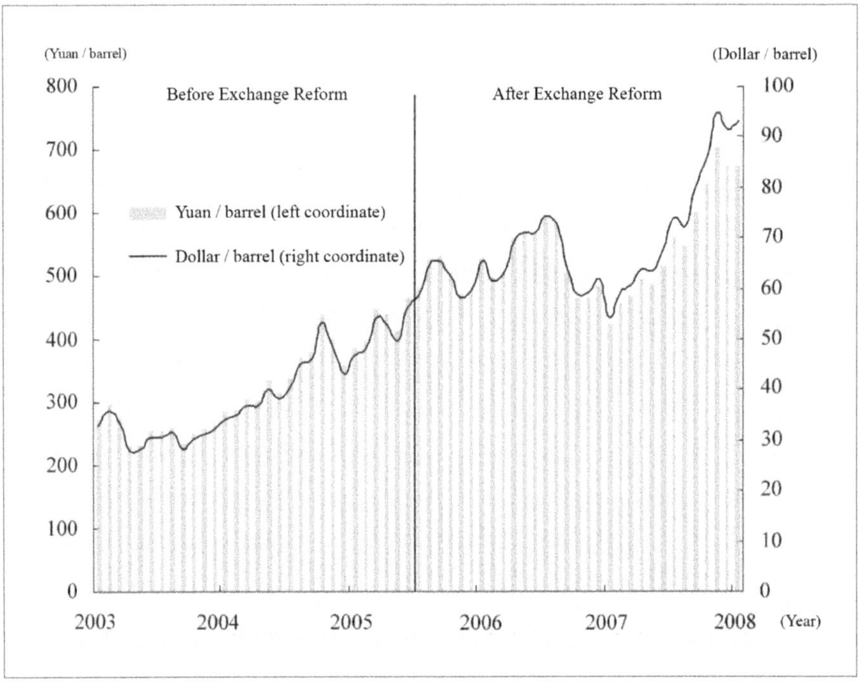

Figure 26. Comparison of U.S. Dollar price and RMB price of crude oil (Comparison of crude oil prices in U.S. Dollar and RMB) (WTI)

Data source: IMF, CEIC, author's calculation.

On the other hand, the appreciation of the exchange rate leads to less export and more imports, resulting in a decrease in the trade surplus and the contribution of net exports to GDP, as well as having a tightening effect on the economy. However, China's trade surplus did not shrink significantly under a small appreciation of the real effective exchange rate, suggesting that the tightening effect through this channel is not obvious for the time being. Empirical studies have shown (Shi, 2006) that the appreciation of the RMB real effective exchange rate has a tightening effect on the economy but once considering the correlation in international finance such as capital inflow caused by appreciation and monetary expansion in the case of incomplete hedging, the tightening effect is diminishing.

4. The Impact of International Interest Rates

Adopting an inflexible exchange rate regime, China seems to be "outsourcing" monetary policy to the Federal Reserve (FED) (Wang Qing, 2008). Such outsourcing is harmless when China is at the same stage of the cycle as the United States, but it can be problematic when they are at opposite cycles. For example, when the United States is experiencing the subprime mortgage crisis and keeps cutting interest rates, in the face of excessive price increases, China raising the interest rate as requested by the public is as much as adding fuel to the flames of domestic inflation. And low interest rates in the United States will nurture global inflation in the future.

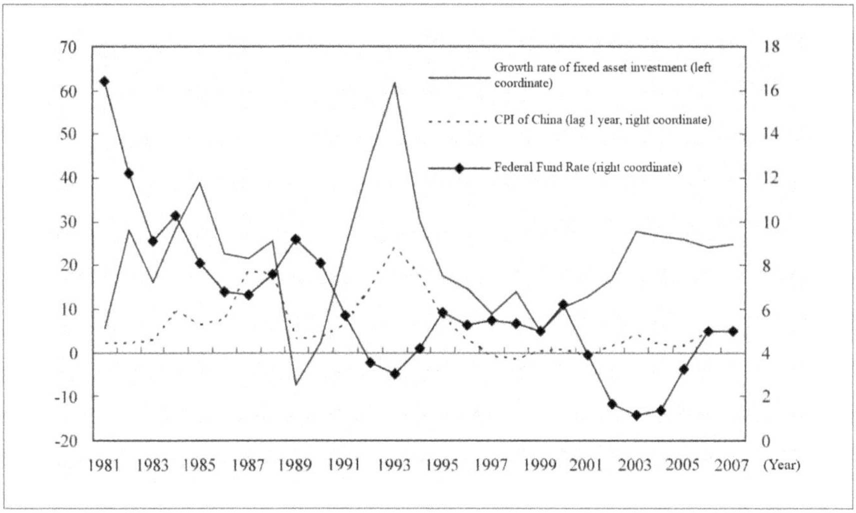

Figure 27. Federal funds rate and investment and inflation rates in China

Source: National Bureau of Statistics, CEIC.

Figure 27 shows that the federal funds rate follows an opposite trend to China's fixed asset investment growth rate and China's one-year lagged inflation rate, indicating that China's cyclical fluctuations, including price, are deeply affected by the federal funds rate of the United States. From this perspective, the effect of the international interest rate on domestic inflation cannot be ignored.

5. Price Distortion Amplified by External Shocks

To catch up with the developed economies, developing countries tend to depress factor prices and implement low-cost industrialization strategies (Growth Frontier Group, 2003). But this distortion, on the one hand, brings macro efficiency loss and is unsustainable; on the other hand, under open conditions, this distortion will also amplify the effect of external shocks and aggravate macroeconomic fluctuations (Growth Frontier Research Group, 2004 and 2005).

At present, China has not straightened out the distortion relationship of factor prices, but meanwhile brings out new price control, which will inevitably aggravate the distortion. The price controls will result in hoarding, or production cuts, both of which will lead to a reduction in supply, thereby exacerbating supply-demand tensions and further driving inflation. A typical case is that the control of resource prices worsens the contradiction between supply and demand: As the government controls prices, rising demand for domestic investment has led to an increase in resource and energy prices, driving up resource and energy prices in other countries while China's prices remain unchanged. So, China becomes more competitive, more of its products are demanded, and the profits of domestic companies have increased, attracting more investors. As investment grows, world demand for resources and energy expand and its prices rise, leading to inversion of resources and energy prices at home and abroad, especially crude oil prices ... This cycle will go on and on. And the more international resource energy prices rise, the greater the pressure on domestic price adjustment; this is positive feedback that will ultimately make price controls unsustainable.

Therefore, we should pay special attention to the amplification effect of external shocks on price distortions. In particular, in an era of globalization, the excessively depressed and distorted price system is in some ways a subsidy to the world. Instead of truly easing the pressure of domestic cost, it will promote the further rise of domestic (investment) demand, exacerbate economic overheating, and thus ramp up the pressure of inflation. In particular, distorted prices perpetuate an extensive growth pattern that leads to high economic growth, while high growth builds inflationary pressures. From the simple Phillips curve equation (Zhang, 2008), we can see that faster economic growth will drive up the inflation rate. Over the past five years, China's economy has maintained a double-digit growth, averaging 10.6%. If measured by the potential growth rate of 9.4 % (steady-state inflation rate of 5%) in Figure 23, then China's economy has been running above the potential growth rate (1–2 percentage points) in the past five years, which undoubtedly accumulates inflationary pressure, leading to the outbreak of inflation. What surprises some scholars is not the emergence of inflation, but why only now it shows up.

Table 14. GDP growth rate under different steady-state inflation rates[2] (%)

Inflation rate	0	1	2	3	4	5	6	7	8	9	10
GDP growth rate	7.38	7.78	8.18	8.59	8.99	9.39	9.80	10.20	10.60	11.01	11.41

Source: Zhang Xiaojing (2008).

4.4 Econometric Analysis

What are analyzed above are the channels through which different external shocks affect inflation. Extended Phillips curve model and VAR model are used below to make an empirical observation.

1. Extended Phillips Curve

The Phillips curve is a classic model for inflation study. Many variations of the curve are adopted in different scenarios. For example, Gordon (1990, 1997) attributes inflation to three factors in his "triangular model": inflation inertia, demand pull and supply shock. A large number of domestic researchers have estimated the dynamic characteristics of inflation through the Phillips curve model (Liu Shucheng, 1997; Wang Shaoping, 2001; Zeng Lifei et al., 2006; Xu Jiangang et al., 2006). This chapter draws on the "triangular model" from Gordon to get the following extended Phillips curve:

$$\pi_t = c + \alpha(L)\pi_{t-1} + \beta(L)D_t + \gamma(L)x_t + \varepsilon_t \quad (1)$$

Where, c is a constant term with π_t as the inflation rate, D_t as the economic growth rate gap. While x_t denotes other control variables, like supply shock variables of international oil prices, food prices and production, and dummy variables can be included to embody system change. $\alpha(L)$, $\beta(L)$ and $\gamma(L)$ denote the lag coefficients of each variable.

2 The data of 2007 are adjusted (GDP growth rate is 11.4 %, inflation rate is 4.8 %), and the results are slightly different from Zhang (2008).

In equation (1), the economic growth rate gap D_t is equal to the actual economic growth rate minus the potential economic growth rate. Many methods are available to calculate the potential economic growth rate, and the results vary, thus the obtained economic growth rate gap is uncertain. To avoid this uncertainty, we can replace D_t by the GDP growth rate directly, and since equation (1) is linear, all uncertainties about the potential growth rate are transferred to the constant term c and the error term ε_t.

Based on the previous analysis of stylized facts, the external shocks are summarized as oil prices, international food prices, exchange rate revaluation and increased liquidity[3]. These variables can be included in vector X_t.

Model variables are comprised of inflation rate (CPI), actual GDP growth rate (GD-PGTH), real oil price (OILR), real food price index (FOODR), real effective exchange rate of RMB (REER), and money supply (M1). The model quotes quarterly data (refer to appendix Schedule 1 in this chapter for data sources). Firstly, seasonally adjust the IMF crude oil price index, international food price index as well as money supply, and then adjust the first two indices with the American real effective exchange rate to obtain the real oil and food price indices. In this way, the obtained price indices not only eliminate the effect of exchange-rate on the U.S. dollar but remove the effect of relative changes between inflation in the United States and in its major trading countries. On this basis, calculate the year-on-year and chain growth rates for each variable separately, and indicate the former one with "_TH" after the code name of these variables and the latter one with "DL" before them. Perform unit root test to all variables (see appendix Schedule 2 of this chapter).

Firstly, calculate the autoregressive AR (2) model with only CPI lag term, which reflects the influence of price lag; secondly, add the GDP growth rate to derive the benchmark model, which reflects the price lag factor and the impact of economic growth rate on prices in the triangular model. To illustrate the impact of external shocks, we calculated an "external shock model" that includes CPI lag factors and external shocks only, and a "hybrid extended model" that includes above factors as well as the GDP growth rate. For the two models, both calculate the equation containing the 4th order lag factor in external shocks, then delete insignificant variables and finally get the estimation results. As the equations include lag factors about explained variable, the D.W. value cannot fully reflect the residual autocorrelation. Therefore, we calculated LM test probability values for residual autocorrelation (see Table 15 for the results).

---

3 When applying international interest rates in VAR analysis, price distortions do not show in the model directly.

The CPI autoregressive AR (2) model shows a high fitting, with the corrected R^2 reaching 0.9691. Since the LM test for residual autocorrelation fails to reject the null hypothesis of no autocorrelation for residuals, the AR (2) model seems to be quite efficient. The benchmark model including GDP growth rate can increase 0.005 for corrected R^2, and 0.54 for probability value F of the LM test for residual autocorrelation.

The results of the external shock model are equivalent to adding some external shock variables to the AR (2) model. The three external shock variables of oil prices, international food prices and the real effective exchange rate are all significant, with an increase of 0.0067 for corrected R^2 over the benchmark model. And although the probability value F of the LM test for residual autocorrelation is reduced by 0.23, the null hypothesis of no autocorrelation for residuals cannot be rejected. The result at least suggests that the impact of external shocks on the domestic CPI is statistically significant.

Based on the benchmark model and external shock model, replace the year-on-year growth rates with chain growth rates in three external shocks of oil prices, international food prices and the real effective exchange rate[4], and add the year-on-year growth rate of the liquidity scale M1 to obtain the hybrid extended model. The results show that the coefficients of the three external shocks and the liquidity scale on the domestic CPI are still significant, with the corrected R^2 increasing by 0.0057 over the benchmark model and the probability value F of the autocorrelation LM test increasing by 0.016. In addition, in the "external shock model" and "hybrid extended model," the influence coefficients of oil price and international prices are both positive, indicating that higher oil prices and international food prices can drive up CPI; and the influence coefficient of liquidity scale M1 is positive, which is in line with economic theory; with a positive influence coefficient, the real effective exchange rate cannot tighten CPI in the short term.

The estimation results of the extended Phillips curve model show that the lagged factor of inflation rate itself is the major factor influencing short-term inflation[5], and the impact of the economic growth rate cannot be underestimated. Given a high corrected R2 of the benchmark model, though the external shock model and the hybrid expansion model are not efficient in improving the

4 We experimented with regression models of year-on-year growth rates and found that the statistical significance of its external shocks declined.

5 This reflects both inflation expectations and the price stickiness determined by institutional factors such as labor markets, price systems as well as enterprise pricing mechanisms.

Table 15. Estimation results of Phillips curve

Sample interval: 1995Q1–2007Q4, with a total of 52 sample points					
Variable name	**Variable symbol**	**AR (2) model**	**Benchmark model**	**External shocks Model**	**Hybrid extended Model**
Intercept term	C	0.002 (1.488)	−0.028 (-2.970***)	0.006 (0.446)	−0.026 (2.419**)
Inflation rate lag of one phase	CPI (-1)	1.139 (10.485***)	1.021 (9.617***)	0.850 (8.504***)	0.911 (9.164***)
Inflation rate lag of two phases	CPI (-2)	−0.285 (-2.941**)	−0.211 (-2.300**)	−0.081 (-0.944)	−0.146 (-1.729*)
Economic growth rate	GDPGTH		0.341 (3.220***)		0.217 (1.877**)
Year-on-year growth rate of real oil price	OILR_TH			0.0057 (1.689*)	
Chain growth rate of real oil price	DLOILR (-1)				0.020 (2.033**)
Year-on-year growth rate of real international food prices	FOODR_TH			0.050 (5.295***)	
Chain growth rate of real international food prices	DLFOODR (-2)				0.0868 (3.272***)
Year-on-year growth rate of real effective exchange rate	REER_TH			0.06 (2.393**)	
Chain growth rate of real effective exchange rate	DLREER (-2)				0.131 (2.359**)
Year-on-year growth rate of M1	M1_TH (-1)				0.051 (1.897*)
Coefficient of determination R^2		0.9703	0.9756	0.9827	0.9826
Corrected R^2		0.9691	0.9741	0.9808	0.9798
D.W. Statistics		1.95	2.037	2.10	2.024
LM test probability[b]		0.401	0.941	0.71	0.957

Note: a.*, * * *and * * * indicate that the t-statistics of each coefficient are significant at 1%, 5% and 10% levels, respectively.

b. The probability of LM test reports the F probability value of Lagrange multiplier test with lag of two phases, and the null hypothesis is that the residuals have no autocorrelation.

determination coefficient of the equation, the short-term impact of external shock on CPI is statistically significant and can improve residual autocorrelation.

2. VAR Analysis

Note that the one-equation model of Phillips curve only describes statistical relations between CPI and the exogenous variables, but it fails to reflect the interaction of variables. The econometric results in Table 15 also provide only the historically explained variance of the fitted sample, but they fail to provide dynamics of the forecast variance in the mid-and-long term. In fact, in the economic system, CPI, GDP, international oil prices, international food prices and monetary policy variables may influence each other. To overcome the shortcomings of a single equation, VAR model is used to estimate the impact of external factors on domestic inflation, assuming that each variable is endogenous.

We adopted the following p-order vector autoregressive model:

$$y_t = c + \sum_{i=1}^{p} \Psi_i y_{t-i} + \varepsilon_t \tag{1}$$

In this equation, y_t is a column vector combined by one $(n\times 1)$-dimensional endogenous variable, $c = (c_1, c_2, \cdots c_n)$ is the intercept vector of VAR model, Ψ_i constitutes the $(n\times n)$ dimensional coefficient vector of the model, and $\varepsilon_t = (\varepsilon_{1t}, \varepsilon_{2t}, \cdots, \varepsilon_{nt})$ is a random factor of the model, which is assumed to be a white noise vector.

The previous analysis shows that international oil prices, representative of commodity prices, keep an intrinsic connection with food prices. Therefore, we choose international crude oil and food prices as proxy variables for external price shocks. To reflect the impact of exchange rate shocks, we choose the real effective exchange rate of RMB as a proxy variable. In addition, China has long practiced the policy of pegging to U.S. dollar, and the policy of "crawling peg" after the exchange rate reform, making funds outstanding for foreign exchange a proxy variable for global liquidity transformation shocks on China's economy. And considering the impact of international interest rates on the domestic economy, the Federal Fund Rate (FFR) is adopted here as a proxy record for international interest rates. Finally, in monetary policy, the role of interest rate variables cannot be ignored, so we use one-year time deposit rate as an indicator of interest rate variables. As inflation is essentially a monetary phenomenon, money supply indicator should also be added to the model to measure the impact of monetary factors on inflation.

Much literature about VAR models uses level data of variables such as GDP and prices as the initial basis for analysis. Some models analyze the quantitative relation between the first-order log differences of variables, and others join the cointegration relationships to analyze the relationship between the level data of variables. Because of the cumulative quarterly data of China's nominal GDP, it may be unreliable to adjust China's GDP to a single quarterly value by a simple method, and the quarterly real GDP index is not available. Therefore, the VAR model (as well other data) here adopts year-on-year GDP growth rates instead of using the level variables of GDP as initial data. As the first-order log-difference VAR model essentially analyses the quantitative relationship between chain growth rates of variables, the VAR model constructed by year-on-year data does not violate the basic principles of the first-order log-difference VAR model.

The model variables include actual GDP growth rate, real oil price shock (OILR_TH), real food price index growth rate (FOODR_TH), inflation rate (CPI), real effective exchange rate growth of the RMB (REER_TH), funds outstanding for foreign exchange growth rate (FEXA_TH), Federal Fund Rate (FFR), China's one-year deposit rate (R) and M2 growth rate (M2_TH). The model uses quarterly data from 1994Q1 to 1997Q4. The unit root test shows that all variables are stationary series (see appendix Schedule 2 of this chapter), which allows for the construction of the VAR model.

The impulse response function allows analyzing the impact of external shocks on inflation, where the ordering of the variables is important. Literature generally analyzes impulse response functions in the following variable ordering: the first variable is not affected by all other variables at the same time, but shocks to the first variable affect other variables; the second variable affects the remaining variables (except the first one), but it is not affected by them at the same time; and so on for the rest variables. We also make the following ranking based on this principle: actual GDP growth rate, OILR_TH, international FOODR_TH, CPI, FFR, real effective exchange rate, FEXA_TH, R, and M2_TH. This choice of order is in line with the general practice of relevant literature. The actual output does not respond simultaneously to the shocks of other variables in the model; oil prices as well as international food prices have a direct effect on inflation. The inflation rate and international interest rates impose a potential impact on China's real effective exchange rate. In response to changes in inflation and economic growth rates, the central bank adjusts the exchange rate, funds outstanding for foreign exchange and interest rates, while controlling the money supply, which eventually feeds back on actual output.

Due to the sample size limitations, the maximum lag is assumed to be 3 phases. According to the selection criteria of the lag phase of the model, LR, FPE, AIC, and HQ statistics are all 3 phases (see Schedule 3 in the appendix of this chapter), so 3 periods lag is determined as the benchmark model①, with the sample interval adjusted for lag phase as 1995Q4–2007Q4. The inflation response of VAR model (Figure 28) shows that: (1) the impact of GDP growth rate on CPI is significant and has a lasting effect; (2) rising oil prices drives up inflation rate; (3) China's CPI can respond quickly to international food price increases and it lasts for a long time with international food price shocks waning after about 12 quarters; (4) the lagged impact of CPI itself declines rapidly, reaches the market bottom at the 12th quarter, and eventually fades off. (5) FFR increases have tightening effect on China's inflation; (6) The tightening effect of real effective exchange rate appreciation of RMB on inflation has a short-term lag. The exchange rate appreciation can curb inflation after 1 quarter, and the tightening effect reaches its maximum in about 7 quarters; (7) CPI barely responds to the impact of funds outstanding for foreign exchange in the short 1–5 quarters, but then reacts positively, indicating that the central bank's hedge is effective; (8) CPI reacts to interest rates with a lag, and the tightening of interest rates increase on CPI takes effect about 4 quarters later. (9) CPI responds positively to supply increase, and reaches a maximum around the 8th quarter, conforming to the basic theory.

The impact of each factor on inflation can be reflected by the decomposition results of forecast variance (see Table 16). The GDP factor takes up an increasing proportion in forecast variance and rises to be the maximum variance ratio factor in the 16th quarter and the variance ratio approaches 40% in the 40th quarter, indicating that the GDP growth rate is decisive for CPI in the mid-to-long term. The variance ratio of oil price factor remains at around 8%. The impact of international food prices on CPI is prominent. In four quarters, the variance ratio of international food prices exceeds 30% and then gradually decreases, falling below 20% after the 20th quarter. This suggests that international food prices are the major factor influencing CPI in the short term.

As the largest initial variance ratio of all variables, CPI lag factor reached 55.34 %, but then declined gradually. And after the 12th quarter, it retreated behind the variance ratio of shocks in GDP growth rate, international food prices and real effective exchange rate. The variance ratio of the real effective exchange rate rose gradually, reaching a maximum of 18.8% in the 8th quarter, which shows that the real effective exchange rate has an obvious tightening effect on CPI. The funds outstanding for foreign exchange have a constantly low and the smallest variance ratio, which stands at only 3.11% by the 40th

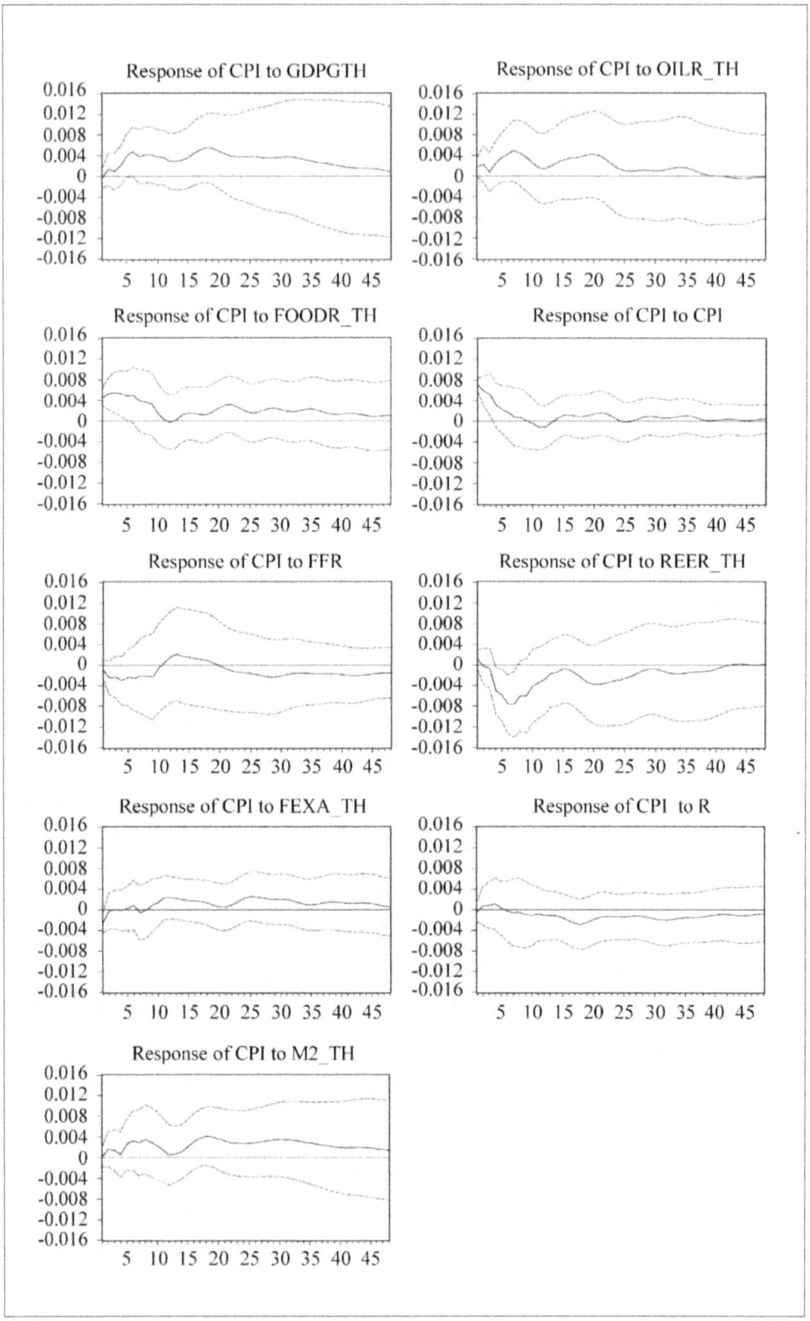

Figure 28. Inflation response in VAR (3) model with three lag phases

Table 16. VAR (3) Model prediction variance decomposition—percentage of each factor to prediction variance (%)

Date	Standard deviation	Economic growth rate GDPGTH	International oil price OILR_TH	International food prices FOODR_TH	Inflation rate CPI	Federal funds rate FFR	Deposit interest rate R	Real effective exchange rate REER_TH	Foreign exchange FEXA_TH	Generalized Currency M2_TH
1	0.00	0.12	8.32	36.22	55.34	0.00	0.00	0.00	0.00	0.00
2	0.01	1.97	8.26	44.34	39.79	1.20	0.77	0.06	1.92	1.69
3	0.01	1.93	5.80	52.68	31.01	0.83	1.40	0.10	2.03	4.22
4	0.01	3.48	5.98	51.70	22.93	1.69	1.37	7.10	1.50	4.24
8	0.01	15.19	9.41	29.28	11.67	2.54	0.97	18.14	0.96	11.85
12	0.01	20.41	8.62	24.44	11.35	3.38	1.24	18.46	1.48	10.63
16	0.01	24.35	8.73	21.11	9.80	5.67	1.33	16.08	3.74	9.20
20	0.01	32.03	9.12	17.57	8.08	5.31	2.32	13.82	3.24	8.50
24	0.01	34.42	9.10	17.42	7.40	4.69	2.57	13.03	3.08	8.30
28	0.01	36.63	8.45	17.32	7.10	4.45	2.82	12.19	3.27	7.78
32	0.02	38.41	7.85	17.41	6.60	4.20	3.46	11.47	3.27	7.33
40	0.02	39.68	7.36	17.73	6.15	4.05	4.38	10.51	3.11	7.02
48	0.02	39.17	7.53	18.04	5.93	4.29	4.83	10.42	3.06	6.74
Cholesky Ordering: GDPGTH, OILR_TH, FOODR_TH, CPI, FED, R, REER_TH, FEXA_TH, M2_TH										

quarter, further indicating that the explanatory power of funds outstanding for foreign exchange on CPI was not high, and the central bank's hedge was effective. The impact of FFR on domestic CPI is insignificant at the beginning, but the variance ratio can reach 5.67% by the 16th quarter, indicating that the impact of international interest rates on China's CPI is reflected in the mid-and-long term. The variance ratios of domestic interest rates and money supply to CPI also rise gradually, showing that the impact of interest rates and M2 on CPI is lagged. Changing the order of FFR, one-year deposit rate and the real effective exchange rate has no essential impact on the variance decomposition result, indicating that the result is still robust.

According to the results of extended Phillips curve and VAR analysis: (1) the impact of external shocks, especially short-term international food prices as well as mid-and-long term international crude oil prices increases, on domestic inflation cannot be ignored; (2) the real effective exchange rate has a certain time-lag in curbing inflation; (3) the increase of funds outstanding for foreign exchange has little direct impact on CPI, which shows that the hedging of the central bank is effective; (4) monetary aggregates has a great influence on inflation, while domestic interest rate plays a much smaller role; (5) international interest rate has an impact on domestic prices, indicating that monetary policy is more or less outsourced; (6) GDP growth rate and lagging CPI remains the most important factors that determine inflation.

4.5 Conclusions and Recommendations for Policy Makers

This chapter has discussed how external shocks affect China's inflation through mechanism analysis and empirical research. Some conclusions are drawn, and recommendations are put forward as follows:

First, we should, actively and prudently, draw lessons from the Asian crisis in response to external shocks. China is in the midst of globalization and is increasingly connected with the outside world. That means China will face more external shocks. The spread of the subprime crisis has significantly exacerbated the uncertainty of the international economic landscape. In this context we should cherish the achievements of more than 30 years of reform and opening-up and work hard to avoid the economic regression caused by the Asian financial crisis.

Second, we should pay close attention to the impact of external shocks on domestic inflation, but controlling the expansion of domestic aggregate demand, especially investment demand, remains the key to curbing inflation. Both the extended Phillips equation and VAR analysis show that the impact of external shocks, especially short-term international food prices and medium and long-term international crude oil prices, on China's inflation cannot be ignored. We should, however, meanwhile notice that the CPI is most deeply affected by GDP and lagged CPI (inflation stickiness). This shows that inflation should be fundamentally curbed through controlling aggregate demand, especially rising investment demand with various policy tools (including interest rate hikes) to prevent excessive economic growth.

Third, we should improve the elasticity of the exchange rate mechanism and enhance the independence of monetary policy. Econometric analysis shows that appreciation can play a role in suppressing inflation, but with a time lag; international interest rates also impose certain impact on domestic prices; raising interest rates can suppress inflation, but with weaker effect than appreciation, because of the inelastic exchange rate system. Therefore, the key to dealing with external shocks is to gradually enhance the elasticity of the exchange rate mechanism and improve the independence of monetary policy, making monetary policy the true first line of defense against external shocks.

Fourth, we should adjust the distorted factor prices timely while taking fiscal and taxation measures, to alleviate medium and long-term inflationary pressures. In the past, China adopted a low-cost industrialization strategy that kept factor prices down, which boosted growth but also led to wide price distortions, maintaining the extensive development model.

In response to inflationary pressures, the government has resorted to temporary price intervention, further exacerbating the distortions. Distorted price systems are more vulnerable to external shocks because many shocks come directly for the problems (not conspiracies, but stratagem in the open). Therefore, we should adjust the factor price system timely to straighten out the relationship and take supporting fiscal measures, such as the introduction of taxes on resources together with environmental taxes.

In the short term, this will increase the cost of enterprises and the cost-push inflationary pressure, but in the medium and long term, the increase in the real cost faced by enterprises (the previous price distortion was a subsidy to enterprises) will just restrain excessive investment demand and avoid economic overheating, thus helping to truly alleviate inflationary pressure.

Appendix

Schedule 1. Original data, variable names, and sources

Variable name	Symbol	Data source
Inflation rate	CPI	IMF International Financial Statistics
Real GDP growth rate	GDPGTH	CEIC
Real effective exchange rate	REER	IMF International Financial Statistics
Crude oil price index	OIL	IMF International Financial Statistics
International food price index	FOOD	IMF International Financial Statistics
One-year deposit interest rate	R	IMF International Financial Statistics
U.S. real effective exchange rate	REER_USA	IMF International Financial Statistics
Money supply	M1	CEIC
Money supply	M2	CEIC
U.S. federal funds rate	FDR	IMF International Financial Statistics

Schedule 2. Unit root test of each variable (determining the lag order according to SIC criterion) (1994Q1–2007Q4)

Variable name	Variable symbol	ADF test	Discriminant parameter
Inflation rate (year-on-year)	CPI	−3.299**	With intercept term, maximum hysteresis = 10
GDP growth rate (year-on-year)	GDPGTH	−2.711*	With intercept term, maximum hysteresis = 10
Real crude oil price growth rate (year-on-year)	OILR_TH	−3.633***	With intercept term, maximum hysteresis = 10
International food price index (year-on-year)	FOODR_TH	−1.85**	No intercept term, maximum lag = 20
Real effective exchange rate growth rate (year-on-year)	REER_TH	−2.171**	With intercept term, maximum hysteresis = 10
Real crude oil price growth rate (month-on-month)	DLOILR	−4.374***	No intercept term, maximum lag = 10
Growth rate of international food price index (month-on-month)	DLFOODR	−4.756***	No intercept term, maximum lag = 10
Real effective exchange rate growth rate (month-on-month)	DLREER	−4.908***	No intercept term, maximum lag = 10
Growth rate of money supply (year-on-year)	M1_TH	−3.056**	With intercept term, maximum hysteresis = 10

Continued

Variable name	Variable symbol	ADF test	Discriminant parameter
Growth rate of money supply (year-on-year)	M2_TH	-2.10**	No intercept term, maximum lag = 10
Real interest rate	RR	-1.77*	No intercept term, maximum lag = 10
U.S. federal funds rate	FDR	-3.34*	With intercept and trend terms, Maximum hysteresis = 10

Note: *, * * and * * * represent rejection of the original hypothesis of unit root at 1%, 5% and 10% significance levels, respectively.

Schedule 3. Selection criteria of lag order of VAR model (1995Q4–2007Q4)

Lag order	LogL	LR	FPE	AIC	SC	HQ
0	880.58	NA	2.87 e-27	-35.57	-35.22	-35.44
1	1245.55	580.97	2.80 e-32	-47.17	-43.69*	-45.85
2	1344.06	120.63	1.91 e-32	-47.88	-41.28	-45.37
3	1478.51	115.24*	5.99 e-33*	-50.06*	-40.33	-46.37*
*Indicates the lag order selected according to this standard						
LR: Sequence-adjusted LR test statistic (5% significance level)						
FPE: Final Prediction Error						
AIC: Akaike Information Criterion						
SC: Schwartz Information Criterion						
HQ: Hannan-Quinn Information Criterion						

Real Estate Cycle and Financial Stability

China's real estate overheating has long been a focal issue for all walks of life in China. The central bank has issued a series of measures to regulate the industry and issued the *2004 China Real Estate Financial Report* even though these measures and research reports have also caused considerable controversy. The overheating of real estate is not new in China. The real estate boom in the early 1990s should remain fresh in our memory.

The real estate boom is just one phase in the real estate cycle. The study of the real estate cycle can be traced back to the 1930s, when Kuznets proposed the so-called "building cycles," and since then the literature on the real estate cycle has been sprung up. The real estate cycle is closely related to financial stability. During the American banking crisis in the 1980s, the real estate credit losses and the risks induced were mainly blamed for bank failures. Since the 1990s, real estate has played a critical role behind the bursting of Japan's foam economy and the erupting Asian financial crisis. In the twenty-first century, the international low interest rate and more liquidity drive up the real estate prices in the major developed countries, and the housing mortgage loan plays a pivotal role in the financial sector. If the real estate price is radically adjusted, the asset quality of the banking system in these countries will decline rapidly, and the economy and finance will be seriously impacted. In this case, the global real estate foam will be widely reported and speculated, and China cannot stay out. The problem of China's real estate industry should not be treated as a general industrial problem, but its impact on the overall macroeconomic stability, especially financial stability, should be viewed from a global perspective.

Starting from the real estate cycle in China, this chapter intends to analyze the various driving factors that form the real estate cycle and then use the quarterly data from 1992 to 2004 for econometric analysis. On this basis, it discusses the relationship between the new round of the real estate cycle and the current financial stability and puts forward corresponding policy recommendations.

5.1 A Rough Division of China's Real Estate Cycle

At present there is no recognized common standard for the concept of real estate cycle. Different literature offers their own definitions and measurement indicators, such as real estate investment rate, housing vacancy rate, real estate price, real estate investment rate of return, etc. This chapter only uses the growth rate of real estate investment as a measure to divide China's real estate cycle (see Figure 29).

According to the changes in real estate investment, we believe that since the reform and opening-up, China's real estate market has experienced three cycles:

The first cycle, 1978–1991. In this period, China's real estate industry developed from scratch. The urban economic system reform starting in 1985 gave birth to the real estate industry. The industry came to a climax in 1988 but has been impacted by the national macro-control, monetary tightening and expenditure reduction since 1989.

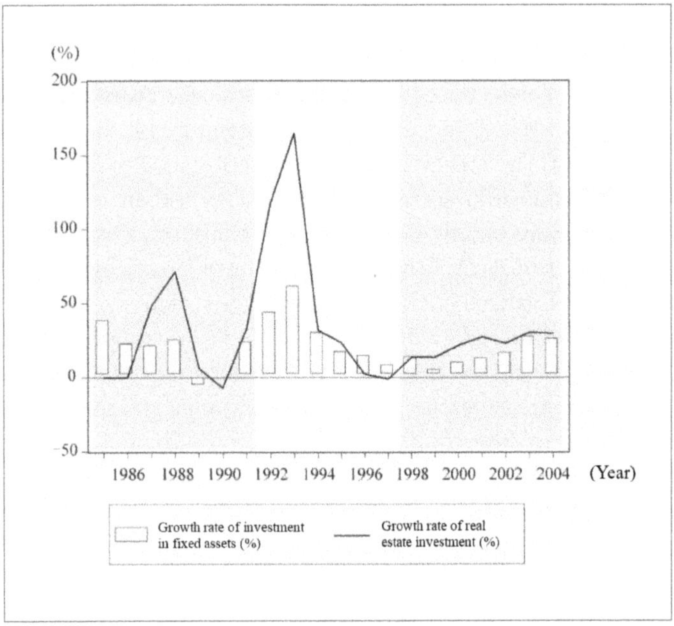

Figure 29. China's real estate cycle

Source: China Statistical Abstract 2005; Statistics of China's Fixed Assets Investment (1950–2000).

The second cycle, 1992–1997. The real estate market has experienced two stages: overheating and adjustment. In 1992, Deng Xiaoping delivered his South Tour speech, and the 14th CPC National Congress was held. The national economy developed rapidly, and the real estate industry grew at full steam especially in large and medium-sized coastal cities. Since 1992, the People's Bank of China has allocated a portion from the social credit plan for the real estate credit department of professional banks to issue entrusted loans. A "development zone" craze and enclosure craze spread across the whole country and reached the peak in 1993. Commercial banks flung themselves in enclosure and speculation through loans beyond the scale, illegal lending and self-run companies. In the second half of 1993, the overheated economy led to high inflation. The country rolled out a moderately tight policy and focused on the regulation of the real estate industry. The country strictly tightens the monetary policy and stipulated that real estate companies could not be listed for financing. Banks faced a large number of non-performing assets. In 1996, the real estate investment grew only by 2.1% and bottomed out in 1997 with a negative growth (−1.2%).

The third cycle (i.e., the new real estate cycle), went from 1998 to this day. Driven by the reform of the national housing system and commercial banks' opening of housing mortgage loans and other businesses, the growth rate of real estate investment began to rise in 1998.

Although this is not the only way to divide the cycle, we can reach a consensus that since 1998, the growth rate of real estate investment has exceeded that of fixed asset investment, implying the beginning of a new round of real estate cycle. If we compare these three cycles, the current cycle since 1998 appears to be much smoother, which is very similar to the characteristics of the entire economic growth cycle, namely just a relatively stable cycle, no big ups and downs in the past. However, even so, this round of real estate overheating still deserves close attention.

5.2 Driving Factors of the New Real Estate Cycle

For the new round of the real estate cycle, it is worth noting how the real estate industry has become overheated and will this overheating continue. But first, we should know: what are the driving factors of the new real estate cycle? Which of these factors are sustainable and which are not?

Different from ordinary assets, real estate has the dual characteristics of physical assets and financial assets, so the interpretation of the real estate cycle becomes more complex. Moreover, the driving factors of the real estate cycle will vary in different economies. For example, it is generally believed that in developed economies, the rapid rise in housing prices mainly comes from the investment demand of surplus funds. In recent years, the global stock market has continued to decline, especially after the myth of the high-tech stock market in the United States burst, a large number of funds flowed out of the stock market, eager to find suitable investment channels. Traditionally, the relatively stable real estate market soon became the paradise of these funds. This drive can be seen as a "portfolio effect." Compared with developed countries, the rise of housing prices in some developing countries in Asia is considered to be the result of a combination of policy incentives, demand growth and investment drivers.

The driving factors for China's new round of the real estate cycle, we believe, are growth, macro, and institutional factors.

1. Analysis of Growth Factors

The so-called growth factors are the impact of China's economic growth on the real estate market.

First, urbanization. Urbanization, as an engine of growth, is a very important growth factor. Since 1998, there has been a trend of accelerated urbanization in China. We can divide the urbanization process from 1978 into three stages based on simple calculation: from 1978 to 1987, the urbanization rate increased by 7.4%, with an average annual increase of 0.74 percentage points. From 1988 to 1997, the urbanization rate increased by 6.1%, with an average annual growth of 0.61 percentage points. From 1998 to 2004, the urbanization rate increased by 8.41%, with an average annual growth rate of 1.2 percentage points. This speed is almost twice the average annual growth rate of the last decade, which fully demonstrates the acceleration of urbanization in China since 1998. The rapid growth of the urban population has brought huge housing demand, thus promoting the development of the real estate industry.

Second, residents' income increased. With the economic growth and the increase in residents' income, the per capita GDP in 2003 exceeded USD 1000. The rise in personal disposable income and the decline of Engel's coefficient mean that housing expenditure is increasing and housing demand is rising. However, the increased per capita disposable income is obviously not enough to purchase houses. Only with the support of housing consumption credit can housing demand be fulfilled.

2. Analysis of Macro Factors

Macro factors are mainly reflected in the expansionary macro policies and a large amount of foreign capital inflows.

Since 1998, in order to cope with the impact of the Asian financial crisis and expand domestic demand, the government has adopted expansionary fiscal policy and monetary policy, which have played a very important promoting role. This expansionary policy also foreshadowed the overheating of real estate. First, expansionary fiscal policy is mainly reflected in the issuance of long-term construction bonds. According to the data, from 1998 to 2004, China issued totally 910 billion yuan of long-term construction bonds. The total investment generated by this part of bonds reached about 5 trillion yuan, driving up annual GDP growth of 1.5–2 percentage points. This ensures that the country can concentrate its efforts on building a large number of major infrastructure projects of overall significance and also drives real estate investment. Second, expansionary monetary policy, mainly interest rate policy and housing consumption credit policy. The downward trend of interest rates has supported macro growth and overheating. The promotion of housing consumption credit has further driven the development of real estate (see Figure 30 and Figure 31).

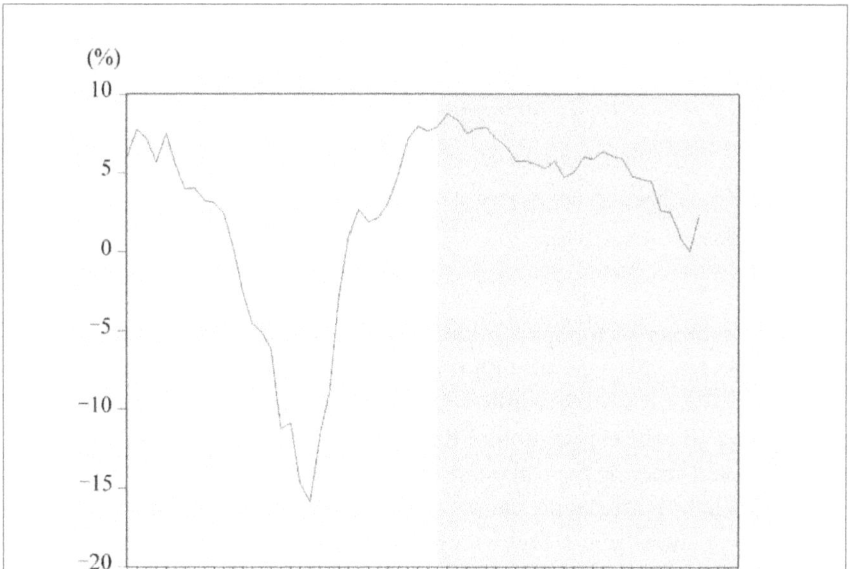

Figure 30. Change of real loan interest rate

Source: China Statistical Yearbook

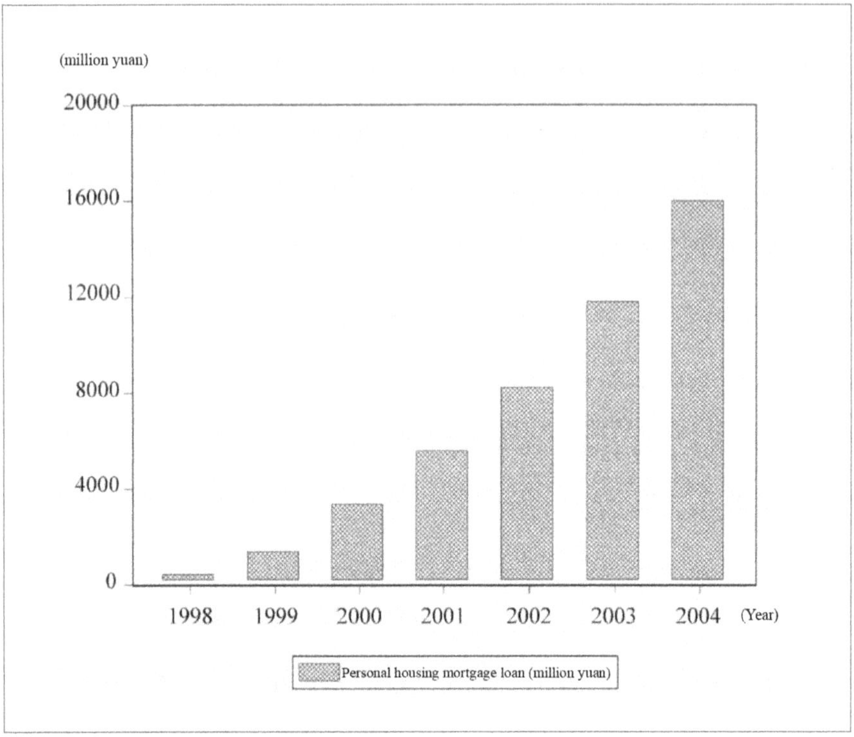

Figure 31. Personal housing mortgage loan (1998–2004)

Source: The People's Bank of China.

A large number of foreign capital inflows under the expectation of RMB appreciation have played a driving role in the current real estate cycle.

In recent years, the massive inflow of foreign capital is related to both China's high growth and the expectation of RMB appreciation (Zhang Xiaojing, 2005). Foreign capital entering the real estate industry is expected to obtain at least: the benefits brought by the appreciation of the RMB; and the income brought by the rise of real estate prices. Due to the lack of data, it is difficult to comprehensively evaluate the impact of foreign investment on China's real estate industry. However, what is certain is that the massive inflow of foreign capital has notably driven the overheating of China's economy and plays a role in promoting the real estate overheating in some regions, although it may not be the most important driving factor.

Overseas funds enter the real estate market in Shanghai, Beijing and other big cities through various channels. According to the survey of the Financial Market

Department of the People's Bank of China, the proportion of overseas funds in Shanghai in the total funds for house purchase rose from 8.3% in the first quarter of 2003 to 23.2% in the fourth quarter of 2004. According to the statistics of the Shanghai Branch of the People's Bank of China, from January to November 2004, a total of over 22.2 billion yuan of foreign funds flowed into the Shanghai real estate market, an increase of 13.5% over 2003, of which about 15 billion yuan was used for real estate development, accounting for 12.8% of the total real estate development in the whole year. About 7 billion yuan of foreign capital was used to purchase houses, mainly villas, apartments and other high-priced commercial houses. In the first two months of 2005, the area and amount of new commercial houses purchased by foreign funds in Shanghai with a unit price of more than 11000 yuan/square meter increased by 47.6% and 73% year on year, and the area and amount of second-hand houses purchased with a unit price of more than 11000 yuan/square meter increased by 2.8 times and 3.1 times year on year (Real Estate Financial Analysis Group of the People's Bank of China, 2005).

3. Analysis of Institutional Factors

China is in the process of development, and many systems are deficient or even distorted, in that: (1) the investment and financing channels are single, which limits the effective asset portfolio of residents; (2) the current institutional framework determines the distortion of local government behavior. Both these have had an impact on the current real estate cycle.

3.1. Investment and Financing Channels

Any rational economist, whether in developed countries or developing countries, will maximize the benefits through an effective asset portfolio. In China, banks

Table 17. Composition of residents' financial assets (%)

Type	1997	1998	1999	2000	2001	2002	2003	2004
Cash in hand	6.6	6.7	12.1	11.5	11.2	11	10.7	10.5
Savings deposit	76.9	75.5	75.2	69	71.6	73.3	73.7	73.3
Bond investment	9.7	10.6	4.9	6.3	5.8	5.7	5.6	6.1
Stock investment	5.4	5.5	6.2	9.5	7.7	6.5	6.4	6.5
insurance investment	1.4	1.6	0.8	1.6	1.7	1.8	1.8	2
Customer margin	—	—	0.9	1.9	2	1.7	1.8	1.6

Source: China Financial Yearbook; Relevant issues of *Quarterly Variable Tracking Analysis* edited by Fan Gang.

are dominant (bank deposits account for more than 70% of residents' financial assets, see Table 17). The entire financial market is underdeveloped, and residents lack diversified investment channels. Therefore, under falling interest rates, a low stock market, foreign exchange investment control and an underdeveloped bond market, they naturally choose to invest in real estate.

3.2. Problems of Local Governments

Local governments have played a critical role in this round of the real estate cycle. Reviewing the economic cycle in history, the local governments always played a role in the "ups" of the economy. The reason why local governments always have such an investment impulse lies in their assessment system and soft budget constraints.

Under the current system, namely fiscal responsibility system and fiscal system of delineating income and expenditure, local governments inevitably pursue fiscal maximization, which leads to the maximization of growth rate and investment. In addition, the local government performance is often assessed based on GDP, fiscal and employment growth indicators. Now it is plus GDP indicator which is difficult to put into practice though. As a result, local governments always have a strong investment impulse. The market-oriented reform of factors has facilitated this government-led investment impulse, and land revenue has become the "second finance" of local governments.

The loosen constraints of local government budget have encouraged local governments to expand regardless of costs and consequences. Now, the local government is not an economic entity that can be responsible for its own profits and losses, with no liability for the debt or fiscal revenue of the next government. The interests of the next generation and the next government are not considered in its decision-making process. No one represents the interests of the next government in the current decision-making process. These interests are not included in the current economic decision-making interest balance. This is why the current government approves all land usage for the next 20 years and stuff all construction projects for the coming 20 years on the current 5 years.

Local governments are obviously "too positive" in the current round of real estate cycle. Land acquisition at low prices and transfer at high prices have become a shortcut for the localities to create political achievements and increase financial revenue. A booming real estate industry can drive the overall growth of the local economy, including GDP, finance and employment. All these have provided incentives for local governments to develop the real estate industry. Some local governments have also expanded the demand for real estate through forced demolition under the guise of urbanization.

Based on the above three factors driving the current round of the real estate cycle, namely, growth, macro and institutional, we come to the following conclusions.

First, growth factors play a decisive role in the development of the real estate industry. For a long time in the future, China will still maintain steady and rapid growth, so growth factors will continue to play their role. For example, continuous urbanization, the increase in people's income and housing demand remain an irresistible long-term trend.

Second, with the promotion of marketization, the institutional factors will play a weakened role in driving the development of real estate. On the one hand, the investment channels will be gradually broadened, and the assets available will not be limited to real estate, especially the recovered current stock market offers new investment opportunities. In addition, the evolving bond market and the more attractive foreign exchange investment brought by the change in the exchange rate formation mechanism will enrich the investment portfolio and discourage the old "one-sided" investment in the real estate industry. On the other hand, the behavior of local governments is also gradually standardized, and the reform of the financial system has also more or less restrained the impulse of local governments to invest excessively in real estate. These changes in institutional factors will, in general, make the investment and demand for real estate more rational.

Third, many macro factors have changed at present, for example, the original expansionary policy is now replaced by a neutral one. With the steady progress of the reform of the RMB exchange rate formation mechanism, the risk of two-way fluctuations in the RMB exchange rate has also played a certain role in restricting the inflow of foreign capital into the real estate industry.

In general, among the factors driving the current round of the real estate cycle, growth factors will still play a role for a long time in the future. They are well sustainable, while the sustainability of institutional factors is poor[1], and many macro factors are no longer sustainable. Given the decisive role of growth factors in the future development of the real estate industry, after weighing, we believe that both the development of the real estate industry and the overall level of real estate prices will still stay in a stable and rising trend in the long term.

---

1 Although the promotion of marketization will standardize the behaviors of general consumers, real estate developers and local governments, and the supply and demand of real estate will return to rationality, there is still a long way to go before the real realization of marketization of the real estate industry (including the regulation of the real estate industry).

5.3 Quantitative Analysis

In order to make the above analysis of the driving factors of the real estate cycle more convincing, we use relevant data for econometric analysis.

To establish an econometric equation, in general, we should select indicators to measure real estate development, including real estate price, real estate sales area, or real estate investment, as dependent variables, and growth factors including urbanization level, GDP, or urban per capita disposable income, etc., macro factors including interest rate, housing mortgage loans, real estate development loan, etc. and institutional factors including currency expectation factor, local government behavior distortion factor, etc., as explanatory variables.

1. Data Description

Through the channels of the China Economic Network, CEIC, People's Bank of China and various statistical yearbooks, we have obtained the time series data from the first quarter of 1992 to the fourth quarter of 2004 (see Table 18). For a more convenient analysis, we process some raw data, like the quarterly growth rates of g_ houseinvest and g_ sales are calculated based on the level data to eliminate seasonal factors, and realrate is the difference of loan interest rate minus CPI.

Considering that China's foreign exchange integration on January 1, 1994, a major structural change, imposed great impact on the whole macroeconomy

Table 18. Basic information of data

Variable	Meaning	Stability
g_housinvest	quarterly year-on-year growth rate of real estate development investment	I(1)
g_sales	quarterly year-on-year growth rate of sales area of commercial housing	I(1)
housloan	housing mortgage loan amount	I(2)
devploan	loan amount of real estate development	I(2)
longloan	medium and long-term loans from financial institutions	I(2)
totaloan	loan amount of financial institutions	I(1)
totalratio	(housing mortgage loan + real estate development loan)/loan amount of financial institutions	I(1)
realrate	real loan interest rate	I(1)
reer	real effective exchange rate	I(1)
shstock	Shanghai Composite Index	I(1)

Note: I (n) means that the sequence is stationary after n times of difference.

(including the real estate industry), we add a dummy variable Dummy, taking January 1, 1994, as 1, and other time as 0.

Unfortunately, other expected indicators, like real estate prices, urbanization level, GDP growth rate, per capita disposable income and indicators to measure the distortion of local government behavior, have no sufficiently long quarterly time series. This more or less limits our efforts to expand the data sample.

2. Quantitative Results and Economic Implications

We perform a unit root test for the above variables (see Table 18). We divide the variables in Table 18 into stationary variables and then use PcGets for econometric analysis in which as many variables and hysteresis as possible should be sampled. Through repetitive attempts, we found that with the real estate development investment as the dependent variable, the main statistics (t value, DW value, R2, etc.) are relatively satisfactory, with clear economic implication. See Table 19 for econometric results.

Table 19 lists the econometric results of dependent variables of nominal real estate investment growth rate and real estate investment growth rate. We find

Table 19. PcGets econometric analysis results (%)

	Dependent variable	
	Nominal real estate investment growth rate(Δg_housinvest)	**Real real estate investment growth rate[Δ(g_housinvest—cpi)]**
Constant	—	-0.09674(-4.279)
reer	-0.01295(-1.717)	-0.02284(-3.026)
Δreer_2	-0.02694(-3.502)	-0.02927(-3.810)
Δrealrate_1	0.03437(3.401)	0.04581(4.539)
Δtotalratio	0.06976(2.063)	0.14236(3.607)
Δtotalratio_1	—	0.07020(1.784)
dummy	-0.51780(-4.101)	-0.62347(-4.877)
R^2		
Adjusted R^2	0.52301	0.68163
DW value	0.48153	0.63822
Sample period	1.98	2.11
Constant	1992Q2-2004Q4	1992Q2-2004Q4

Note: t statistics are in brackets.

that the explanatory power of the latter as the dependent variable is nearly 16 percentage points higher than that of the former, that is, the adjusted R2 increases from 48.2% to 64.2%. Therefore, we will take the real estate investment as the dependent variable to analyze the econometric results.

First, if the real effective exchange rate index changes by 1 unit, the real estate development investment growth rate will change in an opposite direction by 5.2 percentage points (i.e., sum of Δ Reer and Δ reer_ 2). Considering the response of real estate investment changes to currency expectations, especially the impact of foreign investment under open conditions, we include the real effective exchange rate variable in the econometric equation. Since the integration from 1994 until 1998, the real effective exchange rate has shown an upward trend, indicating an expectation of depreciation of the RMB in this period. The Asian financial crisis saw grim expectation of RMB depreciation. At the expected stage of depreciation, a large amount of funds flowed out and real estate investment became less attractive. Since China is in the stage of "soft landing" of macroeconomics in this period, and the growth of real estate investment has been greatly restrained by government regulatory factors, the negative impact of the expected depreciation of RMB on real estate investment should not be overemphasized. However, after 1998, the real effective exchange rate fell, and there was an expectation of appreciation of the RMB. Both domestic and foreign funds believed that the appreciation expectation would raise the future real estate price, so a large amount of funds flooded into the real estate industry, driving up real estate investment in a short time. Many analysts pointed out that the entry of foreign capital into real estate is an important reason for the overheating of real estate, which nevertheless supported by no convincing quantitative test. We believe that the analysis of the impact of real effective exchange rate changes on real estate investment here can serve as assertive evidence of the impact of foreign investment on real estate.

Second, when the real loan interest rate of the previous period changes by 1 percentage point, the current real estate investment growth rate will change by 4.58 percentage points in the same direction. The coefficient sign of the real loan interest rate should be contrary to our expectation. According to the general economic theory, a rising real loan interest rate will lead to a decrease in investment. Therefore, the two should change in the opposite direction. How does the change toward same direction happen? On the one hand, for a long time, China's interest rate has not been market-oriented, and as the price of capital, interest rate cannot fully reflect the cost of capital. On the other hand, many of China's investments are government-driven, and real estate investment seldom considers interest rate factors. Even real estate investment rises following higher interest rates. The following analysis shows that the loan to the real estate industry instead of interest rate has become an important factor affecting real estate investment.

Third, when the ratio of real estate loans to total credit changes by 1 unit, the growth rate of real estate investment will change by 21.3 percentage points in the same direction. Real estate investment is mainly affected by real estate loans, showing that bank loans are the main source of real estate investment, and the financial risks arise from high growth of real estate investment. The ratio of real estate loans to the loans of all financial institutions is also known as the risk exposure of real estate loans. According to the econometric equation in this chapter, the greater the risk exposure, the higher the real estate investment. The close relationship between the two provides a strong basis for the later analysis of real estate risks.

Fourth, the dummy variable shows that exchange rate integration imposes a great negative impact on real estate investment, resulting in a 62.3 percentage point decline in real estate investment in the current period.

The above econometric analysis is different from other real estate econometric analyses in that it takes the real effective exchange rate as a variable and emphasizes the impact of the expected factors of currency changes and foreign capital factors on real estate investment, which is consistent with economic reality, especially in the past two years. In addition, we introduce the proportion of real estate loans, emphasize their importance in real estate investment, and measure it as an important indicator of real estate risk exposure, which is not practiced in some studies.

5.4 Real Estate Cycle and Financial Stability

The development of real estate cannot do without financial support, and the cyclical changes of real estate will also impose a great impact on financial stability. When the market is booming, bank credit funds are poured into real estate, and the funds raised by listed companies are also injected into real estate development in large quantities. In the downturn of the market, bank funds were stuck, forming non-performing assets, and the real estate listed companies delivered poorer performance. The real estate cycle impacts financial stability by the following channels: (1) financial development must rely on the development of the real economy. An expanding real estate industry drives the expansion of the real estate financial business and promotes financial innovation. For example, since 1998, the rising China's real estate credit has served as a new "growth point" of bank credit expansion. The low non-performing rate of real estate loans is also an important factor in the decline of bad debt rates. (2) The development of the real estate market affects financial stability. The bursting of China's real estate foam in 1993 resulted in substantial bad debts. During the Asian financial crisis, all countries saw an excessively rising then falling real estate price. Following the plummet in real estate prices, banks engaged in real estate finance had bad debts, and the quality of assets in the banking system declined, even fueling a banking crisis. The bank-led economy, the form of real estate finance is single, and commercial banks shoulder almost all the burden of real estate finance. A considerable portion of the funds required by the whole real estate industry, such as real estate development loans, working capital loans, construction enterprise loans and housing mortgage loans, is provided by the banks. The risk of the real estate market can be easily converted into bank credit risk, dumping the risks in the real estate cycle fluctuations in the banking system.

For the current round of real estate overheating, ordinary people are worried when they can afford to buy a house given the excessive rise of housing prices, while the government and the central bank are concerned more about what impact a bursting real estate form will have on financial stability, and how the current real estate cycle will jeopardize financial stability. We believe that the risks of the real estate industry can be analyzed from the perspective of consumers, producers (developers) and the government, while the main risks are reflected in the risk exposure of real estate credit, the problem of government guarantee and the mismatch of deposit and loan terms.

1. Housing Mortgage Loan (From the Perspective of Consumers)

Since 1998, personal housing mortgage loans have served not only as an important force to promote the development of the real estate industry, but also a critical means for the banking industry to expand the scale of credit and reduce the non-performing loan rate. All Chinese banks and regulators consider mortgage loan as an excellent way of lending, with high asset quality. As of the first quarter of 2005, the bad debt ratio of personal housing mortgage loans in China stood merely at 1.5%. Compared with the conventional state-owned economic loans and other forms of loans guaranteed by the government, personal housing mortgage loans indeed have much lower risk. However, the potential risks of housing mortgage loans cannot be ignored.

Some believe that since the introduction of mortgage loans facilitates the debt of residents, China has produced more and more "Fu Weng (debtors)," that is, a large number of liabilities may lead to negative total assets of residents. This statement seems reasonable but fail to observe that the proposition and concern of "Fu Weng" have mainly developed based on the concept of stock, namely the ratio of residents' total existing assets to their total liabilities. In fact, bank risk mainly stems from the concept of flow, that is, whether the residents can pay the corresponding debt with their cash flow at certain time point, for example, to what extent can the "monthly installment" be repaid by the monthly disposable income. From the perspective of traffic, the proposition and concerns of "Fu Weng" are exaggerated.

But this is not to say that the risks of personal housing mortgage loans can be ignored. First of all, people buy houses not only for accommodation, but also for investment (speculation). According to the survey of the Ministry of Construction in 2004, the proportion of commercial residential purchase for investment in Beijing stood at about 17%, and the proportion in major cities of the Yangtze River Delta reached about 20%. Investment demand is often more susceptible to the impact of future income expectations and other economic expectations such as the trend of interest rates and is quite risky. Secondly, some house buyers elicit loans from different banks by various means to fund their investment.[2] This kind of deceptive behavior also increases the risk of bank credit. Resources cannot be shared among banks, and information investigation is not effective, providing opportunities for such people.

2. Developer Loans from the Perspective of Producers

Real estate finance is blamed for developers working on land development and real estate development being highly dependent on bank loans. Statistics show that the bank funds obtained by Chinese real estate developers through various channels account for more than 70% of their assets. Let's come to the following detailed analysis of the potential risks of real estate developers' loans.

1. Loan risk of land development. The land consolidation and reserve center mainly gets the funds needed through the following channels: a certain amount of start-up funds allocated by the municipal finance; advance payment of land use right transfer fee; bank loans as main source; operating

---

2 For example, when applying for loans to buy houses, buyers generally choose developers' phased guarantees and mortgages. Some loopholes in the program are easily exploited by some investors. Say someone buys a house with a loan of 1 million yuan from Bank A, according to the 20% down payment rule, the buyer pays 200000 yuan to Bank A. In principle, the property right is mortgaged to the bank during the repayment period after the buyer completes the property right certificate. However, the certification authority issues the property right certificate to individuals rather than directly sends it to the bank. Therefore, some buyers mortgage the property right certificate to Bank B, to get about 70% of the loan for a house from Bank B (assuming 700000 yuan), and the buyers can use the 700000 yuan as the down payment for other three houses, and so on.

income from reserved land. The land reserve center is often run with high debt. China's land reserve loan reached 82.837 billion yuan at the end of 2004, with a larger comprehensive credit line. Most of these quotas are realized in the name of government guarantees. In fact, such government guarantees are generally ineffective because the guarantees of finance or other departments do not comply with the Guarantee Law. Meanwhile, the land use right operated by the land reserve center can be used as collateral for the bank loans, but according to the current laws and regulations, the pledged land does not belong to the land consolidation and reserve center.

2. The loan risk of real estate development enterprises. Take Beijing as an example. From 2000 to 2002, the average asset-liability ratio of real estate development enterprises in Beijing reached 81.2%. The debt management of real estate development enterprises got more serious. The debt ratio of the 20 largest real estate development loans in China exceeded the average level in Beijing. The high-liability operation of real estate development enterprises nurtures great potential risks (Real Estate Financial Analysis Group of the People's Bank of China, 2005).

3. Exposures of Real Estate Credit Risks

The possible risks of real estate credit can be measured by the proportion of real estate loans, that is, personal housing mortgage loans plus real estate development loans, to the loans of the entire financial institutions, namely the real estate credit risk exposure. The previous econometric analysis shows that it is the expansion of real estate credit risk exposure that drives the growth of real estate investment. In turn, the rapid growth of real estate investment will inevitably lead to the rapid expansion of credit risk exposure. According to our calculation, the real estate credit risk exposure was only 2.9% in 1998 but reached 10% in 2002 and 13.5% in 2004 (see Figure 32). Although China's current real estate credit risk exposure is not so worrying compared with the 30% - 55% credit risk exposure of some countries before the Asian crisis. Given the bulky cumulative bad debts in China's banking system, a financial system far less robust than that of developed market economy countries, especially the much higher real estate credit risk exposure ratio of some banks, we need to pay close attention to this risk exposure ratio.[3]

[3] In 1996, the proportion of real estate credit in bank loans was: Hong Kong (40–55%), Malaysia (30–40%), Singapore (30–40%), Taiwan (35–45%), and Thailand (30–40%). Quoted from Koh et al. (2004).

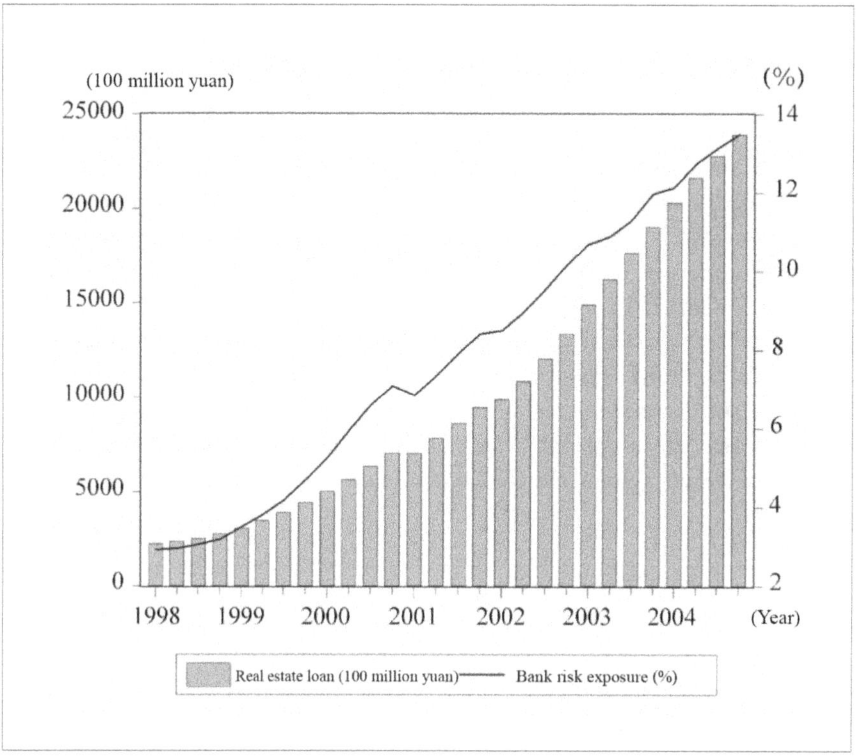

Figure 32. Real estate credit risk exposure

Source: The People's Bank of China.

4. Potential Risks of Government Guarantee

Since 1998, the rapid growth of medium and long-term loans has been quite prominent (see Figure 33), thanks to some measures taken by the government to expand domestic demand, such as reinforcing infrastructure construction and promoting personal consumption loans. Among them, major project loans in infrastructure construction are closely related to government guarantees or government ties. It is estimated that more than 80% of the medium and long-term loans of financial institutions are related to government guarantees. Some of these guarantees are tangible, like letters of guarantee issued by local governments and people's congresses. Some are intangible, like the oral assurance of "it's alright" by the Secretary-General of the government.

It is difficult to estimate how much of the total real estate loans are related to government guarantees. At the very least, the loans from the land consolidation and reserve center mentioned above and a large number of infrastructure construction loans related to real estate development are guaranteed by the government. So, who will be responsible for the bad debts of the bank arising from the projects guaranteed by the government? Obviously, these liabilities will eventually become comprehensive national liabilities, aggravating the financial risk of the entire economic system.

In China, many risks are ridden with government-guaranteed risks, like the government guarantee in land development loans and the government implicit guarantee under the fixed exchange rate system, which was lifted in July 2005). The government credit or guarantees make this risk more implicit than explicit. Moreover, "over trusting" the government or relying on the government guarantee leads, the banks seldom consider such risks. Moreover, even if such risks break out, the banks won't feel headache, as the saying goes "although the meat is rotten, it is still in the pot." Under this mindset and especially the chronic disorder of the old system, the risks related to government-guaranteed loans are

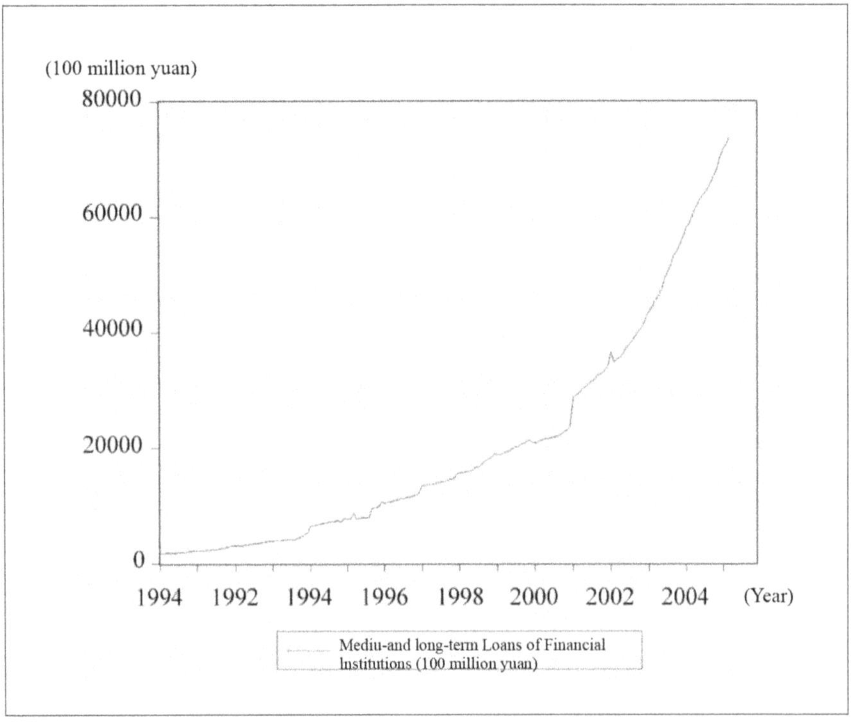

Figure 33. Medium- and long-term loans from financial institutions

Source: The People's Bank of China.

not taken seriously. Banks have issued more government-guaranteed credit but ignored the possible risks. The risk of government guarantee is an institutional problem and an important factor affecting future financial stability.

5. Mismatch of Deposit and Loan Terms

The term mismatch of deposits and loans of commercial banks refers to the term mismatch problem when commercial banks rely on short-term deposits to finance long-term loans. As shown in Figure 34, since 2001, the medium- and long-term loans have been growing more rapidly, and their proportion in the total loans of financial institutions has also been rising, to 40% by 2004. The rapid rise in the proportion of medium- and long-term loans is prone to the so-called term mismatch and the resulting risks. The financial crisis caused by the mismatch of deposit and loan terms is a lesson from the past. For example, in South Korea in 1997, its banking system borrowed mainly short-term debt including foreign

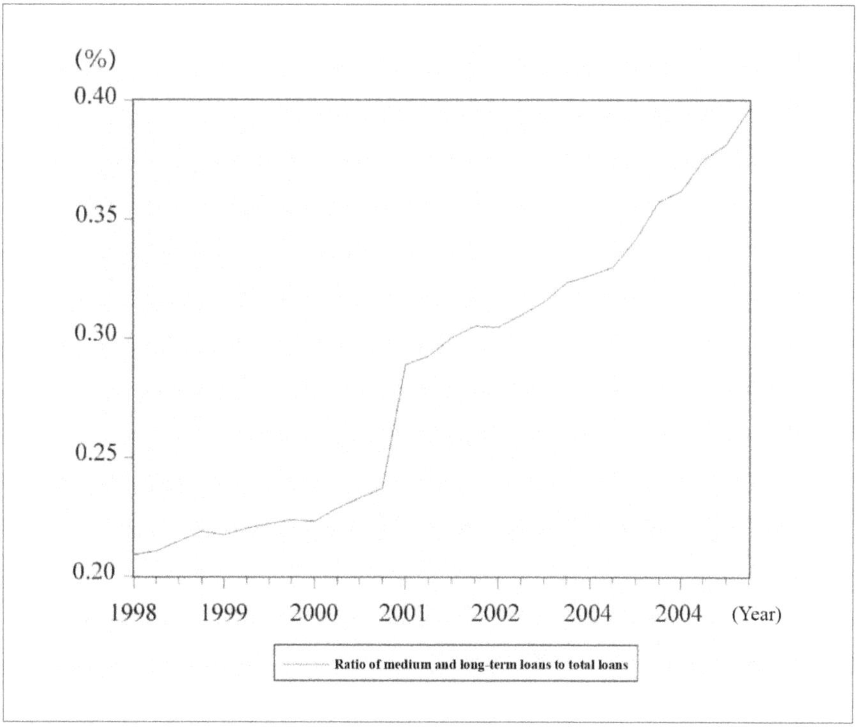

Figure 34. Changes in medium- and long-term loans

Source: The People's Bank of China.

debt) and supported mostly long-term investment. Therefore, when the Asian financial crisis broke out, the foreign funds flowing into South Korea dropped sharply, eventually throwing South Korea's finance into the liquidity trap, and the currency depreciated significantly.

Then, how can the medium- and long-term loans rise rapidly? On the one hand, more than 80% of medium- and long-term loans are related to government guarantees. On the other hand, the growth of real estate loans is obviously an important explanatory factor. According to Figure 35, real estate loans accounted for about 36% of the total medium- and long-term loans in 2004. This shows that the term mismatch of deposits and loans is more or less caused by the real estate cycle, and this risk deserves close attention.

Based on the above analysis, the housing mortgage loan risk, real estate development loan risk, government guarantee risk, and term mismatch risk, in the

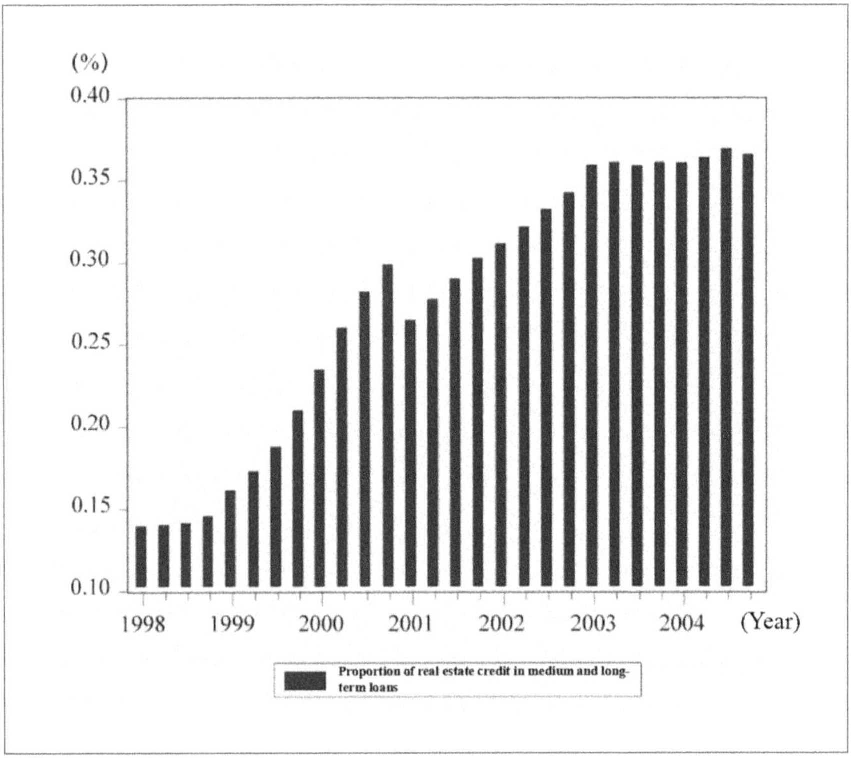

Figure 35. Proportion of real estate credit in medium and long-term loans

Source: The People's Bank of China.

final analysis, are all first reflected and most concentrated in bank risk; while driving up the national comprehensive liabilities, government guarantee risk can ultimately be a financial risk. This highlights that the new round of the real estate cycle is closely related to China's current sound operation of banks and financial stability.

5.5 Conclusion and Policy Recommendation

This chapter examines China's real estate cycle, especially the driving factors of the new round of the real estate cycle. The research shows that the comprehensive effect of growth, macro and institutional factors will, in the long run, remain in a stable and rising trend in both the development of real estate industry and the overall level of real estate prices.

The impact of the new round of the real estate cycle on financial stability is mainly reflected in the risk exposure of real estate credit, the problem of the government guarantee and the problem of term mismatch. All these potential risks will, in the final analysis, be first reflected and most concentrated in bank risks. In order to effectively resolve the risks of the real estate industry and maintain financial stability, we propose the following policy recommendations.

1. Working Hard to Solve the Problems of the Banking Industry

On the one hand, banks should be more prudent in lending, and thus actively improve their corporate governance structure, financial supervision and financial ecology. On the other hand, the rise of real estate credit as a medium - and a long-term loan can easily give rise to the term mismatch problem. Therefore, it is necessary to promote the development of medium- and long-term direct financing. Meanwhile, to curb the excessively high proportion of medium- and long-term loans of banks, measures such as asset securitization, which is currently being trialed with initiatives like the mortgage asset securitization of China Construction Bank and the credit asset securitization of China Development Bank, should be employed to facilitate the flow of this portion of assets.

2. Regulating the Behaviors of Local Governments

The investment impulse of local governments shall be corrected, in a stepped manner, as an important driving force of the real estate boom, which requires modification of the original system model, regulation of the soft budget constraints of local governments and reversion of the government officials' endeavor to only focus on growth. Only by adopting such measures can the distorted behavior of the government be corrected, and real estate investment be made more rational.

This approach addresses the old impulse toward real estate investment, which was also considered "rational" but within the context of a soft budget constraint, thereby reducing the cyclical fluctuations and financial risks associated with government expansion impulses.

3. Monitoring the Entry of Foreign Capital into the Real Estate Industry

Our econometric analysis shows that the real effective exchange rate plays an important role in explaining the growth of real estate investment. Therefore, stabilizing the exchange rate expectation is obviously an important measure to effectively curb the large inflow of foreign capital into the real estate industry. The current exchange rate formation mechanism in China has changed, especially since the exchange rate is no longer subject to one-way changes like appreciation but now carries the risk of two-way fluctuations. Therefore, the incentive of foreign capital to enter the real estate industry through the appreciation of the RMB to gain its benefits will be weakened. However, as appreciation is still expected, the foreign capital should still be refrained from entering the real estate industry for speculation through capital control measures. From the perspective of international experience, in order to prevent the loss of national wealth and curb the real estate speculation, 137 of the 187 member-countries of the International Monetary Fund regulate foreign investment in real estate. As the purchase of domestic commercial housing by overseas institutions and individuals is registered under the capital account, we can regulate the transaction and exchange of foreign capital entering real estate according to the principle of capital account management and strengthen the investigation and punishment of illegal capital outflow (inflow) under real estate to curb speculation.

Empirical Analysis of Cross-Border Capital Flows: A Case Study of the "Hong Kong Path"

6.1 Introduction

With ongoing economic globalization, cross-border capital flows are becoming more frequent and larger in scale. So, what factors affect cross-border capital flows? According to neoclassical theory, capital should flow to the places where yields are highest. In the era of economic globalization, capital will be effectively allocated on a global scale. Since the marginal returns of capital diminish, capital should flow to places where capital is scarce, indicating that cross-border capital flows should head for poor countries rather than rich countries.

However, this is not the case at all. According to the data from the World Bank, in 2001, the global FDI stock reached $6.15 trillion, including $4 trillion for the developed countries. In 2004, the global FDI inflow stood at $648 billion, of which $233 billion went to developing countries, and its share increased to 36%, the highest since 1997. The United States has maintained its position as the largest recipient of FDI. In addition, the International Monetary Fund's survey on Portfolio investment also shows that in 2001, the global stock of securities investment reached $12.55 trillion, of which the stock of securities investment absorbed by developed countries accounted for nearly 95% of the world, while developing countries only accounted for 5%. Similarly, capital flows between Hong Kong and the mainland have seen the Hong Kong banks changing from the net creditor to the mainland in 1999 to the net debtors to the mainland, namely the mainland has become the net supplier of capital for Hong Kong banks. Since 2000, the Hong Kong banks has owed significantly more debts to the mainland. In July 2004, their net debts increased to HK $112.2 billion, five times that of 1999 (Hong Kong Monetary Authority, 2005).

Why is the trend of cross-border capital flows inconsistent with neoclassical theory? Lucas (1990) suggested that human capital is crucial. Even if capital flows to underdeveloped areas with insufficient human capital, no higher yields can be earned. Additionally, some scholars explain this phenomenon from various angles, including political factors like political instability and the presence of military governments in some African countries as significant constraints, institutional factors such as the hostility or risk of confiscation to foreign capital, the investment environment encompassing policy transparency, preferential treatment or corruption, and macro factors like GDP growth rate and interest rate. These factors are very explanatory for direct investment or greenfield investment. However, for indirect investments, such as portfolio investments, including some speculative capital, namely short-term profit-seeking capital, the influence factors will be different. Therefore, we should pay more attention to exchange differences, interest rate differences, and to the assessment of a country's investment environment from the perspective of risk, because this short-term cross-border capital is more sensitive to risk.

In essence, what affects cross-border capital flows is the trade-off between risks and profits, and the ultimate goal of capital flows is to make profits. In terms of its influencing factors, besides general factors such as politics, systems, and macro factors, short-term capital will also be strongly affected by such factors as expectations, rumors in the market, emergencies and so on. Taking the cross-border capital flows between the mainland and Hong Kong as an example, this chapter analyzes the channels and scale of cross-border capital flows and applies the quarterly data from 1993 to 2004 for econometric analysis, to identify the influencing factors of cross-border capital flows and accordingly puts forward corresponding policy suggestions.

6.2 Channels and Scale of Cross-Border Capital Flows between Hong Kong and the Mainland

The capital flows between Hong Kong and the mainland are mainly through trade and finance. An "under-table channel", namely the informal financial channel, also serves this purpose.

1. Trade Channel

The trade channel, through which capital flows in both directions, includes products and services exchanges, namely bilateral trade, as well as personnel exchanges, that is, tourism. In terms of bilateral trade, the total import and export volume of the two places has increased from HK $250 billion in 1993 to over HK $875 billion in 2004, and the mainland has become the largest export destination and import source of Hong Kong. 45% of Hong Kong's exports are to the mainland and 44% of its imports come from the mainland. In recent years, its offshore trade with the mainland has been expanding. In 2004, Hong Kong's entrepot and offshore trade accounted for 38% of GDP. In terms of personnel exchanges, namely tourism, after the mainland authorities lifted the restrictions on mainland residents' groups visiting to Hong Kong in 2002, the number of mainland tourists to Hong Kong has surged. In 2004, nearly 15 million mainland citizens traveled to Hong Kong, spending HK $50 billion, accounting for 60% of Hong Kong's tourism revenue in the same period. Up to 52.556 million Hong Kongers traveled to the mainland in the same year, spending HK $53.7 billion.

2. Financial Channel

The financial channel includes investment between the mainland and Hong Kong, listing of mainland enterprises in Hong Kong to raise funds, and credit exchanges between banks in the two places.

Firstly, direct investment. Direct investment between the two places increased from HK $33.7 billion in 1993 to HK $49.6 billion in 2004. In 2004, more than 1/3 of Hong Kong's foreign investment came from the mainland, and more than 50% of Hong Kong's foreign investment went to the mainland. The mainland is not only the largest source of investment in Hong Kong, but also the largest investment destination and the largest source of investment income in Hong Kong.

Secondly, the credit scale in the mainland and Hong Kong. This scale can be presented by the relation of creditors' rights and debts between Hong Kong banks and mainland banks. Foreign debt of banks the obligations they undertake for overseas non-resident entities, including deposits and loans from oversea clients, and stocks, securities and capital instruments held by non-residents which are issued by foreign banks. Foreign assets refer to creditor's rights of foreign entities, including foreign currency, loans and other credits to foreign entities, stocks, debt securities and capital, foreign debt issued by foreign entities, and creditor's rights from current accounts and capital and financial account activities of the entire economic system. According to this standard, statistics calculated and sorted by Hong Kong Monetary Authority show that the total amount of bank creditor's rights and debts between Hong Kong and the mainland rose from HK $293.7 billion in 1993 to HK $496 billion in 2004, reaching HK $538.8 billion in the first nine months of 2005.

Thirdly, financing in the stock market. The amount of money raised by mainland enterprises in the Hong Kong stock market has risen from HK $15.1 billion in 1993 to HK $25.4 billion in 2004, reaching HK $28.7 billion in the first nine months of 2005.

3. "Under-Table" Channel (Informal Channel)

The "under-table" channel of capital flow between Hong Kong and the mainland, namely the informal channel, refers to the capital deposit and exchange system formed in Hong Kong and Macao changers and private banks, which have greatly enhanced the scale of two-way capital flow between the two places.

3.1. The Way Informal Capital Flows Between the Two Places

According to the statistics made by Hong Kong Monetary Authority, there were about 500 changers in Hong Kong at the end of 2004, of which 167 changers operated the RMB exchange business and provided integrated services, including remittance, exchange, etc. These changers can remit a large amount of RMB such as 10 million yuan from the mainland to Hong Kong within one day and change it into dollars on the same day and remit it to the United States.

The procedure for remitting money to Hong Kong involves the following steps: firstly, a remitter deposits money at a mainland bank designated by a changer, after consulting the changer in Hong Kong by telephone to determine the mainland bank account for deposit; secondly, the remitter faxes the deposit receipt, which could be from banks like the Industrial and Commercial Bank of China (ICBC), to the changer in Hong Kong; thirdly, the changer converts RMB into any foreign currency, such as U.S. dollars or Hong Kong dollars, based on the day's exchange rate, allowing the payee to receive an equivalent amount of the chosen foreign currency along with relevant certificates that include the name and other evidence provided by the remitter, all within half an hour; finally, leveraging Hong Kong's developed financial system, the changer can remit money globally. The procedure for clients in Hong Kong to remit dollars to the mainland and receive RMB in the mainland is: firstly, the remitter hands over U.S. dollars to a changer, collects a bank slip issued by the changer, and faxes it to the mainland payee; secondly, the changer informs the mainland trader to deposit the equivalent RMB into the account of a mainland bank; thirdly, the mainland bank informs the payee to withdraw the money; finally, the payee withdraws money with a relevant slip.

In the process of the above exchange operations, the changer bears the exchange risk, but the remitter does not bear any risk because there is a deposit certificate issued by ICBC; The payee also does not bear the risk but only collects the money when informed.

3.2. Estimation of the Scale of Informal Capital Flow in "Two Places"

From the perspective of international transaction experience, it is usually difficult to estimate the actual scale of capital circulating through informal remittance channels, let alone accurately estimate the debt asset and transaction volume of both parties. However, the following factors can help us judge the scale of capital exchange between the two places.

The first is the "common knowledge" of China in racial ties, cultural background, demographic characteristics, or remittance systems. In this aspect, the mainland maintains a high correlation with Hong Kong. The close historical and cultural ties, including language, population, historical awareness can greatly facilitate the remittances between the two places. Secondly, the main source of private exchange is the number of residents working overseas; the exchange system of the two places undertakes such a function as mainland people working in Hong Kong remit money to relatives with limited amount. Thirdly, the ability and cost of banks and other formal financial intermediaries to provide remittances service efficiently. Compared with Hong Kong, financial intermediaries in the mainland offer poor service and experience strict regulation. Both the two places demand a more efficient remittance and exchange service system. For example, the formal banking system can basically meet the requirements of Hong Kong enterprises to remit large amount of money to mainland enterprises to pay workers' wages and buy raw materials. Fourthly, the existence of a dual foreign exchange market. The more the official exchange rate deviates from the real exchange rate, the stronger the motivation of market participants to transfer funds through the informal system, and the higher the risk of the black market. The mainland's capital account management system, fixed exchange rate system and the expectation of RMB appreciation or devaluation exist drive up or keep down the black-market risk and further determine the inevitability of capital circulation through the informal remittance system. Whether the RMB is under the pressure of devaluation or appreciation, this kind of black capital market will inevitably operate. Therefore, the scale of capital flow in the two places is also large.

The above four factors decide the scale of capital circulation through informal remittance systems in the two places. We learned from the field investigation that a changer can process exchange transactions of millions of dollars in one day. If the changer can exchange USD 3 million every day, around 150 changers can transact RMB exchange and can swap up to USD 15 billion (about HK$ 120 billion) in one year.

At present, there are no statistics at home and abroad on the scale of cross-border capital flows between Hong Kong and the mainland. This chapter roughly estimates such scale according to the composition of the Balance of Payments (BOP), that is, the scale of capital flows between the two places = the volume of bilateral trade + bilateral tourism expenditure + bilateral FDI + the funds raised by mainland companies listed in Hong Kong + the volume of Hong Kong banks' creditor's rights and debts.

According to the above method, the scale of cross-border capital flows between Hong Kong and the mainland (Figure 36) increased from HK $798.5 billion in 1994 to HK $1.55 trillion in 2004, accounting for more than 10% of the GDP of the mainland in 2004. In the narrow sense, cross-border capital flows generally do not include capital flows caused by bilateral trade. Even removing the trade factor, total capital flows between Hong Kong and the mainland rose from HK $474.9 billion in 1994 to HK $674.7 billion in 2004 (Figure 37). Cross-border capital flows between the two places generally show an upward trend, but there are also fluctuations. In particular, the capital flows rose before and declined after the Asian financial crisis, and reached a high point in 2000, which has a lot to do with mainland companies listing in Hong Kong to raise funds.

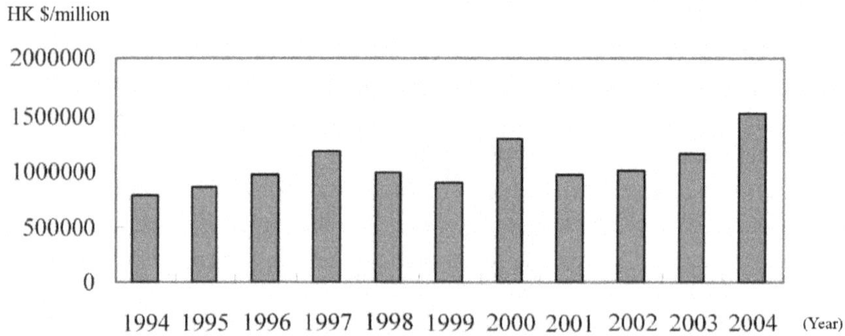

Figure 36. Total scale of capital flows between Hong Kong and the mainland (including trade)

Source: CEIC; Hong Kong Monetary Authority (HKMA); Hong Kong Exchanges and Clearing (HKEX).

It should be noted that when estimating the scale of capital flows between Hong Kong and the mainland, we will face a statistical problem of double summation because the creditor-debtor relationship between the banks of the two places has in fact partially reflected other channels and scale of capital flows.[1] Therefore, the

[1] For example, in the past few years, Hong Kong's trade surplus with the Chinese mainland (adjusted to exclude foreign processing trade) has been increasing, which means that the current account statistics are positive, and the capital account statistics are correspondingly negative. Some of these funds may return to invest in the Chinese mainland, forming the creditor's rights of Hong Kong banks to the Chinese mainland. FDI from Hong Kong to the mainland forms the creditor's rights of Hong Kong banks to the mainland. However, part of this part of FDI will be deposited in the banking system of the Chinese mainland in the form of funds, and the latter may deposit a part of it in Hong Kong banks, thus causing

figures on the scale of cross-border capital flows should be used carefully. This also brings some difficulties to the later econometric analysis.

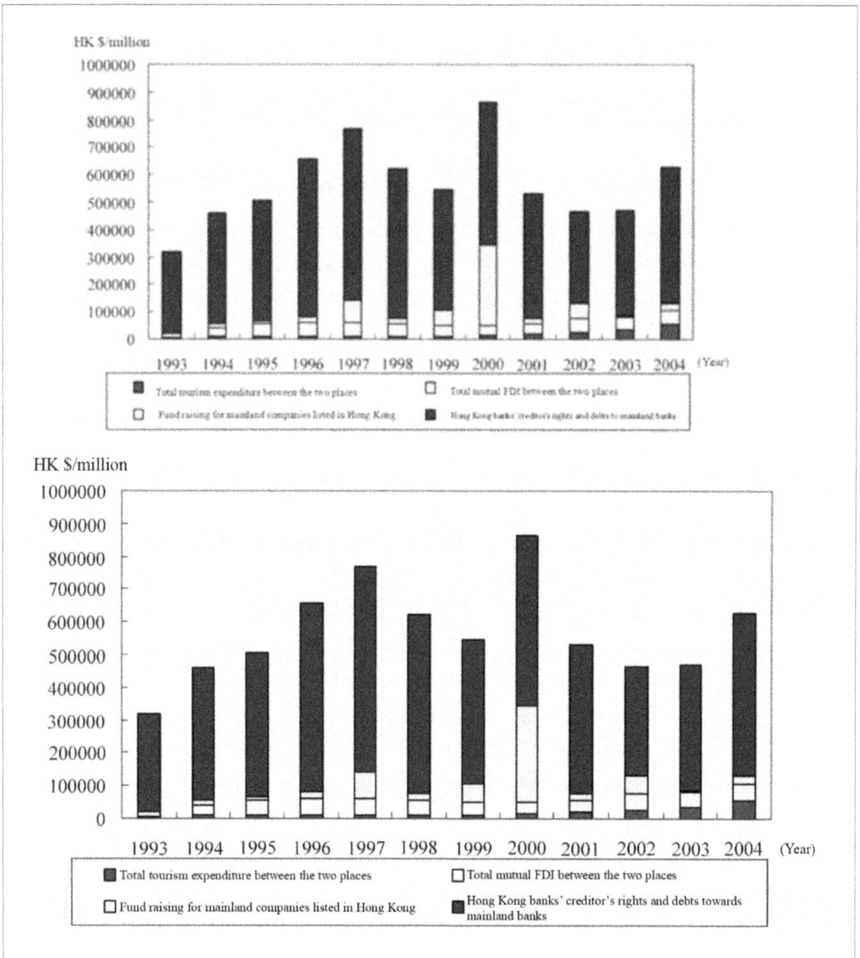

Figure 37. Scale of capital flows in different channels between Hong Kong and the mainland (excluding trade)

Note: The amount of creditor's rights and debts between banks in Hong Kong and the mainland is the largest, and the financing of mainland enterprises in the Hong Kong stock market fluctuates greatly.
Source: CEIC; Hong Kong Monetary Authority (HKMA); Hong Kong Exchanges and Clearing (HKEX).

Hong Kong banks to form debts to the Chinese mainland. But the value after offsetting the creditor's rights and debts should still be the creditor's rights of Hong Kong banks to the Chinese mainland (the amount is less than Hong Kong's FDI to the Chinese mainland).

6.3 Analysis of Influencers of the Capital Flow Between Hong Kong and the Mainland

As pointed out in the introduction, many factors affect cross-border capital flows. We will mainly analyze the factors influencing the cross-border capital flows between Hong Kong and the mainland in terms of GDP growth, expectations of RMB currency change, interest rate spreads, stock market performance and changes in some institutional rules (e.g., RMB business and CEPA in Hong Kong).

1. Economic Growth in Hong Kong and the Mainland

The mainland maintains a much higher GDP growth than Hong Kong. The rapid economic growth in the mainland has always been an important factor for attracting Hong Kong funds. In fact, partial rather than whole capital flow from developed countries to developing countries, aiming to, among others, share the high growth benefits of developing countries.

2. Expectation of RMB's Value Fluctuations

During the depreciation of RMB, a large amount of funds flowed out of the mainland. The expectation of depreciation of the U.S. dollar and appreciation of Hong Kong dollar and RMB attract capital to flow into Hong Kong, specifically: Firstly, the depreciation of the U.S. dollar drives up the investment value of Hong Kong dollar. Since 2002, the U.S. dollar has been depreciating continuously. Since the Hong Kong dollar is pegged to the U.S. dollar, the investment value of Hong Kong dollar assets has increased with the depreciation of the U.S. dollar. As a result, Hong Kong dollar assets were highly pursued and funds flowed into Hong Kong, thus increasing the potential size of capital inflows to the mainland. Secondly, the expectation of RMB appreciation attracts foreign investment to Hong Kong's financial market. Since the second half of 2003, the expectation of RMB appreciation has increased. With the inflow of FDI into Hong Kong and investment in RMB assets or Hong Kong dollar assets that were closely related to RMB, like purchase of shares of Chinese listed companies in Hong Kong, objectively increasing the capital stock in Hong Kong (Figure 38).

3. Differences Between the Three Stock Markets in Hong Kong and the Mainland

Hong Kong stocks fell by more than half during the Asian financial crisis and began to bounce back on September 22, 1998. By 2005, they had recovered sharply. When international hot money expects RMB appreciation, they will buy RMB or "RMB assets" as much as possible. Because RMB is not a freely convertible currency at present, it is still difficult to buy RMB. However, it is much easier to buy RMB assets, and investing in H-shares is the most convenient channel. H-shares are "RMB assets" denominated in U.S. dollars or Hong Kong dollars. When the RMB appreciates, the price of U.S. or HK dollars-denominated H shares also rises accordingly. Meanwhile, given the poor performance of the mainland stock market, some of the funds from the mainland stock market turned to the Hong Kong stock market, increasing the scale of capital flows between Hong Kong and the mainland.

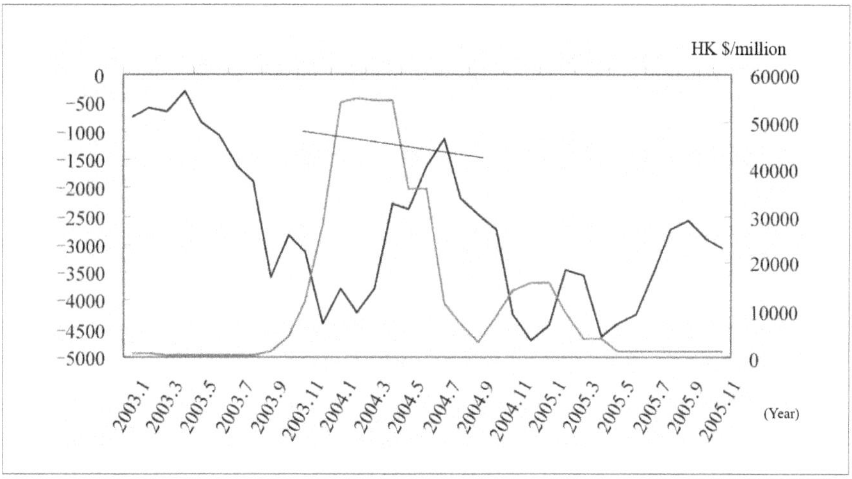

Figure 38. RMB NDF and aggregate balance of Hong Kong banks (2003–2005)

Note: The Aggregate Balance of the banking system in Hong Kong has increased significantly since mid-2003, during the period when the RMB appreciation was more widely expected, and the banking system had sufficient liquidity.
Source: HKMA website and Reuters database.

4. Changes in Institutional Regulations

The flow of funds between Hong Kong and the mainland will also be affected by changes in institutional regulations, mainly the expected clearing arrangements of People's Bank of China for Hong Kong banks to handle personal RMB business, and the implementation of CEPA.

With the increasingly close economic and trade relations between the mainland and Hong Kong, RMB has been circulating and used in Hong Kong at a certain scale. On November 19, 2003, the People's Bank of China (PBOC) issued the No.16 [2003] Announcement of the People's Bank of China (hereinafter referred to as the "Announcement"), declaring that PBOC will provide clearing arrangements for banks in Hong Kong to handle individual RMB business.

Since February 25, 2004, banks in Hong Kong have embarked on personal RMB deposit, exchanges and remittances for Hong Kong residents. Since the end of April 2004, banks in Hong Kong have launched RMB bank card services. In addition to the above four businesses, RMB cards with the UnionPay logo issued by banks in the mainland can also be used in Hong Kong since January 18, 2004. At the end of 2005, the balance of deposits of the clearing bank (Bank of China (Hong Kong) Limited, BOCHK) in banks of Shenzhen had reached RMB 23 billion, and the average household deposit amount exceeded RMB 50,000. The opening of RMB business in Hong Kong has changed the amount of RMB in overseas circulation, increased China's foreign exchange reserves and realized the cross-border RMB flow. The cross-border use of RMB bank cards has increased tourism expenditure and scaled up the capital flow. In addition, the CEPA arrangement launched by the mainland in 2002 has greatly promoted the exchanges of personnel and capital between the mainland and Hong Kong, serving as another driving force for the further expansion of capital scale between the two places.

5. Differences in Financial Management Systems and Development Between the Two Places

The large scale and multiple channels of capital between the two places are also related to the differences in financial management systems and development between the two places, which are manifested by:

Firstly, Hong Kong is a free trade zone, and the largest international financial center in Asia; the mainland still implements capital account regulation, and the internal management capacity of the financial system still needs to further improve.

Secondly, there are both legal normal channels and so-called illegal channels, as well as integrative channels combing the two in the two places in which funds transference is conducted through formal banking systems by illegal private banks or exchange stores.

Thirdly, the informal financial flow channels between the two places, in terms of the mainland, mainly come into being due to China's foreign exchange control system, such as exchange rate system, banking problems, lagging development of small and medium-sized banks, unfinished interest rate liberalization and other factors. In contrast, informal finance in Hong Kong, where the financial system is developed and free, is much less extensive than its counterpart in the mainland. For example, its exchange store is a formal financial intermediary supervised by the Hong Kong Police Station, but this kind of finance is considered informal in the mainland. Therefore, informal finance in

Hong Kong mainly refers to gray finance. The combination of formal finance in Hong Kong and informal finance in the mainland has created a chain of informal remittance channels. The gray channel of capital flow between the mainland and Hong Kong has become an integral part of China's informal remittance channels.

6.4 An Econometric Analysis

To better illustrate the influencing factors of cross-border capital flow through the "Hong Kong Channel," we use the quarterly data from 1993 to 2004 for econometric analysis. We first selected the total scale of capital flow between the two places as a dependent variable for regression, but the results were not satisfactory. Then, we selected the total amount of creditor's rights and debts of banks in Hong Kong to the mainland and regressed respectively and found that the results were better with the debt of banks in Hong Kong to the mainland as the dependent variable. As a result, the debt of banks in Hong Kong to the mainland has become a proxy variable for cross-border capital flow between the two places. Figure 37 also shows that after excluding trade factors, the creditor's rights and debts of banks in Hong Kong to the mainland have always accounted for a very high proportion of the scale of capital flow between the two places. From this perspective, it can serve as a representative proxy variable. The following is a specific econometric analysis.

1. Data

Through CEIC, IFS, HKMA website, the People's Bank of China, and various statistical yearbooks, we obtained quarterly time series data from 1993 to 2004 (Table 20).

It should be noted that the purpose of using Difstockh, that is, the difference between the quarter-on-quarter growth rate of Shanghai's stock index and that of Hong Kong Hang Seng's stock index, is to illustrate the impact of the difference between the mainland and Hong Kong stock markets on the capital flow between the two places. The reason for considering this indicator is that in reality, when the mainland stock market is in depression, capital flows to Hong Kong, and vice versa. Moreover, in 2002 and 2003, the mainland introduced the CEPA policy in Hong Kong, and banks in Hong Kong started RMB business. This is a great structural change that is helpful to analyze the impact of institutional changes on the capital flow between the two places. Therefore, we added two dummy variables, CEPA and RMBbusi, taking 2002 and 2003 as 1 respectively and other years as 0.

Table 20. Basic information of data

Variable identification	Variable meaning	Stability
DLHKBL	Growth rate of total debt of banks in Hong Kong to the mainland	I (0)
Difstockh	The difference between the quarter-on-quarter growth rate of Shanghai stock index and that of Hong Kong Hang Seng stock index in Hong Kong	I (0)
DLRMBREER	Year-on-year growth rate of RMB's real effective exchange rate	I (0)
GDPdiff	The difference between the GDP growth rate of the mainland and that of Hong Kong	I (0)
LInteratediff	The difference between the mainland loan interest rate and that of Hong Kong	I (0)

Note: I (n) means that the sequence reaches smoothness after n times difference.

2. Measurement Results and Economic Implications

Unit root test was carried out on the above variables (see Table 20 for the results). In econometric analysis with PcGets software, we found that with the growth rate of Hong Kong banks' total debt obligations to the mainland as the dependent variable, the statistical indicators (t-value, DW-value, R2, etc.) of the main independent variables are satisfactory, with clear economic implications (see Table 21 for the econometric results).

Table 21 shows the econometric results with the growth rate of total debt of Hong Kong banks to the mainland as the dependent variable. The analysis of the econometric results is as follows.

1. R^2 was 0.62 and turned into 0.52 after adjustment. This shows that 52% of the changes in Hong Kong banks' debt to the mainland can be explained by interest rate spread, GDP difference, real effective exchange rate, RMB business and CEPA factors.
2. Interest rate spread, equal to the value of mainland interest rate minus Hong Kong interest rate, has a positive relationship with debt, because the combined effect of the current period, lag period I and lag period III of interest rate spread is positive. The rise in interest rate spreads and capital flowing to the mainland should drive up Hong Kong banks' creditor right to the mainland, but according to the econometric results, Hong Kong banks' debts to the mainland has increased. This is out of keeping with intuition.

Table 21. Results of quantitative analysis of PcGets

Dependent variable	**DLHKBL**
Independent variable	
LInteratediff	0.01327 (3.018)
LInteratediff_1	-0.02930 (-5.148)
LInteratediff_3	0.02994 (4.684)
GDPdiff_3	-0.01540 (-3.029)
DLRMBREER_2	1.42093 (2.937)
Difstockh	0.16765 (-2.605)
Difstockh_2	-0.08583 (-2.022)
Difstockh_3	-0.10716 (-2.605)
RMBbusi	0.1 1993 (3.111)
CEPA	-0.06147 (-1.843)
R^2	0.61937
Adjusted R^2	0.51861
DW value	1.91
Sample period	1993Q1-2004Q4

Note: t statistics are in brackets.

However, because the interest rate in the mainland is not market-oriented, these results can be explained partially.

3. GDP difference, amount to the value of GDP growth rate of mainland minus GDP growth rate of Hong Kong is inversely related to debt. The rising GDP gap between the mainland and Hong Kong means that the mainland economy performs better, so more funds flow to the mainland, keeping down the debt of Hong Kong banks to the mainland. Vice versa, declines of the GDP gap mean a recession in the mainland economy, so more funds flow to Hong Kong and increase debt.

4. REER has a positive relationship with debt. That means when the REER growth rate rises and depreciation is expected, funds flow out of the mainland and Hong Kong banks owe more debts to the mainland. Or, when REER drops and there is an expectation of appreciation, capital flows to the mainland and debt drops.
5. The effect of the stock market on capital flow is not obvious, but the net effect is negative, which accords with economic logic. That is, when the mainland stock market performs better than Hong Kong, the capital flows to the mainland, which leads to the decline of Hong Kong banks' debt to the mainland. Vice versa, capital flows into Hong Kong because the Hong Kong stock market performs better than the mainland, and the Hong Kong banks owe more debts to the mainland.
6. RMB business: the promotion of RMB business in Hong Kong has made the funds flow to Hong Kong and the Hong Kong banks owe more debts to the mainland. This positive relationship is obvious.
7. CEPA: The implementation of CEPA provides more channels and more favorable policies for Hong Kong funds to enter the mainland. As a result, more funds flock to the mainland, thus reducing the debts of Hong Kong banks to the mainland, showing a negative relationship.

The above econometric analysis shows the important factors affecting cross-border capital flows range from interest rate spread, GDP difference, RMB appreciation expectation, stock market difference between the two places to mainland policy toward Hong Kong.

6.5 Conclusions and Policy Recommendations

Through empirical research, this paper analyzes the channels and scale of cross-border capital flow through the "Hong Kong Channel." Using the quarterly data from 1993 to 2004, this chapter further discusses the influencing factors of cross-border capital flows, and points out that the important factors affecting the capital flows of the two places especially the debts of Hong Kong banks to the mainland include the performance of overall economic growth (GDP difference), stock market performance (stock return rate), the expectation of RMB value change and the change of institutional regulations. Since the "Hong Kong Channel" of cross-border capital flow has become a fait accompli, on the one hand, the authorities should have a clear understanding on this and pay attention to the financial risks and put forward corresponding countermeasures on the other hand.

1. "Hong Kong Channel" More or Less Breaks Through the "Firewall" of Capital Control in the Mainland

We believe that although the cross-border flow of funds is restricted due to the capital control in the mainland, the "Hong Kong Channel" actually more or less breaks through this "firewall." Therefore, the government should pay close attention to the large-scale cross-border capital flows through the "Hong Kong Channel" and the possible impact on financial stability.

2. The Flow of Mainland Funds to Hong Kong Deserves Attention

The flow of capital from the mainland to Hong Kong, where Hong Kong banks maintain net debts to the mainland, can undeniably promote Hong Kong's prosperity. However, while the mainland still requires funds to support its development, it must reflect on the reasons behind the capital outflow, with Hong Kong being just one of the destinations. Our analysis indicates that the poor performance of the mainland stock market and the expectation of changes in the value of the RMB, especially the anticipation of depreciation, are significant factors contributing to the outflow of capital. Therefore, on the one hand, we should standardize the development of the stock market to make it perform better and become more attractive; on the other hand, we should continue to promote the reform of the RMB exchange rate system and realize the two-way floating of the RMB exchange rate, discouraging the capital flow for speculating on the one-way change of the RMB value.

3. The "Hong Kong Channel" Needs to be Regulated

There are both formal, that is, through standardized and legal channels, and informal funds through the "Hong Kong Channel," especially the channels of illegal private banks mentioned above. At present, the "Hong Kong Channel" should be gradually regulated by means of diversion. On the one hand, we are required to vigorously dredge and develop formal channels, such as promoting the development of RMB business in Hong Kong rapidly, so that capital can flow between the two places through the formal banking system as much as possible; on the other hand, illegal private banks and money laundering should be resolutely cracked down. In addition, since both formal and informal financial systems develop from each other's defects, and the distortion caused by financial regulation in the mainland can notably expel funds out of China through illegal channels. Therefore, the mainland regulatory authorities should take measures to gradually correct the distortion and deal with the deficiencies in the formal financial sector.

The Impact of the Subprime Crisis on Stock Markets in the Mainland and Hong Kong

7.1 Introduction

The subprime crisis, which erupted in the summer of 2007, merely exposed the problems of the U.S. financial market and institutions at its onset. However, the initial internal problems in the U.S. soon spread abroad, evolving into a global financial crisis. Although the impact of the Asian financial crisis is local, and the impact of the IT bubble burst in the United States has not caused global economic and financial turmoil, the global impact of the financial crisis that started on Wall Street has intensified, and it is not known when it will end.

After the outbreak of the crisis, the correlation between emerging market economies and developed economies has been hotly debated. Some people think that the epicenter of the subprime crisis was Wall Street, and those companies and developed economies with high financial openness that undertake most subprime business are hardest hit by the crisis, while emerging markets seem to be less affected (Wang & Ji, 2008) and may even have veered away from the crisis to some extent. Other people believe that continuous financial integration has made the emerging market economies more vulnerable to external shocks, especially the reversal of market confidence related to the subprime crisis. Therefore, the distant subprime crisis in the United States could still affect emerging markets (IMF, 2008b; IMF, 2008d).

Given their distinctive economic development and economic structures, developed economies and emerging market economies are bound to response differently the impact of the subprime crisis. Then, what kind of evidence can support such a different mechanism and effect? Taking Hong Kong SAR and mainland stock markets as an example, we now discuss the impact effect of the U.S. stock market during the subprime crisis.

The choice of Hong Kong SAR and Chinese mainland stock market is based on the fact that Hong Kong SAR is a relatively developed economy, with a mature financial market and a high financial openness. Hong Kong SAR has been rated as the freest market in the world for years. On the other hand, although its open economy has developed greatly in both breadth and depth, the Chinese mainland is still largely an emerging market economy given its relatively cautious and gradual financial opening and the resulting less developed and open financial market. They represent two different types of economy. In addition, Hong Kong SAR and the Chinese mainland are now more integrated, which involves the correlation and interaction between the two markets. Therefore, by investigating these two markets, we can grasp the impact of the sub-prime crisis on these two markets, and we can further understand the correlation or spillover effects between these two markets.

A core question related to the above analysis is whether the subprime crisis in the United States has a significant impact on Hong Kong SAR's stock price trend relative to that in the Chinese mainland. Because both the Chinese mainland and Hong Kong SAR have experienced a long period of rising stock prices. This upward trend continued when the subprime crisis broke out. However, with the spread of the subprime crisis, the negative impact on these two markets showed up.

Based on the above background, this chapter examines the impact of the U.S. subprime crisis on the daily returns and conditional volatility of stocks in the mainland and Hong Kong SAR. In order to capture the spillover effect of the subprime crisis in the United States, we adopt a two-step approach: first, we estimate a set of univariate GARCH models (represented by UGARCH); second, a set of multivariable GARCH models (represented by MGARCH) are established to further identify the source and magnitude of such spillovers.

The results of both the univariate model and the multivariable GARCH model show that: (1) The Chinese mainland stock market is not immune from the impact of the subprime crisis, and the so-called decoupling theory is not true, which can be supported by the spillover effect of the price level and volatility of the American stock market on the Chinese mainland. (2) From the perspective of the stock price level and volatility, the Hong Kong SAR market is more affected by the American market than the Chinese mainland market. Moreover, the historical fluctuation of the American market has a more lasting impact on the future fluctuation of the Hong Kong SAR market than on the Chinese mainland market, showing that as an international financial center, Hong Kong SAR is more susceptible to external risks. (3) From the perspective of volatility persistence, the degree of cross-volatility between Hong Kong SAR and the Chinese mainland is lower than that between the United States and the

Chinese mainland, mainly because the United States is the source and center of the subprime crisis. (4) As expected, the conditional correlation between stock returns in Hong Kong SAR and Chinese mainland is higher than that between them and the United States, indicating a higher financial integration between Hong Kong SAR and the Chinese mainland.

This chapter has made a breakthrough beyond the existing literature in the following three aspects.

1. As far as we know, this chapter is the first literature that attempts to estimate the impact of the U.S. subprime crisis on the stock markets in Chinese mainland and Hong Kong SAR with univariate and multivariate GARCH models.
2. By comparing the different responses of the Chinese mainland and Hong Kong SAR markets to the sub-prime crisis, this chapter reveals the different financial openness of the Chinese mainland and Hong Kong SAR and their correlation with the outside world.
3. The analysis in this chapter provides some reference to the authorities on how to formulate policies to deal with external shocks, especially in the background of increasing liberalization of the capital account in the Chinese mainland.

This chapter is organized as follows: section 2 reveals the performance of the Chinese mainland and Hong Kong SAR stock markets, the channels through which the sub-prime crisis affected the Chinese mainland and Hong Kong SAR markets, and the basic characteristics of the Chinese mainland and Hong Kong SAR markets; section 3 briefly reviews the relevant literature; section 4 introduces the data characteristics and methods; section 5 summarizes the empirical analysis and main conclusions; section 6 puts forward the conclusions and policy recommendations.

7.2 The Performance of the Stock Markets in the Mainland and Hong Kong: Stylized Facts and Basic Observations

How did the Chinese mainland and HK SAR stock markets perform in the face of the subprime crisis? We first compare the performance of some developed economies to emerging market economies in the stock market by showing the peaks and troughs of the stock indexes from September 15 to October 31, 2008. This date is seen as a starting point, mainly because of the global panic caused by the collapse of Lehman Brothers on that day (see Figure 39 and Table 22).

Table 22. High and low points of stock markets in emerging markets

	From high to low (October 31st, 2007, to October 31st, 2008)	During the bankruptcy of Lehman Brothers (from September 12th, 2007, to October 31st, 2008.
Brazil	-43.00	-28.94
Hong Kong SAR, China	-55.45	-27.82
Korea	-46.09	-24.69
Mexico	-35.56	-20.77
South Africa	-33.00	-20.36
China	-70.97	-16.87
India	-50.66	-30.09
Russia	-65.21	-42.36
Germany	-37.80	-20.00
Japan	-46.48	-26.34
Britain	-34.88	-19.19
America	-37.73	-22.92

Sources: Bloomberg and calculation of the authors.

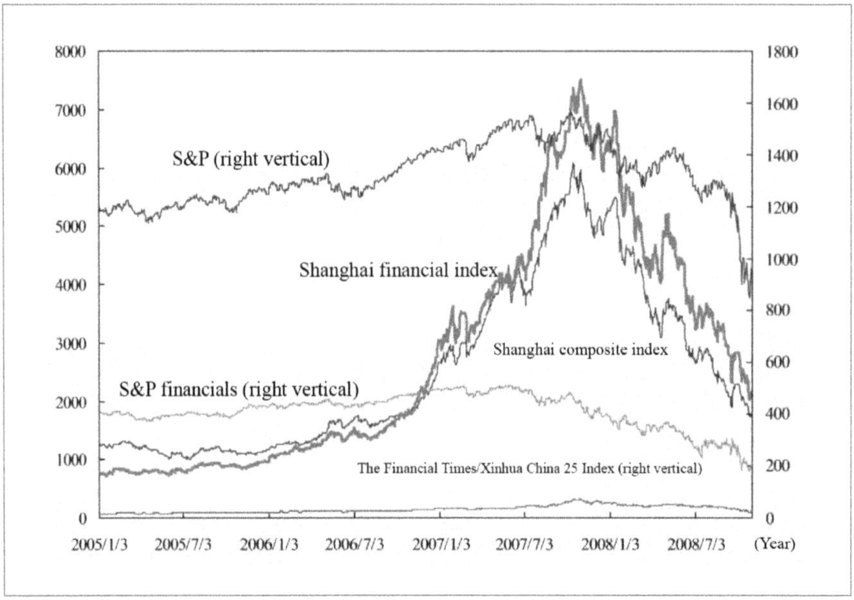

Figure 39. A-shares Index trend

Source: Bloomberg.

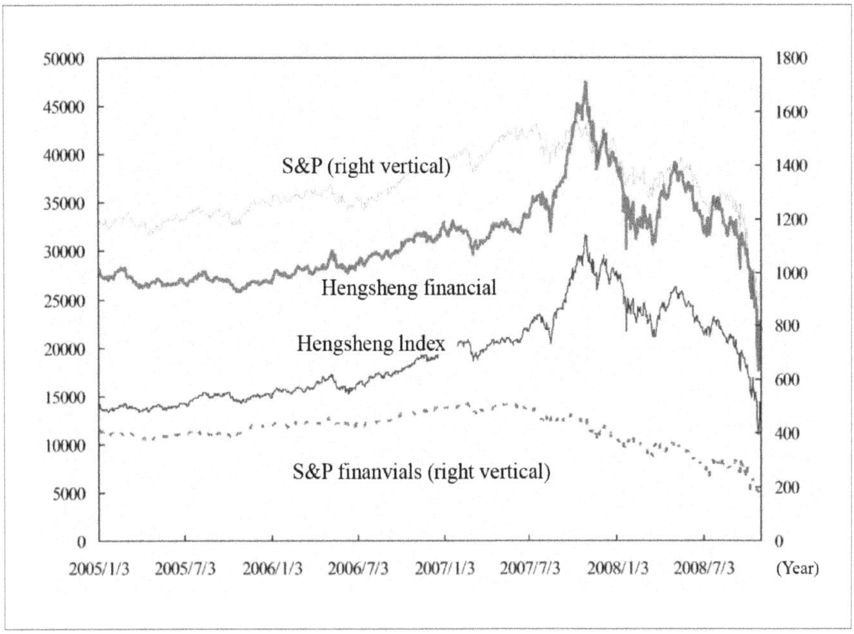

Figure 40. B-shares Index trend

Source: Bloomberg.

In contrast, the financial systems of the Chinese mainland and Hong Kong SAR have performed relatively well in responding to the impact of international capital markets thanks to their low exposure to securities products. However, these two markets are not entirely immune. As shown in Table 22, the stock prices in major developed countries have dropped by at least 30% from the high point in October 2007, while those in Chinese mainland and Hong Kong SAR stock markets fell even more by 71% and 56% respectively. Following the declining stock prices, the U.S. stock market has become more volatile since the end of 2006, especially when the subprime crisis broke out in mid-2007 and Lehman Brothers collapsed in mid-September 2008 (see Figure 41).

This resonance between emerging markets (including the Chinese mainland and HK SAR) and developed markets is no coincidence. There are many transmission channels between the two. The followings are some channels of the impact of the U.S. subprime crisis on the Chinese mainland and Hong Kong SAR markets.

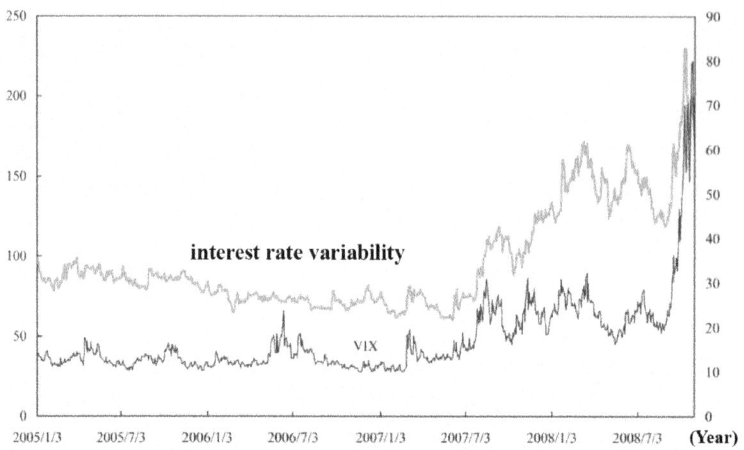

Figure 41. U.S. financial market volatility

Source: Bloomberg.

1. Insignificant Direct Losses and Substantial Potential Losses

With low financial openness and little "going global" progress, China is not impacted seriously by and only suffers limited loss from the U.S. subprime crisis. According to the 2007 annual report of Bank of China, it lost about 15.5 billion yuan in the U.S. subprime crisis. After the collapse of Lehman Brothers, four Chinese banks, namely Bank of China, Industrial and Commercial Bank of China, China Merchants Bank and Industrial Bank announced that they held totally USD 380 million of Lehman-related bonds, of which ICBC, including foreign-funded institutions, held USD 151.8 million, which, the highest among the four banks, but only accounted for ten-thousandth of its total assets. According to the statistics of the China Banking Regulatory Commission, the assets of overseas institutions of Chinese-funded banking financial institutions, which are vulnerable to the impact of international financial turmoil, accounted for only about 3.7% of total assets (in 2008). In addition, according to preliminary estimates, central enterprises have accumulated more than $ 1 trillion in assets overseas, many of which have been involved in derivatives trading, so there are some losses. If all these factors are taken into consideration, China will be more exposed to the risks in the sub-prime crisis. However, while developed economies suffer from 4 trillion-dollar asset losses, China only experiences much lower direct losses related to subprime mortgages (2009). However, it should be noted that although the direct losses are insignificant, the potential losses cannot be ignored, especially in the case of the devaluation of the U.S. dollar, the reserve assets are shrinking sharply. Currently, about 60% of China's $ 2 trillion in foreign exchange reserves are in U.S. dollars.

Regardless of their total subprime exposure well below 0.5% of overall bank assets (IMF, 2008), Hong Kong SAR banks still experienced some shocks. For example, counterparty risk has pushed up the inter-bank interest rates, while the deteriorating market environment has hindered IPO issuance, resulting in the loss of local bank fees. On September 24, 2008, rumors of a liquidity shortage resulted in a run on the Bank of East Asia. Risk-averse behavior and liquidity needs led to an increase in risk-averse investment behavior. High-quality collateral, such as Hong Kong SAR Government Exchange Fund Paper (HKGEFP), was highly sought after. Investors in Hong Kong SAR also suffered losses from "Minibonds" related to the bankruptcy of Lehman Brothers.

2. Market Pessimism Induced by Negative Mindset

Another impact of the subprime crisis was a blow to the mindset of investors. Before the United States took over Fannie Mae and Freddie Mac, Lehman Brothers collapsed, and the U.S. government issued a $ 700 billion bailout plan, the subprime crisis only demonstrated destructive power of limited range, then after these events broke out and measures were taken, the world and China had a new understanding of the seriousness and contagion of this financial crisis. In particular, the collapse of Lehman Brothers caused global panic and market pessimism. These blows to investors' confidence undoubtedly exerted a significant negative impact on China's financial markets (including stock and housing markets) and physical investment.

3. Uncertainties of Capital Flow

Subprime crisis has two effects on capital flow: one is the risk aversion effect, in which the international capital in the epicenter of subprime crisis flows to the Chinese mainland and Hong Kong SAR markets to hedge against risks; The other is the credit crunch effect in developed countries, which makes foreign capital (such as capital from the Chinese mainland and Hong Kong SAR) flow back to developed markets to solve the liquidity shortage. For example, in the first two quarters of 2008, the inflow of hot money from the Chinese mainland reached USD 130 billion, exceeding the inflow of hot money in 2007. However, by the third and fourth quarters of 2008 and the first quarter of 2009, another USD 7.56 billion, USD 89.99 billion and USD 80.8 billion of hot money flowed out respectively (see Figure 42). Net trading of U.S. residents' stocks abroad (an indicator of capital flows to the Chinese mainland and Hong Kong SAR) shows that the capital flows to Hong Kong SAR have become more volatile since the outbreak of the subprime crisis (see Figure 43). In addition, the increase of capital flow may also make the stock prices in the Chinese mainland and Hong Kong SAR more volatile.

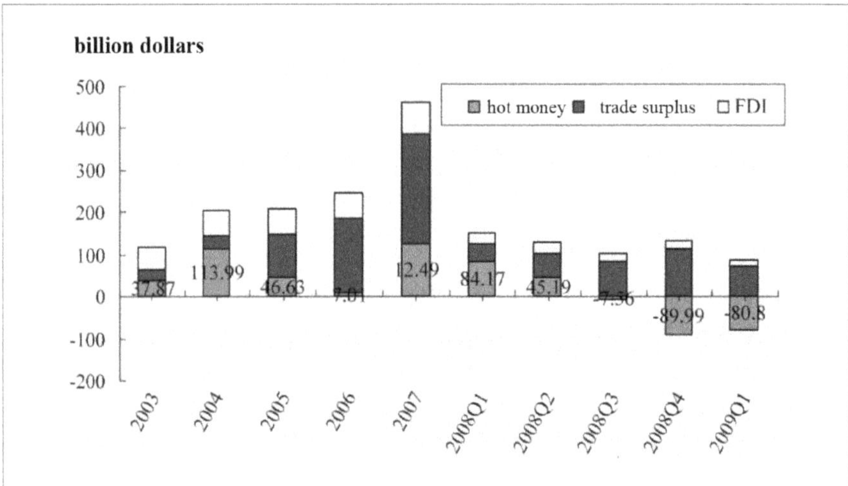

Figure 42. Hot money flows in Chinese mainland (U.S.$ billions)

Note: New foreign exchange reserves = FDI + trade surplus + hot money.
Source: State Administration of Foreign Exchange

4. The Slow Growth of Global Economy and the Increasing Pressure of External Demand

China's rapid economic growth over the past few years is inseparable from the strong global economic growth and the resulting contribution of external demand. Statistics show that China's external demand (net exports) has contributed an average of 21.3% to GDP over the past three years. In 2007, the dependence of China on foreign trade reached 66.8%. With the spread of the subprime crisis, the U.S. economy is declining, and the global economy is slowing down, China's foreign demand will certainly be affected. And HK SAR, as the center of entrepot trade, will also be affected by the decline in Chinese mainland's foreign demand. All of these will have an impact on the stock market in HK SAR and the Chinese mainland.

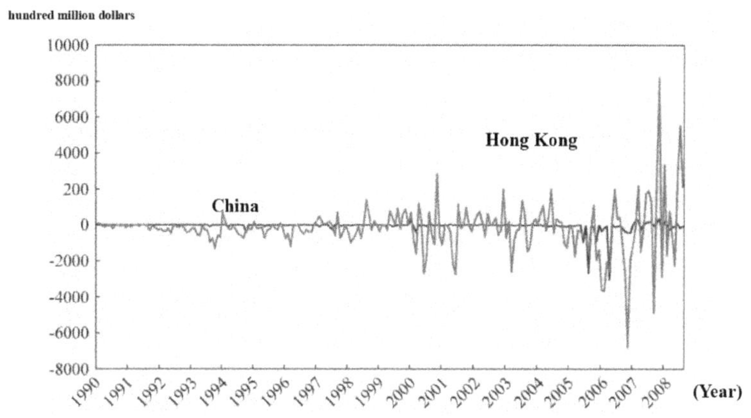

Figure 43. Net foreign exchange transactions of U.S. residents in mainland of China and Hong Kong SAR

Note: Net foreign exchange transactions by U.S. residents in the stocks of Chinese and Hong Kong SAR companies are used here as a proxy for capital inflows to both countries.
Source: Haver database; U.S. Department of the Treasury.

In addition, for understanding the transmission channels of the subprime crisis, we should pay attention to the following characteristics of the Hong Kong SAR and Chinese mainland markets.

First, as a major structural change in the Chinese mainland stock market, the reform of the shareholder structure implemented in the past few years has greatly promoted the development of the Chinese mainland stock market. Before 2005, China's stock market was a dual-class structure, with coexisting tradable shares and non-tradable shares. About two-thirds of the shares of listed companies were not tradable, which imposed a great negative impact on the development of the stock market. Such a segmented system brought high uncertainties and people did not know when these non-tradable shares would flood into the market, thus hindering the recovery of the market and adversely affecting the overall credit of China's stock market. The sword of Damocles had been hanging above the head. To solve this problem, the government initiated the reform of the shareholder structure in 2005. As more non-tradable shares were listed and circulated, the real market value of the shares was gradually realized, driving up the stock prices since 2005. Of course, the introduction of exchange rate reform in 2005 also had an impact. In the past few years, the reform of the shareholder structure has been serving as an important impetus for the development of China's stock market.

Second, the Chinese mainland differs greatly from Hong Kong SAR in terms of the degree of market openness. China's capital account is opening up, and there are still some restrictions on capital flow. The Hong Kong SAR market is an open market, which can be accessed by all foreign investors and issuers, and there are no restrictions on Hong Kong SAR residents' overseas investments. In addition, the difference between the two places is also reflected in the fact that Hong Kong SAR's stock market and banking industry are very open to Chinese companies' stock issuance, while the Chinese mainland financial market can only be accessed by some Hong Kong SAR institutions. After the promulgation of the Chinese Mainland-Hong Kong SAR Closer Economic Partnership Arrangement (CEPA), the Chinese mainland is more open but not completely open to Hong Kong SAR.

Third, with the increasing financial integration between the Chinese mainland and Hong Kong SAR, the policy choice and financial market development of the Chinese mainland are crucial to Hong Kong SAR's position as an international financial center. On the one hand, Hong Kong SAR plays a very important role in the opening of capital accounts and the development of financial market in the Chinese mainland. On the other hand, the rapid economic growth and the development of the financial market in the Chinese mainland have created the conditions for Hong Kong SAR to enhance its competitiveness as a major international and regional financial center. This two-way mutual benefit has intensified the co-movement of bilateral stock markets.

7.3 Taking Stock of Relevant Literature

A number of theoretical and empirical studies have been carried out on the transmission of stock yield and volatility among different economies.

From the perspective of theoretical research, some theoretical analyses have been organized based on the "revision of expectations." For example, Kodres & Pritsker (1998) believed that even if the fundamentals do not change, market traders and asymmetric information would amplify the impact through portfolio adjustment. Calvo (1999) and Calvo & Mendoza (2000) proposed that the co-movements of the stock market was caused by the herd behavior of asset managers.

From the perspective of empirical research, the correlation of stock yield in different markets is a common method used to study spillover effects. For example, the study of Baig & Goldfajn (1999), taking into account domestic news and fundamentals, showed that different stock markets were closely and significantly correlated. By analyzing various potential contagion channels in the financial markets of 12 transition countries, Gelos & Sahay (2000) proved that the stock markets were significantly more correlated with financial integration from 1994 to 1999. Chan-Lau, Mathieson & Yao used extreme value theory to analyze the nonlinear relationship and the contagion of the financial market and found that a negative stock yield could lead to higher contagion degree (2004).

In addition to the correlation analysis method, VAR theory is also used to analyze spillover effects in some studies. For example, Guimarae-Filho et al. (IMF, 2008b) used various statistical models (including VAR model) to find that an increasing spillover effect from the United States to Asian countries. For another example, by analyzing the source and scale of spillover effects among developed countries, Bayoumi & Swiston (2007) concluded that the change of the global financial environment was the main source of spillover effects, and the stability of American financial environment contributed to the stability of the global financial environment and reduced the fluctuation of financial market and economic growth.

In addition, the GARCH model is also used to analyze spillover effects. For example, Chan-Lau and Ivaschenko (2003) found that "the Wall Street virus" made the price spillover effect between American and Asian stock markets more pronounced, but the volatility spillover effect between them was not significant. Booth, Martikainen and Tse (1997) used multivariate EGARCH model to analyze stock price and volatility spillover effects among Scandinavian countries and found that the transmission of stock price volatility was asymmetric, and the spillover effect of bad news was far greater than that of good news. Worthington and Higgs (2001) studied the transmission mechanism of stock yield and volatility in Asian stock markets and used MGARCH model to identify the source and scale of spillover effects and analyze the differences between developed countries and emerging market countries in the transmission mechanism of spillover effects.

Besides, other methods are available to study spillover effects. For example, Jobst & Kamil (IMF, 2008c) used the multivariate extreme value theory (EVT) to quantify the extreme values of different stock market returns and found that the American and Latin American stock markets suffered from more serious financial contagion when financial turmoil occurred.

Finally, some latest findings on spillover effects have been released. For example, in the International Monetary Fund's Global Financial Stability Report of October 2008 (IMF, 2008d); Psalida and Sun used panel data from 30 emerging market countries to analyze the contagion channels from developed country stock markets to emerging market countries' stock markets. They also used VAR models to analyze the impulse responses of stock prices to external impacts (market volatility, liquidity and credit risk) in some countries, and concluded that global factors have become important drivers of spillover effects transmitted from stock markets in developed countries to stock markets in emerging market countries.

7.4 Data and Methods

In this chapter, the daily stock price indices of the United States, Chinese mainland and Hong Kong SAR are used to calculate the stock yield, that is, subtracting the logarithm of all stock price indices: $R_t = \text{In}P_t - \text{In}P_{t-1}$ (Figure 44, Figure 45). R stands for stock yield, and P for stock price index.[1]

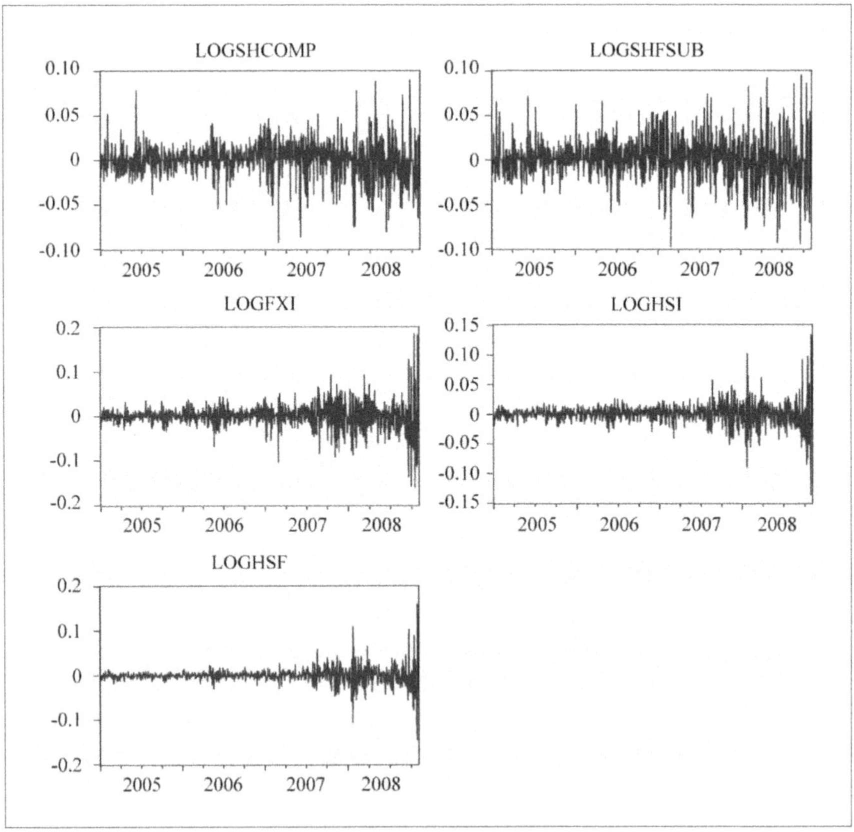

Figure 44. Daily stock yield (January 1, 2007–October 31, 2008)

Source: Bloomberg Consulting database; calculated by the author.

1 Dividend factor is not involved in the stock yield.

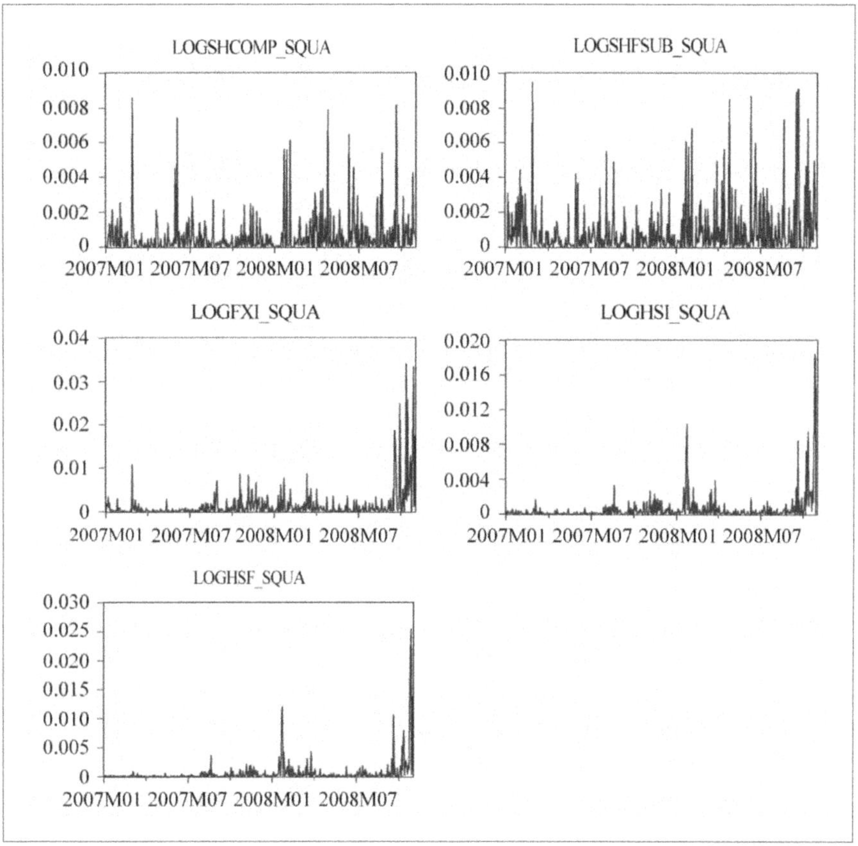

Figure 45. Daily stock yield squared (January 1, 2007–October 31, 2008)

Source: Bloomberg Consulting database; calculated by the author.

The purpose of this chapter is to investigate whether the subprime mortgage crisis has a significant impact on the stock yield and volatility in Chinese mainland and Hong Kong SAR. In order to control domestic macroeconomic variables, such as monetary conditions and economic growth, as well as global financial market volatility, we introduce two sets of independent variables: one is the economic and financial variables of Chinese mainland and Hong Kong SAR, and the other is the variables of global financial market volatility.

Referring to Liu, Pauwels and Chan (2008), we use unexpected domestic economic variables/variables reflecting unexpected impacts. Specifically, we measure unexpected impacts based on the impact of unexpected changes in these macroeconomic and financial variables on stock prices and the difference between actual and market forecast (expected) data on the announcement date of the macroeconomic and financial variables (see the appendix for details on market forecast data). These unexpected variables include the interest-rate spread reflecting interest rate parity, the difference in the growth rate of money supply (M2), the difference in inflation and the difference in industrial production. The impact of the balance of payments on stock prices is expressed by the difference between the growth rate of the Chinese mainland's trade surplus and the growth rate of Hong Kong SAR's imports and exports.[2]

The market forecast data comes from Bloomberg Consulting database and Consensus Forecast The latter regularly surveys financial institutions and asks them to forecast the macroeconomic and financial data of Chinese mainland and HK SAR every month before the official data is disclosed. The sample period is from January 1, 2005, to October 31, 2008, covering the peaks and troughs of the stock index during the subprime mortgage crisis.

With regard to global financial market indicators, we take the Chicago Board Options Exchange's Volatility, VIX and Lehman Brothers Swaption Volatility (LBSPX)[3] as indicators of global financial market volatility. Table 23 shows the detailed domestic and international indicators.

In order to test whether the subprime mortgage crisis has a significant impact on the stock yield and volatility in the Chinese mainland and Hong Kong SAR, we use the GARCH model to analyze the impact of the U.S. market on the stock yield and conditional volatility in Chinese mainland and Hong Kong SAR. In the GARCH model, the stock yield mean and conditional variance (σ_t^2) are set.

We establish two sets of GARCH models: one is the univariate GARCH (UGARCH) model; the other set is the multivariate GARCH (MGARCH) model. The specific structure of the two sets of models is as follows.

---

2 Since there is no forecast data of Hong Kong SAR's current account surplus in Bloomberg database, we use the growth rate of Hong Kong SAR's import and export to reflect the current account surplus.

3 Lehman Brothers' option volatility is a weighted average of interest rate option volatility index for 1–6 months.

Table 23. Data sources and transformations

Name of variables	Description of variables	Unit of data	Source	Transformation
Shanghai Securities Composite Index (LOGSHCOMP)	Shanghai Securities Composite Index	Daily index	Bloomberg Consulting	Difference of logarithms
Shanghai Securities Financial Index (LOGSHFSUB)	Shanghai Securities Financial Index	Daily index	Bloomberg Consulting	Difference of logarithms
iShares FTSE/ Xinhua China 25 Index (FXI)	iShares FTSE/ Xinhua China 25 Index (FXI)	Daily index	Bloomberg Consulting	Difference of logarithms
Hang Seng Index (LOGHSI)	Hang Seng Index	Daily index	Bloomberg Consulting	Difference of logarithms
Hang Seng Financial Index (LOGSPXFINL)	Hang Seng Financial Index	Daily index	Bloomberg Consulting	Difference of logarithms
Standard & Poor's Index (LOGSPX)	Standard & Poor's Index	Daily index	Bloomberg Consulting	Difference of logarithms
Standard & Poor's Financial Index (LOGSPXFINL)	Standard & Poor's financial index	Daily index	Bloomberg Consulting	The difference between the actual number and the predicted number
Sino-U.S. interest rate spread (CHNINTDIFF)	Sino-U.S. interest rate spread	Monthly percentage change	Bloomberg Consulting	The difference between the actual number and the predicted number
Hong Kong SAR-U.S. interest rate spread (HKINTDIFF)	Hong Kong SAR-U.S. interest rate spread	Monthly percentage change	Bloomberg Consulting	The difference between the actual number and the predicted number
China Industrial Production (CHNIP)	China Industrial Production	Monthly percentage change	Bloomberg Consulting	The difference between the actual number and the predicted number
China's money supply (CHNMS)	China's money supply	Monthly percentage change	Bloomberg Consulting	The difference between the actual number and the predicted number

Continued

Name of variables	Description of variables	Unit of data	Source	Transformation
China CPI (CHNCPI)	China CPI	Monthly percentage change	Bloomberg Consulting	The difference between the actual number and the predicted number
China's trade surplus (CHNTRAVOL)	China's trade surplus	Monthly percentage change	Bloomberg Consulting and Consensus Forecast database	The difference between the actual number and the predicted number
Hong Kong SAR money supply (HKMS)	Hong Kong SAR money supply	Monthly percentage change	Bloomberg Consulting	The difference between the actual number and the predicted number
Hong Kong SAR CPI (HKCPI)	Hong Kong SAR CPI	Monthly percentage change	Bloomberg Consulting	The difference between the actual number and the predicted number
Hong Kong SAR's trade surplus (HKTRADE)	Hong Kong SAR's trade surplus	Monthly percentage change	Bloomberg Consulting and Consensus Forecast database	The difference between the actual number and the predicted number
Market Volatility (VIX)	Market volatility	Monthly	Bloomberg Consulting	Horizontal variable
Interest Rate Volatility (LBSPX)	Interest rate volatility	Monthly	Bloomberg Consulting	Horizontal variable
Subprime Mortgage Crisis (EVENT)	Subprime mortgage crisis	Quantity	Bloomberg Consulting	Horizontal variable

Source: Bloomberg Consulting database; Consensus Forecast database.

1. UGARCH model

In the UGARCH model, we add a subprime crisis event variable, which is a time series of 0 or 1. If there is a negative event of the subprime mortgage crisis, we define that day as 1. Otherwise, it is 0. That is, in the UGARCH model:

If there is a negative event of subprime mortgage crisis, event = 1;

If not, event = 0.

The purpose of establishing this UGARCH model about the subprime mortgage crisis is to see whether the stock markets in Chinese mainland and Hong Kong SAR respond to the subprime mortgage crisis. The stock yield equation is equal to its autoregressive variable and other variables. The specific structure of the model is:

$$R_t = \text{constant} + \xi_t R_{t-1} + \lambda X_{t-1} + \phi V_t^f + \phi \text{event} + \epsilon_t \quad (1)$$

Among them, R_t is the stock yield; R_{t-1} is the 1-period lagged stock yield; X_{t-1} is the control variable for the Chinese mainland and Hong Kong SAR; V_t^f represents the indicator of global financial market volatility; the event represents the subprime mortgage crisis event; ϵ_t is the residual.

The conditional variance (σ_t^2) equation of the residual is:

$$\sigma_t^2 = \alpha_0 + \alpha_1 \epsilon_{t-1}^2 + \beta_1 \sigma_{t-1}^2 + \mu \text{event} \quad (2)$$

ϵ_{t-1}^2 is the ARCH term and σ_{t-1}^2 is the GARCH term (component).

2. MGARCH model

After using the UGARCH model to analyze whether the subprime mortgage crisis has a significant impact on the stock yield and volatility in Chinese mainland and Hong Kong SAR, we take the linkage effect among the United States, Chinese mainland and Hong Kong SAR into the analysis framework, and observe whether the stock yield and volatility of the United States have an impact on those of Chinese mainland and Hong Kong SAR from a systematic perspective.

We use MGARCH model. In view of the interactions among markets would provide a better analysis of stock yield and volatility spillovers effects than the UGARCH model (Tse & Tsui, 2002; Bae, Karolyi, & Stulz, 2003), we establish several sets of MGARCH models to further analyze the source and size of spillover effects.

Theoretically, the MGARCH model should be as simple as possible and be flexible. For the analysis of this chapter, we use the diagonal VECH model to limit the coefficient matrices A and B to diagonal matrices. Among them, the coefficient matrix is first order, which is equivalent to the diagonal BEKK model. This model setting can reduce the number of estimation coefficients and ensure that the conditional variance matrix is semidefinite. In addition, the model can identify both the spillover effects of self-volatility and that of cross-market volatility. Finally, since the standard residuals show that the model has an excess kurtosis, we assume that the error term follows the student's t-distribution to model the thick tail in the residuals.

The data we use in the MGARCH model for the U.S., Chinese mainland, and Hong Kong SAR is from January 1, 2005, to October 31, 2008. In order to test the situation during the subprime mortgage crisis, we also shortened the data period to January 3, 2007–October 31, 2008. The explanatory variables for the conditional expected return equation include the 1-period lagged return of each market. The equations for Chinese mainland and Hong Kong SAR contain the same domestic and international macro control variables and international financial market variables as in the previous UGARCH model.

$$R_t = \text{constant} + \zeta_t R_{t-1} + \eta R^f_{t-1} + \lambda X_{t-1} + \phi V^f_t + \epsilon_t \quad (3)$$

$$\sigma^2_t = \alpha_0 + \alpha_1 \epsilon^2_{t-1} + \beta_1 \sigma^2_{t-1} \quad (4)$$

The difference between equations (1) and (3) is that the latter has 1-period lagged returns for the United States, Chinese mainland, and Hong Kong SAR, which act as a source of spillover effects, replacing the subprime mortgage crisis event variables in the UGARCH model.

7.5 Results

According to the method introduced in the previous section, we have built two sets of GARCH models. One group is the UGARCH model, and the other is the MGARCH model. In each group of models, the explanatory variables are subdivided into two categories: one is the yield on a composite stock index (e.g., the S&P stock index); the other is the return on a financial sector stock index (e.g., the S&P financial stock index) (see Table 24).

The autoregressive equations for stock index yields indicate that autoregression occurs in each stock index yield equation. And the ADF test indicates

Table 24. Stock daily yields: Statistics

	S&P Indices	S&P Financial Index	SSE Composite Index	SSE Moneyman Index	iSharcs FTSE/ Xinhua China 25 Index (FXI)	Hang Seng Index	Hang Seng Financial Index
Mean value	-0.0002	-0.0007	0.0003	0.0010	0.0003	0.0000	-0.0003
Medians	0.0004	0.0000	0.0003	0.0000	0.0007	0.0004	0.0000
Max.	0.11	0.12	0.09	0.10	0.18	0.13	0.16
Min.	-0.09	-0.17	-0.09	-0.10	-0.16	-0.14	-0.15
Standard Deviation (SD)	0.01	0.02	0.02	0.02	0.03	0.02	0.02
Partiality	-0.14	-0.31	-0.33	-0.07	-0.02	0.12	0.31
Peakiness	22.05	17.69	6.20	5.06	11.94	16.36	24.00
Jarque-Bera Value Probability	15126.82 <0.0001	9004.53 <0.0001	445.01 <0.0001	177.65 <0.0001	3332.30 <0.0001	7435.98 <0.0001	18389.62 <0.0001
Total	-0.22	-0.68	0.31	1.01	0.29	-0.02	-0.25
Sum Sq. Dev.	0.16	0.43	0.39	0.59	0.76	0.31	0.30

Source: Bloomberg Consulting database; according to author's calculations.

that the difference in stock index returns is I (0), as are the stock volatility (VIX) and interest rate volatility (LBSPX) (see Table 25). The information criteria test of Akaike Information and Schwarz indicates that the explanatory variables in the equation should be taken with a lag of 1 period. (see Table 26).

Clustering also exists in the square of stock index yields in Chinese mainland and Hong Kong SAR. ARCH tests indicate that it is appropriate to utilize the GARCH model here. The distribution of the squared stock index yields shows large skewness and kurtosis, indicating that the error terms are non-normally distributed (see Table 27).

Table 25. Statistical values regarding stock price and volatility: Augmented Dickey-Fuller Test

Variables	ADF Test	Judgment Coefficient (c, t, k)
iSHARESFTSE/Xinbua China 25 Index (FXI)	−39.0***	(c,0,0)
SSE Composite Index	−58.8***	(c,0,0)
Shanghai Financial Index	−35.1***	(c,0,0)
Market Volatility	−4.2***	(c,0,4)
Interest rate volatility	−3.2**	(c,0,1)
U.S.-China spreads	−1.9*	(c,0,12)
China CPI	−9.4***	(c,0,20)
China Industrial Production	−11.1***	(c,0,25)
China Money Supply	−17.8***	(c,0,23)
China Trade Surplus	−26.6***	(c,0,23)
Hang Seng Index (HSI)	−38.7***	(c,0,2)
Hang Seng Financial Index	−36.0***	(c,0,2)
S&P Index	−19.5*	(c,0,1)
Hong Kong SAR-U.S. interest rate spread	−3.6***	(c,0,2)
Hong Kong SAR Trade Surplus	−25.1***	(c,0,22)
Hong Kong SAR Trade Money Supply	−69.9***	(c,0,0)
Hong Kong SAR CPI	−69.9***	(c,0,0)

Source: Bloomberg Consulting database; according to author's calculations.

Table 26. Criteria for selecting the lag period in VAR

	SSE Composite Index	SSE Financial Index	iShares FTSE / Xinhua China 25 Index (FXI)	Hang Seng Index	Hang Seng Finance Indexes
Lags	1	1	1	1	1
Loglikelihood	2524.23	2311.85	2202.56	2624.87	2647.42
Akaikeinfocriterion	−5.03	−4.60	−4.39	−5.23	−5.28
Schwarzcriterion	−4.98	−4.55	−4.34	−5.19	−5.23

Source: Bloomberg Consulting database; according to author's calculations.

Table 27. Distribution of the squared stock yields

	SSE Composite Index	SSE Financial Index	iShares FTSE / Xinhua China 25 Index (FXI)	Hang Seng Index	Hang Seng Finance Indexes
Mean	0.0004	0.0006	0.0008	0.0003	0.0003
Median	0.0001	0.0002	0.0001	0.0000	0.0000
Max.	0.0086	0.0095	0.0341	0.0184	0.0255
Min.	0.0000	0.0000	0.0000	0.0000	0.0000
Standard Deviation (SD)	0.0009	0.0012	0.0025	0.0012	0.0014
Partiality	5.10	3.98	8.22	9.87	11.31
Peakiness	35.91	22.76	88.50	121.51	158.74
Jarque-Bera value probability	49465.32 <0.0001	18910.14 <0.0001	315860.81 <0.0001	601423.76 <0.0001	1031880.16 <0.0001
Total	0.39	0.59	0.76	0.31	0.30
Sum Sq. Dev.	0.00	0.00	0.01	0.00	0.00
Sum Sq. Dev.	0.00	0.00	0.01	0.00	0.00
Number of Observational Data	1000	1000	1000	1000	1000

1. UGARCH Model

Different explanatory variables are used in each set of UGARCH models. Three stock index yields are used in the Chinese mainland equations: the Shanghai Composite Index, the Shanghai Financial Index, and the FXI Index respectively. In the Hong Kong SAR equation, the Hang Seng Index and the Hang Seng Financial Index are used.

In the following parts, the impact of subprime mortgage events on stock yield in Chinese mainland and Hong Kong SAR will be first estimated. And the empirical results will be illustrated with the data period of January 3, 2007, to October 31, 2008, as an example.

Chinese Mainland

(1)Table 28 shows the empirical results for the event equation for the Chinese mainland.

Table 28. Regression results of the event model: China

		January 1, 2007–October 31, 2008			2005年1月1日到2008年10月31日		
		Model 1	**Model 2**	**Model 3**	**Mode 1**	**Mode 2**	**Mode 3**
	Strain Variable	**SSE Composite Index**	**SSE Financial Index**	**iShares FTSE / Xinhua China 25 Index (FXI)**	**SSE Composite Index**	**SSE Financial Index**	**iShares FTSE / Xinhua China 25 Index (FXI)**
Mean Value Equation	Intercept Term	−0.0035 (0.0081)	−0.0012 (0.0095)	−0.0166* (0.0089)	0.0024 (0.0032)	0.0051 (0.0042)	0.0016 (0.0041)
	Daily Stock Yield (1 period lag)	−0.0576 (0.0565)	−0.0188 (0.0577)	−0.2348*** (0.0518)	−0.0298 (0.0328)	−0.0557 (0.0357)	−0.1233*** (0.0352)
	U.S.-China Spread	−0.0036** (0.0017)	−0.0030 (0.002)	−0.0043** (0.002)	−0.0012** (0.005)	−0.0012* (0.0007)	−0.0008 (0.0007)
	Macroeconomic News Industrial Production Growth Rate	0.0002 (0.0045)	−0.0002 (0.0069)	0.0064 (0.0054)	0.002 (0.0008)	0.0001 (0.001)	0.0008 (0.001)
	Trade Surplus	−0.007 (0.0035)	−0.0007 (0.0038)	−0.002*** (0.0007)	0.0004 (0.0007)	0.0005 (0.0009)	−0.0003 (0.0006)
	Broad Money Growth Rate	0.0028 (0.0081)	0.0001 (0.0099)	0.0073 (0.0117)	0.0015 (0.0052)	0.0021 (0.0078)	0.0010 (0.0043)
	Inflation Rate	−0.0117 (0.0095)	−0.0052 (0.0172)	−0.0168* (0.0088)	0.0002 (0.0057)	0.0019 (0.0095)	0.0052 (0.0047)
	Global Financial Market Volatility VIX	−0.0297* (0.0176)	−0.0184 (0.0219)	0.0280 (0.0334)	−0.0286* (0.0151)	−0.0293 (0.0192)	0.0155 (0.0202)
	Interest Rate Volatility	0.0053 (0.008)	0.0024 (0.0099)	0.0066 (0.0107)	0.0007 (0.0046)	−0.0008 (0.006)	−0.0039 (0.0057)
	Subprime Debts	−0.0034 (0.0027)	−0.0051 (0.0032)	−0.0042 (0.0033)	−0.0005 (0.00023)	−0.0016 (0.0028)	−0.0044 (0.0032)
	Intercept Term of Variance Equation	0.0001* (0.0001)	0.0002** (0.0001)	0.0000 (0)	0*** (0)	0** (0)	0*** (0)

Continued

	January 1, 2007–October 31, 2008			2005年1月1日到2008年10月31日		
	Model 1	Model 2	Model 3	Mode 1	Mode 2	Mode 3
Strain Variable	SSE Composite Index	SSE Financial Index	iShares FTSE / Xinhua China 25 Index (FXI)	SSE Composite Index	SSE Financial Index	iShares FTSE / Xinhua China 25 Index (FXI)
ARCH Item (a)	0.081** (0.0358)	0.0962** (0.0468)	0.0761*** (0.0237)	0.0568*** (0.0098)	0.0326*** (0.0075)	0.0941*** (0.0157)
GARCH Term (β)	0.6677*** (0.1482)	0.5782*** (0.1752)	0.8661*** (0.039)	0.9183*** (0.0138)	0.9524*** (0.0129)	0.8579*** (0.0243)
Subprime Debts	0.0001 (0)	0.0002* (0.0001)	0.0002*** (0.0001)	0*** (0)	0* (0)	0.0002*** (0)

Note: The explanatory variable is the daily stock yield lagged by 1 period. All equations are GARCH (1, 1) models with maximum likelihood estimation and Berndt-Hall-Hall-Hausman (BHHH) maximum algorithm. Standard errors are in parentheses.

***, **, and * respectively denote significant at the 1%, 5%, and 10% levels.

We will first pay attention to the intercept term and the lagged daily stock yields. The intercept terms for both the Shanghai Composite Index equation and the Financial Index are not noticeable. The FXI index, on the other hand, is significant at the 10% level. The negative intercept term for the FXI indicates that given other equal conditions, the FXI index falls by an average of 0.02% per day. Also, stock returns with a lag of 1 period are significant in the FXI model. The unique performance of the FXI may be related to the fact that all stocks listed in the FXI are listed in Hong Kong SAR. Evidently, they are all more susceptible to international markets.

Next is the effects of various macroeconomic and financial control variables. Interest rate differentials are statistically significant, however, the coefficients in SSE Composite and FXI equations are negative, which indicates that monetary tightening is effective in controlling stock price inflation. Most of the domestic macroeconomic financial unexpected information variables are also statistically insignificant. These results suggest that unexpected information about domestic macroeconomic finance hardly affects Chinese mainland stock yields.[4]

[4] Other variables may be more explanatory. For example, since 2005, the reform of non-tradable shares has greatly promoted the efficiency of resource allocation in the stock market and the rise of stock prices. Since the purpose of this chapter is to discuss the international

We now take a look at the impact of external shocks on equity yields. Global market volatility and subprime events are insignificant in all these three models, which suggests that the external shocks hardly affect Chinese mainland stock returns.

The variance results of the UGARCH model are shown in the lower part of Table 28. We find that the coefficients of ARCH, GARCH and subprime events are all significantly positive, indicating that subprime events increase the conditional volatility of the Shanghai Financial Index and the FXI Index. Moreover, the coefficients of these variance equations are also positive. In addition, in all cases, $\alpha_1 + \beta_1$ is less than one, yielding an infinite estimate of the positive unconditional variance. Subprime events are significant in both the Shanghai Composite and FXI equations, suggesting that the Shanghai Financial and FXI indices respond to external shocks from the United States.

1.1 Hong Kong SAR, China

Table 29 presents the empirical results on the event equation for Hong Kong SAR. They have some similarities with the results for the Chinese mainland, for example, none of the domestic macroeconomic variables are significant. But they are somewhat different as well. First, the intercept term in the Hong Kong SAR equation is positive, indicating that given all else equal, Hong Kong SAR stock prices increase by 0.01% per day on average. Second, the difference in interest rates between Hong Kong SAR and the United States. is also highly significant, but with a positive sign. It reflects the fact that Hong Kong SAR, as an international financial center, can attract capital to the Hong Kong SAR stock market when interest rates are higher than those in the United States. Third, the VIX variable is highly significant in the Hong Kong SAR equation, indicating that market volatility has a negative impact on Hong Kong SAR stock yields. Fourth, the subprime event variable is significant not only in the variance equation (with a positive coefficient) but also in the mean equation (with a negative coefficient), indicating that subprime events have a significant impact on both the level and volatility of Hong Kong SAR stock returns.

---

transmission of stock prices and volatility, other explanatory variables of the Chinese mainland stock market are not discussed in depth in this chapter.

Table 29. Regression results of the event model: Hong Kong SAR

		January 1, 2007–October 31, 2008		January 1, 2005–October 31, 2008	
		Model 1	**Model 2**	**Model 1**	**Model 2**
	Strain Variable	**Hang Seng Index**	**Hang Seng Finance Indexes**	**Hang Seng Index**	**Hang Seng Finance Indexes**
Mean Value Equation	Daily Stock Yield (lagged one period)	−0.0685 (0.0545)	−0.0288 (0.0546)	−0.0232 (0.0376)	0.0238 (0.0356)
	US-China Spread	0.0047 (0.0018)	0.0052 (0.0016)	−0.0002 (0.0006)	−0.0003 (0.0004)
	Macroeconomic News Trade Surplus	0 (0.0001)	0 (0.0001)	0 (0.0002)	0 (0.0001)
	Broad money Growth Rate	0 (0.0003)	−0.0001 (0.0003)	−0.0001 (0.0001)	−0.0001** (0.0001)
	Inflation Rate	0.0004 (0.0081)	0 (0.007)	0.0039 (0.0038)	0.0029 (0.0029)
	Global Financial Market Volatility VIX	−0.0439*** (0.0162)	−0.0389** (0.0157)	−0.034*** (0.0106)	−0.0221** (0.0092)
	Interest Rate Volatility	0.0027 (0.0034)	0.004 (0.0032)	0.0018 (0.0027)	0.0012 (0.0022)
	Subprime Debts	−0.0043 (0.0021)	−0.0037 (0.0019)	−0.0023 (0.0019)	−0.0019 (0.0017)
	Intercept Term of Variance Equation	0 (0)	0 (0)	0*** (0)	0*** (0)
	ARCH item (a)	0.1556*** (0.0397)	0.1843*** (0.0384)	0.0952*** (0.0176)	0.1174*** (0.0181)
	GARCH Item (β)	0.8068*** (0.0526)	0.7943*** (0.0409)	0.8515*** (0.0292)	0.8327*** (0.0216)
	Subprime Debts	0.0001** (0)	0.0001*** (0)	0.0001*** (0)	0.0001*** (0)

Note: The explanatory variable is the daily stock yield lagged by 1 period. All equations are GARCH (1, 1) models with maximum likelihood estimation and Berndt-Hall-Hall-Hausman (BHHH) maximum algorithm. Standard errors are in parentheses.

***, **, * respectively indicates significant at the 1%, 5%, and 10% levels.

Table 30. Estimated coefficients of the conditional mean equation: Composite Index

	January 1, 2007–October 31, 2008						January 1, 2005–October 31, 2008					
	America (i=1)		China (i=2)		Hong Kong SAR (i=3)		America (i=1)		China (i=2)		Hong Kong SAR (i=3)	
	Coefficient	Standard errors	Coefficient	Standard errors	Coefficient	Standard errors	Coefficient	Standard errors	Coefficient	Standard errors	Coefficient	Standard errors
α	0.00	(0.0004)	0.01	(0.0066)	0.0058**	(0.0026)	0.0005**	(0.0002)	0.00	(0.0028)	0.0038***	(0.0013)
α_{i1}	−0.0868*	(0.0469)	0.2651***	(0.0613)	0.7569***	(0.0465)	-0.0662**	(0.0333)	0.1951***	(0.0445)	0.6051***	(0.0306)
α_{i2}	0.01	(0.0173)	−0.07	(0.0533)	−0.0694***	(0.0265)	0.02	(0.0146)	-0.02	(0.0292)	0.00	(0.0161)
α_{i3}	−0.0531**	(0.0256)	0.01	(0.0513)	−0.04	(0.0397)	−0.0681***	(0.0208)	0.02	(0.0346)	−0.0669**	(0.0276)

Note: The DiagonalVECH model is used. All equations are GARCH (1, 1) models with maximum likelihood estimation and the Berndt-Hall-Hall-Hausman (BHHH) maximum algorithm. Standard errors are in parentheses.

***, **, * respectively indicates significant at the 1%, 5%, and 10% levels.

Source: Bloomberg Consulting database; according to author's calculations.

2. MGARCH model

Two sets of MGARCH models are computed by using the composite and financial indices of Chinese mainland, Hong Kong SAR, and the United States, respectively. The estimated coefficients and standard errors of the conditional mean equations of the composite indices are shown in Table 30.

The price spillover effect from the United States to Hong Kong SAR is more significant than from the U.S. to the Chinese mainland, with coefficients of 0.76 and 0.27, respectively. It reflects the reality of the Chinese mainland's low financial openness.

In this chapter, the conditional variance covariance equation in the UGARCH model effectively captures the volatility of these three markets and cross-market volatility. Table 31 illustrates the estimated coefficients of the variance and covariance integrated index equations. These coefficients quantify the impact of current or lagged own and cross-market shocks on own and cross-market volatility in other markets.

The auto-volatility is large and significant in all three markets, indicating the presence of a significant ARCH effect. Specifically, the coefficient of auto-volatility is 0.04 for the U.S. and 0.13 and 0.16 respectively for the Chinese mainland and Hong Kong SAR. These results are consistent with previous research that the spillover effects of auto-volatility are generally larger in emerging markets than in developed countries (Worthington & Higgs, 2001). In terms of cross-market volatility, the spillover effects between the United States and Chinese mainland, and between the United States and HK SAR are 0.07 and 0.08, respectively. While the spillover effect of cross-market volatility between the Chinese mainland and HK SAR is 0.15, larger than that of its two counterparts. This also indicates that the financial integration between the Chinese mainland and H K SAR is deepening.

Regarding the GARCH equation, most of the estimated coefficients are significant. The coefficients of lagged volatility for the United States and Hong Kong SAR are 0.97 and 0.83, respectively, while the coefficient of lagged volatility for the Chinese mainland is insignificant. This indicates that the lagged volatility between developed and open financial markets is larger. In addition, the spillover effects of cross-market volatility between the United States and China and between the United States and Hong Kong SAR are 0.40 and 0.90, respectively. And the spillover effect of cross-market volatility between the Chinese mainland and Hong Kong SAR is 0.37. That is, the past volatility in the U.S. market has a greater impact on future volatility in Hong Kong SAR than on future volatility in the Chinese mainland, which further indicates that Hong Kong SAR, an international financial center, is more vulnerable to external shocks. In addition, the lower cross-market volatility between the Chinese mainland and Hong Kong

Table 31. Estimated coefficients of variance and covariance equations: Composite Index

	January 1, 2007–October 31, 2008						January 1, 2005–October 31, 2008					
	America (i=1)		China (i=2)		Hong Kong SAR (i=3)		America (i=1)		China (i=2)		Hong Kong SAR (i=3)	
	Coefficient	Standard errors	Coefficient	Standard errors	Coefficient	Standard errors	Coefficient	Standard errors	Coefficient	Standard errors	Coefficient	Standard errors
Mi1	0.00	(0)	0***	(0)	0**	(0)	0	(0)	0	(0)	0	(0)
Mi2	0***	(0)	0***	(0)	0***	(0)	0	(0)	0***	(0)	0	(0)
Mi3	0**	(0)	0***	(0)	0***	(0)	0	(0)	0	(0)	0	(0)
Ai1	0.0408***	(0.0094)	0.0733***	(0.0162)	0.0808***	(0.0144)	0.0385***	(0.0068)	0.037***	(0.0054)	0.0501***	(0.0065)
Ai2	0.0733***	(0.0162)	0.1315***	(0.0496)	0.145***	(0.036)	0.037***	(0.0054)	0.0354***	(0.0076)	0.0481***	(0.0069)
Ai3	0.0808***	(0.0144)	0.145***	(0.036)	0.1598***	(0.038)	0.0501***	(0.0065)	0.0481***	(0.0069)	0.0652***	(0.0105)
Bi1	0.9707***	(0.0073)	0.4028***	(0.1424)	0.8987***	(0.0182)	0.9691***	(0.0052)	0.9628***	(0.0053)	0.9586***	(0.0048)
Bi2	0.4028***	(0.1424)	0.17	(0.1182)	0.3729***	(0.1364)	0.9628***	(0.0053)	0.9565***	(0.0092)	0.9523***	(0.006)
Bi3	0.8987***	(0.0182)	0.3729***	(0.1364)	0.832***	(0.0329)	0.9586***	(0.0048)	0.9523***	(0.006)	0.9482***	(0.0076)

Note: We use the common DiagonalVECH model. All equations are GARCH (1, 1) models with maximum likelihood estimation and the Berndt-Hall-Hall-Hausman (BHHH) maximum algorithm. Standard errors are in parentheses.

***, **, * respectively indicate significant at the 1%, 5%, and 10% levels.

Source: Bloomberg Consulting database; according to author's calculations.

Table 32. Estimated coefficients of the conditional mean equation: Financial Stock Index

	January 1, 2007–October 31, 2008						January 1, 2005–October 31, 2008					
	America (i=1)		China (i=2)		Hong Kong SAR (i=3)		America (i=1)		China (i=2)		Hong Kong SAR (i=3)	
	Coefficient	Standard errors	Coefficient	Standard errors	Coefficient	Standard errors	Coefficient	Standard errors	Coefficient	Standard errors	Coefficient	Standard errors
α	0.00	(0.0005)	0.01	(0.0078)	0.00	(0.0027)	0.00	(0.0003)	0.0074*	(0.0038)	0.0027**	(0.0011)
$\alpha i1$	-0.05	(0.0428)	0.2461***	(0.0423)	0.3353***	(0.0259)	-0.05	(0.0316)	0.2101***	(0.0398)	0.3076***	(0.0183)
$\alpha i2$	0.02	(0.014)	0.00	(0)	0***	(0)	0.01	(0.0126)	0.00	(0)	0***	(0)
$\alpha i3$	-0.1591***	(0.04)	-0.01	(0.0525)	-0.05	(0.0389)	-0.0913***	(0.0323)	0.03	(0.0459)	-0.01	(0.0266)

Note: The DiagonalVECH model is used. All equations are GARCH (1, 1) models with maximum likelihood estimation and the Berndt-Hall-Hall-Hausman (BHHH) maximum algorithm. Standard errors are in parentheses.

***, **, * respectively indicate significant at the 1%, 5%, and 10% levels.

Source: Bloomberg Consulting database; author's calculations.

Table 33. Estimated coefficients of variance and covariance equations: Financial Stock Index

	January 1, 2007–October 31, 2008						January 1, 2005–October 31, 2008					
	America (i=1)		China (i=2)		Hong Kong SAR (i=3)		America (i=1)		China (i=2)		Hong Kong SAR (i=3)	
	Coefficient	Standard errors	Coefficient	Standard errors	Coefficient	Standard errors	Coefficient	Standard errors	Coefficient	Standard errors	Coefficient	Standard errors
Mi1	0.00	(0)	0.00	(0)	0.00	(0)	0	(0)	0	(0)	0	(0)
Mi2	0.00	(0)	0**	(0)	0*	(0)	0	(0)	0	(0)	0**	(0)
Mi3	0.00	(0)	0*	(0)	0.00	(0)	0	(0)	0**	(0)	0**	(0)
Ai1	0.0195***	(0.0054)	0.0317***	(0.0086)	0.0468***	(0.0081)	0.0488***	(0.0082)	0.0292***	(0.0042)	0.0584***	(0.007)
Ai2	0.0317***	(0.0086)	0.0516**	(0.0229)	0.0761***	(0.0189)	0.0292***	(0.0042)	0.0175***	(0.0039)	0.035***	(0.005)
Ai3	0.0468***	(0.0081)	0.0761***	(0.0189)	0.1122***	(0.0218)	0.0584***	(0.007)	0.035***	(0.005)	0.07***	(0.0109)
Bi1	0.9919***	(0.0049)	0.9338***	(0.0268)	0.9487***	(0.0087)	0.9615***	(0.0064)	0.9728***	(0.0037)	0.9488***	(0.006)
Bi2	0.9338***	(0.0268)	0.8791***	(0.0499)	0.8932***	(0.0276)	0.9728***	(0.0037)	0.9842***	(0.0034)	0.96***	(0.0055)
Bi3	0.9487***	(0.0087)	0.8932***	(0.0276)	0.9074***	(0.0159)	0.9488***	(0.006)	0.96***	(0.0055)	0.9363***	(0.0099)

Note: The DiagonalVECH model is used. All equations are GARCH (1, 1) models with maximum likelihood estimation and the Berndt-Hall-Hall-Hausman (BHHH) maximum algorithm. Standard errors are in parentheses.

*** indicates significance at the 1% level; ** indicates significant at the 5% level, and * indicates significance at the 10% level.

Source: Bloomberg Consulting database; author's calculations.

SAR also suggests that the impact of the United States on the Chinese mainland is greater than that of Hong Kong SAR on the Chinese mainland in terms of the persistence of cross-market volatility, which reflects the persistent impact of the Unites States as the flashpoint of the subprime crisis.

Conditional correlation analysis shows that the correlation between the United States, S & P, and the SSE is much smaller than that between the United States, S & P, and the Hang Seng. In addition, the correlation between the SSE and the Hang Seng is the largest among the three markets. These results indicate that the Chinese mainland is less financially open, but the correlation between the Chinese mainland and Hong Kong SAR has exceeded the correlation between the Chinese mainland and the United States, reflecting the increasing financial integration between the Chinese mainland and Hong Kong SAR (Figure 46).

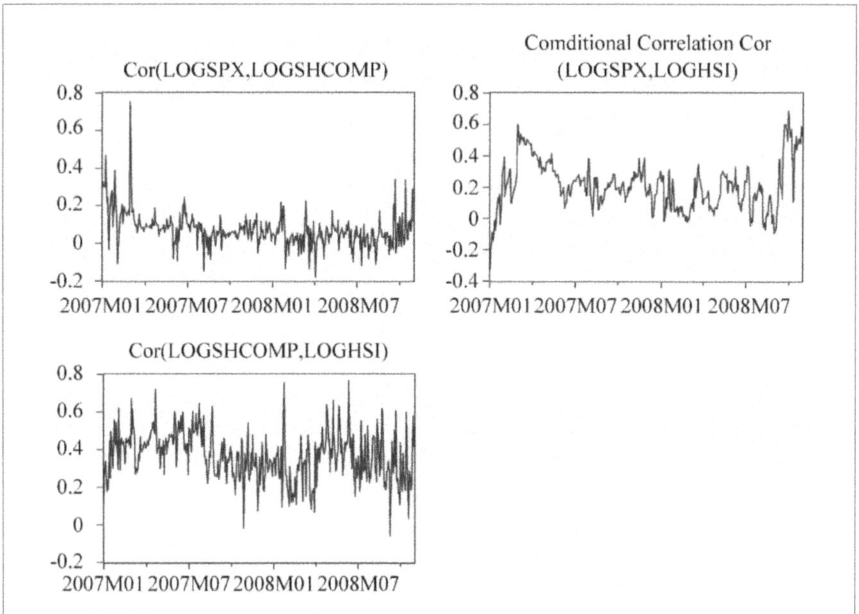

Figure 46. Conditional correlations for each composite index (January 1, 2007–October 31, 2008)

Source: Bloomberg Consulting database; according to author's calculations.

To assess the reliability of these results, robustness tests were conducted. In addition to various explanatory and explained variables, the robustness tests were performed on the UGARCH and MGARCH models by adjusting the sample period with the starting time delayed from 2007 to 2005. The results of the mean and variance equations derived using the financial stock indices are similar to the previous results (Table 32, Table 33, Figure 47). Overall, our results are more robust to both explanatory and explained variables with different sample periods (Table 30 to Table 33).

7.6 Conclusions and Policy Recommendations

This chapter finds that, whether from the perspective of stock price level or stock price volatility, the subprime mortgage crisis in the United States has significantly affected Chinese mainland stock market and more greatly impacted the Hong Kong SAR stock market. And the historical volatility of the American stock market has a more lasting impact on Hong Kong SAR's future volatility than that of Chinese mainland market. These results show that Hong Kong SAR's position as an international financial center is more vulnerable to external impacts. In addition, the volatility of the U.S. stock market has a more lasting impact on the Chinese mainland stock market than the volatility of the Hong Kong SAR stock market, which reflects that the United States is the birthplace of the subprime mortgage crisis. Finally, as one might expect, Hong Kong SAR and the Chinese mainland are more connected than they are to the United States, suggesting greater financial integration between Hong Kong SAR and the Chinese mainland.

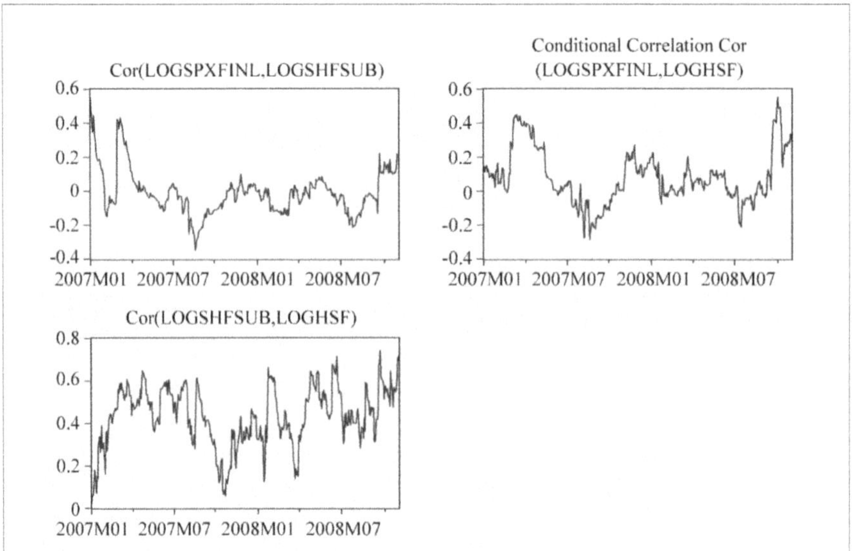

Figure 47. Conditional Correlation of Financial Indices (January 1, 2007–October 31, 2008)

Source: Bloomberg Consulting database; calculated by the author.

1. No economy is entirely immune from the subprime mortgage crisis, as shown by our regression results. Although the Chinese mainland and Hong Kong SAR were not directly affected at the beginning of the subprime mortgage crisis, as the crisis intensified, various direct and indirect impacts became increasingly significant, and financial markets were largely influenced by the monetary and financial conditions in the United States. The Chinese mainland and Hong Kong SAR have involved in the global financial system in greater depth and breadth, and the authorities should pay close attention to the external negative impact.
2. Pay close attention to the impact of the subprime mortgage crisis spreading from the financial sector to the physical sector. Although our research mainly focuses on the financial sector, that is, the impact of the subprime mortgage crisis on the stock market, in fact, the impact of the subprime mortgage crisis has already spread from the financial sector to the real economy. The shrinking volume of global trade, the recession of the world economy, and the following massive unemployment and livelihood problems are all challenges faced by countries all over the world. How to take more effective measures to consolidate and accelerate economic recovery is still the most urgent task for governments of all countries at present.
3. The importance of international policy coordination. The impact of the U.S. subprime mortgage crisis on the Chinese mainland and Hong Kong SAR, and the closer linkage between the Chinese mainland and Hong Kong SAR stock markets, reflect the importance of international policy coordination in an era of economic globalization. An important lesson from the Great Depression of the 1930s was that instead of coordinating their actions, the countries acted individually and even adopted "beggar-thy-neighbor" policies, thus prolonging the depression. After the outbreak of the current subprime mortgage crisis, countries realized the importance of unified action and international policy coordination. Through various platforms such as G20 summits and BRIC summits, governments have done their best to be in the same direction, though the intensity may vary, in terms of bailout plans, fiscal stimulus packages, prevention of trade protectionism and whether to consider policy withdrawal, especially the coordination and cooperation between developed economies and emerging market economies has reached an unprecedented level, all of which have undoubtedly become the important conditions for the world economy to weather the crisis more quickly.
4. China's opening-up to the outside world, especially capital account liberalization, needs to be advanced cautiously. With increasingly open trade and more and more financial spillovers from international markets, the

capital account has in fact become increasingly open, despite government controls (Prasad & Rajan, 2008). In such a natural opening process, it is urgent for policy authorities to strengthen financial markets and related infrastructure, such as governance structure, exchange rate mechanism, regulatory system, etc., to cope with de facto capital account liberalization. It is generally believed that during the Asian financial crisis, China suffered less because it was not open enough. There is another argument that China did not lose because it was not in the game at all. And current smaller losses associated with the subprime crisis are also related to China's low-level financial openness. This seems to suggest that financial non-opening is instead an umbrella against external impacts. But the fact is that in the era of financial globalization, the limited financial openness, that is, the so-called de facto financial liberalization, which has isolated China from the outside world, will be increasingly difficult to maintain in the future. Therefore, the key issue is not to stop the pace of capital opening, but to find the appropriate way and at what pace to promote capital account opening.

Global Imbalances and Financial Crises: A Perspective of Monetary Hegemony

Since August 2007, the U.S. subprime crisis has evolved into a global financial crisis. The developed economies at the center of the crisis and the emerging market economies on the periphery have been greatly impacted. However, the crisis is still spreading from the financial sector to the real economy. The most serious financial crisis since the Great Depression is adjusting the strong global growth cycle in the past few years, and a world recession is inevitable.

Perhaps, people are not unfamiliar with the crisis; its mechanism and consequences have been under investigation for a long while. However, there is not much in-depth discussion of the crisis in orthodox economics, and the textbooks just discuss it in columns. Because orthodox economics assumes that the market operates as usual, and that the crisis is an extreme situation. The emergence of the crisis is the greatest irony and challenge to orthodox economics. Although Summers (1989) made a genius imagination of a more serious financial crisis 20 years ago, and the mechanism and consequences of the crisis envisaged by Summers (1989) are quite consistent with the current subprime crisis, his proposition that the United States institutional "firewall" might prevent the crisis from spreading from the financial sector to the real economy was merely his wishful thinking. As a financial historian, Jindelberg (2007) has a classic summary of the crisis. His story-telling description is now gradually replaced by a large number of empirical analyses by Reinhart and Rogoff (2008a; 2008b; 2009) et al. Although these historical studies with large time span and geographical span are very helpful to establish a real crisis economics, there is little in-depth analysis of the crisis. In fact, when the once-in-a-century major crisis comes up, people still seem unprepared, in theoretical analysis or policy practice. Now, it seems that most academic research and policy measures are trying to answer the following questions: what causes this crisis; is it different from previous crises, or is it just a reproduction of history? How did the crisis spread and how did the economies response? How can we get out of the crisis? How can we avoid the recurrence of the crisis?

This chapter will focus on the above issues. The first section provides the historical review and literature review of global imbalances and financial crises, pointing out the internal relationship between imbalances and crises. The second section reveals the institutional background and underlying causes of the crisis by constructing a mathematical model, especially emphasizing the important role played by the international dollar standard or dollar hegemony. The last part is the summary and policy recommendations of the whole chapter.

8.1 From Imbalances to Crises: A Historical Review

1. Global Imbalances and Global Liquidity Surplus Since the New Century

Global imbalances have become increasingly prominent since the twenty-first century. On the one hand, the current account of the United States continues to deteriorate, and the net external debt continues to build up; on the other hand, emerging market countries including China and some petroleum-exporting countries have continued to run surpluses and accumulated large amounts of U.S. dollar reserves. In absolute terms, China's current account surplus in 2007 was $371.8 billion, and the United States' current account deficit in 2007 reached $731.2 billion. China's surplus was roughly half of the United States' deficit. In terms of relative volume, China's surplus in 2007 accounted for 11.3% of its GDP, and the United States' deficit in 2007 accounted for 5.3% of its GDP (Figure 48). In addition, Figure 48 shows that China's surplus became significant around 2003, and the United States' deficit began to deteriorate rapidly around 1997.

In addition to global imbalances, another noteworthy phenomenon since the twenty-first century is the global liquidity surplus, specifically: First, since the mid-1990s, the real interest rate of the major developed economies has experienced a continuous decline. From 2005 to 2006, the real interest rate of the 10-year national debt of the major countries was generally below 2% and is thus referred to as an unprecedented low-interest rate by many institutions and economists. Second, low-interest rates are only one side of liquidity surplus, which is generally measured from the total amount of money and credit. Since the high-powered money created by the central bank in the modern financial system only accounts for a small part of the total amount of money and credit, liquidity surplus is hard to measure and is more or less debated (Rüffer & Stracca, 2006). Morgan Stanley's research suggested that liquidity surplus can be defined as the ratio of the total

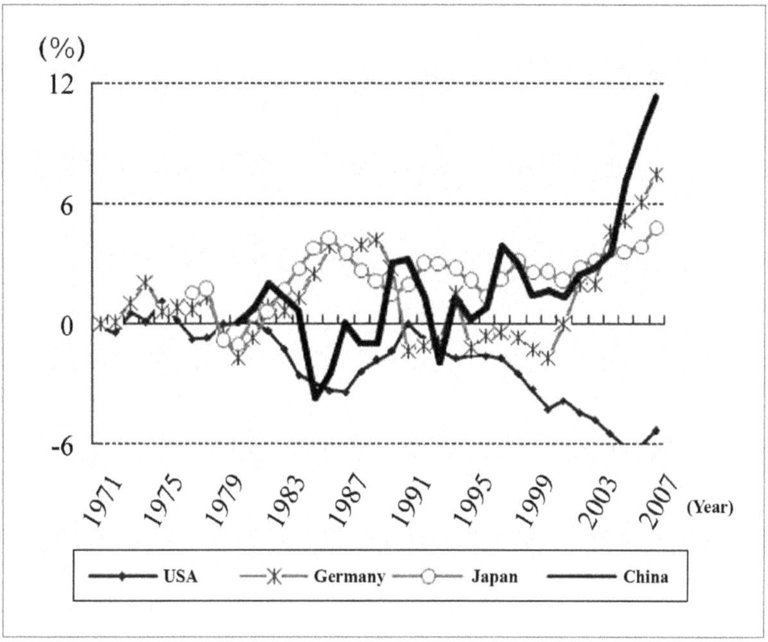

Figure 48. Current account/GDP

Source: IMF World Economic Outlook Databases.

amount of money to nominal GDP, namely "Marshall K value." Their research showed that the world economy experienced an obvious liquidity boom from 2002 to 2006. Driven by this, the asset price foam continued to expand and burst from 2007 to 2008 (Fels, 2005; 2009). Figure 49 shows the year-on-year growth rate of the RMB loan balance of financial institutions in China from 2006 to 2008. As shown in Figure 49, this indicator rose sharply in the middle of 2006, and began to decline in 2008, but quickly returned to its previous high in December. The excess growth of loans, which began to highlight in 2006, partly reflects the impact of the global liquidity surplus on China. The fall in 2008 indicates that a series of previous austerity measures have begun to take effect and may be caused by the impact of other external shocks (this cannot be excluded). The rapid rebound in December should be a result of the government's economic stimulus measures.

2. Global Economic Imbalances Since the Second World War: A Historical Review

From "new economy" to "great moderation," since the new century, the world economy under the leadership of the United States seems to show people an unusual

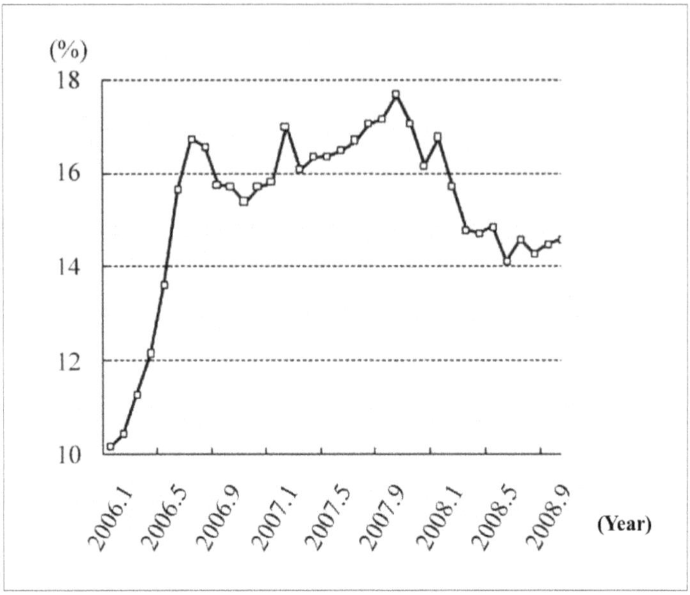

Figure 49. Loan growth rate of financial institutions in China

Source: The People's Bank of China

new future. However, the bursting of the Internet foam has made "new economy" no longer attractive, and the recent outbreak of the global financial crisis has also dissipated the optimism of "great moderation." Facts have proved that the new century is not so different. The words "Great Depression" and "stagflation" have showed up frequently recently, indicating that people have vaguely noted the similarities between the current economic situation and some historical events. Economists with a sense of history prefer to seek inspiration and answers from history. Because those factors at the institutional level are much more stable than the volatile economic phenomena. By examining these factors, we can expose the common nature of those seemingly different economic phenomena.

Like the financial crisis, global imbalances are nothing new. Bergstein (2005: 29) pointed out when talking about global imbalances that: "In fact, after the Second World War, this is at least the fifth time the similar thing comes out: the sharp appreciation of the United States dollar has seriously deteriorated the current account, which in turn has built up the pressure of domestic trade protectionism and growing concern about the collapse of the United States dollar, and then the problem was solved through more or less disorderly exchange rate readjustment and temporary measures of major countries."

Bergstein (2005:30) also noted the relationship between this imbalance and the international monetary system: "In recent years, all the debates on how to strengthen the "international financial structure" have focused on the issue of emerging market economies, ignoring the countries and currencies at the center of the system. In the next few years, the main goal of the United States foreign economic policy should be to study, propose and discuss the improvement of the international monetary system, so as to reduce the possibility of continued serious currency dislocation and economic imbalances."

From the end of the Second World War to 1958, the balance of payments of the United States was neglected in a benign manner. During this period, the production capacity of other major countries was seriously impaired in the Second World War, while the production capacity of the United States was gradually strengthened. These countries had to import large amounts of American goods for post-war reconstruction, so the United States once had a large balance of payments surplus, and its gold reserves also climbed to the peak. Although the credit of the dollar was unquestionable, the United States failed to provide the much-needed liquidity to the world, resulting in a shortage of dollars. This contradiction was eventually resolved through large-scale foreign aid and gifts from the United States, which was mixed with geopolitical factors in the Cold War era, reflecting the consideration of the United States for its long-term strategic interests. Since 1958, the domestic production capacity of Europe and Japan was gradually recovered, so was the convertibility of the currencies of major countries. The aforementioned situation rapidly reversed. Throughout the 1960s, the United States remained or shrinking surplus in the trade balance and current accounts. At the same time, the long-term capital flow balance deficit resulted in a deficit in the basic balance. This led to the continuous reduction of the gold reserves of the United States and the continuous growth of its external debt. The balance of payments problem thus became a malignant priority, drawing the foreshadowing for the final collapse of the Bretton Woods system.[1,2]

Figure 48 shows the current account changes in the United States, Germany, Japan and China from the 1970s to the twenty-first century. Among them, in the 1970s, the United States experienced two relatively mild deficits, corresponding to the surpluses of Germany and Japan. Throughout the 1980s, the United States

---

1 For a detailed discussion of the external imbalances of the United States in the 1960s, please refer to Eichengren (2000).

2 The former is also known as the "savings surplus" view, and the latter is also known as the "double deficit" view. This is similar to the debate between China and the United States in recent years. The comparison of these two periods can be referred to Ito (2009), which supported the "double deficit" view.

had a serious current account deficit, received support from Japan and Germany. In the early 1990s, the current account of the United States improved, and the surpluses of Japan and Germany decreased by varying degrees. Following the Asian financial crisis into the twenty-first century, in addition to Japan and Germany, China and emerging markets in Asia have become the main forces supporting the current account deficit of the United States, resulting in an unprecedented huge deficit in the United States.

Concerning the world economy in the 1970s, it is generally believed that the two oil crises led to "stagflation" in the western world. Recently, some scholars questioned this view and believed that the "stagflation" was mainly caused by the fluctuation of the total amount of money and the reform of the monetary system (Barsky & Kilian, 2001; Knotek, 2006). In 1971, when governments and the public generally lost confidence in the dollar, the Nixon administration finally chose to close the gold window and completely cut the convertibility ties between the dollar and gold. This is a major change in the international monetary system. Since then, the currency issuance of the United States has no longer been subject to its own gold reserves. In 1971 and 1972, the money supply of the United States increased significantly. The growth rate of M2 increased from 4% in 1970 to more than 12%, higher than the average level of 7% in the 1960s. The growth rate decreased in the following three years, but it bounced back above 12% again in 1976 and 1977. Meanwhile, the current account of the United States showed a slight deficit for the first time in 1971, and reached a relatively significant level in 1972, 1977 and 1978. Throughout the 1970s, except Germany, other major developed countries experienced double-digit inflation. The unemployment rate in all countries other than Japan increased significantly and lasted until the mid-1980s. At the same time, the economy slowed down throughout the world. The external imbalances in the 1970s did not attract too much attention, because compared with severe inflation and unemployment, imbalances are just a minor by-product.

In the mid-1980s, the United States had a very serious current account deficit, which could be directly attributed to the sharp appreciation of the U.S. dollar exchange rate. From 1979 to 1985, the real trade-weighted exchange rate of the U.S. dollar rose by more than 70%. Some scholars, from the standpoint of the United States, stress that Japan, the main surplus country, should be responsible for this imbalance, because Japan deliberately manipulated its exchange rate in order to promote exports, and Japan's closed and backward financial markets led to excess domestic savings. Other scholars put forward an opposite view from the standpoint of the late-developing countries, that the imbalance was essentially caused by the huge fiscal expenditure of the United States, which was blamed for the low savings in the United States.2 Feldstein (2000: 58–59) provided a transmission mechanism from budget deficit to trade deficit, that is, the budget deficit drove up real interest rate, which in turn led to the rise of the exchange rate of the U.S. dollar and resulted in the trade deficit. In addition, data shows that despite Volcker's tightening policy in the early 1980s, the growth rate of the money supply in the United States from 1981 to 1986 was not low, with M2 growing by 9.2%, slightly lower than the average growth rate of 10% in the 1970s, but much higher than the 7% in the 1960s. This imbalance was finally corrected through the devaluation of the U.S. dollar. By 1991, the U.S. current account was restored to balance, and the real exchange rate of the U.S. dollar fell back to around the level of 1979. These adjustments were represented by the "Plaza Agreement" in 1985 and the "Louvre Agreement" in 1987. Some economists believe that international policy coordination under these two agreements should be responsible for the collapse of the U.S. stock market in 1987 and the subsequent Japanese asset foam. In addition to the exchange rate, the fiscal deficit of the United States continued to improve from 1987 to 1989, the growth of money supply also declined from 1987, and this trend continued until 1995.[3]

From the above review, we can see that, first of all, because of its special position in the world economy, the United States has always played an important role in past global imbalances. Secondly, after the collapse of the Bretton Woods system, the global economy landscape has undergone major changes.[4] The current account of the United States experienced serious deficits from time to time. Finally, the expansionary monetary and fiscal policies of the United States are often served as the sparks of global imbalances.

Although the opinions on the causes of the subprime crisis vary, the following two views are representative (White, 2008): (1) the current crisis is different, and is caused by some special factors, such as financial innovation and a large number of financial derivatives, and (2) the current crisis is similar, with superficial representation and transmission mechanism. Reinhart and Rogoff (2008a) reviewed the crises of the past eight centuries and believed that they generally arose under the interest rate shocks from the financial center countries and the commodity price shocks. This is also the characteristic of the current round of subprime

3 M2 and M3 caliber. The change of M1 was relatively drastic, with a significant increase in 1992.

4 At least three important changes deserve attention: (1) the exchange rate because more volatile, more sustained, but less correlated with the real economy; (2) financial and economic crises frequently occurred (Goldberg, 2007; Reinhart & Rogoff, 2008); (3) the net income of the United States' external debt has increased significantly, turning the United States into a world's speculative capitalist from a world's banker (Gourinchas & Rey, 2005b).

crisis. Reinhart and Rogoff (2008b) further pointed out that the developed and developing countries experienced crisis of similar incidence.

In the current discussion, the first view is dominant. On the one hand, many people have long complained about the complex and non-transparent financial innovation, and vented their anger based on the ideal subject of the financial crisis. On the other hand, it seems stubborn and stupid to fall again where the predecessors have fallen many times, while making mistakes in new things can always be forgiven. However, we prefer the view of similar crisis. First, the current crisis accurately copied the classic syllogism of previous crises: credit expansion—foam burst—debt default. Secondly, blaming the crisis on financial innovation is somewhat like blaming tulip fever on tulips. Rather, the truth seems to be that financial innovation is not the root cause of the crisis, but it has accelerated the spread of the crisis and deepened the damage of the crisis.

So far, the exploration into root causes of the crisis leads us to the previous global imbalances and the associated global liquidity surplus; the discussion of global imbalances then ultimately leads us to the development and evolution of the entire international monetary system since the Second World War. Therefore, two reference points are available for the study and analysis of the financial crisis, namely examination of the previous global imbalances in recent years, and survey, verification of the international monetary system characterized by the dollar standard since the establishment of the Bretton Woods system dozens of years ago.

8.2 Literature Review: Traditional and New Perspectives

A large number of research literature on global imbalances have emerged since the twenty-first century. Relevant literature covers a vast ground in the field, among others, global savings surplus (Bernanke, 2005), Bretton Woods System II (Dooley et al., 2002s), financial dark matter (Hausmann & Sturzenegger, 2005), the most pessimistic perspective (Noubini & Setser, 2004), and global "hard asset" shortage (Caballero et al, 2008). I selected some representative and enlightening views for the following discussion.[5]

[5] Bagnai (2008) pointed out in a recent study that there are three different perspectives to discuss global imbalances: (1) the savings-investment method, which explains the global imbalances by examining the domestic savings and investment in the countries with imbalances; (2) balance of payments or elastic method, which explains global imbalances by examining exchange rates and trade flows; (3) the global portfolio method, which explains global imbalances through changes in the global financial asset stock. Starting from this division, Bagnai made a relatively comprehensive review of relevant literature. The model in this chapter is mainly constructed using the global portfolio method.

Obstfeld and Rogoff (2000) pointed out early the unsustainability of U.S. current account deficit and the impact of the corresponding adjustment. In the subsequent series of studies (Obstfeld & Rogoff, 2004; 2005), they further improved the theoretical framework and strengthened the previous views. They believed that the sudden reversal of the current account deficit in the United States was becoming more possible, and that such an adjustment would lead to a sharp and substantial depreciation of the real exchange rate of the U.S. dollar, thus bringing huge risks to the world economy. Their research did not touch the root causes of the imbalance, nor did they pay attention to the problems of liquidity surplus. Therefore, they did not expect that the final adjustment would begin with the bursting of the asset price foam and the financial crisis. Blanchard et al. (2005) attributed the current account deficit of the United States to two major factors: the rising demand for foreign products in the United States and the rising demand for U.S. assets in foreign countries. Their model showed that the changes of these two factors could explain the changes of the U.S. current account and the U.S. dollar exchange rate. They also discussed the impact of the sharp depreciation of the U.S. dollar exchange rate and believed that this would cause little damage to the U.S. economy but would cause a great negative impact on the economies of Europe and Japan.

In short, many studies have focused on the potential impact of the U.S. current account deficit and foreign debt accumulation on the U.S. dollar exchange rate from the traditional point of view, rather than the impact of liquidity surplus on asset prices. At present, the crisis is triggered by the asset price foam of global liquidity surplus, rather than the sharp depreciation of the real exchange rate of the U.S. dollar.

Regardless of the different grounds, many economists are pessimistic about the sustainability of global imbalances, but there are also a few optimists. For example, Cooper (2006) believed that the huge deficit of the United States would continue for at least one to two decades and would not be worrying. Globalization was the natural result of intertemporal transactions. Population changes, especially aging, would increase savings until after its peak. Therefore, there is no so-called "global imbalances," which is not an unbalanced state. Dooley et al. (2002; 2004a; 2004b) pointed out that the fixed exchange rate region in Asia as a new periphery has rebuilt the Bretton Woods system with the United States as the center. In this system, peripheral countries implemented export-oriented development strategies through the undervaluation of exchange rates, capital controls and national capital exports. The output of national capital was realized by accumulating central national reserve assets. The reason why peripheral countries were willing to hold low-yield reserve assets was that their domestic capital markets were inefficient and needed to use the capital markets of central countries in the form of FDI. Reserve assets can be seen as an international mortgage to guarantee the entry of private investment in the central country, which corresponded to the current account deficit of the central country. The successful implementation of this strategy would enable the peripheral countries to catch up with the central countries in economy and finally realize financial liberalization and enter the floating exchange rate system of the central countries. After Europe in the 1960s, Japan in the 1980s and emerging economies in Asia today, many countries would repeat this development strategy mistake in the foreseeable future. Therefore, the current account deficit of the United States was the basic feature of a successful international monetary system and was healthy and sustainable. This study mainly focuses on the peripheral countries and does not pay enough attention to the additional benefits gained by the central countries in this process, as well as other risks the economic policies of the central countries will cause to the global economy. The outbreak of the financial crisis shattered this optimistic view. Facts have proved that the stability and sustainability of the so-called Bretton Woods System II is questionable. However, although this study did not make a correct prediction, the research perspective is still enlightening. That is to say, the discussion of global imbalances should have historical depth, and attention should be paid to the institutional level of the international economy, namely the development and evolution of the international monetary system.

Caballero et al (2008a) are among the handful researchers to model the relationship between global imbalances and global liquidity surplus (hereinafter referred to as CFG model). They put forward two key assumptions: economic growth rate as well as supply capacity of financial assets differ from country to country. Their model includes three countries: U (the United States), E (Europe and Japan) and R (the rest economies). Among them, U and E, with the ability to provide "hard assets," are competitors in absorbing global savings, while R has no such ability. R's economic growth is strong, with a large amount of surplus savings, while E's economic growth is slower than U. The model shows that the slower E's economic growth, or the weaker R's asset supply capacity, the larger U's current account deficit, the larger its asset proportion in the global asset portfolio, and the lower the global interest rate level. This study establishes the relationship between imbalances and liquidity surplus, that is, they are the common product of changes in the global economic structure. With the outbreak and spread of the international financial crisis, Caballero et al (2008b) expanded the above model, focusing on how liquidity surplus led to foam in asset prices and sharp fluctuations in commodity prices. The CFG model is very ingenious and provides a valuable explanation for the real economy. However, the model itself also has shortcomings. First of all, the researchers do not make a convincing argument and explanation for the most critical "hard asset" hypothesis in the model. In addition to factors such as the efficiency of the financial market, there are differences in asset supply capacity between countries. Are these differences also related to the international status of currencies? Secondly, the competitive relationship between U and E in asset supply is questionable, which means that if E's economic growth is faster than U, then E will replace U and become a current account deficit country. Thirdly, the model mainly explains the current global imbalances and does not involve other imbalances in history. Do all imbalances arise from differences in growth rates and asset supply capacity of countries? Finally, because there is no money in the model, the model can only describe liquidity from the perspective of interest rate, ignoring the huge impact of money supply on the economy.

McKinnon (2005)'s research provides us with a very valuable reference for thinking about the above issues. He attributed the global imbalances to the international dollar standard. Due to historical reasons, international product trade and capital flows were mainly denominated in U.S. dollars, which made the United States "the only country that can have huge liabilities in its own currency that is immune to the risks that other countries with debts denominated in foreign currencies will generally encounter." In this case, the United States faced soft constraints on international borrowing, which ultimately led to a low savings rate in the United States. Therefore, rather than providing "hard assets," the United States is facing the soft constraint of international borrowing due to the special status of the United States dollar.

8.3 A Big-Country Model of Imbalance and Crisis: A Perspective of Monetary Hegemony

Based on the CFG (Caballero et al., 2008a) model, this section uses the Cambridge equation to introduce a currency and purchasing power parity to introduce an exchange rate and constructs a two-country model with a national currency as the international standard currency.

The model mainly discusses the global imbalances in the case of the central countries of the international monetary system. As the peripheral countries will hold the central national currency, the central country can take this opportunity to collect seigniorage from the world, giving itself the incentive to support government spending by issuing more currencies.

When the currency issue exceeds a certain point, where global liquidity and real interest rate exceed the conditions for steady economic growth, there will be two extreme states: high-interest and low-interest rates. High-interest rates will harm the real economy, and liquidity surplus will cause inflation, which may lead to "stagflation." Under low-interest rates, asset prices will deviate significantly from the real economy, possibly forming asset price foam.

This model and the CFG model are similar in that global imbalances and liquidity surplus are the common results of the same reason, and different in that the CFG model focuses on the differences in economic growth and asset supply capacity of countries. This model focuses on the monetary hegemony of the central country. Therefore, it can be considered a model of monetary hegemony, imbalance and crisis.

The world economy consists of two countries, H and N, which are completely the same except for their monetary statuses. The economies of both countries consist of numerous homogeneous residents, who are born and die with the same probability per unit of time, so the population is constant and standardized to 1. Production is completed by a fixed number of "trees," whose value is V_t^j and the "fruit" produced per unit of time is X_t^j.

The "fruit" is distributed as follows: the owner of the "tree" gets δX_t^j, and the rest is distributed to the newly born residents. Residents do not consume during the whole life and only consume all their life savings until the moment of death. The "fruit" is perishable and must be consumed in the current period. Therefore, residents must convert the "fruit" obtained into assets or money during their lives.

Assets are "tree," and money is issued by the government. The government obtains seigniorage by issuing money, and maintains a budget balance per unit of time, that is, government expenditure equals seigniorage: where, represents time, and time is continuous.

H is the central country of the international monetary system. Its currency has dual attributes: to meet both domestic and international needs. According to portfolio theory, a country's wealth is held in the form of assets or currencies:

$$W_t^N = (1-\alpha)V_t^N + \frac{\beta V_t^H}{E_t} + \frac{\gamma M_t^H}{E_t} + M_t^N \tag{1}$$

$$W_t^H = \alpha E_t V_t^N + (1-\beta)V_t^H + (1-\gamma)M_t^H \tag{2}$$

Among them, α, β and γ are parameters, which represent the holding ratio of assets and currencies in the two countries, and $0 \le \alpha, \beta, \gamma \le 1$. As a peripheral country, N must hold a certain amount of the currency of H as reserves. On the contrary, H will not hold the currency of N.

E_t is the exchange rate, that is, the value of the currency of N expressed in the currency of H. The purchasing power parity is established, that is $E_t P_t^N = P_t^H$. Formula (1) is denominated in the currency of N, and formula (2) is denominated in the currency of H. The holding status of global wealth can be obtained by multiplying formula (1) and E_t then adding formula (2):

$$W_t = V_t + M_t \tag{3}$$

Where, $W_t = W_t^H + E_t W_t^N$, $V_t = V_t^H + E_t V_t^N$, $M_t = M_t^H + E_t M_t^N$. Formula (3) is denominated in the currency of H.

According to the principle of arbitrage trading, the immediate nominal return of held assets i_t meets the following requirements:

$$i_t V_t^j = \delta P_t^j X_t^j + \dot{V}_t^j \tag{4}$$

That is, the return on assets equals dividends plus capital gains. P_t^j is the price of output (i.e., "fruit") in country j. Assuming the exchange rate remains stable, we convert formula (4) to be denominated in the currency of H and add them to obtain:

$$i_t V_t = \delta P_t^H X_t + \dot{V}_t \tag{5}$$

X_t is the "fruit" produced per unit of time in the world, that is, $X_t = X_t^H + X_t^N$.

The wealth change of a country per unit of time consists of three parts: residents' consumption, the "fruit" shared by newly born residents and asset income.[6] So, there are:

$$\dot{W}_t^N = -\theta W_t^N + (1-\delta) P_t^N X_t^N + (1-\alpha) i_t V_t^N + \frac{\beta i_t V_t^H}{E_t} \tag{6}$$

$$\dot{W}_t^N = -\theta W_t^H + (1-\delta) P_t^H X_t^H + \alpha i_t E_t V_t^N + (1-\beta) i_t V_t^H \tag{7}$$

6 Because the government always maintains a balanced budget and consumes the amount of money produced while issuing it, the government's actions have no impact on the total wealth of the economy.

If the exchange rate remains stable, the change of global wealth can be obtained by multiplying Et from formula (6) and adding it to formula (7) and substituting formula (5):

$$\dot{W}_t = -\theta W_t + P_t^H X_t + \dot{V}_t \tag{8}$$

The Cambridge equation is used to introduce the demand for money, and when the global money market is balanced:

$$M_t = kP_t^H X_t \tag{9}$$

The coefficient K, the so-called "Marshallian K," is the ratio of the total amount of money to nominal output and can also be regarded as the reciprocal of the speed of money circulation.

Combining formula (3) and formula (8), we can obtain:

$$\theta W_t + \dot{M}_t = P_t^H X_t \tag{10}$$

The above formula shows that global output is equal to the consumption of the residents plus the consumption of the governments of the two countries. Regardless of the cost of currency issuance, $\dot{M}_t$ can be regarded as the total income obtained by the governments of both countries in the form of seigniorage, and its actual value is $\dot{M}_t / P_t = kX_t \left(\dot{M}_t / M_t\right)$.

The global economy has three markets: asset, currency and product. Formula (3), formula (9) and formula (10) respectively represent the equilibrium of these three markets. According to the Walras law, under the condition that the first two markets are balanced, the product market is also balanced.

Assuming that the economy is in a steady state, there are $\dot{P}_t^H / P_t^H = \dot{P}_t^N / P_t^N = \rho$ and $\dot{X}_t / X_t = g$, that is, the global economic growth rate and the inflation rate of both countries are constant. Assuming that $\rho + g < i < \rho + g + \theta$, the global equilibrium nominal interest rate i_t and real interest rate r_t satisfy the formula below by virtue of the asymptotic property of the ratio of fictitious economic variables W_t, V_t, M_t, and real economic variables $P_t^H X_t$, (see appendix for derivation process):

$$r_t = i_t - \rho = \frac{\delta\theta}{1 - k\left(\rho + g + \theta\right)} + g \tag{11}$$

When $k = 0$, the real interest rate is determined by δ, θ and g, whose rise will lead to the rise of the real interest rate. The increase in the growth rate of "fruit" output g increases the appreciation rate of "tree" assets, driving up the real interest rate. Formula (5) shows that the rise of δ increases the dividend of "tree" assets, driving up the real interest rate. The increase of θ will reduce the accumulation of total wealth, reducing the value of "tree" assets (indicated by formula (8)) and driving up the real interest rate.

If monetary factors are considered, $k(\rho+g+\theta)$ will also affect the real interest rate. The rise of k will lead to an increase in the amount of money held by residents, reducing the value of "tree" assets (indicated by formula (4)) and driving up the real interest rate. The rise of $\rho+g+\theta$ will strengthen this impact, further driving up the real interest rate.

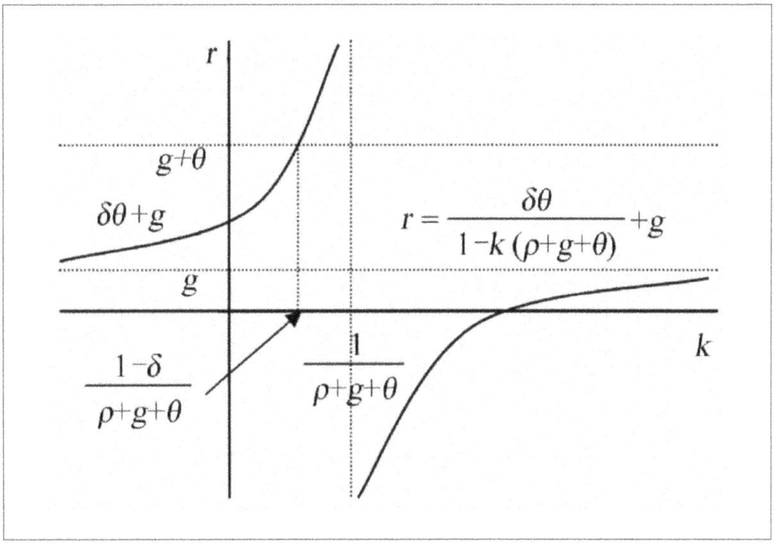

Figure 50. Real interest rate and "Marshallian K"

Given other parameters, we examine the relationship between the real interest rate and "Marshallian K." As shown in Figure 50, $r(k)$ is a hyperbola with $r=g$ and $k=1/(\rho+g+\theta)$ as asymptotes. It can be seen from the appendix that the convergence condition of the whole system is $g<r<g+\theta$, so the k value corresponding to the equilibrium interest rate should meet: $0<k<(1-\delta)/(\rho+g+\theta)$.[7] When

[7] When k=0, there is no currency in the economy, which is reduced to the CFG model. When k<0, it is equivalent to the government providing additional output to the economy in exchange for the ownership of assets, which is not considered in this chapter.

the value exceeds the upper bound of this range, there is no steady growth path in the economic system.

Steady growth requires that the three dummy variables of wealth, asset and currency maintain an appropriate proportion to the real economy and grow simultaneously. High-interest rates will lead to rapid accumulation of wealth and eventually deviate from the synchronization track with the real economy. In the real economy, high-interest rates will cause damage to the real economy, while increasing value means liquidity surplus. Therefore, the global economy may face "stagflation."

The low discount rate will quickly drive up asset value and eventually deviate from the synchronization track with the real economy. In the real economy, low-interest rates have a stimulating effect on the real economy, which will support the rise of asset value and narrow its deviation from the real economy. However, if the growth of the real economy cannot close the gap between the two, the emergence of the foam will be delayed. According to Figure 50 and the above discussion, we divide the economy into the following situations according to the value of the real interest rate and the "Marshall K" (see Table 34).

Table 34. Economic conditions under different values of real interest rate and "Marshallian K" (i.e., monetary aggregate/GDP)

"Marshallian K"	$k<0$	$0<k<\frac{1-\delta}{\rho+g+\theta}$	$k>\frac{1-\delta}{\rho+g+\theta}$	
Real Interest Rate	$g<r<\delta\theta+g$	$\delta\theta+g<r<g+\theta$	$r>g+\theta$	$r<g$
Economic Conditions	**Condition I**	**Condition II**	**Condition III**	**Condition IV**
	The government provides additional output to the economy. (Not discussed hereof)	Balanced growth of fictitious economy and real economy; long-term equilibrium value of interest rate	Wealth growth deviates from the real economy; possible "stagflation"	Asset growth deviates from the real economy; possible low interest rate foam

The above discussion shows that, changes in the money supply will impose a huge impact on the global asset market and ultimately affect the real economy by affecting "Marshall K" and the real interest rate. Because of the dual nature of the currency of H, which accounts for a large share of the global money supply, the impact of the monetary policy of H on the global economy cannot be ignored.

The monetary policy of H should take into account both domestic and international objectives. When these two objectives conflict, H will face a dilemma. For example, when stimulating its economy with loose monetary policy, H also injects liquidity into the global economy. If this policy eventually makes "Marshall K" and the real interest rate exceed the limit required for steady growth, then the global economy may suffer turbulence.

Next, we will discuss the current account and trade balance of the two countries. Current account and trade balance are respectively defined as CA_t^j and TB_t^j, then:

$$CA_t^j \equiv \dot{W}_t^j - \dot{V}_t^j - \dot{M}_t^j \tag{12}$$

$$TB_t^j \equiv P_t^j X_t^j - \theta W_t^j - \dot{M}_t^j \tag{13}$$

That is, the current account is the difference between domestic savings and investment at time t, and the trade balance the difference between domestic output and expenditure at time t. Because the sum of the current accounts and trade balances of the two countries in the same currency is zero, we can understand the global external balance by discussing the condition of H only. Under the condition of a stable exchange rate, the current account of H can be obtained from formula (2) and formula (12), and the trade balance of H from formula (2), formula (7) and formula (13), specifically:

$$CA_t^H = \alpha E_t \dot{V}_t^N - \beta \dot{V}_t^H - \gamma \dot{M}_t^H \tag{14}$$

$$TB_t^H = \delta\left(\alpha - \beta\right) P_t^H X_t^H - \gamma \dot{M}_t^H \tag{15}$$

Obviously, in the model economy, the currency of H held by N has become the trade deficit and current account deficit of H. The maintenance of this deficit means that H has collected seigniorage from N. When increasing money supply, H will collect more seigniorage, expanding its domestic deficit and deepening global imbalances. From formula (14) and formula (15), we can obtain:

$$CA_t^H = TB_t^H + \delta\left(\alpha - \beta\right) P_t^H X_t^H + \alpha E_t \dot{V}_t^N - \beta \dot{V}_t^H \tag{16}$$

This shows that the current account consists of two items: trade balance and net income from external assets and liabilities. The accumulation of a country's current account balance constitutes its external net assets NFA_t^j, which can be obtained by integrating (14):

$$NFA_t^H = \int CA_t^H dt = -\gamma M_t^H \tag{17}$$

According to the efficient market hypothesis, it is impossible for a country to obtain permanent gains through capital gains in the long term and continuously improve its current account, that is, $\alpha E_t \int \dot{V}_t^N dt - \beta \int \dot{V}_t^H dt = 0$. Therefore, in the long run, the currency of H held by N is fully reflected as the net external debt of H. If $\gamma = 0$, then the two countries are completely symmetrical. At this time, a country cannot maintain its current account deficit and net external debt for a long time.

When reaching a certain point, a country's monetary expansion will cause huge risks to its own economy, while imposing relatively low impact on the global economy. When implementing monetary expansion under the opening conditions, the small countries have to fully absorb the consequences and will have no impact on the world economy.

Three main conclusions can be drawn from the model: (1) when the currency of a sovereign country becomes the international standard currency, in order to inject liquidity into the global economy, the country must maintain the current account deficit, which also means that the country collects seigniorage from the world; (2) because of the dual nature of its currency, the monetary policy of the central country will have a huge impact on the global asset market. When reaching a certain point, the country's excess monetary supply will bring huge risks to the global economy; (3) the expansionary monetary policies of peripheral countries have little impact on the global economy, but excessive expansion will bring huge risks to the domestic economy when reaching a certain point.

In short, through the historical review in previous section and the model analysis in this section, we believe that the expansionary fiscal and monetary policies of the United States are the root cause of the global imbalances and financial crisis, and the special status or hegemony of the U.S. dollar has played an important role here. The international dollar standard has two meanings: first, the United States has the responsibility and obligation to provide liquidity for the global economy to meet relevant needs, which requires the United States to maintain certain balance of payments deficit.

Secondly, the United States seek additional benefits taking advantage of its special influence on the global economy, including collecting seigniorage from the whole world. This contradiction of rights and obligations is intertwined with the problems of domestic and foreign policy, placing the U.S. macroeconomic strategies in a dilemma. Over accommodating domestic objectives often puts the global economy at huge risks. This is also why the cry for "super sovereign" international currency is so deafening.

8.4 Conclusions and Policy Recommendations

Based on the above analysis, our conclusions and policy recommendations are as follows. First, global imbalances are the underlying cause of the current subprime crisis, and solving the problem will be the key to avoiding the recurrence of the crisis. Historical review, literature search and our mathematical model all reveal that imbalances and crises are closely related to the hegemony of the U.S. dollar. Therefore, it is essential to reform the international monetary system.

At least, the "exorbitant privilege" of the dollar complained by Charles de Gaulle should be restrained. It is too costly to impose restrictions on the U.S. dollar hegemony by means of ex-post crisis or financial turbulence. We should reform the international monetary system and improve the global governance structure to realize the prior restrictions on the U.S. dollar hegemony.

Second, all economies are locked in and interact with each other. An improved external environment and coordination, cooperation with other countries are one country's way out of the crisis. In the era of globalization, the "decoupling theory" no longer holds, and the cyclical fluctuations of economies become more synchronous.

China needs to cooperate with other countries to get out of the crisis, so we should pay close attention to the changes in the international situation and take countermeasures. In addition, the interaction of cycles also highlights the importance of international cooperation. Separate action and trade protectionism in the Great Depression are painful lessons.

Appendix

By combining formula (3), formula (5), formula (8) and formula (9), we can obtain:

$$\dot{W}_t = \left(i_t - \theta\right) W_t + \left(1 - \delta - i_t k\right) P_t^H X_t \tag{A1}$$

By integrating formula (5) forward and integrating formula (A1) backward, we will have:

$$V_t = \int_t^{\infty} \delta P_s^H X_s e^{-i(s-t)} ds \tag{A2}$$

$$W_t = W_0 e^{(i-\theta)t} + \int_0^t \left(1-\delta-ik\right) P_s^H X_s e^{(i-\theta)(t-s)} ds$$

If $\rho + g < i < \rho + g + \theta$, the following asymptotic property holds:

$$\frac{V_t + M_t}{P_t^H X_t} \underset{t\to\infty}{\to} \frac{\delta}{i-\rho-g} + k \tag{A4}$$

$$\frac{W_t}{P_t^H X_t} \underset{t\to\infty}{\to} \frac{1-\delta-ik}{\rho+g+\theta-i} \tag{A5}$$

Let the right end of formula (A4) and formula (A5) be equal, and then formula (11) can be solved.

Besides, if $i < \rho + g$, then $\frac{V_t + M_t}{P_t^H X_t} \underset{t\to\infty}{\to} \infty$; if $i > \rho + g + \theta$, then $\frac{W_t}{P_t^H X_t} \underset{t\to\infty}{\to} \infty$.

China's National Comprehensive Liabilities and Market-Oriented Reform

Due to historical reasons and system reform, large-scale and complex national comprehensive liabilities remain in China. The concept of national comprehensive liabilities was put forward by Fan Gang (1999) just after the Asian financial crisis, when Fan tried to examine whether a similar crisis would occur in China from the perspective of national comprehensive liabilities, with focus on the non-performing assets of banking sector. However, with the efficient promotion of bank restructuring and reform by the Chinese government in recent years, the non-performing asset ratio of banks has dropped rapidly, from 25.4% in 2001 to about 8% by the end of 2005. In terms of the non-performing assets of banks alone, the current risk of national comprehensive liabilities seems to be less serious, but it is actually an illusion. Because through analysis, we find that it is an only change in the risk composition in national comprehensive liabilities, with some risks rising and some waning. On the one hand, the disposed stock of non-performing assets of banks is not gone, but it is partially transformed into contingent liabilities of other forms. On the other hand, although the ratio of non-performing assets of banks has dropped sharply, problems such as social security expense and local government debt have emerged again. These problems have arisen long ago, but they are becoming more urgent and severe now. Under opening conditions, considering the reform of RMB exchange rate formation mechanism and all-round opening-up of financial industry at the end of 2006, national comprehensive liabilities may have "new members" in its composition. Therefore, the review of the scale, composition of national comprehensive liabilities and resolution and prevention of risks is not a rehash, but a key issue of great practical significance, which is crucial to the sustainable and stable growth of China's economy.

9.1 Literature Review and the Characteristics of This Study

The term of "national comprehensive liabilities" refers to the sum of all liabilities including contingent liabilities accumulated by a country in the course of its economic development. It is called comprehensive liabilities because some liabilities are in the direct form of debts such as domestic and foreign debts of the country, while some are in other forms such as non-performing assets of banks, social security debt, etc. The latter is another form of "liability" and is generally called comprehensive liabilities because they ultimately need to be borne by the national finance, regardless of their non-debt forms (in other forms). From a more rigorous perspective, national comprehensive liabilities are actually equivalent to the sum of all liabilities in the Fiscal Risk Matrix proposed by Polackova (1998), an expert on the World Bank. The Matrix includes both deterministic liabilities that have occurred and contingent liabilities that occur with a certain probability and may eventually evolve into deterministic liabilities. The concept of "comprehensive" liabilities is adopted here, to comprehensively analyze and sum up all kinds of liabilities and make an overall judgment on the national financial risks.

In addition to the study of Fan Gang (1999), Liu Shangxi et al. (2003,2005) also explored the risk of national comprehensive liabilities from the perspective of financial risk. What's more, international institutions have been paying close attention to this subject, such as the studies of the World Bank (2005) and IMF (2006). They adopted different estimation methods and drew new conclusions, but within the analytical framework of Polackova (1998) in general, and considered new factors not considered in previous studies.

Compared with the above research, this study tries to make breakthroughs in the following aspects. First, all kinds of comprehensive liabilities will be thoroughly investigated. This study attempts to cover the "new members" of national comprehensive liabilities shown in recent years, such as social security liabilities, local government liabilities, the pro-cyclical effect of Basel II, and the potential loss of foreign exchange reserves caused by RMB exchange rate appreciation. Through theoretical estimation of these "new members" in accordance with national conditions and international experience, we strive to get a clear picture of the overall scale and nature of national comprehensive liabilities.

Second, the national comprehensive liabilities will be investigated from the perspective of opening-up. Under ongoing reform and opening-up, the composition of comprehensive liabilities is changing, and new comprehensive liabilities risks arise. China's experience in smoothly weathering the Asian financial crisis is simple: we did not lose because we did not participate in the game (Yi, 2004). In other words, China was not involved in the crisis, not because China's financial system was strong enough in resisting risks, but China implemented prudent capital account management policies. However, with the reform of RMB exchange rate formation mechanism, the stepped opening-up of capital account, and the emerging pro-cyclical effect of Basel II, the national comprehensive liabilities will build up risks. Therefore, it is of great significance to study the national comprehensive liabilities risks from the perspective of opening-up at this stage.

Third, the countermeasures to resolve and prevent the national comprehensive liabilities risks will be studied. Previous studies have rarely mentioned countermeasures or only put forward some abstract views in principle. This chapter will discuss this topic, with special emphasis on the necessity and feasibility of a market-oriented approach in stock risk resolution and increment risk prevention.

9.2 Overall Estimation and Dynamic Changes of National Comprehensive Liabilities

The composition of national comprehensive liabilities is complex, with different estimated scales. Under ongoing reform and opening-up, new members will be included and old ones removed dynamically for comprehensive liabilities, and their risks and policy implications deserve close attention.

1. An Overall Estimation

The composition of national comprehensive liabilities is complex, and the scope differs from study to study, which actually reflects that national comprehensive liability is not a very rigorous concept. With reference to the Fiscal Risk Matrix proposed by Polackova (1998), we divide national comprehensive liabilities into the following categories.

1.1. The Central Government's Domestic and Foreign Debts

Table 35 shows that, from the changes of domestic and foreign debts, thanks to our great attention to the lessons of the Asian financial crisis, except that foreign debts exceeded domestic debts in 1998 and 1999, the balance of domestic debts has always exceeded foreign debts since the beginning of the twenty-first century. Notably, the foreign debt, especially short-term foreign debt, has been growing rapidly in recent years, especially, by 22.9% in 2005, and short-term debt accounted for more than half of foreign debt.

It should be pointed out that in the relevant research (Liu, 2005), the balance of foreign debt is only 277.8 billion yuan of sovereign foreign debt borrowed by national ministries and commissions. While our statistics here show 2,303.18 billion yuan, which is quite different from the former. The gap should be the foreign debt balance of private sectors such as Chinese and foreign banks and

Chinese and foreign enterprises. In terms of national comprehensive liabilities, all these foreign debts will be on the country, like in the Asian financial crisis. Therefore, it is rather objective to consider the total foreign debt as a whole.

Table 35. China's domestic and foreign debts and their changes

Year	Domestic debt (RMB)	Foreign debt (RMB)	Foreign debt (USD)	Growth rate of foreign debt (%)
1998	7765.70	12077.51	1460.4	-
1999	10606.85	12556.34	1518.3	3.96
2000	13100	12051.87	1457.3	-4.02
2001	15618.00	14068.1	1701.1	16.73
2002	19366.10	13938.26	1685.4	-0.92
2003	23935.10	16013.2	1936.3	14.89
2004	25777.60	18905.22	2286.0	18.06
2005	28774	23031.77	2810.5	22.94

Data source: Ministry of Finance, State Administration of Foreign Exchange.

1.2. "Quasi-National Debt"

This refers to bonds with a financial guarantee issued by government departments, such as policy financial bonds. Because policy banks' issue bonds based on the market, the scale and pricing of bond issuance are determined according to their own credits, and the funds raised are also used in the market, we do not include such debt into the scope of comprehensive liabilities in this chapter. However, because the credit of policy banks incorporates national credit, we should pay close attention to the medium and long-term credit risk caused by the surge of medium and long-term loans of policy banks. Under poor risk control or impact of domestic and foreign economy and finance, such debt may eventually be transformed into national comprehensive liabilities. That is why in some studies (Liu, 2005), quasi-national debt is listed as contingent liability. In 2005, the balance of financial bonds of policy banks reached around 1.8 trillion yuan. If this part of debt is considered, the national comprehensive liabilities ratio will rise significantly.

1.3. Local Government Debt

Local governments are not allowed to issue bonds on their own under Chinese law. Therefore, local government debts mainly consist of loans borrowed by them at home and abroad through local trust investment institutions, and debts of local state-owned enterprises guaranteed by the financial department. Since this problem has been serious in recent years (Wei Jianing, 2004), we will regard it as a study object. The scale of local government debt is estimated at 800 to 1000 billion yuan.

1.4. Contingent Liabilities in the Form of Financial Non-performing Assets and Other Non-performing Assets

Contingent liabilities include non-performing assets of banks, other financial institutions such as securities companies and insurance companies, and new forms of disposing non-performing assets. Non-performing assets of banks can be disposed of in multiple ways, including stripping off and writing-off non-performing assets, capital injection, issuance of special government bonds, central bank bills, refinancing and other investments attracting financial investors. Consequently, the rate of non-performing assets of banks has declined rapidly. However, these disposals cannot clear non-performing assets on stocks, but most of them have been transformed under disguise. For example, the non-performing assets of commercial banks have become non-performing debts of the central bank and remain a part of the national comprehensive liabilities. Specifically, they are composed of:

A. 270 billion yuan of special government bonds issued: Evidently, this debt will be repaid.
B. Stripped non-performing assets: In 1999, 1429.1 billion yuan of non-performing assets were stripped to asset management companies, most of which could not be recovered. In March 2006, the weighted average asset recovery rate was 23.89% for non-performing assets disposed by four asset management corporations, namely China Huarong, China Great Wall Industry Corporation, Orient Group and China Cinda. Actually, the loss would be valued at 100 billion yuan. In addition, the Bank of China, China Construction Bank and Industrial and Commercial Bank of China stripped non-performing assets of more than 500 billion yuan in the process of financial restructuring from 2003 to 2005. The stripping cost of non-performing assets alone was 1.5 trillion yuan. This is another form of comprehensive liabilities converted from non-performing assets. Obviously, a part of the non-performing assets of original commercial banks has now been converted into the central bank's debt
C. Capital injected by the banks: The Bank of China, China Construction Bank and the Industrial and Commercial Bank of China had invested USD 60 billion, which was more than 490 billion yuan based on the interest

rate back then. Although this capital injection is a kind of investment and obtains benefits (discussed in detail later), it is also a cost expenditure for the central government, so injected capital is also a part of generalized comprehensive liabilities.

D. Written-off non-performing assets: The Bank of China, China Construction Bank and Industrial and Commercial Bank of China wrote off more than 500 billion yuan of non-performing assets. Written-off non-performing assets cause the final loss. Non-performing assets are wrote-off in the accounting account, but the government mixes up the loss, through say fiscal capital injection, owned profits offset by state-owned banks and re-loans issued by the central bank, or additional currency and inflation. From this perspective, the costs of written-off non-performing assets are also comprehensive liabilities.

E. Costs on the reform of Rural Credit Cooperatives: Most of the cashing of central bank bills, special loans and special grants may cause losses in the process of the reform.

F. Capital injected into the restructuring of securities companies: These capitals are basically from conservation funds for securities investors and refinancing of the central bank, of which the equity capital and advance capitals of conservation funds are from financial contributions and refinancing of the central bank.[1]

The total amount of the above items reaches more than 30000 billion yuan. That is to say, while the non-performing asset ratio decreased from 25.4% in 2001 to 8.9% in 2005 (16.5 percentage points), a national comprehensive liability of more than 30000 billion yuan had come into being, with new composition.

1.5. A Shortfall of Social Security Funds Oriented by a Shortfall of Pension

This was not paid close attention to in the late 1990s, at least not included in Fan Gang's (1999) study. However, it is an urgent issue and constitutes the most important part of comprehensive liabilities now. The shortfall of social security funds have been estimated by various individuals or institutions, such as the IMF, the

1 In 2005, China set up Securities Investor Protection Fund, which was established solely by the State Council. The Ministry of Finance contributed 6.3 billion yuan as the registered capital and equity capital on funds, and the Central Bank contributed 61.7 billion yuan as advance funds (which needs to be repaid to the Central Bank in the future).

World Bank and relevant domestic research.[2] The shortfall ranges from 2 trillion to 3 trillion yuan, up to 9 trillion yuan, and we assume it to be 3 trillion yuan.

1.6. Other Contingent Liabilities

We mainly study here the loss of foreign exchange reserves caused by the appreciation of the RMB, a new change not explored by other researchers. At the end of 2005, the amount of foreign exchange reserves reached USD 818.872 billion, and the RMB appreciated for 2.5%, thus the marked-to-market losses of U.S. dollar foreign exchange assets reserved by the central bank amounted to about 100 billion yuan if the U.S. dollar reserves accounted for 60%. Of course, the appreciation of the euro and the yen in the foreign exchange reserves in the same period will offset the loss of foreign exchange assets caused by the depreciation of the dollar.

In the process of forming national comprehensive liabilities, we need to pay close attention to the risks faced by the central bank. Although the loss of foreign exchange reserves caused by the appreciation of the RMB mentioned above accounts for a small proportion (0.67%) of the comprehensive liabilities of the whole country, this loss may be potential future risk for the assets of the central bank. According to the Economic Observer, if we consider both the central bank's refinancing and Huijin's capital injection, the central bank invested nearly a trillion yuan in three state-owned banks in the round of state-owned bank share reform launched in early 2004 (Li, 2006).[3]

Based on the above analysis, we can make an overall estimate of China's current comprehensive liabilities. Meanwhile, we listed the relevant studies in chronological order (Table 36) for comparison. Notably, it is controversial to simply sum up the deterministic liabilities and contingent liabilities to obtain comprehensive liabilities. This is mainly because the probability of contingent liabilities evolving into fixed liabilities is debated. Not only are there differences in reform cost estimates, but also the income estimates vary greatly due to different time and conditions. Therefore, this chapter does not advocate a very accurate estimate of the scale of comprehensive liabilities. Its main purpose is to understand and

---

2 The World Bank's research (2005) believes that China's pension financing shortfall was about 9.15 trillion yuan from 2001 to 2005. In October 2006, the consultation report of the International Monetary Fund estimated that this number was about 5 trillion yuan, while the research of the Ministry of Finance believed that it was 2.5 trillion yuan.

3 Meanwhile, we also see that the state spent big costs on and made considerable gains from the reform of the three state-owned banks. The market value of the three banks after the reform and listing is very high, and the state capital injection was rewarded with relatively high (book) gains.

analyze the dynamic changes and countermeasures of fiscal risks in the reform process from a comprehensive and dynamic perspective.

Table 36. Overall estimate of China's national comprehensive liabilities (%)

Items	1997	1998	2005
1. Domestic debts	7.32	8.78	15.78
2. Specific national debts (Debt not included in the budget)	—	—	1.48
3. Foreign debts	14.7	14.57	12.63
4. Local government debts	—	—	5.48
5. Financial contingent liability	25.05	27.19	19.2
6. Existing non-performing assets of banks			9.87
7. A shortfall of the social security fund	—	—	16.45
8. Book loss of foreign exchange reserves caused by RMB appreciation	—	—	0.55
Total			
Proportion in current year's GDP (%)	47.07	50.53	81.45

Source: Besides the existing non-performing assets of banks which are the data of the CBRC, the other data of 2005 are calculated by the author based on the publicly disclosed data of the Ministry of Finance and the People's Bank of China and the annual report of commercial banks. The data of 1997 and 1998 are quoted from Fan (1999).

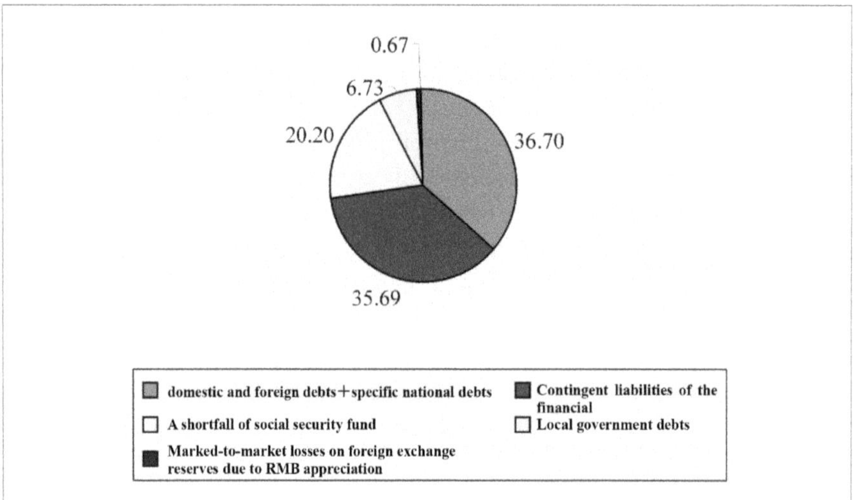

Figure 51. The constitution of national comprehensive liabilities (%)

Source: The author calculated according to Table 36.

Figure 51 shows that the national comprehensive liabilities are dominated by domestic and foreign debts, contingent liabilities of the financial sector and the shortfall of Social Security Fund (SSF), which account for 36.7%, 35.7% and 20.2% of the total comprehensive liabilities respectively. Given that the growth of domestic and foreign debts is within a safe range, it will be essential to reduce the contingent liabilities of the financial sector and make up the gap in the SSF. Notably, although the ratio of non-performing assets has dropped sharply, the national comprehensive liabilities brought by the financial sector have not changed much. Therefore, a new mechanism of bank reorganization and reform for curbing the incremental risk is key to containment of comprehensive debt risks.

2. Dynamic Change

The above analysis of the composition of national comprehensive liabilities is basically a static investigation, but the impact of future changes of various economic parameters on contingent liabilities has not been discussed in detail. We keep an eye on the country's comprehensive liabilities. On the one hand, we want to know exactly how high the share of GDP is now; on the other hand, we also want to further know various new and future macro and micro changes in the open state in comprehensive liabilities, economic growth rate in the open period, population aging, social security system reform and financial reform, and so on.

2.1. Macro Level

Firstly, the slowdown of economic growth may expose the original accumulated problems and risks and form new non-performing asset (NPA). Secondly, the aging problem and the declining trend of high savings rates will also increase explicit liabilities. With expanded population aging and ta declining high savings rate, China's economy may depend more on foreign debt, thus increasing its explicit debt. Thirdly, rising fiscal deficits will also drive up comprehensive liabilities. Many citizen-friendly policies will all increase the fiscal deficit, including the perfection of the national social security system, the payment of pensions, the implementation of the policy of encouraging consumption, and the transfer payment to economically backward areas, thus forming the national comprehensive debt. Fourthly, the cost of responding to financial fluctuations will also lead to a dynamic increase in comprehensive liabilities. Some factors will also increase government expenditure and drive up national comprehensive liabilities, such as oil price fluctuation, the cycle of rising interest rates, exchange rate change, domestic social instability, international financial crisis and its impact on the domestic economy.

Finally, the impact of the openness factor should deserve keen attention, specifically:

A. The depreciation of the U.S. dollar exchange rate leads to the loss of the book value of foreign exchange reserves in RMB. In the process of global economic imbalance adjustment, central bank assets are prone to opportunity cost, exchange rate risk, and interest rate risk. From the perspective of opportunity cost loss, although China now keep much more foreign exchange reserves, its ability to purchase oil and gold has not increased significantly. This does not include the negative impact on the prices and parity of oil and gold if China increases both of their holdings significantly. From the perspective of exchange rate risk, the depreciation of the U.S. dollar exchange rate leads to the loss of the book value of foreign exchange reserves in RMB. From the perspective of interest rate risk, the change of interest rate in the United States will affect the profitability of U.S. dollar assets. Then the yield of international financial bonds will rise, which will lead to a decline in bond prices, thus causing book losses of foreign exchange assets held by the central bank. B. Exchange rate fluctuations have a certain negative impact on the RMB value of capital injected into banks. Since the injected bank entered into an agreement with Central Huijin Investment Ltd. to purchase an option from Huijin: the injected bank has the right to exchange up to the amount of the capital injection in U.S. dollars into RMB at a fixed rate of 8.2769 RMB per U.S. dollar after several years, the exchange rate risk is ultimately taken by Huijin Company. C. In order to hedge the inflow of foreign exchange and prevent inflationary pressure, the central bank issued a lot of bills or repurchased or sold government bonds to repatriate the funds. Accumulating foreign exchange reserves is more or less a process in which the government exchanges foreign currency assets at the expense of expanding debts (issuing currency, central bank bills, or treasury bonds). Gray et al. (2006) mentioned in the latest framework for analyzing macro-financial risks that public sector liabilities include various guarantees, foreign currency debts, local currency debts and base currency, so the government debt will be increased when we issued additional currency. In addition, Fan (1999) adds the inflation factor when examining the financial risk of comprehensive liabilities, which is also similar to the study of Gray.

2.2. Micro Investigation

Firstly, with the further opening of China's banking, securities and insurance industries and the gradual implementation of Basel II, after the transition period of China's entry into WTO, its financial industry will face a more open and brand-new competitive pattern. The intensification of external competition challenges the existing financial supervision concepts, models and effectiveness. When failing the fierce competition, Chinese banks will have greater pressure of the growth of non-performing assets.

Second, the pro-cyclical effect of Basel II will also increase the pressure of credit loss. The implementation of Basel II will aggravate the fluctuation of a credit cycle. Because according to the accord, the ability and scale of bank lending are highly dependent on the capital adequacy ratio. Banks with high capital adequacy ratios lend more, while those with low ratios will lend less. The relationship between this rule and the credit and economic cycle is as follows: when the economy is prosperous, the profitability of banks is enhanced, the capital adequacy ratio is improved, and banks can easily expand credit; In an economic recession, the non-performing assets of banks is increased, profits and provisions decreased, capital adequacy ratio decreased, and bank credit is tightened. Therefore, capital adequacy ratio and credit cycle fluctuation will aggravate investment and economic fluctuation, affect the stability of the macro-economy and increase credit asset loss.

Third, the potential risks of insurance companies have emerged. Some problems of China's insurance industry hide greater risks, such as the historical legacy of China's insurance industry, the capital utilization and the profit and loss in the life insurance industry. If financial reorganization is needed, the comprehensive liabilities of the country will go up.

Fourth, the reorganization of some banks will further increase the comprehensive liabilities. For example, due to historical reasons and considering financial stability, the reorganization and reform of Guangdong Development Bank, China Everbright Bank and Agricultural Bank of China all need financial support from local governments and central governments, and such restructuring will increase the comprehensive liabilities of the country.

In addition, dynamically, other potential financial risks in the financial sector will also lead to a dynamic increase in comprehensive liabilities. The country's comprehensive debts may expand due to the mismatch of deposit and loan term structure of commercial banks, the high-risk assets of industrial departments, such as enterprise stock rights, liquidation assets and accounts receivable, and the risk guarantee provided by local finance for real estate development[4], among others.

In a word, with the continuous expansion of China's opening to the outside world, China is facing more and more external shocks and policy constraints, and China will face more comprehensive liabilities related to macro stability, compliance with international standards and fulfillment of commitments. At present, the weak links of national comprehensive liabilities lie in the following: the micro-subjects of the market have not really dispelled their dependence on the country, the moral hazard is still large, the market restraint is not strong,

---

4 In the current process of real estate development, local municipal and district finance bureaus are the investors and guarantors behind many real estate investment companies and are the real debtors of these companies' high debts. Once the real estate market enters the adjustment period, local finance will be seriously dragged down by these companies.

and the coexistence of regulatory tolerance and regulatory gap. Therefore, it is of great significance to find a fundamental solution to comprehensive liabilities and avoid new liabilities.

9.3 Risk Measurement of National Comprehensive Liabilities

Measure and evaluating the comprehensive debt risk is a difficult challenge. This paper mainly discusses two aspects: total amount and structure. The first is about the calculation of total liabilities. This total does not refer to the absolute amount of the country's comprehensive debt, but to its ratio to GDP, because the absolute amount itself does not have much practical significance. Although China's official government debt.[5] It accounted for less than 18% in 2005 (IMF, 2006), but at the end of the 1990s, the national comprehensive debt ratio was about 50% (Fan, 1999), and this ratio increased further in 2005. Of course, there is a statistical problem, that is, in the late 1990s, some comprehensive liabilities, such as social security debts, were not included. Considering this factor, the actual change of the national comprehensive debt ratio is not as great as the figures show.

However, even considering statistical factors and given other things being equal, is the higher the comprehensive liability ratio, the greater the risk? Currently, China is at a development stage with a national comprehensive liability ratio of 81%, so how much risk is China facing? This question is difficult to answer. For example, in the 1990s, many Western experts on China alarmist the "China collapse theory" according to the non-performing asset ratio or comprehensive liability ratio of Chinese banks, but there was no crisis in China. Clearly, other factors need to be taken into account to measure the risk of a country's comprehensive liability ratio.

The difficulty with risk measurement is also that given the same comprehensive liability ratio, the risk varies from country to country. It is generally accepted that 60%-70% of GDP for comprehensive liability may be an international warning line, but this indicator does not apply to all countries. Different countries, different histories and different levels of economic and financial development level will affect the judgment of comprehensive liability risk. One scholar (Reinhart et al., 2003) introduced the concept of "debt intolerance" to describe this difference.[6]

---

5 The government bond issued to cover the central government's fiscal deficit, special government bonds issued in 1998, and bonds issued for local governments are included.

6 "intolerance" is a medical concept that refers to an allergic reaction to drugs. The so-called "debt intolerance" refers to the allergic reaction of some countries to debt, that

Furthermore, the debt ratio and risk are closely related to a country's history and culture, especially its credit record, for example, whether it likes to default on its debts, and inflation, which is also an important reason why the debt ratio, which is not high by the standards of developed countries, is reflected as high country risk in developing countries.

Besides credit history and inflation, another important factor to measure debt risk is the development level of the financial system. Recent literature mentioned (Mendoza et al., & IMF, 2006) that in the process of financial globalization, the development level of the financial market has a great influence on the measurement and judgment of comprehensive liability risk. Developed financial markets help a country accumulate a large amount of foreign debts, for example, in the United States, the mature and developed financial markets enable the United States to maintain a large scale of external debts at a lower cost for a long period of time. This is a balanced allocation of the market, and the risk of foreign debts is far less than that of other countries in the same circumstances.

The above analysis provides some insight into China's comprehensive liability risk.

Firstly, we cannot judge the degree of comprehensive liability risk merely by looking at the absolute quantity of comprehensive liability or its ratio to GDP, even though the increase in this debt ratio is worth concern. Instead, we should adopt a dialectical and dynamic perspective on comprehensive liability risk in light of China's national conditions. It is necessary to consider the composition of comprehensive liability, distinguishing between short-term risks and long-term risks, and recognize which urgent problems need to be solved immediately and which need to be solved dynamically over time. Among China's current comprehensive liability, what needs to be solved urgently is the restructuring of agricultural banks and the shrinking value of foreign exchange reserve assets due to the depreciation of the U.S. dollar, while the problem of social security arrears will take time to be gradually resolved. In the long run, it is crucial for China's economy to keep growing, because once growth stops, a number of problems and risks will emerge.

Secondly, the main concern of debt intolerance is country risk. Externally, China has a good credit record and rarely experiences high inflation rates for there's no hyperinflation like in Latin America. But China's problem is how to maintain the soundness of its financial system, especially in improving the quality of bank assets. Therefore, when measuring the comprehensive liability

---

is, they cannot stand excessive debt. If the debt ratio is high, there will be problems and crises.

risk, we should pay attention to the influence of the development level of China's financial market on the comprehensive liability risk: there is a big gap between China's financial market and mature market, and China's ability to resolute, diverse and share risks is weak, which is the "Achilles' heel" of China's national comprehensive liability.

In summary, recent financial reforms, social security system reforms, and economic reforms have greatly reduced risks in the economic and financial system and have made remarkable achievements worldwide. However, the underdeveloped financial markets and high comprehensive liability ratios make China's financial stability highly dependent on economic growth, and changes in the domestic and international environment bring potential variables for economic growth. Therefore, in the process of economic and financial reform in the future, it is the key to further improve China's financial stability to prevent the risk of country's comprehensive liability through a market-oriented approaches.

9.4 Risk Disposition of National Comprehensive Liabilities and Market-Oriented Reform

Regarding the disposal of China's comprehensive liability risk, in the past, China had no clear risk disposal plan and excessively relied on the lender-of-last-resort function of the central bank, and its legal systems were deficient. After continuous exploration and trial and error, the Chinese government is strengthening the role of market-oriented approaches in resolving comprehensive liability risks and put them into practice. The process of financial risk disposal reflects the change of China's plan on addressing comprehensive liability risks. The disposal of contingent liabilities in the financial sector and contingent liability, mainly non-performing assets of banks, has undergone a transformation process from write-off to divestment and then to market-oriented reform. The attraction of strategic investors and listing of banks fully reflect the market-oriented policy orientation and have achieved significant and positive results.

1. Establishment of Asset Management Company

In 1998, a total of 1.4 trillion yuan of non-performing assets were divested to have asset management companies revitalize these non-performing assets. In 2003–2005, market-oriented approach was added to the process of bank restructuring to avoid divestiture from becoming a windfall (Table 37). For example, in 2005, when disposing of doubtful loans, ICBC adopted a bidding approach, not only improving the recovery ratio but also greatly promoting the market-oriented process of non-performing assets disposal.

Table 37. Several large-scale divestitures of non-performing assets that have occurred

Year	Assets Divestiture Banks	Total Amount (Trillion yuan)	Receiving Institutions	Asset class
1999	Four state-owned commercial banks and China Development Bank	14291	Four companies	Doubtful
2004	Bank of Communications	641	China Cinda Asset Management Co., Ltd.	Doubtful and loss
	Bank of China, China Construction Bank	2787	China Cinda Asset Management Co., Ltd.	Doubtful
	Bank of China	1424	China Oriental Asset Management Co. Ltd.	Loss
	China Construction Bank	569	China Cinda Asset Management Co., Ltd.	Loss
2005	Industrial and Commercial Bank of China	4590	Four companies	Doubtful
		2460	74.hina Huarong Asset Management Co., Ltd	Loss
2005	Banks of Shanghai	30	China Cinda Asset Management Co., Ltd.	Doubtful

Source: Financial Risk Research Center, China Cinda Asset Management Corporation, Financial Risk Research, No. 11–12, 2006.

2. Capital Injection by Banks

If the divestiture of non-performing assets is to remove the bad debts from the bank's assets, then capital injection is meant to improve the bank's balance sheet. However, either divesting bad loans or adding capital is largely an administrative approach, ultimately government pay exceeding indemnity. Essentially, state funding is a cost to taxpayers: direct state injection is spending current fiscal money, while debt capital injection is increasing the burden on taxpayers in the future. Therefore, the market-oriented risk-sharing mechanism is not yet evident.

3. Banks' Bailout, Restructuring and Exit

This is still largely a case of the government taking the losses, and thus not yet very marketization. However, this disposal can more effectively control incremental risk (i.e., generation of non-performing assets in the future).

4. Subsidizing Banks by Using the Spread Between Interest Rates for Savings Deposits and Loans

In recent years, there has been a spread of about 300 points between banks' one-year deposit rates and lending rates, which is actually a subsidy to banks from their customers. To some extent, this method harms the interests of bank customers and reduces the financial efficiency (Ma, 2006). The trend of interest rate marketization tends to reduce or even eliminate such policies.

5. Issuance of Subordinated Debt

In December 2003, China Banking and Insurance Regulatory Commission issued the Notice on Inclusion of Subordinated Term Debt into Tier 2 Capital. Issuance of subordinated debt[7] has become an important way for China's commercial banks to replenish capital. Replenishing funds through subordinated debt is obviously more market-oriented than direct capital injection. Moreover, subordinated debt is raised from institutional investors, which means that the risk of non-performing assets of banks is shared through marketization.

6. Attracting Strategic Investors and Public Listing

The financial reorganization of state-owned commercial banks and joint-stock banks, attracting strategic investors and public listing all reflect the principle of market-oriented risk sharing, and mainly aim to share the future incremental risks. This way has achieved good results: the market value of the equity of the three banks held by Central Huijin Investment Ltd. has exceeded the total investment of the central bank including Central Huijin Investment Ltd.'s capital injection and central bank refinancing through the successive listing of three banks, especially overseas listing. This reflects the confidence of market investors in the Chinese government's ability and credit standing to promote financial reform and shows recognition of the market-oriented reform orientation.

---

[7] The so-called subordinated debt refers to the long-term debt of commercial banks with a fixed term of not less than 5 years (including 5 years). It is not used to make up for the daily operating losses of banks unless the banks fail or liquidate, and the claim right of this debt ranks after deposits and other liabilities.

7. A Market-Oriented Limited Compensation Mechanism

7.1. Banking

The government is studying the establishment of a deposit insurance system, which can help the affected institutions with the premiums paid by deposit financial institutions, relieve' the pressure on the government and the central bank, and avoid moral hazard. At the same time, the state implicit compensation should be abolished, and a market-oriented limited compensation mechanism should be established, so as to promote market entities to enhance their risk awareness, make investment decisions according to the risk status of financial institutions, and give full play to the role of market constraints. According to the risk degree of deposit financial institutions, the deposit insurance system sets different insurance rates, which is conducive to the formation of a positive incentive mechanism.

7.2. Securities Industry

In order to strengthen the market restraint of securities companies, promote the survival of the fittest in the securities industry and effectively protect the legitimate rights and interests of securities investors, the People's Bank of China vigorously promotes the establishment of a securities investor protection system. On June 30, 2005, the CSRC, the People's Bank of China, the Ministry of Finance and other ministries and commissions jointly studied and formulated the Administration Measures for Securities Investor Protection Funds. On September 29, 2005, China Securities Investor Protection Fund Corporation was formally established. The Protection Funds established offer clear regulations on protecting the legitimate rights and interests of public investors, playing a positive role in stabilizing and enhancing investors' confidence and preventing the transmission and diffusion of risks of securities companies.

7.3. Insurance Industry

In December 2004, China Insurance Regulatory Commission promulgated the Administration Measures for Insurance Guarantee Funds referred to as "Administration Measures," initially establishing the insurance investor protection system in the form of insurance guarantee funds. Insurance guarantee fund is a statutory fund formed by insurance companies in accordance with the requirements of Insurance Law. According to the principle of "central management and coordinated employment," the guarantee fund is used to provide relief to policy holders or policy transferee companies when insurance companies are revoked or declared bankrupt. The establishment of the insurance guarantee fund further deepens the reform of the insurance industry and helps to establish the exit mechanism of insurance companies in line with the principle of marketization. The insurance guarantee fund system can alleviate the social shock caused by the withdrawal of insurance companies from the market and enhance the public's confidence in the insurance industry.

However, not all comprehensive liabilities can be solved through marketization. The "market failures" will limit the solution scope of market-oriented reform. Some social responsibilities and the resulting comprehensive liabilities must also be mainly borne by the government (Zhang Xiaojing et al., 2006). It is necessary to distinguish the boundaries of market-oriented reform, so as to avoid the situation of declining comprehensive liabilities ratio declines + aggravated social instability. Market-oriented sharing is the fundamental way to reduce and solve the national comprehensive liabilities in the end.

9.5 Conclusions and Policy Recommendations

1. The Country's Comprehensive Liabilities Are Still Grim from an Open Perspective

According to our estimation, China's national comprehensive liabilities ratio reached 81% in 2005. We cannot directly tell the size of the country's comprehensive liabilities only from this figure, but structural analysis offers a glimpse of the grimness: (1) Although the sharp decline in the non-performing asset ratio of banks more of less reflects the reduction of the national comprehensive debt risk, since this was achieved at the expense of more than 3 trillion yuan of comprehensive debt, so resolving and preventing the contingent liabilities from the financial sector remains a grim challenge. (2) The transition from economic catch-up to social construction means a substantial increase in social expenditure in the future, especially the high proportion of social security fund gap in national comprehensive liabilities, which should be paid close attention to. (3) As of now, we should concern most the new national comprehensive debt risk brought about by further opening-up, especially the challenges posed by the devaluation of China's foreign exchange reserves due to changes in the U.S. dollar exchange rate, the comprehensive opening of the financial industry, and the implementation of the Basel Accord. In the era of economic globalization, the crisis is often associated with the impact of external factors. Therefore, the current national comprehensive liabilities are still grim from an open perspective. We must not be blinded by the illusion that the sharp decline in the non-performing asset ratio of banks may reduce the risk of national comprehensive liabilities.

2. Market-Oriented Reform: A Potential Approach to Resolve National Comprehensive Liabilities

We have tried a variety of approaches to deal with national comprehensive liabilities. At first, we basically focused on administrative arrangements (verification, divestiture, etc.), but administrative arrangements are prone to: first, moral hazard, and everyone is looking forward to windfalls; second, inability to solve the national comprehensive liabilities well, and which will be transferred. Therefore, it is necessary to adopt the way of market reforms. Experience at home and abroad shows that a sound cost-sharing institutional framework can promote the medium and long-term stability of the financial system, and market-oriented reform under opening-up is more important. We propose the following future market-oriented reforming methods: (1) breaking the monopoly of state-owned financial departments, developing private finance and promoting the development of financial markets; (2) standardizing the market exit mechanism of financial institutions and making budget constraints more accurate; (3) establishing and improving the investor protection system; (4) improving the corporate governance and regulatory governance of the financial sector; (5) reducing government intervention and breaking the "pot of risks" (the government shouldering all the responsibilities.)

3. The Government Responsibility in Dealing with the National Comprehensive Liabilities

Although market-oriented reforming is the basic way to solve the national comprehensive liabilities, not all liabilities can be resolved through marketization. After all, the market also has its limitations. From economic catch-up to the transition stage of social construction, a large number of social expenditures need to be borne by the government, including social security, medical education and so on. Therefore, while upholding market-oriented management of social security funds, we should be clear that social security is still the responsibility of the government. We cannot simply buck pass the task of establishing and perfecting the social security system to the market, and we should learn past lessons in education, medical care and social security.

4. Rapid and Stable Economic Growth Is the Fundamental Guarantee to Deal with the National Comprehensive Liabilities

Rapid economic growth, like that faster than comprehensive liabilities, is conducive to the decline of the country's comprehensive liabilities ratio; stable economic growth and less volatility, also helps to slow down the growth rate of the country's comprehensive liabilities. In fact, many bad debts of banks are born in the "expansion-contraction" cycle. Therefore, stable and sustained economic growth means that we can effectively ensure that the national comprehensive liabilities are within a controllable range in the dynamic.

Growth Imbalance and Government Responsibility: A Perspective of Social Expenditure

The welfare arrangement "from cradle to grave" had always been regarded as an important symbol of socialism. As the decision-maker of China, the government has taken on all things related to the lives of the people (except farmers). As the market-oriented reform advances, more and more market arrangements have emerged to balance the government and the market. Besides, charging system of some public goods and such services as education and health care have come into force. Amid the widening gap of income, the way of financing public services by charging their users is increasingly hindering people with low incomes from necessary services (World Bank, 2005), causing the inadequate access to medical services, education and other livelihood issues. It also gives rise to people's reflection on the reform and growth pattern. On the one hand, remarkable progress has been made in economic growth measured by GDP. On the other hand, people's access to basic living standards, including compulsory education, basic health insurance, social insurance, and other public services, is not promising. The imbalance between the economic growth of the nation and people's livelihoods is the essence of the ongoing imbalances[1]. It is also the most important and eye-catching "growth imbalance" in the rapid growth.

China, as a developing country, growth imbalance is an inevitable economic reality. There are several contributing factors, among others, taking economic construction as the center and implementing the catch-up strategy, GDP growth has become the supreme goal of the government. Accordingly, the assessment

1 The ongoing imbalances in the economic growth of China include the following: urban-rural and regional imbalance, imbalances in investments and consumption, manufacturing and service industry development imbalance, external imbalance featured twin surpluses and high foreign exchange reserves, and economic and social development imbalance.

indicators of government officials are mainly economic indicators rather than social indicators. The guiding principle of "giving priority to efficiency and giving consideration to fairness" often turns into "efficiency only, no fairness" in practical work. All this will inevitably lead to a situation where the economic growth indicators have reached or far exceeded the expectations of the plan, while some social development indicators such as environmental protection have not met the requirements of the plan, and there are even no quantitative requirements in social security, public health and medical treatment (Wang, 2005).

Because of this, we believe that in order to promote social development directly related to people's livelihood, the government should take more responsibilities, that is, the government should adjust the expenditure structure, increase social expenditure, and play a fundamental role in providing public goods and services, so that low-income people can also access equal services. This chapter is organized as follows: the first section discusses the government's responsibility from historical and theoretical perspectives; the second section analyzes the current situation and existing problems of Chinese government's social expenditure from an empirical perspective; the third section discusses the importance of social expenditure for the improvement of people's livelihood and the formation of human capital from the perspective of the model, and analyzes the macro impact of fiscal structural adjustment, that is, increasing social expenditure and reducing economic expenditure; the fourth section puts forward conclusions and policy recommendations.

10.1 Government Responsibility: Historical and Theoretical Perspectives

The study of the role or responsibility of the government cannot do without the relationship between the government and the market, which has been a controversial topic in the long history of economic development. Therefore, it is necessary to discuss the role of the government from a historical perspective.

From the night watchman government of Smith to the government intervention of Keynes, to the privatization of Reagan and Thatcher, to the new state interventionism and the "left turn" of some countries, the role of the government has changed from time to time. In essence, it is just a trade-off between dealing with government failure and market failure. Market failure has justified government intervention legally. However, practice shows that government intervention will also bring about government failure. Many scholars have pointed out that the late-developing countries are in the catch-up stage and need government leadership, which seems to provide new grounds for government intervention.

However, the results of government intervention to make up for the deficient market mechanism and market failure of late-developing countries are not ideal. In fact, the intervening government should first do the right things, but it is difficult to meet this condition. Moreover, the problem caused by improper government intervention is no less serious than market failure (Datta Chaudhuri, 1990). This is an important reason why many developing countries preferred neoclassicism and market mechanism to structuralism and government intervention in the 1950s and 1960s.

There is no essential difference between government failure and market failure in both developed and developing countries. The best choice should be to find an optimal balance between government failure and market failure. Acemoglu et al. (2000) pointed out that we should not blindly emphasize the coverage of public finance, but he considered what kind of public expenditure is effective. The optimal government intervention would lead to government failure provided: (1) government intervention required bureaucrats to collect information and implement policies for it; (2) at least some people who enter the bureaucracy could be eroded by corruption, which meant that they might misreport information at the right price; (3) bureaucrats were somewhat heterogeneous. These three conditions meant that government intervention would create opportunities for corruption, create room for the rent-seeking of civil servants and lead to the misallocation of resources. Compared with the situation where there were no opportunities for corruption, corruption may lead to the expansion of the government and the rise of civil servants' wages. They then pointed out that the government failure did not necessarily mean that government intervention was harmful, because the government was taxing some behaviors and subsidizing others to make up for market failure.

Tanzi et al. (2005) summarized the historical changes of the role of government from the perspective of experience by discussing the growth of public expenditure in industrialized countries from the 1870s to 2005.

During the First World War in 1870, the average share of public expenditure in GDP increased slowly, from 10.7% in 1870 to 11.9% in 1913. The "Great Depression" provided the most sufficient reason for the expansion of the government. By 1937, public expenditure had increased to an average of 22.8%, about twice that of 1913. After the Second World War, especially during the period from 1960 to 1980, people showed unprecedented enthusiasm for active spending policies. As a result, the share of public expenditure in GDP increased from 28% in 1960 to 43% in 1980. Throughout the 1980s and early 1990s, excessive government spending and the expensive welfare plans were increasingly criticized, and the government also committed to and launched multiple reforms (including the privatization of social security). Therefore, on the whole, the level of public expenditure continued to rise, but at a markedly slower pace. The unweighted average public expenditure reached 44.8% of GDP in 1990 and 45.6% in 1996 (Tanzi et al., 2005). From 1997 to 2004, the proportion of government expenditure to GDP in G7 countries experienced a slow growth or a slight decline (Tanzi et al., 2005).

Similar to the theoretical analysis of Acemoglu et al. (2000), Tanzi et al. (2005) also pointed out a trade-off between the government and the market through empirical analysis: the increase of public expenditure will have two effects: firstly, more taxes will be levied, which will lead to the decline of personal disposable income; secondly, the demand of those who benefit from public expenditure to take actions according to their own capabilities to prevent various risks has been weakened. In this case, public action has to some extent replaced private action. Therefore, they believed that increasing public expenditure would not automatically improve public welfare. Through the study of government scale and performance, Tanzi et al. (2005) further pointed out that although large governments generally did better in providing fairness, small governments could also achieve welfare growth satisfactorily. However, with regard to the prospect of future government functions, they did not agree to return to the "Hobbes jungle" era, but they suggested that the functions and public expenditure of the country should be more moderate and targeted, so that the country might usher in a vibrant economy and social welfare would increase. In this way, people would live a more stable life, enjoy the freedom of choice and revitalize the market, and benefit from the security provided by public goods and social safety nets.

The above analysis reveals the debates about the size of the government and the coverage of government public expenditure. Although these debates have not ended so far, the understanding of the basic responsibilities of the government has gradually formed a consensus from the historical perspective, that is, no matter how the role and size of the government change, the government is responsible for guaranteeing expenditure on:

1. public goods and services, including pure public goods such as national defense, public order, and security, and general public services such as administrative management and legislation.
2. merit goods and services, including education and health services, as well as housing and community living facilities, entertainment and cultural affairs.
3. social security and welfare, also known as income maintenance.
4. economic services, such as rural infrastructure with strong externalities.

Considering the theme of this chapter, we do not intend to discuss all aspects of government responsibility, but focus on the second and third aspects, namely education, medical care and social security, which are related to people's livelihood.

Theoretically, we should first examine government responsibility from the perspective of market failure in a general sense.

In terms of high-quality goods and services, market failure is mainly reflected in its strong positive externalities. The social marginal income often exceeds the private marginal income. With insufficient awareness and evaluation of social income, individuals are unwilling to spend on consumer goods, for which the government should provide subsidy or the said high-quality goods and services free of charge.

Social security usually includes two types of intervention measures: social insurance and social assistance. The former primarily helps reduce the fluctuation of personal income and expenditure and realizes risk protection through the mandatory participation of a large number of individuals and enterprises under the organizational management and financial support of the government giving necessary financial support and bearing the ultimate responsibility. Of course, the weak correlation (non-equivalence) between contributions and benefits in the process of social insurance also reflects the intention of income redistribution, including the redistribution at the horizontal level between the rich and the poor, and the redistribution at the vertical level between generations or different stages of the life cycle. While social assistance is to realize altruistic assistance or income redistribution through government transfer payments supported by general taxes. The market failure related to social security, especially social insurance, is mainly reflected in three aspects: first, the strong, lasting and wide impact of social risk causes difficulties in identifying the incidence, predicting the consequences of events, conducting currency measurement and effectively dispersing risks, so such risk is generally uninsurable from a commercial perspective; second, due to information asymmetry, adverse selection and moral hazard problems lead to failure of the insurance market; third, the collective nature of social risk makes the prevention of social risk a public product including collective product or common goods, or more precisely a club product, which must be prevented by some social collective action.

When considering the responsibility of the government, "social justice" or "social fairness" is another important dimension that requires meticulous survey, serving as an important base for this chapter.

The theory of social justice can be traced back to the classical utilitarianism proposed by Bentham, who believed that social welfare was the simple sum of the welfare or utility of all social members, and that society should pursue "the maximum happiness of the largest number of people," that is, the maximization of the total utility of all social members. Although utilitarianism believes that the welfare of any member of society should be treated equally, it only cares about the total amount of utility and thus ignores the issue of welfare distribution.

The modern theory of social justice has been far away from utilitarianism, emphasizing the importance of social justice. Representatives are John Rawls, Amartya Sen, etc.

Rawls' theory of justice (1971) is based on two principles: first, everyone should have the broadest fundamental freedom equally; second, the difference in social distribution among individuals should be based on the principle of not harming the interests of the most vulnerable group in society, and the status and position should be accessible to all. Under the principle of difference or maximum, Rawls' social welfare function assumed that people were risk-averse and chose under the "veil of ignorance" proposed by Hasanyi (1955). The level of social welfare depended on the welfare level of the people with the lowest utility in society. In Rawls' view, the allocation of resources agreed upon by all members of society without knowing their social situation was fair. Justice referred to some fundamental concepts, such as the equal distribution of primary goods to all citizens.

Sen's theory of social justice (1999a) mainly focuses on "freedom." In Sen's view, there were different types of human freedom at various levels, including both "instrumental freedom" and "substantive freedom." Regarding instrumental freedom, Sen listed five important forms: (1) political freedom; (2) economic conditions; (3) social opportunities; (4) transparency assurance; (5) protective guarantee. As for substantive freedom, Sen introduced the core concept of "capability." A person's "capability" refers to the combination of various possible functioning that the person is likely to achieve. "Capability" is therefore a kind of freedom, the substantial freedom to realize the combination of various possible functioning. It is from the perspective of "capability" that Sen looks at the issue of fairness. Sen argued that through public behavior, the government should pay more attention to the improvement of people's "capability" or substantive freedom, such as access to education, medical care, etc.

In addition, there is the social justice theory of the supremacy of freedom, represented by Robert Nozick. Nozick's social justice theory can also be summarized as the entitlement theory (1974). This theory evaluates fairness not from the perspective of procedures instead of results, that is, procedural justice. In Nozick's view, the result was the product of the process, so the focus on fairness should be on the aspect of process fairness. He believed that as long as the basic rights of individuals were guaranteed and respected, it was fair. These basic rights included the right to survival, the right to obtain individual products of labor and the right to free choice. Nozick believed that these rights and the "due" derived from them were sacred, inviolable, unconditional and absolute. The evaluation of fairness did not depend on whether to satisfy individual preferences, but on whether to ensure the exercise of freedom and rights. Further, if a distribution started from a fair state and went through a fair process, then the distribution result should be considered fair, even if it may be unequal.

So, how do the basic education, medical care, and social security that citizens enjoy reflect social fairness? This can be understood from the following three aspects.

First, the equality of civil rights or the guarantee of survival rights. The right of citizens to enjoy education, health, and minimum living security is collectively referred to as "welfare rights" or "social rights" in the West and is regarded as an extension of basic civil rights or a part of social citizenship. The "welfare clause" in the United Nations Declaration of Human Rights explicitly stipulates this right, such as Article 22: "Every person, as a member of society, has the right to enjoy social security and the realization of various economic, social and cultural rights necessary for his personal dignity and the free development of his personality"; Article 25: "Everyone has the right to enjoy the standard of living necessary to maintain the health and welfare of himself and his family, including food, clothing, housing, medical care and necessary social services, and to enjoy security in the event of unemployment, disease, disability, widowhood, aging or loss of livelihood under other uncontrollable circumstances"; Article 26: "Everyone has the right to education. Education should be free, at least at the primary and basic stages." The right of citizens to enjoy education, health and minimum living security is mainly reflected in the value of survival: everyone's certain survival needs must be met by using public resources to reach a socially determined minimum value, and no one should fall below the minimum value of nutrition, housing, medical care, education and other aspects. This "basic need" that must be met is mainly a reflection of the social preference of "risk aversion" that is manifested in response to certain uncertainties in economic life. It is derived from certain moral norms and belongs to the category of bottom-line justice or bottom-line ethics. In this sense, the right of citizens to enjoy education, health and minimum living security based on the value of survival is first of all a moral right, and this right is often prescribed in the form of national laws, thus rising to legal rights. Respecting and protecting this right will also realize the procedural fairness that Nozick emphasized.

Second, fairness or equality of opportunity. The so-called fair opportunity means that a person's achievements should be the result of efforts and talents, rather than determined by his own background including some natural conditions and social relations. In general, education and health are important tools for equal opportunities. They directly affect a person's ability to survive, participate in the economy, and create income and wealth, or the capability that Sen emphasized. The social security system changes or enhances people's opportunities by providing people with safety nets and improves their ability by helping people manage risks. Therefore, education, medical care and social security are all conducive to achieving equal opportunities or fairness in the sense of starting point. However, it should be emphasized that only when all members of society, regardless of their background, have equal access to education, health and social security, will their guarantee mechanism for (achievement) equality of opportunity work. In other words, equality of opportunity in the first sense is the premise of equality of opportunity in the second sense. Public action should be committed to the equalization of opportunities at the first level, ensuring equal opportunities for all members of society to receive education, health and social security, so as to ensure equal opportunities for their progress and achievements in the future.

Third, avoid extreme poverty. In the real world, absolute equality of opportunity is often difficult to achieve. Even if there is real equality of opportunity, there always come different results due to different talents, efforts and luck. In this case, the Rawls doctrine, which is very disgusted with absolute poverty or inequality of results, shows that it is necessary to protect the extremely poor people in society, that is, the groups below the absolute survival demand line, through public intervention, namely the income redistribution mechanism. Not only does absolute poverty itself require public intervention, but absolute poverty also has an impact on shaping opportunities. Because compared with high-income groups, low-income and vulnerable groups tend to have lower average years of education, fewer health services and the most deficient protection from risk management. This means that inequity of results leads to inequity of opportunities, and may lead to new inequity of results, thus falling into the so-called "poverty trap" or "unfairness trap." To get rid of this vicious circle, the government must implement income redistribution to ensure a fair result to a certain extent. This fair mechanism is most obvious in social relief.

It is based on the demand for social fairness that the responsibility of the government is highlighted. Since the market cannot solve the problem of fairness automatically, or the market failure is the most serious in providing the public goods of "social justice," it is necessary for the government to assume its responsibility and play a major role in actively promoting fairness.

10.2 Government Social Expenditure: Status Quo and Problems

The structure of government expenditure can be generally divided into maintenance expenditure dominated by administrative expenditure and national defense expenditure; economic expenditure dominated by government investment; social expenditure dominated by education, health and social security. Social expenditure also generally includes housing expenditure such as subsidies for low-rent housing. The government itemized expenditure shows that the expenditure directly related to people's livelihood, such as education, medical care and social security, is social expenditure. We now analyze the status quo and problems of China from the perspective of social expenditure.

1. Education Expenditure

Figure 52 shows that the proportion of education expenditure in fiscal expenditure has increased from 6.7% in 1978 to 17.8% in 1996 and followed a substantially declining trend since then. In 2004, the proportion was only 13.5%, lower than those of other developing countries, such as Thailand's 22.44% (2000) and Mexico's 25.54% (1999). The share of public education expenditure in GDP has been hovering at 2% - 3% for years, not only far lower than the average level of developed countries and the world, but also lower than the level of

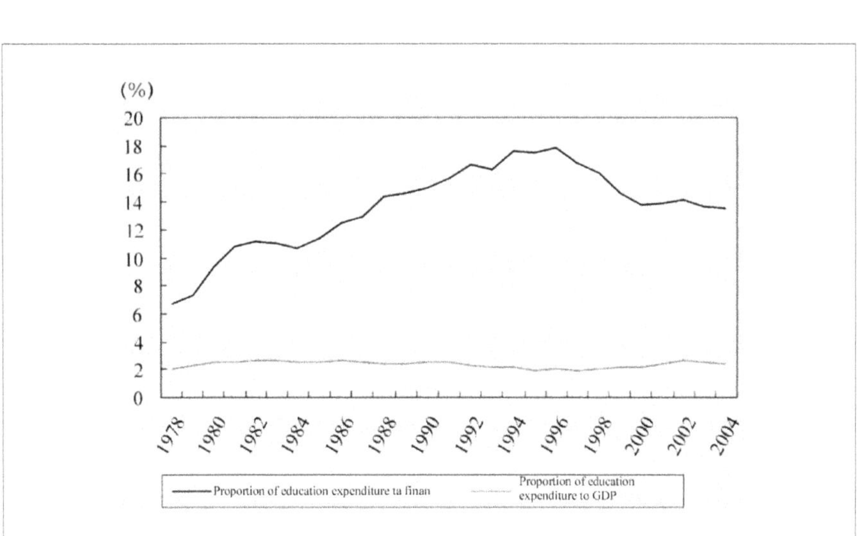

Figure 52. Changes in the share of education expenditure

Source: China Financial Yearbook 2005.

underdeveloped countries [the world average was 4.8% in 1997, 5.4% in high-income countries, 4.8% in middle-income countries, and 3.3% in low-income countries (World Bank, 2001)], This also lags behind the goal of "to achieve 4% of the national financial education expenditure in the gross national product by the year 2000," which was committed in the Outline of China's Education Reform and Development issued by the country as early as 1993.

From the perspective of the source of education funds, on the one hand, the proportion of education funds in the budget to the total education funds dropped from 62.8% in 1978 to 55.6% in 2004, down 7.2 percentage points. On the other hand, the proportion of tuition and miscellaneous expenses in education funds increased from 4.4% in 1978 to 18.6% in 2004, up 14.2 percentage points (see Figure 53). Obviously, in terms of education financing, the government's share is decreasing, while the individual's share is increasing.

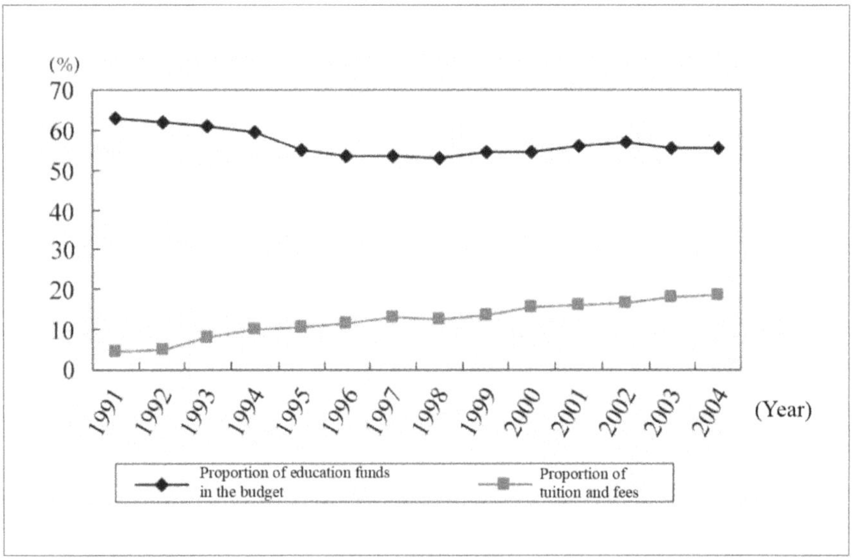

Figure 53. Changes in sources of education funds

Source: China Statistical Abstract (2006), Compilation of statistical data of the fifty-fifth year of the People's Republic of China.

From the perspective of education expenditure structure, on the one hand, the proportion of basic education expenditure is low. On the other hand, there is a large gap between urban and rural education expenditure. In the mid-1990s, with regard to education fund allocation in OECD countries: the average expenditure for primary education students reached about 36% of that for higher education, and that for secondary education reached about 50%. In 1996, the corresponding ratio in China was only 6% in primary school, 11% in junior high school and 24% in senior high school. In 2001, the corresponding rates changed to 6% in primary school, 9% in junior high school and 23% in senior high school (China Education Expenditure Statistical Yearbook 2002). This reflects our inadequate allocation of funds for basic education. From the perspective of urban and rural distribution, schools in the municipalities directly under the Central Government received the highest education expenditure per student, followed by counties directly under the Central Government, then other urban areas and rural areas. The average expenditure per student in urban areas of municipalities directly under the Central Government is more than three times that in rural areas (China Human Development Report 2005). The gap is huge.

2. Health Expenditure

The absolute amount of China's financial investment in health has increased year by year. However, from the perspective of the composition of health expenditure, the proportion of government budget health expenditure has shown an

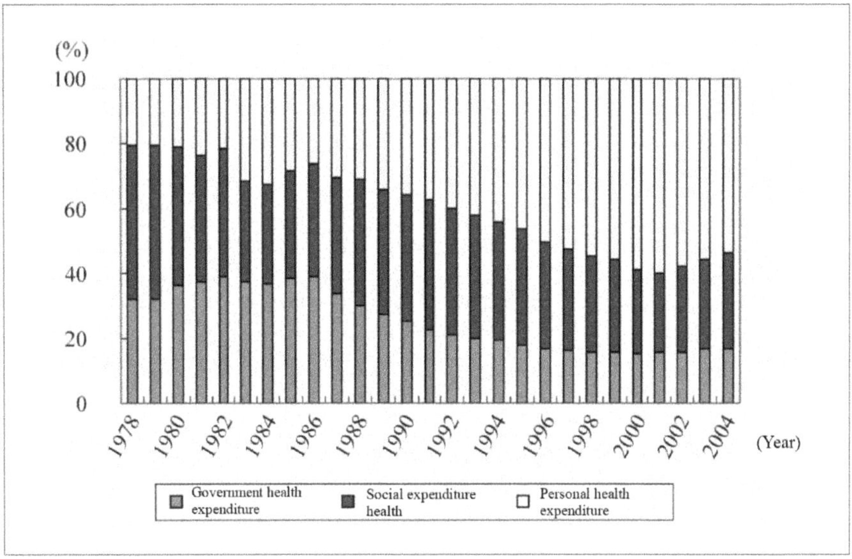

Figure 54. Composition of health expenditure

Source: *China Health Statistics Summary (2006)* (Du, 2004).

obvious downward trend, while the proportion of personal health expenditure has increased significantly. Figure 54 shows that government health expenditure accounted for 32.2% of the total health expenditure in 1978 and increased to 38.7% in 1986. Since then, the proportion of government health expenditure has declined year by year, falling to 15.7% in 2002, and rising slightly after 2003. At the same time, the proportion of personal health expenditure increased from 20.4% in 1978 to 60% in 2001 and then decreased slightly to 53.6% in 2004. Social health expenditure dropped from 47.4% to 29.3% in 2004. From the perspective of changes in the composition of health costs, apparently the costs borne by the government are declining, while the costs borne by individuals are rising. Be it education or medical care, this change is closely related to the reform of the charging system.

Internationally, government and social health expenditure accounts for the vast majority of total health expenditure in both developed and middle-income countries, and even in many low-income countries. Table 38 shows that, compared with the world average, the proportion of individuals and the government in China's health expenditure is just supplementary: China's personal expenditure accounts for 60.6%, and government expenditure accounts for 39.4%. However, the world average is 38.2% for personal expenditure and 61.8% for government expenditure. According to the statistics of the World Health Organization in 2002, China's per capita government health expenditure is ranked 131st among the 191 member-countries, while China's personal health expenditure ranked 15th. The shortage of Chinese government health expenditure can also be indicated by the international comparison of the proportion of public health expenditure to GDP: in 2000, the world average level of this proportion was 5.4%, 6.0% in

Table 38. Comparison of health expenditure structure among countries in 2000 (%)

	Proportion of total health expenditure in GDP	Proportion of personal expenditure	Proportion of government expenditure
China	5.3	60.6	39.4
Developed countries	8.5	27.0	73.0
Transitional countries	5.3	30.0	70.0
Least developed countries	4.4	40.7	59.3
Other developing countries	5.6	42.8	57.2
World average	5.7	38.2	61.8

Source: Wang Shaoguang (2003)

high-income countries, 3.0% in middle-income countries, 2.7% in low-middle-income countries, and only 1.9% in China (World Bank, 2004).

Notably, there is a big gap between urban and rural areas in terms of health investment: the absolute difference between urban and rural per capita health expenditure has been increasing since 1990, from 120 yuan in 1990 to 664 yuan in 2002, resulting in a great difference in the use of medical services between urban and rural areas. According to the Third National Health Service Survey, the hospitalization rate of rural residents was lower than that of urban residents - the former was 34%, and the latter was 43%. In addition, 14% of the patients in rural areas did not receive any medical treatment, while the index in urban areas was 10%. Among the patients who should not be discharged from the hospital, 34.5% of the patients in the city requested to be discharged from the hospital, of which 53% were due to financial difficulties. In rural areas, 47% of patients requested to be discharged, of which 67.3% were due to financial difficulties.

3. Social Security Expenditure

Table 39 shows China's financial social security expenditure. The financial social security expenditure mainly refers to the part of the social security expenditure borne by the government, so it is a narrow caliber. According to this caliber, the financial social security expenditure in 2004 stood at 344.026 billion yuan, only 2.15% of GDP. Internationally, in the public finance system of developed market economy countries, public consumption or income support expenditure on social security and welfare is the most important expenditure item of the government, accounting for 30%-50% of the fiscal expenditure and 10%-30% of GDP.

Table 39. China's financial social security expenditure from 1998 to 2004

Year	Financial social security expenditure (100 million yuan)	Proportion in GDP (%)	Proportion in fiscal expenditure (%)
1998	77.488	0.92	7.18
1999	137.553	1.53	10.43
2000	191.841	1.93	12.08
2001	222.868	2.03	11.79
2002	289.397	2.40	13.12
2003	293.826	2.16	11.92
2004	344.026	2.15	12.08

Source: China Financial Yearbook (2005), China Statistical Abstract (2006).

On a broader caliber, namely the social security expenditure of the country and society (mainly enterprises), China reached 731.82 billion yuan in 2002, accounting for 7.15% of its GDP (Cai Shewen, 2004). However, even so, compared with the international community, China's social security expenditure was still very low. Table 40 shows that in the 1960s, social security expenditure accounted for more than 10% of GDP in countries with a per capita GDP of more than USD 1000 (except Japan), while China accounted for only 7.15%.

Table 40. Comparison between the level of social security expenditure of some developed countries in 1960 and that of China in 2002

Country	Year	GDP per capita (USD)	Proportion of social security expenditure in GDP (%)
UK	1960	1363	13.9
Sweden	1960	1641	12.8
Finland	1960	1110	12.7
Denmark	1960	1298	12.5
U.S.	1960	2783	10.3
Japan	1960	458	8.0
France	1960	1297	13.4
German	1960	1345	20.5
China	2002	≈1000	7.15

Source: According to IMF: *Government Finance Statistics Yearbook (2001)* and United Nations: *Statistical Yearbook (1965)*. Quoted from: Cai Shewen (2004).

In addition to the low total level of China's social security expenditure, there are also great structural inequalities. On the one hand, the social security costs of urban workers are getting higher and higher, which exceeds the level that enterprises and society can afford. On the other hand, migrant workers, township enterprise workers and farmers, who account for the vast majority of China's labor force, are hardly covered by the social security system. In terms of old-age security, according to the data of the China Aging Research Center's sampling survey of the country's urban and rural elderly population at the end of 2000, the coverage rate of old-age insurance for the urban elderly reached more than 70%, while the coverage rate of the rural elderly was less than 4%. If we consider that some rural residents who enjoy old-age insurance transferred the insurance they obtained when they were employed in cities and towns back to the countryside, the coverage rate of old-age insurance among real farmers may be lower. In terms of medical security, the overall coverage level is not high, and the gap between urban and rural areas is not small. The Third National Health Service Survey found that 30.2% of the urban population enjoyed basic medical insurance for urban workers, 4.0% enjoyed free medical care, 4.6% enjoyed labor insurance, 5.6% enjoyed commercial medical insurance, and 44.8% without any medical insurance. In rural areas, 9.5% of the rural population participated in cooperative medical care, 3.1% in various social medical insurance, 8.3% in commercial medical insurance, and 79.1% without any medical insurance. In terms of social relief, the expenditure on urban minimum living security in 2004 stood at 17.27 billion yuan, while the sum of rural minimum living security expenditure and rural regular relief expenditure was 3.07 billion yuan, accounting for only 17.8% of the urban minimum living security expenditure.

The social security system aims to build a social safety net.[2] In China, since the government took charge of everything under the traditional planned economy, social security was not considered. However, as China turned to a market economy, the social security network was weakened, and the market security network has not yet been put in place. In this case, a strong social security system would be necessary. In the West, people are worried that the strong and improperly designed social safety net has reduced savings and weakened the motivation of saving. However, China has gone too far in the other direction (Stiglitz, 2006), that is, the social safety net is weak, thus individuals have to take more responsibilities, increasing savings and reducing consumption. From this point of view, we believe that one of the important reasons for the current high domestic savings is the insufficient government expenditure on social security.

4. Overall Situation of Social Expenditure

The above respectively discussed the low expenditure on education, medical care and social security. On the whole, China maintains a low financial social

[2] Social safety net (SSN) generally refers to the social security system formed by the government as the main body. From a worldwide perspective, the concept of social safety net has been widely adopted since the 1980s and is closely linked with social policies. In China, with the deepening of structural adjustment and reform, the concept of "social safety net" first appeared in the form of an official document in the Ninth Five-Year Plan. It is also from this period that the national finance has been adjusted accordingly: first, a new category of "social security subsidy expenditure" has been added to the government budget since 1998, and then the national social security fund has been supplemented for several consecutive years since the end of the Ninth Five-Year Plan, so as to further improve the subject of financial and social security expenditure and enrich the financial and social security investment to a certain extent (although the gap is still large).

Table 41. Financial social expenditure and its proportion

Year	Total social expenditure (100 million yuan)	Proportion of social expenditure to fiscal expenditure (%)	Proportion of social expenditure to GDP (%)
1978	94.07	8.38	2.60
1979	112.89	8.81	2.80
1980	134.42	10.94	2.98
1981	149.88	13.17	3.08
1982	177.69	14.45	3.36
1983	203.41	14.43	3.43
1984	237.34	13.95	3.31
1985	305.84	15.26	3.41
1986	372.52	16.90	3.65
1987	392.04	17.33	3.28
1988	46.006	18.47	3.08
1989	54.057	19.14	3.20
1990	59.849	19.41	3.23
1991	68.896	20.34	3.19
1992	78.086	20.87	2.93
1993	95.266	20.52	2.70
1994	123.328	21.29	2.56
1995	145.436	21.31	2.39
1996	173.193	21.82	2.43
1997	206.052	22.32	2.61
1998	249.218	23.08	2.95
1999	309.489	23.47	3.45
2000	380.889	23.98	3.84
2001	450.997	23.86	4.11
2002	510.836	23.16	4.25
2003	552.469	22.41	4.07
2004	639.517	22.45	4.00

Note: Social expenditure= Social, cultural and educational expenditure - scientific research expenditure

Source: *China Financial Yearbook (2005)*

expenditure. Table 41 shows that in the 1990s, the fiscal social expenditure[3] accounted for 20% -24% of the total fiscal expenditure. Its share in GDP was a little more than 4%. Comparison among countries show that China's financial social expenditure accounts for a low proportion compared with countries at all income levels (see Table 42).

Table 42. Proportion of financial social expenditure of countries with different incomes

	High-income countries		Mid-income countries		Low-income countries	
Items	% of GDP	% of total expenditure	% of GDP	% of total expenditure	% of GDP	% of total expenditure
Social expenditure	21.1	49.5	11.5	42.1	7.6	27.5
Education	4.3	11.0	3.8	14.9	3.9	14.7
Health	3.4	8.3	2	7.7	1.7	6.3
Social security	12.2	27.5	4.6	15.7	1.3	4.2
housing	1.2	2.7	1.1	3.8	0.7	2.3

Source: IMF: *Government Finance Statistics Yearbook (1995)*.

Through a large number of data above, we have shown that in the process of economic growth, the whole social expenditure has not achieved a corresponding rapid growth, thus social and economic development are not commensurate, specifically: first, in social expenditure, the share of the government is relatively low, or even declining; second, in terms of the benefits from the increase in social expenditure, there is severe inequality between different classes or income groups. Therefore, we believe that the government should expand the proportion of social expenditure, provide basic public services such as education, medical care and social security, and promote the accessibility of these services for low-income groups to achieve social equity in a stepped manner.

3 The total social expenditure here is not equal to the sum of education, medical care and social security expenditure in the previous analysis. Because there is an overlap between social security expenditure and medical expenditure. In addition, in the international comparison, social, cultural and educational expenses do not include relevant housing subsidies. This leads to certain incompatibility between these groups of data. However, this does not affect the overall trend.

10.3 Government Social Expenditure, Human Capital Accumulation, and Growth

The previous section emphasized the importance of government social expenditure and pointed out that the proportion of social expenditure should be expanded in the fiscal expenditure structure. It is less controversial to improve people's livelihood through more social expenditure. However, this practice may also be questionable, that is, it is likely to raise the proportion of social expenditure, the so-called "non-productive" expenditure[4], hinder future economic growth, thus causing the deterioration of people's livelihood in the future. Below we will reveal the macro prospect of fiscal structure adjustment through model analysis.

Government social expenditure was also mentioned in the past literature, but it is still controversial. The biggest controversy among them is the division of the so-called productive expenditure and non-productive expenditure. To promote growth, the government should increase the proportion of productive expenditure. However, the problem lies in the classification of productive expenditures and non-productive expenditures. In fact, whether a public expenditure is productive or non-productive depends on the relative scarcity of the expenditure in the total expenditure. The empirical research shows that the proportion of public investment in education, health, culture, social security and other aspects by the governments of developing countries is too low and should be increased (Zou, 1996). Baqir (2002) also emphasized the role of social expenditure in economic growth, especially in eliminating income inequality.

We have identified the formation of human capital as the key link through a further investigation of the relationship between social expenditure and growth.

The role of social expenditure in promoting human capital accumulation is supported by a series of empirical studies. Sen (1999b) pointed out in a recent article that because infant mortality, severe malnutrition and widespread illiteracy would directly interrupt people's lives, economic resources should be first allocated to support the affected people in these areas, especially basic education and basic health care services. IMF (1999) pointed out through the empirical analysis of panel data of 50 developing countries and transitional countries that public expenditure on basic education, such as primary and secondary education, and basic health care played a very important role in improving school enrollment and reducing infant mortality. These were also critical for human

[4] The actual meaning of "productive" or "non-productive" expenditure used here in this chapter is "promoting growth" or "non-promoting growth" expenditure.

capital accumulation. Based on micro-data, Strauss & Thomas (1998) believed that health at least had the same explanatory power for changes in wage levels like education. The macro data further supports the positive externality of intervention in the health sector. Bloom and Canning (2003), Bloom and Canning (2004), Gyimah–Brempong and Wilson (2004) found that there was a positive correlation between health capital indicators and total output. They found that the growth rate of 22%–30% can be explained by health capital.

Based on a simple social planner model, we analyze the impact of fiscal expenditure structure adjustment on long-term economic growth through the link of financial social expenditure and corresponding human capital accumulation. We ignore the maintenance expenditure such as administrative expenditure and divide the government expenditure into economic expenditure and social expenditure. The former mainly refers to the infrastructure and basic research provided by the government. The enterprises must use this part of public goods or services in production, which is shown by stock G_Y. The latter, expressed by stock G_H, includes expenditures on compulsory education, basic medical care and social security. These expenditures affect human capital accumulation. In order to simplify the analysis and model setting, we use G_h, G_p, I_k, respectively to represent the flow of financial social expenditure, financial economic expenditure and new material capital investment. K and C respectively represent the stock of material capital investment and residents' consumption. We assume that the (human) capital depreciation rate formed by financial social expenditure, the capital depreciation rate formed by financial economic expenditure and the material capital depreciation rate are expressed as δ.

Assume the government uses lump-sum tax payments to balance the budget expenditure according to the optimal expenditure level of "revenue based on expenditure," thus the distortion effect of tax on household labor supply can be ignored, and the impact of tax can be simplified. Families are both consumers and producers. Assume that households do not invest in human capital, all human capital investment will be paid for by the government.[5]

Based on the above assumptions, we can build a differential dynamical system composed of the following equations (1) to (6):

$$Y = AK^{\alpha}G_H^{\beta}G_Y^{\xi}$$

[5] This assumption may not be completely consistent with the reality. More realistically, it may be that the human capital investment of the family itself and the human capital investment of the government maintain a fixed proportion, but the above assumption will not affect the conclusion.

Provide: $\alpha + \beta + \xi = 1$[6] (1)

Economic resource constraint is:

$$Y = C + I_k + G_b + G_p \tag{2}$$

The equations of state are:

$$\dot{K} = I_K - \delta K \tag{3}$$

$$\dot{G}_H = G_b - \delta G_H \tag{4}$$

$$\dot{G}_Y = G_p - \delta G_Y \tag{5}$$

Assume the government is omniscient and knows the utility function of the family, the government maximizes the goal function of the family under the constraint of the resource equation (2) by selecting the appropriate consumption level, economic expenditure and social expenditure:

$$W = \max \int_0^{\infty} e^{-\rho t} u\left[C(t)\right] dt \text{ [7]} \tag{6}$$

Where $u\left[C(t)\right]$ is the household utility function and:

$$u(C) = \left(C^{1-\theta} - 1\right)/\left(1-\theta\right)$$

Simplify the first-order conditions of the above differential dynamic system, and we can get (see the appendix):

$$\frac{\dot{C}}{C} = -\frac{1}{\theta}\frac{\dot{v}}{v} - \frac{\rho}{\theta} = -\frac{1}{\theta}\frac{\dot{\lambda}}{\lambda} - \frac{\rho}{\theta} = \frac{1}{\theta}\left[\alpha A K^{\alpha-1} G_H^{\beta} G_Y^{\xi} - \delta - \rho\right] \tag{7}$$

6 This regulation makes the production function have the characteristic of constant return to scale, which is beneficial to explain the relationship between financial social expenditure and long-term growth.

7 Among them, "ρ" is a common discount rate in utility function, also known as time preference rate.

Among them, $\alpha AK^{\alpha-1}G_H^{\beta}G_Y^{\xi}-\delta$ is the net marginal product of material capital. The first-order condition shows that $\frac{\dot{\upsilon}}{\upsilon}=\frac{\dot{\lambda}}{\lambda}=\frac{\dot{\eta}}{\eta}=\frac{\dot{\gamma}}{\gamma}$, and the further solution is:

$$\begin{cases} \alpha G_H = \beta K \\ \beta G_Y = \xi G_H \\ \alpha G_Y = \xi K \end{cases} \tag{8}$$

Equation (8) can be further written as:

$$\begin{cases} \frac{G_Y}{G_H} = \frac{\xi}{\beta} \\ \frac{G_Y}{K} = \frac{\xi}{\alpha} \text{ and } \frac{\dot{G}_H}{G_H} = \frac{\dot{G}_Y}{G_Y} = \frac{\dot{K}}{K} \\ \frac{G_H}{K} = \frac{\beta}{\alpha} \end{cases} \tag{9}$$

The above equations show that under the constraint of maximizing household utility, the optimal growth path requires that financial social expenditure, financial economic expenditure and material capital stock must maintain a certain proportion. Under the assumption of the same capital depreciation, the long-term balanced growth requires that the three kinds of capital growth maintain the same proportion. If we take into account the rule that returns to scale remains unchanged namely $\alpha+\beta+\xi=1$, combing equation (9) with the production function $Y=AK^{\alpha}G_H^{\beta}G_Y^{\xi}$, we have:

$$Y = AG_H \cdot \left(\frac{\alpha^{\alpha} \cdot \xi^{\xi}}{\beta^{\alpha+\xi}} \right) \tag{10}$$

This result is equivalent to the well-known AK model. It implies that the increase of government social expenditure is not only endogenous in the long-term growth path, but also conducive to the stability of economic growth.[8] Moreover, in view

[8] Here, we actually regard G_H as an alternative variable of human capital accumulation, thus forming an endogenous sustainable growth path of technological progress with increasing returns to scale.

of the special nature of the AK model, in the long run, the balanced growth of output is consistent with both the growth of financial social expenditure and the growth of economic expenditure and material capital.

This simple model answers the question of whether the structural adjustment of fiscal expenditure will reduce the long-term growth rate. In fact, the government's social expenditure constitutes the force to support long-term economic growth by increasing human capital. Of course, the human capital investment formed by government social expenditure is not the more the better. Under the condition of diminishing marginal output of human capital, excessive social expenditure will inevitably lead to "excess of human capital," making the net marginal product of human capital lower than the net marginal product of material capital, resulting in efficiency loss. At the same time, if the government's tax factors are taken into account, too much social expenditure will inevitably require more taxes. In reality, taxes are generally not a lump-sum tax and mainly include commodity tax or income tax. These taxes distort consumers' demand for goods and labor supply. Therefore, too much social expenditure will also cause efficiency loss due to too much tax. Our conclusion is that the human capital formed by government social expenditure must maintain a coordinated growth with the material capital, neither too much nor too little.

10.4 Conclusion and Policy Recommendations

Through theoretical and empirical analysis, this chapter points out that the current development of China is characterized by an imbalance in the relationship between the country's wealth and the people's livelihood. Although this is caused by a variety of factors, the lack of government social expenditure is undoubtedly an important one. Therefore, the burden that the government has lifted under the financial pressure[9] and the promotion of market-oriented reform needs to be shouldered again in the new stage of development, which means that the

[9] The reform of the charging system for medical care and education and the social security system basically began in the mid-1990s, when the central finance was in dire straits. Schumpeter (1918) pointed out in the article "The Crisis of the Tax Country" that the study of fiscal history enabled people to "understand the laws of social existence and social change, and the driving force of the country's destiny." Schumpeter also made a particularly brilliant comment: "The research method starting from the national finance is particularly effective when it is used to study the turning point of social development … At the turning point of the society, the existing forms have successively disappeared and changed into new forms, and the turning point of the society always contains the crisis of the original financial policy … "

government should take the basic responsibility in providing public services such as compulsory education, basic medical care and social security, to improve the people's livelihood and correct the imbalance in growth. The government should promote human capital accumulation and long-term healthy development of the economy through the increase of social expenditure.

The direct policy implication of this chapter is to accelerate the transformation of the fiscal expenditure structure and increase the proportion of compulsory education, basic medical care and social security expenditure in fiscal expenditure. Under the excessively fast and overheated growth of government-led investment, falling marginal efficiency of investment and aggravated imbalance between departments, the development strategies should be readjusted, the construction of the public financial system accelerated, and more social expenditure should be made to increase the contribution of human capital to economic growth.

In the process of policy implementation, more attention should be paid to.

First, the transformation of economic growth path and growth power. The growth of social expenditure, on the one hand, will promote human capital accumulation, promote the transformation of the growth path from factor input-driven to productive efficiency improvement, and achieve stable and sustained economic growth on this basis; on the other hand, will be conducive to building a strong social safety net, reducing uncertainty in the future, thereby reducing savings, promoting consumption, and bringing about changes in the driving force of growth—growth is driven by domestic demand (especially consumption) instead of investment and export. Although human capital formation and consumption growth will take time, the positive role of social expenditure growth in the transformation of the growth path and the transformation of growth power will take effect.

Second, the limit of government responsibility. This chapter emphasizes the basic responsibility of the government, not necessarily meaning it should take charge of everything just like in the past but stress the payment responsibility of the government in the fundamental education and health services and social security. It is because, on the one hand, in a developing country, the government is constrained in financial expenditure. More importantly, it is necessary to avoid negative incentives and moral hazard problems caused by excessive security. The lessons of insufficient economic vitality and sluggish economic growth in some high-welfare countries are worth learning, and the harm of populism in Latin America necessitates keen alert. We believe that we should mobilize the joint forces of the state, market and society (public domain, private domain and third domain) so that individuals, governments and the third sector [mainly non-governmental organizations (NGOs)] take joint responsibility in social expenditure.

Third, the structure of government social expenditure. While emphasizing the expansion of total social expenditure, we should also pay attention to the structural adjustment of social expenditure to improve the efficiency of expenditure: in the field of education, we should further increase the proportion of expenditure on basic education compared with the expenditure on higher education; in the field of health care, we should further increase the proportion of expenditure on preventive health care [compared to the expenditure on curative health care]. At the same time, in view of the huge urban-rural differences and group differences in social expenditures, in the process of expanding social expenditures, we should give more consideration to rural population and the poor, to ensure fair social expenditure.

Fourth, the way of government social expenditure. This involves the distinction between positive social expenditure and negative social expenditure. Taking employment as an example, active social expenditure aims to reduce the barriers to labor market access, creating more jobs for beneficiaries. For this purpose, we should implement active labor market policies, such as employment training, helping the unemployed find jobs, providing rehabilitation services for disabled workers, providing wage subsidies and other work incentives, as well as providing family care, especially childcare, reducing the cost of working outside, and providing entrepreneurial support. The negative social expenditure is only a transfer payment or income support. This negative social expenditure often has no impact on the inequality of market income, and sometimes even expands the inequality of market income when the labor supply decreases, or the savings decrease. Its impact on the final income inequality depends on whether the transfer payment can offset the possible expansion of the inequality of market income. The inequality of market income and final income can be both reduced through active social expenditure. Therefore, in the process of government social expenditure, more emphasis should be placed on "teaching people how to fish" rather than "giving people fish."

Fifth, government provision of public goods and services does not mean government production. This chapter mainly studies the payment methods of education and medical services from the perspective of consumption, and advocates rebalancing between the government payment methods supported by tax and the individual payment methods supported by consumer payment, increasing the proportion of government burden and reducing the proportion of individual burden. In fact, in addition to the payment problem in the consumption link, for education and medical services, the supply for raw quasi-public products for production is also a problem. In this regard, we should not overemphasize the supply responsibility of the government but more encourage market operation mechanisms such as competition and private participation. The government only needs to more faithfully fulfill its regulatory responsibility. Of course, when adverse selection and moral hazard problems arise from incomplete information or incomplete contracts, lowering the quality of private supply services (especially in medical services), the way of in-house provision instead of private participation such as contracting out should be adopted. In this case, we should also strive to improve the quality of public supply by giving some incentives and strengthening accountability.

Sixth, the respective roles of the central and local governments. In line with the trend of decentralization reform, in terms of social expenditure, the role of local governments should be given full play, for: (1) according to the public choice theory, the "small collective" with fewer members can supply public goods more efficiently than the "large collective" with more members. (2) the huge differences between regions will inevitably lead to different preferences of users in various regions for social services. Giving full play to the role of local governments can more accurately respond to local needs and make decisions and can more effectively provide social services that meet local preferences and local specific conditions, so as to better serve users, and ensure that local governments are more efficient in the supply of social services. At the same time, for national social services, the central government has the main responsibility for payment. In view of the different financial resources among regions, the central government also needs to assist local governments to assume the responsibility for payment of regional social services through transfer payments.

Appendix

The Hamilton equation of the dynamic system is composed of equations (1) to (6):

$$J = e^{-\rho t} \cdot u(C) + v(I_k - \delta K) + \lambda(G_b - \delta G_H) + \eta(G_p - \delta G_Y) + \gamma\left(AK^{\alpha} G_H{}^{\beta}\, G_Y{}^{\xi} - C - I_k - G_b - G_p\right)$$

where, v, λ, and η are the shadow prices of material capital, government social expenditure and government economic expenditure, respectively. γ is Lagrange multiplier.

The first-order conditions are:

(I) For C:

$$e^{-\rho t} u'(C) = \gamma$$

(II) For K:

$$-\delta v + \alpha A K^{\alpha-1} G_H^{\beta} G_Y^{\xi} \cdot \gamma = -\dot{v}$$

(III) For G_H:

$$-\delta\lambda + \beta A K^{\alpha} G_H^{\beta-1} G_Y^{\xi} \cdot \gamma = -\dot{\lambda}$$

(IV) For GY:

$$-\delta\eta + \xi A K^{\alpha} G_H^{\beta} G_Y^{\xi-1} \cdot \gamma = -\dot{\eta}$$

(V) For I_k:

$$v = \gamma$$

(VI) For G_h:

$$\lambda = \gamma$$

(VII) For G_p:

$$\eta = \gamma$$

The relationship between the first-order conditions is as follows:
From (V), (VI), and (VII),

$v = \lambda = \gamma$ and $\frac{\dot{v}}{v} = \frac{\dot{\lambda}}{\lambda} = \frac{\dot{\eta}}{\eta} = \frac{\dot{\gamma}}{\gamma}$ (i) can be obtained.

From (I), (i), and the definition of utility function:

$\frac{\dot{C}}{C} = -\frac{1}{\theta}\frac{\dot{v}}{v} - \frac{\rho}{\theta} = -\frac{1}{\theta}\frac{\dot{\lambda}}{\lambda} - \frac{\rho}{\theta} = -\frac{1}{\theta}\frac{\dot{\eta}}{\eta} - \frac{\rho}{\theta} = \frac{1}{\theta}\left(\alpha A K^{\alpha-1} G_H^{\beta} G_Y^{\xi} - \delta - \rho\right)$ (ii) can be obtained.

From (II), (III), (IV), and (i),

$\begin{cases} \alpha G_H = \beta K \\ \beta G_Y = \xi G_H \\ \alpha G_Y = \xi K \end{cases}$ (iii) can be obtained.

From (iii),

$$\begin{cases} \dfrac{G_Y}{G_H} = \dfrac{\xi}{\beta} \\ \dfrac{G_Y}{K} = \dfrac{\xi}{\alpha} \\ \dfrac{G_H}{K} = \dfrac{\beta}{\alpha} \end{cases} \text{ and } \frac{\dot{G}_H}{G_H} = \frac{\dot{G}_Y}{G_Y} = \frac{\dot{K}}{K} \text{ (iv) can be obtained.}$$

Connecting (iv) and production function $Y = AK^{\alpha}G_H^{\beta}G_Y^{\xi}$ and its provision $\alpha + \beta + \xi = 1$,

$$Y = AG_H \cdot \left(\frac{\alpha^{\alpha} \cdot \xi^{\xi}}{\beta^{\alpha+\xi}} \right) \text{ (V) can be obtained.}$$

Optimal Wealth Distribution and Harmonious Social Welfare Function

11.1 Introduction

The theoretical research circle in China now pays close attention to three interrelated and interactive subjects namely: (1) a widening income gap, (2) insufficient domestic demand and (3) ways to build a harmonious society. It is generally believed the excessive income disparity will cause the rich reluctant to spend money and the poor to aspire after the impossible consumption, which is an important cause for insufficient domestic demand. And further widening income gap may also lead to polarization, aggravate social problems and affect the building of a harmonious society. This study on the optimal wealth distribution and harmonious social welfare function is of great theoretical and practical significance and can provide practical reference for the future formulation of China's inheritance tax law and the ongoing VAT reform.

The research on income distribution is traditionally carried out from three perspectives: First, in microeconomics, the distribution of production results among various production factors is studied from the perspective of maximizing producer profits, forming the initial distribution of national wealth. Second, in microeconomics, how individual consumers allocate their work fruits to maximize personal utility is studied from the perspective of consumer utility maximization. Due to the scarcity of resources and inequality of opportunities, the result of initial distribution is generally unfair, with some people occupying too many social resources while others are scrambling to make both ends meet. Therefore, from the perspective of the whole society, the initial distribution pattern formed in the production field may not be optimal. According to Pigou, the total social welfare depends not only on total national income, but also on the distribution of national income among social members (Wang, 2006). Social welfare may be improved through income redistribution, which requires intervention in the initial distribution of national income, realizing fairness through income and wealth redistribution, and improving social welfare. Therefore, the third perspective of income distribution research is from social welfare to study how to redistribute wealth to maximize social welfare.

Since the revival of neoclassical utilitarianism in the 1970s, many forms of social welfare functions have been developed, including the social welfare function of neoclassical utilitarianism, elites, Rawls, Nash and Akenson.

The classical utilitarian social welfare function regards social welfare as the simple sum of the welfare or utility of all social members, with the welfare of any member being treated equally. The classical social welfare function can be formulated as:

$$W = U_1 + U_2 + \cdots + U_n \text{ or } W = \left(U_1 + U_2 + \cdots + U_n\right) / n$$

Nash's social welfare function is defined as the product of the utility levels of all social members, that is, $W = U_1 \times U_2 \times \cdots \times U_n$.

The social welfare function of elites follows the Maximax principle, that is, social welfare is aimed at maximizing the welfare of elites (the richest in society), that is, $\text{Max}\left\{U_1, U_2, \cdots, U_n\right\}$.

Rawls' social welfare function (Rawls, 1971) takes the welfare of the poorest class as the objective function of social welfare $W = \text{Min}\left\{U_1, U_2, \cdots, U_n\right\}$, and follows Maxmin as the decision-making principle, that is, social welfare is aimed at maximizing the welfare of the poorest.

Bergson (1938) and Samuelson (1947) regard social welfare as a function of the individual utility function. They do not give specific form or formation mechanism of social welfare function, but keep flexibility of its selection (Yao, 2005). It is this flexibility that provides a large room for later researchers. When individual utility is measured by income, Bergson-Samuelson defines the social welfare function as the individual income function $W = V\left\{y_1, y_2, \cdots, y_n\right\}$, where $\left(y_1, y_2, \cdots, y_n\right)$ denotes the income vector of all social members. When the utility function is the linear homogenous function of each individual's income, if the ratio of social welfare to its theoretical maximum (expressed by E) is used as the measure of social fairness, the social welfare function can be expressed as the product of average income and fairness (Deaton, 2005). Sen Amartya (Sen Amartya, 1973), winner of Nobel Prize for Economics in 1998, takes (1–*G*) (*G* is Gini coefficient) as a measure of fairness, and obtains social welfare function: $W_{gini} = \mu\left(1 - G\right)$, where μ is average income. Foster (Foster James E., 1996) suggests adopting Atkinson's index (a measure of inequality). Because of the relation between Atkinson's index and Theil index (another measure of inequality), Foster expresses the social welfare function directly as $W_{Theil-L} = \mu e^{-T_L}$ or $W_{Theil-T} = \mu e^{-T_T}$, where T_L and T_T are two kinds of Theil indices. The drawback of these social welfare functions is that they all rely on the homogeneity assumption (Deaton, 2005), and the choice of inequality measures is arbitrary. In addition, there is no economic criteria to judge the quality of these inequality indices.

Judging from the forms, the social welfare functions of classical, neoclassical, elites, Rawls, or Sen and Foster all have their own strengths and weaknesses. The classical utilitarian welfare function only considers the simple sum and average of individual utilities and ignores the differences among social individuals. The elite welfare function has been widely criticized for considering only efficiency but ignoring equity. Rawls' welfare function emphasizes the welfare of the lowest income earners and nit-picks fairness, which may lead to the insufficient incentives mechanism and inefficiency in society. Sen's and Foster's social welfare functions, as binary functions under the same category of social average income and income difference with different indicators of income difference, pay insufficient attention to the relation between welfare status and income distribution of the lowest income class.

In research of welfare optimization theory, the old welfare economics, under the premise of utility comparability, obtains the conclusion that average distribution maximizes social welfare. Louis Kaplow (1996) studied the optimal distribution of wealth among family members from expected utility maximization and concluded that the wealth optimization conformed to one-point distribution when the preferences of family members were consistent, that is, each family member enjoyed equal share of income. Wold and Whittle (1957) explained how wealth distribution followed Pareto distribution. As for the general study of continuous optimal wealth distribution under constraints, the author has not seen any valuable results.

At present, domestic and international studies on income and wealth distribution mainly focus on empirical analysis and are dominated by international and inter-regional comparative studies. There is not much literature studying the optimal distribution of income and wealth from the perspective of consumers. In empirical research, some assume that wealth distribution follows the Pareto distribution, some assume that income distribution follows exponential distribution and gamma distribution, others assume that wealth obeys logarithmic distribution (Zhang, 2003). Some of these assumptions conform well to reality, but they fail to deliver a reasonable theoretical explanation.

The article Best Theoretical Value of the Gini Coefficient - One Third (Hu, 1993) was published on Chinese and Foreign Management Herald, No. 3, 1993. The Gini coefficient, or the "best theoretical value," was obtained following the so-called theoretical basis that assumed the income of all people in the society was arranged according to the arithmetic series specified by the author. The author strongly disagreed with the author because no relations between "arithmetic series arrangement" and economic "best theoretical value" could be concluded based on Economics. The article On the Best Theoretical Value of Gini Coefficient - by Discussing with Mr. Hu Zuguang (Zhao Zhijun, 1994) was published on Chinese and Foreign Management Herald, No.1, 1994, pointing out the serious defects of Hu's article. However, Mr. Hu Zuguang published another article Research on the Optimal Values of Gini coefficient and its Simple Calculation Formula on Economic Research, No.9, 2004. This article consisted of two parts: "Best Theoretical Value of Gini Coefficient" and "Simple Calculation Formula." The first part was largely consistent with the article Best Theoretical Value of Gini Coefficient - One-third published in 1993 on Chinese and Foreign Management Herald, while the second part, "Simple Formula," was of certain practical significance and is not introduced here. While failing to provide a final explanation to the "best theoretical value" of Gini coefficient, their debate did lead to an important question that had not yet been addressed in economic theory circles, namely, what is the theoretical basis behind the empirical income distribution identified in empirical analysis? Can we give a reasonable explanation to the empirical distribution type of income from the perspective of economics? The author argues that since economics studies the behavior of rational economic man, the economic phenomenon is the result of rational economic man's pursuit of optimal personal interests. Therefore, as a result of rational economic man's behavior, income or wealth distribution should at least be partially explained by their optimal behavior; However, the existing economic theories have not established the relationship between social welfare, income distribution and Gini coefficient.

The questions in this chapter follow this logic: since Gini coefficient is calculated from the income and wealth distribution, if there is indeed a "best theoretical value" of Gini coefficient, there must be a corresponding "best theoretical distribution and Lorenz curve." However, there is no such thing as "one-to-one" correspondence between the Gini coefficient and income distribution, that is, infinite forms of probability distributions or Lorenz curves correspond to the Gini coefficient, while only one Gini coefficient corresponds to a Lorenz curve. This leads to a new theoretical question: given a Gini coefficient, is there an optimal distribution among the infinite probability distributions (or Lorenz curves) corresponding to the Gini coefficient? If yes, what kind of distribution is it? What is the corresponding social welfare function?

The answer to the above questions is closely related to two fundamental issues in economics: one is resources scarcity, because the distribution only makes sense under scarcity. If wealth is infinite and inexhaustible, then there is no need for distribution. The other is the relationship between the consumption preferences of social individuals and social welfare. The distribution form of income and wealth is intuitively inseparable from consumers' preferences. In the era of a socialist planned economy, people's basic values and mainstream social values were egalitarian, and the Gini coefficient was very low. After the launch of reform and opening-up, the mainstream social value orientation changed to "let some people get rich first and then achieve common prosperity" advocated by Deng Xiaoping, but so far, the first half of this value is substantially realized, resulting in a larger and larger Gini coefficient and an increasingly unfair income distribution, which has led to a series of social challenges. Now that we have entered the stage of building a harmonious society following the scientific concept of development, the goal of "common prosperity" is vigorously pursued, and the pattern of the income distribution will also undergo new changes. This shows that income distribution is closely related to social preferences for consumption, and different social preferences will result in various income distributions, thus corresponding to different Lorenz curves and Gini coefficients. Therefore, it is of no theoretical and practical significance to discuss the best theoretical value of Gini coefficient, leaving social preference and optimal wealth distribution aside. Once the optimal distribution type is determined, the preferences of individual consumers can be summed according to the probability distribution based on given consumer preference, to obtain the optimal expression form of social welfare function.

The rest of this chapter is organized as follows: Section 2 mainly discusses the relationship between optimal wealth distribution, social welfare function and consumer preferences, wealth level as well as Gini coefficient. In the first part, the objective function of wealth distribution is put forward; The second part presents the constraints faced by wealth problems. In the third and fourth parts, the general expressions of optimal distribution and social welfare function are obtained for two types of wealth distribution problems; The fifth part discusses the determination of the minimum subsistence line and the policy meaning of its social welfare function. In section 3, inspired by this study, the author points out some existing problems in macroeconomics and puts forward some ideas on rebuilding the micro-foundation of macroeconomics. The last section concludes this chapter and summarizes the main findings of the chapter.

11.2 Consumer Preference, Gini Coefficient, and Optimal Wealth Distribution

1. The Objective Function of Optimal Wealth Distributions

The utility function in this chapter is expressed by indirect utility function, and the utility of each individual depends on its preference for money. Due to the differences between individuals, a common benchmark, which is equivalent to the Galilean frame of reference in Newtonian mechanics, must be selected for interpersonal comparison of utility. Therefore, it is assumed that the preference of each individual in society is expressed by the utility function of wealth $U = U(y)$. The utility function is a second-order continuously differentiable function that satisfies the property of utility function, that is, the first derivative $U'(y) > 0$, second derivative $U''(y) > 0$ and Inada Conditions $\lim_{y\to\infty} U'(y) = 0$.

In terms of the need for workers to sustain human survival and development, any society requires a minimum standard of living that sustains that need. Modern society generally stipulates the minimum living security level from the perspective of law and policy. Assume that $y_m > 0$ is the wealth owned by the poorest people in society, which can guarantee a person to maintain the minimum standard of living stipulated by law and policy, then every individual wealth in a society can be expressed by a random variable $Y \in [y_m, \infty]$. The wealth distribution of the whole society is represented by a probability distribution function $F(y)$, denoted as $Y \sim F(y)$. $F(y)$ is continuously differentiable on $[y_m, \infty)$, and satisfies $F(y_m) = 0$, $F(\infty) = 1$. Probability distribution density function of $F(y)$ is $f(y)$, and their relation is $F'(y) = f(y)$ or $dF(y) = f(y)dx$. Due to the uncertainty of $F(y)$, that is, there are infinite distributions corresponding to a given Gini coefficient, then all distributions satisfying this condition form a distribution set, which is denoted as:

$$\mathrm{P} = \left\{ F(x) \left| \int_{y_m}^{\infty} yF'(y)dy = \mu; \int_{y_m}^{\infty} y\left[1 - F(y)\right]F'(y)dy = \frac{1}{2}\mu(1-G) \right. \right\}$$

The derivation of the constraint conditions will be discussed in "II."

Social welfare function is generally defined as the sum of all individual utility.[1] Given a fixed total number, we can use the average welfare level to

---

1 The social welfare function regards social welfare as the sum of individual welfare, so social welfare is the function of the sum of all individual welfare. Assume there are "n" people in society, the classical social welfare function W can be written as: $W = U_1 + U_2 + \cdots + U_n$

represent the welfare level of the whole society, which is expressed by the following formula:

$$W(F) = \underset{F \in P}{Max}\, EU(y) = \int_{y_m}^{\infty} U(y) f(y) dy = \int_{y_m}^{\infty} U(y) F'(y) dy \tag{1}$$

Note that $W(F)$ is not an ordinary function, but an expression with distribution function as a variable, an integral functional of social welfare about wealth distribution. The expected utility function generated by the optimization problem under probabilistic uncertainty is different from the traditional utility function and is generally a nonlinear mathematical expectation or "G expectation." Peng Shige (Peng, 1997, 1999), a famous Chinese mathematician and an academician of the Chinese Academy of Sciences, discovered the relationship between this nonlinear mathematical expectation and backward stochastic differential equations. One of the main tasks of this chapter is to find the distribution function that maximizes the objective function (1) from the infinite distributions corresponding to a specific Gini coefficient. Such a distribution function is called the optimal wealth distribution function, and the corresponding social welfare function is called the optimal social welfare function.

In addition, equation (1) is an infinite integral and whether the integrand is integrable depends on the nature of the utility function. Except for Inada conditions, the general literature on stochastic economic phenomena study assumes that the utility function is bounded (see Aiyagari, 1993; Huggett, 1997; Huggett & Ospina, 2001; Miao, 2006). These conditions ensure that the utility function is consistent with the equilibrium growth path. Richard M. H. Suen (2009) defined a family of utility functions $U\left[\sigma(y)\right]$ that is: (1) a strictly increasing function; (2) a quadratic differentiable function; (3) the solution of the following second-order linear differential equation:

$$U''(y) + \frac{\sigma(y)}{y} U'(y) = 0$$

When $y > 0$, the equation can be established.

Where $\sigma(y)$ is the function defined in the interval $(0, \infty)$, representing the elasticity of marginal utility. Richard M. H. Suen (2009) proved the following proposition: Assume that $\sigma(y)$ is a nonnegative continuous bounded function, and if $x \geq 0$, for any $y > x$, there is $\sigma(y) > 1$. Therefore, then any function $U\left[\sigma, (y)\right]$ in $U = U(y)$ has an upper bound. Conversely, if $\sigma(y) \leq 1$, then any function $U = U(y)$ in $U\left[\sigma(y)\right]$ has no upper bound. So, to ensure that (1) is meaningful, this chapter holds that $\sigma(y)>1$ is tenable, that is, the utility function $U=U(y)$ has an upper bound[2].

2. The Constraints of Social Welfare Maximization

As mentioned above, the first constraint on optimization (1) is the finiteness of resources and the average level of social wealth. In a given period and a given social group, if wealth is finite, then the average level of social wealth exists:

$$EY=\int_{y_m}^{\infty} yF'(y)dy=\int_{y_m}^{\infty} yf(y)dy=\mu<+\infty^3 \tag{2}$$

We showed earlier that for a given Gini coefficient, there are an infinite number of Lorentz curves and probability distribution functions corresponding to this coefficient. So, the other constraint is on the Gini coefficient. To find the optimal distribution among the infinite number of Lorentz curves and distributions, it is necessary to introduce the second constraint of social welfare maximization problem (1), namely the Gini coefficient constraint. More generally, it is difficult to strike a proper balance between equity and efficiency. If equity is overstressed, the output efficiency in the production field will be affected. Otherwise, social challenges may be intensified due to polarization, which will ultimately have a negative impact on social welfare.

Therefore, theoretically, the government as a social manager can moderate the income distribution based on the initial income distribution; in other words, it should maximize the social welfare on the basis of certain degree of allowed inequality. If the Gini coefficient is used to express the degree of inequality, the structural fine-tuning of government policy is governed (restricted) by the condition $G_1 \le G \le G_2$, that is, in the pursuit of equity, the productive efficiency must not be over affected, and the condition $G_1 \le G$ has to work. In the pursuit of productive efficiency, social differences are not allowed to widen too much and condition $G \le G_2$ has to come into play. In this chapter, we focus on how to regulate the structure of income distribution or wealth structure in a way that maximizes social welfare without compromising efficiency. The constraint on this problem is $G_1 \le G$. As for the production area, we'll discuss it in another paper.

The Gini coefficient is graphically expressed as the ratio of the area between the social equalization curve and the Lorentz curve to the area below the social

---

2 Because the utility function is strictly increasing, $U=u(y)$ has upper bound, so there is a constant 1, making $\lim_{y\to\infty} U(y)=1$

3 Usually, the formula given in the literature is for the case $y_m=0$, $EY=\int_0^{\infty}\left[1-F(y)\right]\mathrm{d}y=\mu$

equalization curve. The Gini coefficient = 0 indicates that social wealth distribution is completely equal, and Gini coefficient = 1 indicates extreme inequality, that is, social wealth is held by one person. According to the definition of Gini coefficient, the continuously distributed Gini coefficient can be expressed as the integral of Lorentz curve. The Lorentz curve is defined as:

$$L\left[F(y)\right]=\frac{\int_{y_m}^{y} tF'(t)dt}{\int_{y_m}^{\infty} tF'(t)dt}=\frac{1}{\mu}\int_{y_m}^{y} tF'(t)dt$$

If we transform the probability distribution function $F(t): F(t)=x,\ F(y)=p$, then $t=F^{-1}(x), y=F^{-1}(p)$. And the Lorentz curve can be written as:

$$L(p)=\frac{\int_0^p F^{-1}(x)dx}{\int_0^1 F^{-1}(x)dx}=\frac{1}{\mu}\int_0^p F^{-1}(x)dx$$

Gini coefficient can be expressed as:

$$G=1-2\int_0^1 L(p)dp=1-\frac{2}{\mu}\int_0^1\left[\int_0^p F^{-1}(x)dx\right]dp$$

As verified, Gini coefficient can be expressed equivalently as:

$$G=1-\frac{2}{\mu}\int_0^1(1-p)F^{-1}(p)dp=1-\frac{2}{\mu}\int_{y_m}^{\infty} y\left[1-F(y)\right]F'(y)dy$$

Thus, we obtain the second constraint of the optimization objective:

$$\int_{y_m}^{\infty} y\left[1-F(y)\right]F'(y)dy=\frac{1}{2}\mu(1-G) \tag{3}$$

The constraint condition (3) is equivalent to $\int_{y_m}^{\infty}\left[1-F(y)\right]^2 dy=(1-G)\mu-y_m$.

3. Optimal Wealth Distribution Problem Without Gini Coefficient Constraint

First of all, we hope to extend the discrete distribution results of Louis Kaplow (1996) on the optimal distribution of household wealth to the case where the distribution of social wealth is continuous. The problem of Louis Kaplow (1996) is expressed by the variational continuous function as follows. The maximum objective is:

$$\underset{F\in P}{Max}\, EU(y)=\int_{y_m}^{\infty}U(y)F'(y)dy \tag{1}$$

The boundary condition:

$$F(y_m)=0,\ F(\infty)=1$$

$$L=U(y)F'(y)-\lambda\left[yF'(y)\right]$$ [4]

The Euler-Lagrange equation corresponding to this problem is $\frac{\partial L}{\partial F}-\frac{d}{dy}\left[\frac{\partial L}{\partial F'}\right]=0$
Or:

$$U'(y)=\lambda \text{ (constant)}$$

Since λ is a constant and $U'(y)$ is monotonically decreasing, y must be equal to the constant. In this case, the distribution function cannot be a continuous function. Therefore, when the wealth distribution is discrete, the optimization objective is:

$$\underset{p_i}{Max}\, EU(y)=\underset{p_i}{Max}\sum_{i=1}^{n}U(y_i)p_i$$

Where $P(Y=y_i)=p_i$ represents the wealth distribution. For the sake of convenience and generality, assume n = 2 (it can be extended to the general case by mathematical induction), $p_1=p,p_2=1-p$. $\alpha_i=y_i/\mu$ represents the ratio of the income of individual i to the average income, obviously, $\alpha_1+\alpha_2=2$. This can be transformed into finding the value of α and p to make $W=pU(\alpha\mu)+(1-p)U\left[(2-\alpha)\mu\right]$ reach its maximum.

Rewrite the above equation as $W=p\{U(\alpha\mu)-U\left[(2-\alpha)\mu\right]\}+U\left[(2-\alpha)\mu\right]$, and now we should proof that α = 1. And we can use proof by contradiction, Assume that $\alpha\neq1$, if $\alpha>1$, $U(\alpha\mu)-U\left[(1-\alpha)\mu\right]>0$. When p = 1, we will get the maximum social welfare. And $p(Y=y_1)=1$ is one-point distribution, which means that social wealth is distributed equally among its members. So, there must be α = 1, which contradicts hypothesis $\alpha\neq1$. $\alpha=1$, $p=1$ are corresponding

[4] Both the maximum principle and variational method can prove that the costate varible under an integral constraint is constant (see Jiang Zhongyi, 1999).

with social welfare function $W = U(\mu)$. This result is the same as that of old welfare economics and can be written as theorem 1.

Theorem 1: Under the condition that the total social wealth is certain and no restriction is imposed on the Gini coefficient, the distribution that maximizes social welfare is a single-point distribution, that is, the average distribution of wealth in the whole society.

4. The Optimal Wealth Distribution Problem with Given Gini Coefficient

The idea expressed in Theorem 1 is absolute egalitarianism, which is not the case in the real world and contradicts the incentive mechanism in the production field. Usually, there is a certain difference in the distribution of wealth in society, that is, to improve efficiency while taking into account social equity. The mathematical expression of this idea is equal to the assumption that the Gini coefficient is given or does not exceed a given constant in Theorem 1. The social welfare objective function (1), constraint conditions (2) and (3), together with boundary conditions $F(y_m) = 0$ and $F(\infty) = 1$, constitute the standard form of dynamic optimization. The problem can be expressed as follows.

The maximization goal:

$$\underset{F \in P}{Max}\, EU(y) = \int_{y_m}^{\infty} U(y) F'(y) dy \tag{1}$$

Constraint conditions:

$$EY = \int_{y_m}^{\infty} y F'(y) dy = \mu < +\infty \tag{2}$$

$$\int_{y_m}^{\infty} y\left[1 - F(y)\right] F'(y) dy = \frac{1}{2}(1 - G)\mu \tag{3}$$

Boundary conditions: $F(y_m) = 0, F(\infty) = 1$

The variational integrand function corresponding to this problem is:

$$L = U(y)F'(y) - \lambda_1\left[yF'(y)\right] - \lambda_2\left\{y\left[1 - F(y)\right]F'(y)\right\} \text{ [5]} \tag{6}$$

5 Both the maximum principle and variational method can prove that the sum of common variables of integral constraints is constant (see Jiang Zhongyi, 1999).

The corresponding value function is:

$$\overline{W}\left(F;\lambda_1,\lambda_2\right)=\int_{y_m}^{\infty} Ld y \tag{7}$$

The first-order condition of the optimization problem is the Euler-Lagrange equation:

$$\frac{\partial L}{\partial F}-\frac{d}{dy}\left[\frac{\partial L}{\partial F'}\right]=0 \tag{8}$$

Calculated:

$$\frac{\partial L}{\partial F}=\lambda_2 yF'\left(y\right) \tag{9}$$

$$\frac{\partial L}{\partial F'}=U\left(y\right)-\lambda_1 y-\lambda_2 y\left[1-F\left(y\right)\right] \tag{10}$$

$$\frac{d}{dy}\left[\frac{\partial L}{\partial F'}\right]=U'\left(y\right)-\lambda_1-\lambda_2\left[1-F\left(y\right)\right]+\lambda_2 yF'\left(y\right) \tag{11}$$

Substituting Eq. (9) and Eq. (11) into Euler-Lagrange Equation (8), we obtain:

$$U'\left(y\right)-\lambda_1-\lambda_2\left[1-F\left(x\right)\right]=0 \tag{12}$$

$$1-F\left(x\right)=\frac{U'\left(y\right)-\lambda_1}{\lambda_2} \tag{13}$$

Boundary conditions $F\left(y_m\right)=0, F\left(\infty\right)=1$ and Inada condition $U'\left(\infty\right)=0$ are applied to (13):

$$1=\frac{U'\left(y_m\right)-\lambda_1}{\lambda_2} \tag{14}$$

$$0=\frac{-\lambda_1}{\lambda_2} \tag{15}$$

The solution of the equations composed of equation (14) and (15) is: $\lambda_1=0$ [6] and $\lambda_2=U'\left(y_m\right)$, substitute them into (13) to obtain the optimal distribution function:

6 $\lambda_1=0$ shows that the first constraint is superfluous because $U'\left(\infty\right)=0$.

$$F^*(y) = 1 - \frac{U'(y)}{U'(y_m)} \tag{16}$$

y_m is determined by the constraint condition (3). Obviously, $F^*(y) = 1 - \frac{U'(y)}{U'(y_m)}$ satisfies the properties of distribution function: $F'(y) > 0, F(y_m) = 0$ and $F(\infty) = 1$.

To prove that the distribution function satisfying the first-order condition is the optimal solution, it is necessary to verify the sufficient conditions for the existence of extreme values. We know that $\frac{\partial^2 L}{\partial F^2} = 0$, $\frac{\partial^2 L}{\partial F'^2} = 0$, $\frac{\partial^2 L}{\partial F \partial F'} = 0$, $\frac{\partial^2 L}{\partial F' \partial F} = \lambda_2 y$, $\frac{d}{dt}\left(\frac{\partial^2 L}{\partial F \partial F'}\right) = \lambda_2 = U'(y_m) > 0$. Therefore, for any given perturbation curve ($p(y)$) satisfying $p(y_m) = 0$, $\lim_{y \to \infty} p(y) = 0$ and any (arbitrarily small) ε, it is defined as $F(y) = F^*(y) + \varepsilon p(y)$ (see Jiang Zhongyi, 1999),

so:
$$\begin{aligned}\frac{d^2 \overline{W}(F, \lambda_1, \lambda_2)}{d\varepsilon^2} &= \int_{y_m}^{\infty} \left[\left(\frac{\partial^2 L}{\partial F^2} - \frac{d}{dy}\frac{\partial^2 L}{\partial F \partial F'}\right) p^2(y) + \frac{\partial^2 L}{\partial F'^2} p'^2(y)\right] dy \\ &= \int_{y_m}^{\infty} \left[-\lambda_2 p^2(y)\right] dy < 0\end{aligned} \tag{17}$$

This proves the sufficient condition for the problem to satisfy the maximum value, that is, when $F^*(y) = 1 - \frac{U'(y)}{U'(y_m)}$, $\overline{W}(F; \lambda_1, \lambda_2) = \int_{y_m}^{\infty} L dy$ is maximizing.[7] Therefore, $1 - \frac{U'(y)}{U'(y_m)}$ makes $W(F)$ as the optimal probability distribution under the constraint condition. And the author obtains the following theorem 2 under general conditions, which is called the optimal wealth distribution representation theorem.

Theorem 2 (optimal wealth distribution representation theorem): For a given utility function $U = U(y)$, under the conditions of wealth scarcity and given Gini coefficient [i.e., satisfying conditions (2) and (3)], the wealth distribution

---

[7] For this problem, $\frac{\partial^2 L}{\partial F'^2} = 0$

function that maximizes social welfare is uniquely determined by the marginal utility of consumers, which is expressed as $F^*(y)=1-\frac{U'(y)}{U'(y_m)}$.

The optimal wealth distribution (16) given above is abstract, because the utility function form is not specific but is universal. When the specific form of the utility function is given, the corresponding specific distribution can be obtained. In the study of economic theory, the commonly used univariate utility functions include the constant relative risk aversion (CRRA) utility function and the constant absolute risk aversion (CARA) utility function. The multivariate utility functions include the quasi-linear utility function and homothetic utility function.

Corollary 1: If the utility function is constant relative risk aversion (CRRA), the corresponding optimal distribution is Pareto distribution. If the utility function is constant relative risk aversion (CARA), assume that the utility function can be expressed as $U(y)=\frac{y^{1-\sigma}-1}{1-\sigma}$, and $\sigma>0$ [8], then the corresponding optimal distribution function is $F(y)=1-\left(\frac{y}{y_m}\right)^{-\sigma}$, which is the standard Pareto probability distribution function.

Corollary 2: If the utility function is constant absolute risk aversion (CRRA), the optimal distribution follows exponential distribution. If the utility function is constant absolute risk aversion (CARA), assume that the utility function is $U(y)=1-e^{-ay}$, and $a>0$, then the corresponding optimal distribution function is $F(y)=1-e^{-a(y-y_m)}$, which is the standard exponential distribution function.

With the optimal wealth distribution function, we can find the social welfare function corresponding to the optimal distribution, which is expressed as:

$$\begin{aligned}
W_{\max} &= \int_{y_m}^{\infty} U(y)F'(y)dy \\
&= \int_{y_m}^{\infty} U(y)\left[\frac{-U''(y)}{U'(y_m)}\right]dy \\
&= \frac{-1}{U'(y_m)}\int_{y_m}^{\infty} U(y)dU'(y) \\
&= \frac{-1}{U'(y_m)}\left\{U(y)U'(y)\Big|_{y_m}^{\infty} - \int_{y_m}^{\infty}\left[U'(y)\right]^2 dy\right\}
\end{aligned}$$

8 In this paper, to ensure the boundedness of the utility function, the utility function needs to satisfy $\sigma>1$.

$$= U(y_m) + U'(y_m)\int_{y_m}^{\infty}\left[\frac{U'(y)}{U'(y_m)}\right]^2 dy$$
$$= U(y_m) + U'(y_m)\int_{y_m}^{\infty}\left[1 - F(y)\right]^2 dy$$
$$= U(y_m) + U'(y_m)\left[(1-G)\mu - y_m\right]$$
$$= U(y_m) - U'(y_m)y_m + U'(y_m)\left[(1-G)\mu\right]$$
$$= R(y_m) + U'(y_m)\left[(1-G)\mu\right]$$

Where $R(y_m) = U(y_m) - U'(y_m)y_m$ represents the consumer surplus of the lowest income earners. In the derivation of the above results, $\lim_{y\to\infty} U(y)U'(y) = 0$ is used at the fifth equal sign, which is determined by the boundedness of $U(y)$ and Inada condition $\lim_{y\to\infty} U'(y) = 0$. And we can obtain:

Theorem 3 (Optimal Social Welfare Representation Theorem): The optimal social welfare function W is jointly determined by the consumer surplus of the lowest income earners $R(y_m)$, the average wealth level μ and the Gini coefficient G. Its expression is:

$$W(y_m, \mu, G) = R(y_m) + U'(y_m)\left[(1-G)\mu\right] \tag{18}$$

Theorem 3 tells us that there are three ways to improve the level of social welfare: first is to increase the consumer surplus of the lowest income earners $R(y_m) = U(y_m) - U'(y_m)y_m$; second is to improve the average level of social wealth μ; third is to reduce relative wealth inequality (G). The level of social welfare increases with the increase of consumer surplus and average wealth of the lowest income earners and decreases with the increase of the Gini coefficient. It is easy to draw the following two inferences from the optimal social welfare function:

Corollary 3: When $G = 0$, that is, wealth is equally distributed throughout society($\mu = y_m$), the optimal social welfare function is the Rawls' welfare function: $W(y_m, \mu, G) = U(y_m)$.

Corollary 4: When consumer preference tends to be risk neutral, that is, the utility function is a linear function in the vicinity, then $U(y_m) = ky_m$, $U'(y_m) = k$, the optimal social welfare function is Sen's welfare function $W(y_m, \mu, G) = k(1-G)\mu$.

These two corollaries show that Rawls' welfare function and Sen's welfare function are two special cases of the optimal social welfare function. Therefore, the results of this chapter are more general and universal.

5. Determination of the Minimum Living Security Line and Its Social Welfare Meaning

Substitute the optimal social welfare function into the equivalent condition of constraint condition (3), and let $h = \mu(1-G)$, we have:

$$h = y_m + \frac{1}{U'(y_m)} \int_{y_m}^{\infty} \left[U'(y)\right]^2 dy \tag{19}$$

Intuitively, equation (19) has two meanings: first, it indicates that h is a function of y_m and y_m is the inverse function of h. Thus, the social welfare function can be written as a function of y_m as well as a function of h. Therefore, if y_m is regarded as the minimum living security level, the minimum living security or minimum wage policy is endogenous to the average wealth level and inequality. Second, it indicates $(1-G)\mu > y_m$, that is because:

$$\frac{dh}{dy_m} = \frac{-2U''(y_m)\left[h - y_m\right]}{U'(y_m)} > 0 \text{ Or } \frac{dy_m}{dh} = \frac{U'(y_m)}{-2U''(y_m)\left[h - y_m\right]} > 0 \tag{20}$$

The minimum subsistence guarantee increases as the average income level rises, and in turn, increasing the minimum subsistence guarantee is an effective way to reduce income disparities.

Let's look at the impact of raising the minimum living security on social welfare. The derivative of the social welfare function (18) is as follows:

$$\frac{dW}{dy_m} = U''(y_m)\left[y_m - h\right] > 0$$

Therefore, the income distribution policy aimed at raising the minimum level of consumer security will not only increase the consumer surplus of the poor but also improve the level of social welfare. From this point of view, Rawls' welfare function does not contradict the social welfare function in this chapter, but Rawls fails to grasp the overall state of the income distribution.

When comparing the optimal social welfare function obtained in this chapter $W = R(y_m) + U'(y_m)[(1-G)\mu]$ with the above welfare function, we note that the social welfare function in this chapter takes into account the average level and distribution of social wealth and takes the welfare of the lowest income class, that is, the so-called vulnerable groups, as an endogenous variable, which has obvious policy implications. Therefore, the welfare function obtained by the author combines the advantages of the above social welfare functions, overcomes their shortcomings, and is by far the most comprehensive welfare function (see Table 43).

Table 43. Comparison of advantages and disadvantages of various welfare functions

Name of Benefit Function	Advocate	Welfare function expression	Characteristics of welfare function
Classical utilitarian social welfare function	*Mashall, Pigou, Pareto*, etc.	$W = U_1 + U_2 + \cdots + U_n$	Summation and arithmetic average of individual utility, ignoring income difference
Nash social welfare function	Nash (*John Forbes Nash Jr.*.)	$W = U_1 U_2 \cdots U_n$	Social welfare is the product of the utility of all members of society
Social welfare function of elite		$W = Max\{U_1, U_2, \cdots, U_n\}$	Maximize the welfare of the highest earners and ignore the vulnerable groups
Rawls' social welfare function	*John Rawls*	$W = Min\{U_1, U_2, \cdots, U_n\}$ Or $W(y_m, \mu, G) = U(y_m)$	Maximize the welfare of the lowest income group and only consider the interests of vulnerable groups
Sen's (*Sen, Amartya K*) Social welfare function	*Amartya K Sen*	$W_{gini} = \mu(1-G)$	Take into account the differences of the total social average level
Foster Social welfare function	*James E. Foster*	$W_{Theil-L} = \mu e^{-T_L}$	Take into account the differences of the total social average level
Optimal social welfare function	Author	$W = R(y_m) + U'(y_m)(1-G)\mu$	Considering the welfare, average wealth and inequality of vulnerable groups.

11.3 Conclusion

This chapter has discussed two problems concerning social welfare maximization: One is the optimal wealth distribution without Gini coefficient constraints; the other is the optimal wealth distribution with given mean value of wealth and Gini coefficient. This chapter proves that under the premise that individual ability difference is acknowledged and a degree of opportunity disequilibrium is reasonable (i.e., the Gini coefficient is not equal to 0), the distribution state of wealth is completely determined by its marginal utility. This chapter further demonstrates that the Pareto distribution is optimal when the utility function is constant relative risk aversion; and the exponential distribution is optimal when it is constant absolute risk aversion. These two utility functions are the most commonly used utility functions in theory, corresponding to two common probability distributions in practice. This finding answers why Pareto distribution can better fit the real wealth distribution. Pareto distribution can well describe the phenomena in sociology, political science, information science, biology and other fields. The author believes that the reason is similar.

The acquisition of general social welfare function, another important result of studying optimal wealth, is unexpected to the author. The social welfare function derived by the author is a function of the welfare of the lowest income, the average wealth level and Gini coefficient. It combines the advantages of various social welfare functions proposed by previous authors, overcomes their shortcomings, and is more suitable as a criterion for comparing social welfare in different societies and at different development stages. In addition, the inference in this chapter shows that several welfare functions proposed by previous authors are special cases of the welfare functions obtained in this chapter.

The social welfare function in this chapter is, in form, essentially different from the utility function of representative consumers. The utility function of representative consumers and the welfare function obtained by summing up the utility functions of representative consumers are defined at different levels. The former depends only on wealth level, while the latter depends not only on it but also on Gini coefficient, which clearly better reflects reality and illustrates major defects in the micro-foundations of traditional macroeconomics.

Optimal wealth distribution is of great significance for guiding the government to formulate inheritance tax, personal income tax and other tax system reforms. First, if the income gap caused by the primary distribution of society is too large, as manifested by a large Gini coefficient, the government can reduce it and raise the minimum subsistence level through progressive income tax as well as inheritance tax policies. Second, under the Gini coefficient with an after-tax target, tax rate policy should also optimize the after-tax income distribution.

References

Chapter One References

Aghion, Philippe, Philippe Bacchetta, and Abhijit Banerjee (2004), "*Financial Development and the Instability of Open Economies,*" NBER Working Paper, 10246,

Brooks, Ray, and Ran Tao (2003), "*China's Labor Market Performance and Challenges,*" IMF Working Paper, *WP*/03/210.

Cai, Fang, Du, Yang and Wang, Meiyan, 2001, "*The New Stage of Population Transformation and the Characteristics of Human Capital Formation,*" the Institute of Population and Labor Economics, Chinese Academy of Social Sciences, Working Paper Series *No*. 6.

Growth Frontier Research Group (written by Zhang Ping and Zhang Xiaojing), 2003, "*The Cumulative Effect of Economic Growth and Structural Adjustment and Capital Formation,*" Economic Research, *Vol*. 8.

Krugman, Paul (1986), "*Is the Japan Problem Over?,*" NBER Working Paper, *No*. 1962.

Krugman, Paul (1997), "*What Ever Happened to the Asian Miracle?,*" Fortune, *Vol*. 136 (4), *pp*. 26–29.

Institute of Economics and Resource Management of *Beijing Normal University*, 2003, *Report on the Development of China's Market Economy in 2003*, China Foreign Economic and Trade Press.

Lin, Yifu, and Li Yongjun, 2002, "Exports and China's Economic Growth: A demand-oriented analysis," China Economic Research Center, Peking University, Working Paper Series *No*.C002008.

Liu, Xiahui, 2004, "*Has the RMB appreciation reached the stage of long-term appreciation expectations?*" Economic Research, *Vol*. 2.

Madison, 1997, *A Review of the World Economy in Two Hundred Years*, Reform Press.

Prasad, Eswar, Kenneth Rogoff, Shang-Jin Wei and M. Ayhan Kose (2003), Effects of Financial Globalization on Developing Countries: Some Empirical Evidence, *IMF. March* 17.

Prasad, Eswar, and Thomas Rumbaugh (2003), *Beyond the Great Wall*, Finance and Development, *December*.

Shen, Lisheng, and Wu Zhenyu: "*The Contribution of Exports to China's GDP Growth: An Empirical Analysis Based on the Input-Output Table,*" Economic Research, *Vol*. 11.

Song, Guoqing, 2003, "*Going out of deflation and RMB exchange rate*," discussion paper of the research group of China Economic Research Center, Peking University.

Wang, Xiaolu, and Fan Gang, 2020, *The Sustainability of China's Economic Growth: A Cross-century Review and Outlook*, Economic Science Press.

World Bank, 1995, *The East Asian Miracle: Economic Growth and Public Policy*, China Financial and Economic Press.

World Bank (Joseph Stiglitz, Shahid Yusuf), 2003, *Reflections on the East Asian Miracle*, Renmin University of China Press.

World Bank, 2003, *World Development Report 2003*, China Financial and Economic Publishing House.

Yasheng, Huang (2001), "*The Benefits of FDI in a Transitional Economy: The Case of China*," *OECD Global Forum on International Investment, New Horizons and Policy Challenges for Foreign Direct Investment in the 21st Century, Mexico City*, November 26–27, 2001.

Young, Alwyn (1995), "*The Tyranny of Numbers: Confronting the Statistical Realities of the East Asian Growth Experience*," *The* Quarterly Journal of Economics, *Vol.* 110 (3), *pp.* 641–680.

Young Rok, Cheong, and Geng Xiao (2003), *Global Capital Flows and the Position of China, Prepared for FONDAD-KIEP-SNU conference, March* 2003.*Yu, Yongding*, 2003, "*Eliminating the Fear of RMB Appreciation and Realizing the Transition to Balanced Economic Development*," International Economic Review, *Vol.* 9–10.

Zhang, Jun, 2002, "*Capital Formation, Industrialization and Economic Growth: Characteristics of China's Transition*," Economic Research, *Vol.* 6.

*<http://www.nber.org/papers/w*10246>.

Chapter Two References

Aghion, Philippe, Philippe Bacchetta, and Abhijit Banerjee, 2004, "*Financial Development and the Instability of Open Economies*," NBER Working Paper, 10246.

Bernanke, Ben, Mark Gertler, and Simon Gilchrist, 1998, "*The Financial Accelerator in Aquantitative Business Cycle Framework*," NBER Working paper, 6455.

Demigüc-Kunt A. and E. Detragiache, 1998, "*Financial Liberalization and Financial Fragility*," IMF Working Paper.

Edwards, S., 2001, *"Capital Mobility and Economic Performance: Are Emerging Economies Different?,"* NBER Working Paper, 8076.

Fernandez-Arias, Eduardo, and Peter, J. Montiel, 1995, *"The Surge in Capital Inflows to Developing Countries-Prospects and Policy Response,"* Policy Research Working Paper, 1473, *World Bank.*

García, Clara, 2004, *"Capital inflows, Policy Responses, and their Ill Consequences: Thailand, Malaysia, and Indonesia in the Decade before the Crises,"* PERI Working Paper Series, *No.* 81.

Glick R. and M. Hutchison, 1999, *"Banking and Currency Crises: How Common Are Twins?,"* Financial Crises in Emerging Markets, *Reuven Glick, Ramon Moreno, and Mark Spiegel eds., N. Y.: Cambridge University Press.*

Goldstein, Morris, 1995, *"Coping with too Much of a Good Thing, Policy Responses of Large Capital inflows to Developing Countries,"* Policy Research Working Paper, 1507, *World Bank.*

Growth Frontier Research Group (written by Zhang Xiaojing and Zhang Ping), 2004, "Economic Growth and Policy Choices in Opening," Economic Research, *Vol.* 4.

Hellmann, T., Murdock, K., and Stiglitz, J. E., 2000, *"Liberalization, Moral Hazard in Banking and Prudential Regulation: Are Capital Requirements Enough?,"* American Economic Review, *Vol.* 90 (1), *pp.* 147–165.

IMF, 2004, Global Portfolio Investment Survey, *August.*

Jin, Luo, 2004, *"Research on the Intensity of Capital Regulation,"* Financial Research, *Vol.* 12.

Kaminsky and Schmukler, 2002, *Short-Run Pain, Long-Run Gain "The Effects of Financial Liberalization," Preliminary, May* 28.*Prasad, Eswar., Kenneth Rogoff, Shang-Jin Wei and M. Ayhan Kose*, 2003, Effects of Financial Globalization on Developing Countries: Some Empirical Evidence, *IMF, March* 17.

Prasad, Eswar, Thomas Rumbaugh, and Qing Wang, 2005, *"Putting the Cart Before the Horse? Capital Account Liberalization and Exchange Rate Flexibility in China,"* IMF Policy Discussion Paper.

Sun, Tao, 2004, *The Construction of Financial Intermediary System in the Era of Financial Globalization*, Social Science Literature Press.*Tornell Aaron Frank Westermann Lorenza Martinez* 2004, *"The Positive Link between Financial Liberalization, Growth and Crises,"* NBER Working Paper, *No.* 10293.

Williamson, John, and Molly Mahar, 1998, *"A Survey of Financial Liberalization,"* Princeton Essays in International Finance, *No.* 211, *November.*

Zhang, Qi, He, Fan and Liu, Mingxing, 2003, "*Financial Liberalization, Vulnerability and Policy Coordination*," World Economy, *Vol.* 12.

Zhao, Min, 2004, "*Policy Options under Capital Inflow*," Economic and Social System Comparison, *Vol.* 2.

Chapter Three References

Agénor, P., McDermott, C. J., and E. S. Prasad, 2000, "*Macroeconomic Fluctuations in Developing Countries: Some Stylized Facts*," The World Bank Economic Review, *Vol.* 14 (2), *pp.* 251–285.

Alan Heap, 2005, *China-The Engine of a Commodities Super Cycle*, *<www.minecon.com>*, *March*.

Fidrmuc, J., Korhonen, I., and I. Bátorová, 2008, *China in the World Economy: Dynamic Correlation Analysis of Business Cycles, BOFIT Discussion Papers 7.*

Gregory, A. W., A. C. Head, and J. Raynauld, 1997, "*Measuring World Business Cycles*," International Economic Review *Vol.* 38, *pp.* 677–702.

Growth Frontier Research Group (written by Zhang Ping and Zhang Xiaojing), 2003, "*The Cumulative Effect of Economic Growth and Structural Adjustment and Capital Formation*," Economic Research, *Vol.* 8.

Growth Frontier Research Group (written by Wang Hongju), 2005, "*High Investment, Macro Cost* and *Sustainability of Economic Growth*," Economic Research, *Vol.*10.

Guo, Qingwang, and Jia, Junxue, 2005, "*Analysis of Dynamic Factors in the Economic Cycle of China's Provinces*," Management World, *Vol.* 11.

Hans, Genberg, Li-gang, Liu, and Xiangrong, Jin, 2006, "*Hong Kong*'s *Business Cycle Synchronisation with Mainland China and the U.S.*," Hong Kong Monetary Authority Quarterly Bulletin, *September*.

Heathcote, J., and Perri, F., 2003, *Why Has the U. S. Economy Become Less Correlated with the Rest of the World?* American Economic Review Papers and Proceedings, *Vol.* 93 (2), *pp.* 63–69.

Kose, Ayhan, Christopher Otrok, and Charles H. Whiteman, 2008, *Under-standing the Evolution of World Business Cycles*, Journal of International Economics, *Vol.* 75 (1), *pp.* 110–130.

Kose, M. A., Otrok C., and C. H. Whiteman, 2003, "*International Business Cycles: World, Region, and Country-Specific Factors*," American Economic Review, *p.* 4.

Kwek, Kian Teng, and Cho Cho Wai, Trade Integration and Business Cycle Synchronization: The Case of India, China with ASEAN-5, FAEA conference paper November 2005.

Leitner, S. M., 2005, *The Business Cycle in the Philippines, PIDS, Discussion Paper Series, No.* 2005-10.

Otrok, Christopher, and Charles Whiteman, 1998, *"Bayesian Leading Indicators: Measuring and Predicting Economic Conditions in Iowa,"* International Economic Review, *Vol.* 39 (4).

Ren, Zhixiang, and Song Yuhua, 2004, *"On China's Economic Fluctuation and the World Economic Cycle under Economic Globalization,"* Technical Economy, *Vol.* 3.

Stock, James H., and Mark W. Watson, 1989, *"New Indexes of Coincident and Leading Economic Indicators,"* NBER Macroeconomics Annual 1989, *The MIT Press, pp.* 351–394.

Stock, James H., and Mark W. Watson, 1993, *"A Procedure for Predicting Recessions with Leading Indicators: Econometric Issues and Recent Experience," in James H. Stock and Mark W. Watson eds.*, Business Cycles, Indicators, and Forecasting, *The University of Chicago Press, pp.* 95–153.*Xu Xianchun*, 2009, *"How to understand the GDP growth rate of the first-quarter expenditure method,"* China Business Daily, May 14.

Yin, Zhang, 2003, China's *Business Cycles: The International Dimension*,

<www.wider.unu.edu/conference>.

Chapter Four References

Bernanke, Ben S., 2005, *"The Global Saving Glut and the U. S. Current Account Deficit," Remarks at the Sandridge Lecture, Virginia Association of Economics, Richmond, Virginia.*

Bi, Yujiang, and Zhu, Zhongdi, 2006, *"The price transmission effect of RMB exchange rate changes: an empirical study based on the cointegration and error correction model,"* Financial Research, *Vol.* 7.

Borio, Claudio, and Andrew Filardo, 2007, *"Globalization and Inflation: New Cross-Country Evidence on the Global Determinants of Domestic Inflation,"* BIS Working Paper, *No.* 227, *May* 2007.

Caballero, Ricardo J., 2006, *"On the Macroeconomics of Asset Shortages,"* NBER Working Paper, *No.* 12753.

Chen, Dazhong, 2005, *"The Asymmetry of the Impact of Crude Oil Price on the Economy - Literature Review,"* International Petroleum Economics, *Vol.* 8.

Chen, Liufu, and Liu Houjun, 2007, *"The price transmission effect of the RMB exchange rate: an empirical analysis based on the VAR model,"* Financial Research, *Vol.* 4.

Citigroup, 2008, *"Emerging Markets: Not a Safe Haven for Macro Investors,"* Global Macro Trading Strategy Focus, *March* 25, 2008.

Fan, Gang, 2008, *"The Impact of the US Economic Recession on China's Economy,"* speech at the 2008 Annual Meeting of the China Development Forum, March 22.

Federal Bank of Kansas City, <http://www.kansascityfed. org/>Feng, Beilin, 2006, *"Analysis of the Effect of Exchange Rate Transmission Effect and Macroeconomic Impact on Inflation,"* World Economy, *Vol.* 12.

Gordon, Robert J., 1990, *"The Phillips Curve Now and Then,"* NBER Working Paper, *No.* 3393, *June* 1990.

Gordon, Robert J., 1997, *"The Time-Varying NAIRU and its Implications for Economic Policy,"* The Journal of Economic Perspectives, *Vol.* 11, *No.* 1, *Winter*, 1997, *pp.* 11–32.

Growth Frontier Research Group (written by Zhang Ping and Zhang Xiaojing), 2003, *"Economic Growth, the Cumulative Effect of Structural Adjustment and Capital Formation—Analysis of Current Economic Growth Situation,"* Economic Research, *Vol.* 8.

Growth Frontier Research Group of the Institute of Economics, Chinese Academy of Social Sciences (written by Zhang Xiaojing and Zhang Ping), 2004, *"Growth and Policy Options in the Opening up—Analysis of Current Economic Growth Situation,"* Economic Research, *Vol.* 4.

Growth Frontier Research Group (written by Zhang Xiaojing), 2005, *"International Capital Flow, Economic Distortion and Macrostability - Analysis of Current Economic Growth Situation,"* Economic Research, *Vol.* 4.

He, Nianru, and Zhu, Runlong, 2006, *"Analysis of the Impact of the Rising World Crude Oil Price on* China's Economy," World Economic Research, *Vol.* 2.

IMF, 2006, *"How Has Globalization Affected Inflation?,"* World Economic Outlook, *Chapter* 3, *April* 2006.

IMF, 2007, *"Globalization and Inequality,"* World Economic Outlook, *Chapter* 4, *Oct.* 2007.

Liu, Jinquan, Jin, Chunyu, and Zheng, Tingguo, 2006, *"The Dynamics of China's Phillips Curve and the Track of Inflation Rate Expectation: A Study Based on the State Space Zoning Transfer Model,"* World Economy, *Vol.* 6.

Liu, Qiang, 2005, *"Model Research on the Impact of Oil Price Change on China's Economy,"* Quantitative Economic and Technological Economic Research, *Vol.* 3.

Liu, Shucheng, 1997, "On China's Phillips Curve," Management World, *Vol. 6.*

*Liu, Shucheng, Zhang, Xiaojing, and Zhang, Ping,*2005, *"Realizing the Smoothing of Economic Cycle Fluctuations at Moderate High Levels,"* Economic Research, *Vol.* 11.

Mankiw, Greg., 2007, *Globalization and the Phillips Curve: Comment on Ball, Oct.* 28, 2006, http://gregmankiw.blogspot.com/2006/10/globalization-and-phillips-curve.html

Rajan, Raghuram G., 2006, *Is There a Global Shortage of Fixed Assets? Remarks at the G-*30 *meetings in New York, December* 1, 2006.

Roberts, John, 2006, *"Monetary Policy and Inflation Dynamics," International Journal of Central Banking, September, Vol.* 2 (3), *pp.* 193–230.

Rogoff, Kenneth, 2004, *"Globalization and Global Disinflation," in* Monetary Policy and Uncertainty: Adapting to a Changing Economy, *Jackson Hole Symposium sponsored by the Federal Reserve Bank of Kansas City.*

Rogoff, Kenneth, 2006, *"Impact of Globalization on Monetary Policy,"* The New Geography: Effects and Policy Implications, *Jackson Hole Symposium*, *Federal.*

Shi, Jianhui, 2006, *"Are Currency Appreciations Concretionary in China?"* NBER Working Paper, *No.* 12551.

Taylor, John B., 2008, *The Impacts of Globalization on Monetary Policy, prepared for presentation at the Banque de France Symposium on "Globalization, Inflation and Monetary Policy," March* 7, 2008.

Wang, Qing, 2008, *"Inflation should be curbed by appreciation," Caijing Magazine, Vol.* 2.

Wang, Shaoping, Tu, Zhengge, and Li, Zina, 2001, *"The Expected Expanded Phillips Curve and Its Applicability Test for China,"* China Social Sciences, *Vol.* 4.

Wang, Xiaolu, and Fan, Gang, 2000, *The Sustainability of China's Economic Growth,* Economic Science Press.

Woodford, Michael, 2007, *"Globalization and Monetary Control,"* NBER Working Paper, *No.* 13329.

Zeng, Lifei, Xu, Jiangang, and Tang, Guoxing, 2006, *"China's New Keynesian Hybrid Phillips Curve under the Open Economy,"* Quantitative Economic and Technological Economic Research, *Vol.* 3.

Zhang, Ping, and Wang, Hongmiao, 2007, *"The Challenge of 'Double Inflation' and Macro-policy Choices,"* Economic Dynamics, *Vol.* 12.

Zhang, Xiaojing, 2008, *"Inflation Situation, Potential Growth Rate and Challenges of Macroeconomic Control,"* Economic Dynamics, *Vol.* 1.

Chapter Five References

Davis, E. Philip, and Haibin Zhu, 2004, *"Bank Lending and Commercial Property Cycles: Some Cross-Country Evidence,"* BIS Working Papers, *No.* 150.

Helbling, F., 2003, *"Housing Price Bubbles-A Tale Based on Housing Price Booms and Busts," This paper draws on Chapter II of the April* 2003 World Economic Outloo*k (IMF).*

Herring, Richard, and Susan Wachter, 2002, *"Bubbles in Real Estate Markets,"* Zell/Lurie Real Estate Center Working Paper, *No.* 402, *March* 2002.

Koh, Winston T. H., Roberto S. Mariano, Andrey Pavlov, Sock Yong Phang, Augustine H. H. Tan, and Susan M. Wachter, 2004, *"Bank Lending and Real Estate in Asia: Market Optimism and Asset Bubbles,"* Forthcoming in Journal of Asian Economics.

National Bureau of Statistics, 2002, *Statistical Code of fixed assets investment in China (1950–2000)*, China Statistics Press.

National Bureau of Statistics, 2005, *China Statistical Abstract 2005*, China Statistics Press. Edited by *Fan, Gang, Quarterly Variable Tracking Analysis*, relevant issues.

Quigley, John M., 2001, *"Real Estate and the Asian Crisis,"* Program on Housing and Urban Policy Working Paper Series, *Working, No. W*99-008.

Real Estate Finance Analysis Group of the People's Bank of China, 2005, China Real Estate Finance Report 2004.

Statistics of China Economic Network, CEIC and the People's Bank of China.

Zhang, Xiaojing, 2005, *"International Capital Flow, Economic Distortion and Macro Stability,"* Economic Research, *Vol.* 4.

Chapter Six References

CEIC database.

Deutsche Bank, "The Hong Kong Bond Market," December 2004.

Guorong, Jiang, Nancy Tang, and Eve, Law, "Cost-Benefit Analysis of Developing the Hong Kong Debt Market," August 31, 2001.

IMF, 1998, *"Financial Crises: Characteristics and Indicators of Vulnerability."*

Lucas, Robert, 1990, *"Why Doesn't Capital Flow from Rich to Poor Countries?,"* The American Economic Review, *May* 1990 (*Papers and Proceedings*), *Vol.* 80 (2), *pp*. 92–96.

Jiang, Shuxia, 1995, *Chin's Underground Finance*, Fujian People's Publishing House.

Li, Yang, and Yin, Zhongli, 2004, "Analysis of the Underground Financial Market between Shenzhen and Hong Kong," China Financial Development Report.

Carlson, Mark, and Leonardo Hernandez, "Determinants and Repercussions of the Composition of Capital Inflows," IMF working paper, *WP//02/86*.

Warr, Peter, "Crisis Vulnerability," Asian Pacific Economic Literature, Vol. 16 (1), *May* 2002.

Reuters database.

Website of the Hong Kong Monetary Authority.

Chapter Seven References

Andrew, Worthington, and Helen Higgs, 2001, *"A Multivariate GARCH Analysis of Equity Returns and Volatility in Asian Equity Markets," Queensland University of Technology School*, Economics and Finance Discussion Papers and Working Papers, *No.* 089.

Annastiina, Silvennoinen, and Timo Terasvirta, January 2008, *"Multivariate GARCH Models," SSE/EFI Working Paper Series in Economics and Finance no.* 669.

Bae, K.-H., G. A. Karolyi, and R. M. Stulz, 2003, *"A New Approach to Measuring Financial Contagion," The Review of Financial Studies, Vol.* 16, *pp*. 717–763.

Baig, T., and I. Goldfajn, 1999, *"Financial Market Contagion in the Asian Crisis,"* IMF Staff Papers, 46, *pp*. 167–195.

Brenda, Gonzalez-Hermosillo, "Investors' Risk Appetite and Global Financial Market Conditions," IMF Working Paper/08/85, *Washington: International Monetary Fund.*

Calvo, G. A, 1999, *"Contagion in Emerging Markets: When Wall Street is a Carrier,"* University of Maryland (*mimeo*).

Calvo, G.A., and E. Mendoza (2000), *"Rational Contagion and the Globalisation of Securities Markets,"* Journal of International Economics, *Vol.* 51 (1), *pp*. 79–113.

China Banking Regulatory Commission, October 2008.

Eswar, S. Prasad, and Raghuram Rajan, *A Pragmatic Approach to Capital Account Liberalization*, NBER Working Paper, *No.* 14051.

G. Geoffrey, Booth, Teppo, Martikainen, and Yiuman, Tse, 1997, *"Price and Volatility Spillovers in Scandinavian Stock Markets,"* Journal of Banking & Finance, *Vol.* 21, *pp.* 811–823.

Hamao, Y., R. W. Masulis, and V. Ng, 1990, *"Correlations in Price Changes and Volatility Across International Stock Markets,"* Review of Financial Studies, *Vol.* 3, *pp.* 281–307.

International Monetary Fund (IMF), 2008 *a*, *"Staff Report for the* 2007 *Article IV Consultation Discussions," Washington, October.*

——, 2008*b*,*"Can Asia Decouple? Investigating Spillovers from the United States to Asia," Regional Economic Outlook-Asia and Pacific, World Economic and Financial Surveys, Washington, April.*

——,2008 *c*,*"Latin American Linkages to Global Financial Market Turbulence," in Regional Economic Outlook-Western Hemisphere, World Economic and Financial Surveys, Washington, April.*

——, 2008*d*, *Chapter* 4, *"Spillovers to Emerging Equity Markets," Global Financial Stability Report, World Economic and Financial Surveys Oct* 2008, *Washington, October.*

Jorge A. Chan-Lau, Donald J. Mathieson, and James Y. Yao, 2004, *"Extreme Contagion in Equity markets,"* IMF Staff Papers, *Vol.* 51 (2), *IMF.*

Jorge, Chan-Lau, and Iryna, Ivaschenko, 2003, *"Asian Flu or Wall Street Virus? Tech and Non-tech Spillovers in the United States and Asia,"* Journal of Multinational Financial Management, *Vol.* 13 (4–5), *pp.* 302–322.

Kodres, L. E., and M. Pritsker, 1998, *"A Rational Expectations Model of Financial Contagion," Finance and Economics Discussion Paper Series* 98/48 (*Washington, D.C.: Board of Governors of the Federal Reserve System*); *forcecoming in Journal of Finance.*

Li-gang, Liu, Laurent, Pauwels, and Jun-yu, Chan, 2008, *"Do External Political Pressures Affect The Renminbi Exchange Rate?,"* Hong Kong Monetary Authority Working Paper,05/2008.

Kalra, Sanja, 2008, *"Global Volatility and Forex Returns in East Asia," IMF Working Paper, WP/08/208.*

Taimim, Bayoumi, and Andrew, Swiston, *"Foreign Entanglements: Estimating the Source and Size of Spillovers Across Industrial Countries,"* IMF working paper, *WP/07/182.*

Taimur, Baig and Ilan, Goldfajn, 1999, *"Financial Market Contagion in the Asian Crisis,"* IMF Staff Papers, *Vol.* 46 *No* 2, *Washington: International Monetary Fund.*

Tse, Y. K., and K. C. Tsui, 2002, *"A Multivariate Generalized Autoregressive Conditional Heteroscedasticity Model with Time-varying Correlations,"* Journal of Business and Economic Statistics, *Vol.* 20, *pp.* 351–362.

Wang, Xinghua, and Ji, Qian, 2008, *The impact of the US subprime crisis on China is limited*, People's Daily (overseas edition), May 5, 2008.

Gelos, Gaston, and Ratna Sahay, 2000, *"Financial Market Spillovers in Transition Economies,"* IMF Working Paper/00/71, *Washington: International Monetary Fund.*

Chapter Eight References

Allen, Franklin, and Douglas Gale, 2000, *"Bubbles and Crises,"* Economic Journal, *Vol.* 110 (460), *pp.* 236–255.

Bagnai, Alberto, 2008, *"The Role of China in Global External Imbalances: Some Further Evidence,"* China Economic Review, *forthcoming.*

Barsky, Robert B., and Lutz Kilian, 2001, *"Do We Really Know that Oil Caused the Great Stagflation? A Monetary Alternative,"* NBER Working Paper, *No.* 8389.

Bernanke, B. S., 2005, *"The Global Saving Glut and the US Current Account Deficit," Updates speech given on March* 10, 2005, *at the Sandridge Lecture*, Virginia Association of Economists, Richmond, *Virginia.*

Bernanke, 2007, *The Great Depression*, Northeast University of Finance and Economics Press.

Blanchard, Olivier, Francesco Giavazzi, and Filipa Sa, *"International Investors, the U. S. Current Account, and the Dollar,"* Brookings Papers on Economic Activity, *Vol.* 2005 (1), *pp.* 1–49.

C. Fred, Bergstein (ed.), 2005, *The United States and the World Economy: America's Foreign Economic Policy in the Next Decade*, Economic Science Press.

Caballero, Ricardo J., Emmanuel Farhi, and Pierre-Olivier Gourinchas, 2008 *a*, *"An Equilibrium Model of 'Global Imbanlances' and Low Interest Rates,"* American Economic Review, *Vol.* 98 (1), *pp.* 358–93.

Caballero, Ricardo J., Emmanuel Farhi, and Pierre-Olivier Gourinchas, 2008*b*, *"Financial Crash, Commodity Prices and Global Imbalances,"* NBER Working Paper, *No.* 14521.

Charles, P. Jindelberg, 2007, *Crazy, Panic and Collapse - History of Financial Crisis (Fourth Edition)*, China Financial Press.

Cai, Fang, 2009, "Scientific development is the fundamental way to resist the financial crisis," Red Flag Manuscript, *Vol.* 6 (total 150).

Cole, Harold L., and Lee E. Ohanian, 2004, "*New Deal Policies and the Persistence of the Great Depression: A General Equilibrium Analysis*," Journal of Political Economy, *Vol.* 112 (4), *pp.* 779–816.

Cooper, Richard, 2006, "*Living with Global Imbalances: A Contrarian View*," Journal of Policy Modeling, *Vol.* 28 (6), *pp.* 615–627.

Dooley, Michael P., David Folkerts-Landau, and Peter M. Garber, 2002, "*An Essay on the Revived Bretton Woods System*," NBER Working Paper, *No.* 9971.

Dooley, Michael P., David Folkerts-Landau, and Peter M. Garber, 2004*a*, "*Direct Investment, Rising Real Wages and the Absorption of Excess Labor in the Periphery*," NBER Working Paper, *No.* 10626.

Dooley, Michael P., David Folkerts-Landau, and Peter M. Garber, 2004*b*, "*The U. S. Current Account Deficit and Economic Development: Collateral for a Total Return Swap*," NBER Working Paper, *No.* 10727.

Eichengreen, Barry, 2000, "*From Benign Neglect to Malignant Preoccupation: U. S. Balance -of-Payments Policy in the* 1960*s*," NBER Working Paper, *No.* 7680.

Eichengreen, Barry, 2004, "*Global Imbalances and the Lessons of Bretton Woods*," NBER Working Paper, *No.* 10497.

Fels, Joachim, 2005, "*Is Global Excess Liquidity Drying Up?*," *Morgan Stanley Global Economic Forum, November* 8.

Fels, Joachim, 2009, "*A New Global Liquidity Cycle*," *Morgan Stanley Global Economic Forum, January* 16.

Gourinchas, Pierre-Olivier, and Hélène Rey, 2005*a*, "*International Financial Adjustment*," NBER Working Paper, *No.* 11155.

Gourinchas, Pierre-Olivier and Hélène Rey, 2005*b*, "*From World Banker to World Venture Capitalist: U.S. External Adjustment and the Exorbitant Privilege*," NBER Working Paper, *No.* 11563.

Hausmann, Ricardo, and Federico Sturzenegger, 2005, "*U. S. and Global Imbalances: Can Dark Matter Prevent a Big Bang?*," *<http://www.cid.harvard.edu/cidpublications /darkmatter_051130.pdf>*.

Ito, Hiro, 2009, "*U. S. Current Account Debate With Japan then, with China Now*," Journal of Asian Economics, *forthcoming*.

Knotek, Edward S. II, 2006, "*Regime Changes and Monetary Stagflation*," *the Federal Reserve Bank of Kansas City Economic Research Department, Research Working Paper, RWP* 06-05.

Liu Shucheng, 2009, "*Analysis of Domestic and Foreign Economic Trends from 2008 to 2009*," China Economic Research Report, Department of Economics, Chinese Academy of Social Sciences, *Vol.* 78.

Martin, Feldstein (ed.), 2000, *American Economic Policy in the 1980s*, Economic Science Press.

Obstfeld, Maurice, and Kenneth Rogoff, 2000, "*Perspectives on OECD Capital Market Integration: Implications for U. S. Current Account Adjustment*," *in Federal Reserve Bank of Kansas City, Global Economic Integration: Opportunities and Challenges, March, pp.* 169–208.

Obstfeld, Maurice, and Kenneth Rogoff, 2004, "*The Unsustainable U.S. Current Account Position Revisited*," *NBER Working Paper, No.* 10869.

Obstfeld, Maurice, and Kenneth Rogoff, 2005, "*Global Current Account Imbalances and Exchange Rate Adjustments*," *Brookings Papers on Economic Activity, Vol.* 2005 (1), *pp.* 67–123.

Reinhart, Carmen M., and Kenneth S. Rogoff, 2008*a*, "*This Time is Different: A Panoramic View of Eight Centuries of Financial Crises*," NBER Working Paper, *No.* 13882.

Reinhart, Carmen M., and Kenneth S. Rogoff, 2008*b*, *Banking Crises: An Equal Opportunity Menace, manuscript, Harvard University, December* 2008.

Reinhart, Carmen M., and Kenneth S. Rogoff, 2009, "*The Aftermath of Financial Crises*," American Economic Review, *forthcoming.*

Research Group of the Macroscopic Department of the Institute of Economics, Chinese Academy of Social Sciences, 2009, *International Relevance of China's Business Cycle.*

Roubini, Nouriel and Brad, Setser, 2004, "*The US as a Net Debtor: The Sustainability of the US External Imbalances*," *<http://pages.stern.nyu.edu/~nroubini/papers/Roubini-Setser-US-Exter- nalImbalances. pdf>.*

Rüffer, Rasmus and Livio Stracca, 2006, "*What is Global Excess Liquidity, and Does It Matter?*," European Central Bank Working Paper Series *No.* 696.

Summers, Laurence, 1989, "*Planning for the Next Financial Crisis*," *in The Risk of Economic Crisis, Edited by Martin, Feldstein, University of Chicago press*, 1989.

V. McKinnon, Ronald I., 2005, "*Trapped by the International Dollar Standard*," Journal of Policy Modeling, *Vol.* 27, *pp.* 477–485.

White, William R. 2008, "*Past Financial Crises, the Current Financial Turmoil, and the Need for a New Macrofinancial Stability Framework*," Journal of Financial Stability, *Vol.* 4, *pp.* 307–312.

Zhang, Ping, 2009, "*The Effectiveness of Macro Policies and the Choice of Incentive Targets*," China Economic Research Report, Department of Economics, Chinese Academy of Social Sciences, *Vol*. 82.

Zhang, Xiaojing, 2008, "*The Periodic Adjustment of China's Growth, Future Trends and Policy Choices*," Finance and Trade Economy, *Vol*.10.

Chapter Nine References

China Cinda Asset Management Corporation Financial Risk Research Center, 2006, "*China's Non-performing Assets Market Development Report 2006*," Financial Risk Research, *Vol*. 11–12.

Fan, Gang, 1999, "*On the Comprehensive Liabilities of the State and How to Deal with the Bad Assets of Banks*," Economic Research, *Vol.5*.

Gray, Dale F., Robert C. Merton, and Zvi Bodie, 2006, "*A New Frame- work for Analyzing and Managing Macrofinancial Risks of an Economy*," *NBER Working Paper, No*. 12637.

Hana 1998. "*Government Contingent Liabilities: A Hidden Risk to Fiscal Stability*," *Policy Research Working Paper, World Bank, Washington, D. C.*

IMF, 2006, *Article IV Consultation-Staff Report, October* 2006, *IMF Country Report No*. 06/394. 15. *Polackova*.

Li, Liming, 2006, "*Huijin's three major banks made money and lost money*," Economic Observer, October 30, 2006.

Liu, Shangxi, 2003, "*Financial Risk: An Analytical Framework*," Economic Research, *Vol.5*.

Liu, Shangxi, 2005, "*Financial Risk: Analysis from the Angle of Economic Aggregate*," Management World, *Vol.7.Ma, Guonan*, 2006, "*Who Pays* China's *Restructuring Bill?*," *CEPII WP*2006-04.

Mendoza, Enrique G., Vincenzo, Quadrini, and Jose-Victor Rios-Rull, 2006, Financial Integration, Financial Deepness and Global Imbalances, *forthcoming*.

Reinhart, C K Rogoff and M, Savastano, 2003, "*Debt Intolerance*," *Brookings Papers on Economic Activity, January*.

Sun, Tao, 2004, *The Construction of Financial Intermediary System in the Era of Globalization*, China Social Science Press

The People's Bank of China: China Financial Stability Report (2005) and (2006), China Financial Publishing House.

Wei, Jianing, 2004, "*The number one killer" exposes the serious hidden debt risk of local government*," China Business Times, February 23, 2004.

Yi, Gang, 2004, "*Thoughts on China's Banking Reform (I)*," China Economic 50 Forum, <http://www.50forum.org.cn, 2004–6–23>.

Yvonne Sin, Pension Liabilities and Reform Options for Old Age Insurance, *Paper No.* 2005-1, *The World Bank, Washington D. C., USA, May* 2005.

Zhang, Xiaojing, Chang, Xin and Wang, Hongju, 2006, "*Growth imbalance and government responsibility: an analysis from the perspective of social expenditure*," Economic Research, *Vol.*10.

Chapter Ten References

Acemoglu, Daron, and Thierry Verdier, 2000, "*The Choice Between Market Failure and Corruption*," *American Economic Review*, *Vol.* 90 (1).

Atkinson, A., and J. Stiglitz, 1980, Lectures on Public Economics, *New York: McGraw Hill.*

Baqir, Reza, 2002, "*Social Sector Spending in a Panel of Countries*," *Working Paper WP/02/35, International Monetary Fund, Washington.*

Bloom, David, and David Canning, 2003, "*The Health and Poverty of Nations: From Theory to Practice*," Journal of Human Development, *Vol.* 4 (1), *pp.* 47–71.

——, *and Jaypee Sevilla*, 2004, "*The Effect of Health on Economic Growth: A Production Function Approach*," World Development, *Vol.* 32 (1), *pp.* 1–13.

Cai, Shewen, 2004, "*Analysis of China's Social Security Expenditure Level*," Monthly Journal of Budget Management Accounting, *Vol.* 7.

China Development Research Foundation, United Nations Development Programme, 2005, *China Human Development Report: Pursuing Fair Human Development*, China Foreign Translation and Publishing Corporation.

China Financial Yearbook Compilation Committee, 2006, *China Financial Yearbook 2005*, China Financial Journal Press.

China's economic growth and macroeconomic stability research group, 2006, "*Learning by doing, low-cost competition and growth path transformation*," Economic Research, *Vol. 4*.

Department of Finance of the Ministry of Education, Department of Population and Social Science and Technology Statistics of the National Bureau of Statistics, 2003, *China Education Expenditure Statistical Yearbook 2002*, China Statistics Press.

Department of National Economic Comprehensive Statistics of the National Bureau of Statistics, 2005, *Compilation of Statistical Data of the Fifty-five Years of the People's Republic of China*, China Statistics Press.

Du Lexun, *"Accounting Results and Analysis of China's Total Health Expenditure,"* Economist website, May 16. <http://www.jjxj.com.cn/news.detail.jsp?keyno=3348>.

Growth Frontier Research Group, 2003, *"The Cumulative Effect of Economic Growth and Structural Adjustment and Capital Formation,"* Economic Research, *Vol.* 8.

Growth Frontier Research Group, 2004, *"The Supply Effect of Fiscal Policy and Economic Development,"* Economic Research, *Vol. 9.*

Growth Frontier Research Group, 2005, *"High Investment, Macro Cost and Sustainability of Economic Growth,"* Economic Research, *Vol. 10.*

Growth in Sub-Saharan African and OECD Countries," Quarterly Review of Economics and Finance, *Vol.* 44 (2), *pp.* 296–320.

Gyimah-Brempong, Kwabena, and Mark Wilson, 2004, *"Health Hu-man Capital and Economic*

Harsanyi, John C., 1955, *"Cardinal Welfare, Individualistic Ethics, and Interpersonal Comparisons of Utility,"* Journal of Political Economy, *Vol.* 63 (4), *pp.* 309–321.

IMF, 1999, *"Does Higher Government Spending Buy Better Results in Education and Health Care?," By Sanjeev Gupta*, *Marijin Verhoevern*, *and Erwin Tiongson*.

Ministry of Health of the People's Republic of China, 2006, *China Health Statistics Summary 2006*, website of the Ministry of Health of the People's Republic of China. <http://www.moh.gov.cn/>

Mrinal, Datta-Chaudhuri, 1990, *"Market Failure and Government Failure,"* Journal of Economic Perspectives, *Vol.* 4 (3). *National Bureau of Statistics*, 2006, *China Statistical Abstract 2006*, China Statistics Press.

Nozick, Robert, 1974, *Anarchy, State and Utopia*, *New York*: *Basic Books.*

Rawls, John, 1971, *A Theory of Justice*, *Cambridge, M. A.*: *Harvard University Press.*

Sen, *Amartya*, 1985, *Commodities and Capabilities*, *Amsterdam*: *North-Holland.*

——, 1999*a*, *Development as Freedom*, *New York*: *Alfred A. Knopf Inc.*

——, 1999*b*, *"Economic Policy and Equity: An Overview," in* Economic Policy and Equity, *ed. By Vito Tanzi*, *Ke-young Chu*, *and Sanjeev Gupta*, *Washington*: *IMF.*

Stiglitz, 2006, *China has crossed the river*, Caijing Magazine, *Vol.* 155.

Strauss, John, and Duncan Thomas, 1998, *"Health, Nutrition, and Economic Development,"* Journal of Economic Literature, *Vol.* 36 (2), *pp.* 766–817.

Tanzi, Veto, 2005, *"The Coming Fiscal Crisis?"Paper provided for the conference "The Long -Term Budget Challenge: Public Finance and Fiscal Sustainability in the G-7," June* 2–4, 2005, *Washington, D. C.*

Vito, Tanzi and Ludgar, Schuknecht, 2005, *Public Expenditure in the 20th Century*, Commercial Press.

Wang, Mengkui, 2006, *"The keynote of China's social and economic policy: keynote speech at the China Development Forum,"* China Economic Times, March 27, 2006.

Wang, Shaoguang, 2003, *"The Crisis and Turn of Public Health in China,"* Comparison, *Vol.* 7.

World Bank, 2001, *World Development Report*, China Financial and Economic Publishing House.

World Bank, 2004, *World Development Report*, China Financial and Economic Publishing House.

World Bank, 2005, *China: Deepening the Reform of Public Institutions and Improving Public Service* Provision, CITIC Press.*World Bank*, 2006, *World Development Report*, Tsinghua University Press.

Zou, Hengfu, 1996, *"The Composition of Public Expenditure and Economic Growth,"* Journal of Monetary Economics, *Vol.* 37, *pp.* 313–344.

Chapter Eleven References

Aiyagari SR. 1994, *"Uninsured Idiosyncratic Risk and Aggregate Saving,"* Quarterly Journal of Economics, *Vol.* 109 (3), *pp.* 659–684.

Arrow, Kenneth J., 1951, 2nd ed., 1963, Social Choice and Individual Values, Yale University Press, New Haven.

Atkinson, Anthony B., 1975, The Economics of Inequality, *Oxford University Press, London.Huggett, M*, 1997, *"The One-Sector Growth Model with Idiosyncratic shocks," Steady states and dynamics*, Journal of Monetary Economics, *Vol.* 39 (3), *pp.* 385–403.

Foster, James E., and Amartya Sen, 1996, On Economic Inequality, *expanded edition with annexe, ISBN* 0-19-828193-5.

Huggett, M, Ospina, S., 2001, *"Aggregate Precautionary Savings: When is the Third Derivative Irrelevant?,"* Journal of Monetary Economics, *Vol.* 48 (2), *pp.* 373–96.

Hu, Zuguang, 2004, *"Research on the Optimal Value of Gini Coefficient Theory and Its Simple Calculation Formula,"* Economic Research, *Vol. 9.*

Hu, Zuguang, 1993, *"The theoretical best value of the Gini coefficient — one third,"* Global Management Review, *Vol. 3.*

Miao, J. 2006, *"Competitive Equilibria of Economies with a Continuum of Consumers and Aggregate Shocks,"* Journal of Economic Theory, *Vol.* 128 (1), *pp.* 274–298.

Ng, Yew-Kwang, 1979; *rev. ed.*, 1983, *Welfare Economics*, *London: Macmillan.*

Peng, S., 1997, *"BSDE and Related G-expectation,"* Pitman Research Notes in Mathematics Series, 364, *pp.* 141–159.

Peng, S. 1999, *"Monotonic Limit Theorem of BSDE and Nonlinear Decomposition Theorem of Doob-Meyers Type,"* Probability Theory & Related Fields, *Vol.* 113 (4), *pp.* 473–499.*Raols, J.*, 1972, A Theory of Justice, *Oxford University Press, Oxford, UK.*

Samuelson, Paul A., 1947, *Enlarged ed.* 1983, *"Welfare Economics," Foundations of Economic Analysis, Harvard University Press, Cambridge, M. A., Ch. VIII, pp.* 203–253.

Samuelson, Paul A., 1981, *"Bergsonian Welfare Economics," in S. Rosefielde (ed.)*, Economic Welfare and the Economics of Soviet Socialism: Essays in Honor of Abram Bergson, *Cambridge University Press, Cambridge, pp.* 223–266.

Sen, Amartya, K., 1973, *"Distribution, Transitivity and Little's Welfare Criteria,"* Economic Journal, *Vol.* 73 (292), *pp.* 771–778.

Suen, Richard M. H., 2009, *"Bounding the CRRA Utility Functions," February*, *<http://mpra. ub.uni-muenchen. de/*13260/1/*Bound _CRRA. pdf>.*

Wang, Guisheng,2006, *Welfare Economics*, China Social Labor and Social Security Press.

Wold H. O. A. and P. Whinle, 1957, *"A Model Explaining the Pareto Distribution of Wealth,"* Econometrica, *Vol.* 25 (4), *pp.* 591–595.

Yao, Mingxia, 2005, *Welfare Economics*, Economic Daily Press.

Zhang, Ping: Growth and Sharing, 2003, *Theory and Demonstration of Resident Income Distribution*, Social Science Literature Press.

Zhao, Zhijun, 1994, *"The Theoretical Best Value of Gini Coefficient,"* Global Management Review, *Vol.* 1.

Epilogue

The original Chinese text was rendered into English by an MTI team led by Professor Shiying Liu from Chongqing University of Posts and Telecommunications. As the project leader, Professor Liu oversaw the whole translation process, coordinated the efforts and took charge of quality control. Qing Zhao, Cunwei Liu, Yi Wang, and Jing Wang reviewed and refined the chapter layouts with their practical editorial skills, while Fei Gao and Yongheng Tan worked hard to proofread the final draft of the work, to identify and sort out errors and grammatical mistakes.

The preface and reference list were translated by Qing Zhao. Chapter 1, 6, and 9 were rendered into English by Pingting Li, Xi Yang, Xingyue Zhu, Gaojie Yang, and Qingyu Qian. Chapter 3, 8, and 10 were translated by Yukun Qiu, Min Li, Jiayu Xu, Shuang Cai, Dai Li, and Wenmin Zhao. The English versions of Chapter 2 and 7 were completed by Feifei Du, Manru Wei, and Lulu Zhou. Chapter 4 and 11 were translated by Xinran Liu and Yuanyuan Li. And the translation of Chapter 5 was jointly completed by Qingqing Li and Chuan Jia.

Together, this dedicated team of translators worked tirelessly to produce a polished work of trusted quality. Their expertise in the subject matter and linguistic quality have ensured that the translated text accurately conveys the original message. Moreover, the team's attention to detail and their modern text processing and translation techniques make the book accessible to readers at all levels of proficiency in the target language.

www.ingramcontent.com/pod-product-compliance
Ingram Content Group UK Ltd.
Pitfield, Milton Keynes, MK11 3LW, UK
UKHW020839290926
15470UKWH00004B/1440

9 783034 356077